The Heretic's Handbook of Quotations

(Expanded Edition)

Cutting Comments on Burning Issues

Charles Bufe

Editor

Copyright © 1988, 1992 by Charles Q. Bufe. All rights reserved.

For information contact: See Sharp Press, P.O. Box 1731, Tucson, AZ 85702

Expanded Edition — First Printing

The Heretic's handbook of quotations / edited by Charles Bufe. —
     1992 Rev. ed. — Tucson: See Sharp Press, 1992.

     245 p. : ill. ; 25 cm.

     1. Quotations, English. 2 Radicalism — Quotations. 3. Capitalism —
Quotations. 4. Anarchism — Quotations. 5. Christianity — Quotations.
6. Free Thought — Quotations. 7. Feminism — Quotations. I. Bufe,
Charles.

ISBN 0-9613289-4-0   808.882

All materials not written, translated, or drawn by the editor, Charles Bufe, remain the property of their copyright holder(s). Anyone wishing to use any of the materials in this book *must* directly contact the relevant copyright holder(s).

In *The Heretic's Handbook of Quotations* we have done our best to use *only* materials in the public domain; materials written, translated, or drawn by the editor of this book, Charles Bufe; and copyrighted materials for which we have received proper reprint permission(s). Due to the nature of this book it is, however, possible that we have used copyrighted materials without being aware of the fact, and hence without receiving reprint permission(s). If we have done this, we regret it. Please contact us as soon as possible if we have inadvertently used your copyrighted material without receiving permission to do so, in order that the matter can be resolved.

Cover by Charles Bufe and J.R. Swanson. Cover graphic by J.R. Swanson.

Printed on acid-free paper with soy-based ink by Thomson-Shore, Inc., Dexter, MI.

This book is dedicated to everyone working to make this a truly free world, and to the memory of those who have died in the effort.

Contents

Introduction to First Edition

This book was produced to fill an unmet need. For decades, "progressive" writers of all types—labor activists, anarchists, socialists, feminists, pacifists, atheists, etc.—have lacked a reliable, large source of quotations on such issues as war, politics, militarism, women's rights, labor, capitalism, sex, religion, science and the arts. *The Heretic's Handbook of Quotations* fills that until-now unmet need. This book contains well over 2000 quotations by several hundred authors on a myriad of important topics.

Another reason I produced this book is that every succeeding generation of radicals seems to reinvent the wheel. They laboriously generate theories and insights very similar to those produced by earlier progressives—but of which they are unaware. Considering the miseducation system and the quality of the mass media in the U.S., this isn't surprising. In school and in the media, one rarely hears a truly dissenting voice. At "best," one will hear "responsible" liberal intellectuals who will challenge the *methods* of the government and corporate capitalism, but not the theories and assumptions upon which those institutions are based. So, most people grow up—and many live their entire lives—without ever hearing genuine dissent. And those sufficiently intelligent and perceptive to be dissatisfied with the status quo find themselves in a near vacuum; they often waste hour upon hour reinventing old theories, and often fall prey to the first leftist political sect they encounter.

I would be very happy if this book were to help anyone avoid these pitfalls. My hope is that *The Heretic's Handbook of Quotations* will introduce its readers to ideas of which they weren't aware. I also hope that many readers will be stimulated to investigate at least a few of the works from which the quotations in this book were taken.

The quotations in *The Heretic's Handbook* were chosen with several things in mind: 1) Are they potentially of use to writers?; 2) Are they insightful or revealing?; 3) Do they have a bite?; and 4) Are they amusing? Of course, not every quotation meets all of these criteria; but they all meet at least one.

The selection of writers in this volume may surprise some readers. Many well known politicians and political commentators are not represented for the simple reason that, in my judgment, they have nothing worthwhile to say. Thus, you won't find the likes of Walter Lippman, George Will, Arthur Schlesinger (Sr. or Jr.), Jimmy Carter, or John F. Kennedy represented here. But you will find important, but almost forgotten, 19th-century writers such as Andrew Dickson White, W.E.H. Lecky, and Robert Ingersoll; unjustly neglected early and mid-20th-century figures like Alexander Berkman, Errico Malatesta, John Flynn, Charles Sprading, Joseph McCabe, and Jay Fox; and many important contemporary writers with whose works most readers will be unfamiliar. You'll also find many quotations from that most prolific of all writers, Anonymous, for the reason that s/he has much of value to say.

Some readers will be dismayed by the lack of a chapter on racism in this book. The primary reason I didn't include such a chapter is that I didn't find enough good quotations on the subject. That was due in large part to my researching methods—I restricted myself, after some bad early experiences, to searching through books either in the public domain or for which I was reasonably sure I could easily obtain reprint permissions. (Even taking this approach, I encountered hideous problems.) So, I did not go through the works of writers such as Malcolm X, whom I would have enjoyed seeing represented in this volume.

For similar reasons, relatively few contemporary feminists are quoted in the chapter on women. I'm generally sympathetic to feminist goals and am aware of the many worthwhile works produced by present-day feminists, but I'm male and therefore can't expect friendly responses to requests for reprint permissions. So, I bypassed a large number of books by feminists from which I would have liked to have taken quotations.

Also, perhaps 15 percent of the quotations in *The Heretic's Handbook* do not have a listed source. Almost all of these are quotations I collected in years past simply because I liked them or because I used them in one or another article or pamphlet. I've attempted to find the sources for these quotations without success—I ran down the sources for perhaps an equal number—but I'm satisfied that the vast majority are genuine. (I should note that most of the no-source-listed quotations by religious figures come from the voluminous and reliable writings of Joseph McCabe.) I have doubts about the authenticity of a few quotations, and I've indicated the questionable status of these by labeling them "attributed."

If I had had the time and resources, I would have done more work in the areas of women, racism, and checking sources. But, I'm a low-income working person. I've already spent over two years of my "spare" time on *The Heretic's Handbook*; and if I had explored every possibly fruitful avenue of investigation, I would have never finished this project. As it is, I've already invested well over 2000 hours of work in this book. In addition to compiling/editing this volume, I've also translated many excerpts, spent seemingly endless hours on clerical work and necessary correspondence, and designed, typeset, and laid out the entire book myself (with the exception of the cover—thanks to J.R. Swanson for help there; thanks also to Fred Woodworth and Kata Orndorff for help with proofreading).

But undoubtedly the worst aspect of preparing this book was dealing with copyright permissions. It was nightmarish. Most of the copyright holders I contacted were responsive and helpful. But others were simply impossible. Some didn't have the courtesy to respond to repeated queries; others refused permission for no apparent reason; and still others demanded what I consider exorbitant fees to reprint decades-old, out-of-print material. For example, George Orwell's heirs simply refused my requests to reprint several quotations from his works; the publisher holding rights to a decades-old, long out-of-print translation of Bakunin's writings wanted several hundred dollars to use excerpts from this work whose author has been dead for over 100 years and whose translator has been dead for nearly 40; the copyright holder to *The State,* by Randolph Bourne (now remembered chiefly for his aphorism, "War is the health of the state") wanted $100 to reprint a few excerpts from this essay which was first published in 1919 and is now out of print, and whose author has been dead for over six decades.

The lessons to be drawn from this are that progressive writers should *never* give control of their works (especially control of reprint rights) to commercial publishers. Such publishers often treat literary and political works purely as commodities—often their only interest is in the monetary value of the material to which they hold rights. Neither should progressive writers leave reprint rights (financial rights, perhaps—reprint rights, definitely not) to family members. Such heirs can show both timidity and obtuseness in their treatment of inherited works, and can end up completely losing sight of why the works they control were ever written. The best course for writers to follow seems to be to retain control of their writings while alive, and to leave the rights to their works to trusted political allies in their wills.

There was, however, also a positive side to dealing with copyright holders. Several went out of their way to offer suggestions and assistance. Of these, I would especially like to thank Fred Woodworth, editor of *The Match!*, and Robin Murray-O'Hair of American Atheists. I would also like to thank all those who granted me permission to quote from their works, especially those who granted me permission to quote extensively, such as Vernon Richards, Albert Ellis, Sam Dolgoff, Murray Bookchin, and Noam Chomsky. Others deserving thanks include the staff of the San Francisco Public Library, who were without exception courteous and helpful to me in my attempts to track down scores of obscure, long out-of-print books and pamphlets. Most of all, I would like to thank my parents, Walt and Madelyn Bufe, and my brother, David Bufe, without whose financial assistance this book would not have been possible.

But this is not the end of this project. I'm planning to issue a second volume of quotations eventually, and I would greatly appreciate any contributions or suggestion you might care to make. (If you're a writer or cartoonist, don't be shy about sending excerpts from your own works.) If you do send any quotations or graphics, please address them to Charles Bufe, c/o See Sharp Press, P.O. Box 426118, San Francisco, CA 94142, and *please* include the author's full name, full title of the work from which the material is taken, date published, name of the publisher, name of the copyright holder, and the author's blood type and fingerprints. Seriously, materials identified only by the author's name are all but useless, and the more information you can send about the source, the better.

Enjoy the book.

— Charles Bufe, San Francisco, May 16, 1988

Editor's Note: The words "libertarian" and "libertarianism" occur frequently in this book. These terms do *not* refer to members of the so-called Libertarian Party.

Since the late 19th century "libertarian" and "libertarianism" have been used as synonyms for "anarchist" and "anarchism." These words are employed in this sense by all writers quoted in *The Heretic's Handbook of Quotations*.

Introduction to Expanded Edition

Reaction to the first edition of *The Heretic's Handbovok of Quotations* was muted — but what little of it there was was gratifying. When *The Heretic's Handbook* was released four years ago, it was ignored by the daily press and the national media, though it was well received by a number of small, alternative publications. In fact, the largest publication to review the book was *Z Magazine*, which at the time had a circulation of only 15,000.

Due in large part to the media blackout — and a distribution system which systematically discriminates against small publishers — sales of the first edition were slow; but they were also steady, and in fact large enough to justify publication of this new, expanded edition. But the primary reason for publishing this new edition is that in the four years since publication of the original edition I've found several hundred additional quotations as well as a number of graphics which are admirably suited for inclusion in this book.

Despite the addition of this large amount of new material, the organization of this expanded edition remains the same as that of the original. The new material has simply been inserted into the previously existing chapters, with the result that several of them are now substantially longer than when originally published. Over the last few years, several readers have suggested that I include chapters on ecology and racism in this new edition. I would like to have done so, but I did not find enough suitable material to form additional chapters; instead, the new material which I discovered (or readers were kind enough to send to me) is included in the existing chapters.

I would again like to thank all of the writers who were kind enough to grant me permission to reprint excerpts from their works in this book; and I would particularly like to thank one writer who did not appear in the first edition of *The Heretic's Handbook*, Allen Thornton, for permission to quote extensively from his writings. Another person I would particularly like to thank is John Rush, who went to the trouble of sending me several dozen quotations, many of which I chose to include in this edition. As well, I would like to thank all of the cartoonists and artists who were kind enough to allow me to reproduce their works; these include Bill Griffith,

Donald Rooum, Tom Tomorrow, Justin Green, Arthur Moyse, and the gang at *Processed World* magazine — J.R. Swanson, Chris Carlsson, Dennis Hayes, Adam Cornford, Greg Williamson, et al. Finally, I would like to thank everyone who bought a copy of the first edition of *The Heretic's Handbook of Quotations*, the very few writers and publications that chose to review it, and those readers who were good enough to send me quotations for possible inclusion in this expanded edition. Many thanks to all.

— Charles Bufe, Tucson, Arizona, May 1, 1992

Acknowledgements

We would like to thank the following for permission to reprint their copyrighted materials:

Freedom Press for permission to reprint excerpts from *Anarchy in Action*, by Colin Ward; *About Anarchism*, by Nicolas Walter; *Wildcat*, by Donald Rooum; *Malatesta: Life and Ideas*, Vernon Richards editor/translator; *Barbarism and Sexual Freedom*, by Alex Comfort; *Anarchy*, by Errico Malatesta; and *Freedom* monthly.

Farrar, Straus and Giroux, Inc. and the Wilhelm Reich Infant Trust Fund for permission to reprint excerpts from *The Mass Psychology of Fascism* and *The Sexual Revolution*.

Alfred A. Knopf, Inc. for permission to reprint excerpts from *Minority Report: H.L. Mencken's Notebooks*, by H.L. Mencken, © 1956, by H.L. Mencken; *Prejudices: Sixth Series*, by H.L. Mencken; *Prejudices: A Selection*, by H.L. Mencken; and *A Mencken Chrestomathy*, by H.L. Mencken.

Murray Bookchin and Black Rose Books for permission to reprint excerpts from *Post-Scarcity Anarchism*, by Murray Bookchin.

Fred Woodworth for permission to reprint excerpts from *The Match!* and *Rent: An Injustice*.

Thomas D. Flynn for permission to reprint excerpts from *As We Go Marching*, by John T. Flynn.

Albert Ellis for permission to reprint excerpts from *The Case Against Religiosity*.

Liguori Publications for permission to reprint excerpts from *Pornography: A Psychiatrist's View*, by Melvin Anchell.

Oxford University Press for permission to reprint excerpts from *Thou Shalt Not Kill* and *What Is Religion?*, by Leo Tolstoy, Aylmer Maude translator.

Dover Publications for permission to reprint excerpts from *Kropotkin's Revolutionary Pamphlets*, Roger Baldwin, editor.

Michael Coughlin Publisher, for permission to reprint excerpts from *Nationalism and Culture*, by Rudolf Rocker.

Sam Dolgoff for permission to reprint excerpts from *Bakunin on Anarchy*, Sam Dolgoff editor/translator; and *The Relevance of Anarchism to Modern Society*, by Sam Dolgoff.

Acknowledgements continued on next page

Archon/Shoestring Press, Inc. for permission to reprint an excerpt from *The Criminal and His Victim*, by H. von Hentig.

Philosophical Library Publishers for permission to reprint excerpts from *Anarchism and Anarcho-Syndicalism*, by Rudolf Rocker, taken from *European Ideologies*, Feliks Gross, editor.

Houghton Mifflin Company for permission to reprint excerpts from *Mein Kampf*, by Adolf Hitler, translated by Ralph Manheim. Copyright 1943 and copyright © 1971 renewed by Houghton Mifflin Company.

Bay Area Center for Art and Technology for permission to use artwork and cartoons from *Processed World*.

Bill Griffith for permission to reprint an excerpt from *Griffith Observatory*.

Justin Green (who wishes to be known as a "warrior" rather than as a "heretic") for permission to reprint two excerpts from *Binky Brown Meets the Holy Virgin Mary*.

Adam Cornford and Dennis Hayes for permission to reprint "Communications Breakdown" from *Liveware*.

Tom Tomorrow for permission to reprint excerpts from *This Modern World*.

J.R. Swanson for permission to reprint excerpts from *The American Heretic's Dictionary*, definitions copyright 1992 by Charles Bufe, illustrations copyright 1992 by J.R. Swanson.

Allen Thornton for permission to reprint excerpts from *Laws of the Jungle*, by Allen Thornton.

Noam Chomsky for permission to reprint an excerpt from *Media Control*.

All of the above-mentioned materials remain the properties of their copyright holders. Anyone wishing to use any portion of these materials must directly contact the relevant copyright holder(s).

Like a refreshing dip in an open sewer...

Politics

Lord Acton

Power tends to corrupt, and absolute power corrupts absolutely.
— Letter to Mandell Creighton, April 5, 1887

The danger is not that a particular class is unfit to govern. Every class is unfit to govern.
— Letter to Mary Gladstone, April 24, 1881

Gracie Allen

The President of today is just the postage stamp of tomorrow.
— attributed

Grant Allen

Individualism is only logically and consistently possible if it starts with the postulate that all men must, to begin with, have free and equal access to the common gifts of nature.
— quoted by Bool and Carlyle in *For Liberty*

Peter Arshinov

Proletarians of the world, look into the depths of your own beings, seek out the truth and realize it yourselves: you will find it nowhere else.
— quoted by Bool and Carlyle in *For Liberty*

Michael Bakunin

If society had never come into being, man would have remained a wild beast forever, or, what amounts to the same thing, a saint.
— *God and the State*

Until now all human history has been only a perpetual and bloody immolation of millions of poor human beings in honor of some pitiless abstraction —God, country, power of State, national honor, historical, judicial rights, political liberty, public welfare.
— Ibid.

I shall continue to be an impossible person so long as those who are now possible remain possible.
— Letter to Ogarov, June 14, 1868

The urge to destroy is also a creative urge.
— *Reaction in Germany*

Alexander Berkman

...so-called political "action" is, so far as the cause of the workers and of true progress is concerned, worse than inaction. The very essence of politics is corruption, sail-trimming, the sacrifice of your ideals and integrity for success. Bitter are the fruits of this "success" for the masses and for every decent man and woman the world over. .

There is nothing more corrupting than compromise. One step in that direction calls for another, makes it necessary and compelling, and soon it swamps you with the force of a rolling snowball become a landslide.

Our present civilization has, by disinheriting millions, made the belly the center of the universe.

Capitalism robs you and makes a wage slave of you. The law upholds and protects that robbery. The government fools you into believing that you are independent and free. In this way you are fooled and duped every day of your life.
— above quotations from *What Is Communist Anarchism?*

Ambrose Bierce

ALLIANCE, In international politics, the union of two thieves who have their hands so deeply inserted in each other's pockets that they cannot separately plunder a third.

ARENA, In politics, an imaginary rat-pit in which the statesman wrestles with his record.

CONSERVATIVE, A statesman who is enamored of existing evils, as distinguished from the Liberal who wishes to replace them with others.

CONSUL, In American politics, a person who having failed to secure an office from the people is given one by the Administration on condition that he leave the country.

IMPARTIAL, Unable to perceive any promise of personal advantage from espousing either side of a controversy or adopting either of two conflicting opinions.

OPPOSITION, In politics the party that prevents the Government from running amuck by hamstringing it.

OUT-OF-DOORS, That part of one's environment upon which no government has been able to collect taxes.

PASSPORT, A document treacherously inflicted upon a citizen going abroad, exposing him as an alien and pointing him out for special reprobation and outrage.

POLITICS, A strife of interests masquerading as a contest of principles. The conduct of public affairs for private advantage.

POLITICIAN, An eel in the fundamental mud upon which the superstructure of organized society is reared. When he wriggles he mistakes the agitation of his tail for the trembling of the edifice. As compared with the statesman, he suffers the disadvantage of being alive.
— above quotations from *The Devil's Dictionary*

William Blake

Prisons are built with stones of law, brothels with bricks of religion.
— *Proverbs of Hell*

Napoleon Bonaparte

A man like me cares nothing for the lives of millions.
— quoted by Rocker in *Nationalism and Culture*

Simon Cameron

An honest politician is one who, when he is bought, will stay bought.
— attributed

Lord Chesterfield

Let us consider that arbitrary power has seldom or never been introduced into any country at once. It must be introduced by slow degrees, and as it were step by step, lest the people see its approach.
— quoted by Bool and Carlyle in *For Liberty*

Winston Churchill

If I had been an Italian, I am sure I would have been with you [Mussolini] from the beginning to the end of your victorious struggle against the bestial appetites and passions of Leninism.
— quoted in *Literary Digest*, February 26, 1927

Your movement [fascism] has abroad rendered a service to the whole world...Italy has shown that there is a way to combat subversive forces.
— Ibid.

Italy [under Mussolini] has demonstrated that the great mass of the people, when it is well led, appreciates and is ready to defend the honor and stability of civil society. It [fascism] provides the necessary antidote to the Russian virus. Henceforth no nation will be able to imagine that it is deprived of a last means of protection against malignant tumors, and every Socialist leader in each country ought to feel more confident in resisting rash and leveling doctrines.
— Ibid.

...a sheep in sheep's clothing

...a modest man with much to be modest about.

He occasionally stumbles over the truth, but he always hastily picks himself up and hurries on as if nothing had happened.

There but for the grace of god, goes god.

— barbs directed at political rivals

Alex Comfort

The factual history of power in society bears the same relationship to communal health as the works of de Sade bear to individual normality, save that it is real, not fantastic. Either it is true that humanity by intelligence and by the practice of mutual aid and direct action can reverse processes which appear socially inevitable, or humanity will become extinct by simple maladaptation...the rejection of power is the first step in any such intelligent reversal.
— preface to *Barbarism and Sexual Freedom*

Glen A. Dahlquist

We are told by some that when a nation gets too democratic the man on horseback will soon appear. These people should know, for they invite him.

Eugene V. Debs

Too long have the workers of the world waited for some Moses to lead them out of bondage. He has not come; he never will come. I would not lead you out if I could; for if you could be led out, you could be led back again. I would have you make up your minds that there is nothing that you cannot do for yourselves.

—Speech, December 10, 1905

I am willing to be charged with almost anything, rather than to be charged with being a leader... I would be ashamed to admit that I had risen from the ranks. When I rise it will be with the ranks, and not from the ranks.

—Speech, June 16, 1918

At Yoakum, Texas, a few days ago...I passed four or five bearers of the white man's burden perched on a railing and decorating their environment with tobacco juice...One glance was sufficient to satisfy me that they represented all there is of justification for the implacable hatred of the Negro race. They were ignorant, lazy, unclean, totally void of ambition, themselves the foul product of the capitalist system and held in lowest contempt by the master class, yet esteeming themselves immeasurably above the cleanest, most intelligent and self-respecting Negro, having by reflex absorbed the "nigger" hatred of their masters.

—*International Socialist Review*, November 1903

...there is no Negro question outside of the labor question...The class struggle is colorless. The capitalists, white, black, and other shades, are on one side and the workers, white, black and all other colors, on the other side.

—Ibid.

In the Republican and Democratic national conventions principle is subordinated to personality. "Who are the candidates?" is the all-absorbing question. The people, like helpless children, are forever looking for some great man to watch over and protect them.

—*The Comrade*, November 1904

Denis Diderot

And with the guts of the last priest let us strangle the last king.

—attributed

Sen. Everett Dirksen

I am a man of principle. And my first principle is flexibility.

—attributed

Fyodor Dostoyevsky

Every member of the society spies on the rest, and it is his duty to inform against them...All are slaves and equal in their slavery...The great thing about it is equality...Slaves are bound to be equal.

—*The Possessed*

Ralph Waldo Emerson

Democracy becomes a government of bullies tempered by editors.

George Engel

Every considerate person must combat a system which makes it possible for the individual to rake and hoard millions in a few years, while on the other side, thousands become tramps and beggars.

—*The Philosophy of Anarchism*

Friedrich Engels

Terror implies mostly useless cruelty perpetrated by frightened people in order to reassure themselves.

—Letter to Marx, September 14, 1870

Luigi Fabbri

The overriding importance attributed to an act of violence or individual rebellion is the daughter of the overriding importance attributed by bourgeois political doctrine to a few "great men" in comparison to that attributed to society as a whole.

—*Bourgeois Influences on Anarchism*

Francisco Ferrer

The education of today is nothing more than drill...children must be accustomed to obey, to believe, to think according to the social dogmas which govern us.

—*The Modern School*

There is no reason for governments to change their systems. They have succeeded in making education serve their advantage; they will likewise know how to make use of any improvements that may be proposed to their advantage.

It is sufficient that they maintain the spirit of the school, the authoritarian discipline which reigns therein, for all innovations to be turned to their profit. And they will watch their opportunity; be sure of that.

—Ibid.

Ricardo Flores Magon

Capital, Authority, Clergy: This is the hydra which guards the gate of this prison called Earth.

—Speech, October 13, 1911

The world is a prison, a much larger one than those with which we're familiar, but a prison nonetheless. The guards are the police and soldiers; the wardens are the presidents, kings, and emperors,; the watchdogs are the legislators; and in this sense we can exactly equate the armies of prison functionaries and their acts with the armies of government functionaries and their acts. The downtrodden, the plebians, the disinherited masses, are the prisoners, obliged to work to support the army of functionaries and the lazy, thieving rich.

—Ibid.

Ah, order! So whine in these moments the partisans of so-called order. Order for these poor souls can only exist when humanity submits to the clubs of the policeman, the soldier, the judge, the jailer, the hangman, and the governor.

But this is not order. By order I understand harmony; and harmony cannot exist while there exist on this planet some who gorge themselves and others who don't even have a crust of bread to lift to their mouths.

—*Regeneración*, May 13, 1911

The only thing for which authority is needed is to maintain social inequality. Mexicanos: Death to Authority! Viva Tierra y Libertad!

—*Regeneración*, February 24, 1912

In sum, the workers fight over bread, they snatch mouthfuls from each other, one is the enemy of the rest, because each searches solely for his own well-being without bothering about the well-being of the rest; and this antagonism between individuals of the same class, this deaf struggle for miserable crumbs, makes our slavery permanent, perpetuates misery, causes our misfortunes—because we don't understand that the interest of our neighbor is our own interest, because we sacrifice ourselves for a poorly understood individual interest, searching in vain for well-being which can only be the result of our interest in the matters which affect all humanity.

—Speech in El Monte, California, 1917

Indifference forges our chains, and we are our own tyrants because we do nothing to destroy them. Indifferent and apathetic, we watch the parade of events as if it were happening on another planet; and as everyone is interested only in himself, with no concern for the general interest, no one feels the need to unite in the struggle for the interests of all. The result is that there is no solidarity among the oppressed, the government knows no limits to its abuses, and bosses of all types make prisoners of us—they enslave us, exploit us, oppress us, and humiliate us.

When we reflect that all of us who suffer the same evils have the same interests, interests common to all the oppressed, and we resolve to show solidarity, then we will be capable of transforming the circumstances which cause our misfortunes into circumstances favorable to our liberty and well-being.

—Ibid.

My fate has been sealed. I have to die within prison walls...a 21-year sentence is a life-term for me. I do not complain about my fate, however, I am receiving what I have always gotten in my 30 years of struggling for justice—persecution. I knew since the first that my appeals to brotherhood, and love and peace would be answered by the blows of those interested in the preservation of conditions favorable to the enslaving of many by one man. I never expected to succeed in my endeavor, but I felt it to be my duty to persevere...My present and my future are dark, but I am certain of the bright future which is opened to the human race, and this is my consolation...There will not be babies whining for milk, there will not be women selling their charms for a crust of bread; competition and enmity will give way to cooperation and love among human beings. Will this not be great?

—Letter to Winnie Branstetter, March 24, 1921

John T. Flynn

Beneath the skin of many a well-advertised liberal lurk the blue corpuscules of a hardened tory. The tragic evil of these misbranded liberals is that they are able to put into effect reactionary measures that conservatives longed for but dared not attempt. When the conservative statesman seeks to adopt some atavistic policy, liberal groups can be counted on to resist the attempt. But when a liberal premier, marching under the banner of liberalism, attempts this there is no opposition or only a feeble one. He paralyzes the natural resistance to such measures by putting a liberal label on them and by silencing or dividing his followers who constitute the natural opposition to his misbranded product.

—*As We Go Marching*

Let us restate our definition of fascism. It is, put briefly, a system of social organization in which the political state is a dictatorship supported by a political elite and in which the economic society is an autarchial capitalism, enclosed and planned, in which the government assumes responsibility for creating adequate purchasing power through the instrumentality of national debt and in which militarism is adopted as a great economic project for creating work as well as a great romantic project in the service of the imperialist state.

—Ibid.

Anatole France

...moderates are always moderately opposed to violence.

—*Penguin Island*

Benjamin Franklin

We must, indeed, all hang together, or most assuredly we shall all hang separately.

—prior to the signing of the Declaration of Independence

Henry Clay Frick

We bought the s.o.b., but he didn't stay bought.
— in regard to Teddy Roosevelt's 1904 campaign

Victor Garcia

Columbus was the first economist. He didn't know where he was going. He deceived his men. And he travelled on government money.

Edward Gibbon

A nation of slaves is always prepared to applaud the clemency of their master who, in the abuse of absolute power, does not proceed to the last extremes of injustice and oppression.
— *The Decline and Fall of the Roman Empire*

William Godwin

The wisdom of Lawmaking and Parliaments has been applied to creating the most wretched and senseless distribution of property, which mocks alike at human nature and the principles of justice.
— *An Enquiry Concerning Political Justice*

Emma Goldman

Republicanism stands for vested rights, for imperialism, for graft, for the annihilation of every semblance of liberty. Its ideal is the oily, creepy respectability of a Mckinley, and the brutal arrogance of a [Theodore] Roosevelt.
— *Francisco Ferrer and the Modern School*

The majority represents a mass of cowards, willing to accept him who mirrors its own soul and mind poverty.
— Ibid.

Lacking utterly in originality and moral courage, the majority has always placed its destiny in the hands of others. Incapable of standing responsibilities, it has followed its leaders even unto destruction.
— Ibid.

That the mass bleeds, that it is being robbed and exploited, I know as well as our vote-baiters. But I insist that not the handful of parasites, but the mass itself is responsible for this horrible state of affairs. It clings to its masters, loves the whip, and is the first to cry Crucify! the moment a protesting voice is raised against the sacredness of capitalistic authority or any other decayed institution. Yet how long would authority and private property exist, if not for the willingness of the mass to become soldiers, policemen, jailers, and hangmen?
— Ibid.

There is no greater fallacy than the belief that aims and purposes are one thing, while methods and tactics are another. This conception is a potent menace to social regeneration. All human experience teaches that methods and means cannot be separated from the ultimate aim. The means employed become through individual habit and social practice, part and parcel of the final purpose; they influence it, modify it, and presently the aims and means become identical.
— *My Disillusionment in Russia*

Nazism has been justly called an attack on civilization. This characterization applies with equal force to every form of dictatorship; indeed, to every kind of suppression and coercive authority. For what is civilization in the true sense? All progress has been essentially an enlargement of the liberties of the individual with a corresponding decrease of the authority wielded over him by external forces.
— *The Individual, Society and the State*

Individuality is not to be confused with the various ideas and concepts of Individualism; much less with that "rugged individualism" which is only a masked attempt to repress and defeat the individual and his individuality. So-called Individualism is the social and economic *laissez-faire*: the exploitation of the masses by the classes by means of legal trickery, spiritual debasement and systematic indoctrination of the servile spirit, which process is known as "education." That corrupt and perverse "individualism" is the strait jacket of individuality. It has converted life into a degrading race for externals, for possession, for social prestige and supremacy. Its highest wisdom is "the devil take the hindmost."

This "rugged individualism" has inevitably resulted in the greatest modern slavery, the crassest class distinctions, driving millions to the breadline. "Rugged individualism" has meant all the "individualism" for the masters, while the people are regimented into a slave caste to serve a handful of self-seeking "supermen." America is perhaps the best representative of this kind of individualism, in whose name political tyranny and social oppression are defended and held up as virtues; while every aspiration and attempt of man to gain freedom and social opportunity to live is denounced as "un-American" and evil in the name of that same individuality.

— Ibid.

Political absolutism has been abolished because men have realized in the course of time that absolute power is evil and destructive. But the same thing is true of all power, whether it be the power of privilege, of money, of the priest, of the politician or of so-called democracy. In its effect on individuality it matters little what the particular character of coercion is—whether it be as black as Fascism, as yellow as Nazism or as pretentiously red as Bolshevism. It is power that dorrupts and degrades both master and slave and it makes no

Originally published in *Freedom*

"And Sue said to me, 'But Richard how can someone as sensitive as you and a practicing humanitarian take this job?' And I said, 'Sue love, I genuinely believe that by doing so I can alleviate some of the worst excesses of the system.'"

difference whether the power is wielded by an autocrat, by parliament or Soviets. More pernicious than the power of a dictator is that of a class; the most terrible— the tyranny of a majority.
— Ibid.

Praxedis Guerrero

To be dragged in the wake of the passive flock and to pass a hundred and one times beneath the shears of the shepherd, or to die alone like a brave eagle on a rocky crag of a great mountain: that is the dilemma.
— *Regeneración*, February 18, 1911

Who is more responsible, the tyrant who oppresses the people, or the people who produce the tyrant?
— *Regeneración*, October 22, 1910

Auberon Herbert

Who shall count up the evil brood that is born from power—the pitiful fear, the madness, the despair, the overpowering craving for revenge, the treachery, the unmeasured cruelty?
— *Westminster Gazette*, November 22, 1893

Deny human rights, and however little you may wish to do so, you will find yourself abjectly kneeling at the feet of that old-world god, Force—that grimmest and ugliest of gods that men have ever created for themselves out of the lusts of their hearts. You will find yourself hating and dreading all other men who differ from you; you will find yourself obliged by the law of conflict into which you have plunged, to use every means in your power to crush them before they are able to crush you; you will find yourself day by day growing more unscrupulous and intolerant, more and more compelled by the fear of those opposed to you, to commit harsh and violent actions. You will find yourselves clinging to and welcoming Force, as the one and only form of protection left to you...
— Ibid.

Adolf Hitler

Every world-moving idea has not only the right, but also the duty, of securing those means which make possible the execution of its ideas. Success is the one earthly judge concerning the right or wrong of such an effort...
— *Mein Kampf*

It is an absurdity to believe that with the end of the school period the state's right to supervise its young citizens suddenly ceases, but returns at military age. This right is a duty and as such is present at all times. Only the present-day state having no interest in healthy people has neglected this duty in a criminal fashion. It lets present-day youth go to the dogs on the streets and in brothels, instead of taking them in hand...

In what form the state carries on this training is beside the point today; the important thing is that it should do so...This education in its broad outlines can serve as a preparation for future military service.
— Ibid.

Elbert Hubbard

A conservative is a man who is too cowardly to fight and too fat to run.
— *Epigrams*

Robert Ingersoll

There is something wrong in a government where they who do the most have the least. There is something wrong when honesty wears a rag, and rascality a robe; when the loving, the tender, eat a crust, while the infamous sit at banquets.
— *A Lay Sermon*

The history of man is simply the history of slavery, of injustice, and brutality, together with the means by which he has through the dead and desolate years, slowly and painfully advanced. He has been the sport and prey of priest and king, the food of superstition and cruel might. Crowned force has governed ignorance through fear.
— *The Liberty of Man, Woman and Child*

In all ages hypocrites called priests have put crowns upon the heads of thieves called kings.
— *Individuality*

For many centuries the sword and cross were allies. Together they attacked the rights of man.
— quoted in *Ingersoll the Magnificent*

Thomas Jefferson

Whenever a man has cast a longing eye on offices, a rottenness begins in his conduct.
— Letter to Tench Coxe, 1820

John F. Kennedy

Do you realize the responsibility I carry? I'm the only person standing between Nixon and the White House.
— during the 1960 presidential campaign (attributed)

Paul Krassner

Politically, I'm a vegetarian who'll eat meat if it's served.
— Interview for *BSU Arbiter*, 1977

Peter Kropotkin

Most eighteenth-century philosophers had very elementary ideas on the origin of societies.

According to them, in the beginning men lived in small isolated families, and perpetual warfare between them was the normal state of affairs. But one fine day, realizing at last the disadvantages that resulted from their endless struggles, men decided to join forces. A social contract was concluded among the scattered families who willingly submitted themselves to an authority which—need I say?—became the starting point as well as the initiator of all progress...

The fact is that all animals, with the exception of some carnivores and birds of prey and some species which are becoming extinct, live in societies. In the struggle for life, the gregarious species have an advantage over those that are not. In every animal classification they are at the top of the ladder, and there cannot be the slightest doubt that the first beings with human attributes were already living in societies. Man did not create society; society existed before man.

— *The State: Its Historic Role*

That which has been represented as individualism so far has been pathetic and skimpy—and what is worse, contains in itself the negation of its goal, the impoverishment of individuality, or in any case the denial of what is necessary for obtaining the most complete flowering of the individual...the stupid egoist is incapable of understanding his own interest and is like the Zulu king who thought he was "asserting his personality" while eating a quarter of a steer a day.

— Letter to Max Nettlau, March 5, 1902

To contemplate the destruction of Capitalism without the abolition of the State is just as absurd, in our opinion, as it is to hope that the emancipation of the laborer will be accomplished through the action of the Christian Church or of Caesarism.

— quoted by Bool and Carlyle in *For Liberty*

Throughout the history of our civilization, two traditions, two opposing tendencies have confronted each other: the Roman and the popular traditions; the imperial and the federalist; the authoritarian and the libertarian...

Between these two currents, always manifesting themselves, always at grips with each other—the popular trend and that which thirsts for political and religious domination—we have made our choice.

— Ibid.

V.I. Lenin

First we have to convince and then use compulsion.

— quoted by Maximoff in *The Guillotine at Work*

Without an apparatus of compulsion we shall not take what we need. Never! Anyone can see that.

— Ibid.

We need a terroristic purge: trials held on the spot and shooting as an unreserved measure.

— Ibid.

The guillotine only terrorized, it only broke down *active* resistance. *But this is not enough for us.*

...We have to break down passive resistance which doubtlessly is the most harmful and dangerous one.

— Ibid.

...yes, the terror of the Cheka [now the KGB] is absolutely necessary.

— Ibid.

We must wipe off the face of the earth all traces ...of the policy of the Mensheviks and Social-Revolutionaries who speak about individual rights; their policy is dooming us to hunger and starvation.

— Ibid.

...an avowal of Menshevik views should be punished by our courts with shooting...

— Ibid.

There are no morals in politics; there is only expedience.

— quoted in *Time* November 17, 1947

Pope Leo XIII

All Catholics must make themselves felt as active elements in daily political life in the countries where they live. They must penetrate, wherever possible, in the administration of civil affairs; must constantly exert the utmost vigilance and energy to prevent the usages of liberty from going beyond the limits fixed by God's law.

— *Immortale Dei*

Obedience is not servitude of man to man, but submission to the will of God, who governs through the medium of men.

— Ibid.

All public power proceeds from God.

— Ibid.

All Catholics should do all in their power to cause the constitutions of states and legislation to be modeled on the principles of the true Church.

— Ibid.

There is an inequality of right and authority which emanates from God Himself.

— *Quod Apostolici Numeris*

The highest duty is to respect authority.

— *Libertas Praestantissimum*

When, amid the slave multitude whom she has numbered among her children, some, led astray by some hope of liberty, have had recourse to violence and sedition, the church has always con-

demned these unlawful efforts, and through her ministers has applied the remedy of patience.
— Apostolic Letter to Brazilian Bishops, 1888

Abraham Lincoln

I have no purpose, either directly or indirectly, to interfere with the institution of slavery in the states where it exists.
— first Lincoln-Douglas debate, August 21, 1858

I do not now, or ever did, stand pledged against the admission of any more slave states to the union. I do not stand pledged to the prohibiton of slave-trade between the states.
— Ibid.

Martin Luther

An earthly kingdom cannot exist without inequality of persons. Some must be free, some serfs, some rulers, some subjects.
— *Werke, Vol. XVIII*, quoted by McCabe

No one need think that the world can be ruled without blood. The civil sword shall and must be red and bloody.
— *Werke, Vol. XV*, quoted by McCabe

As to the common people, Mr. Everyman, one has to be hard with them and see that they do their work and that under the threat of the sword and the law they comply with the observances of piety, just as you chain up wild beasts so as to get a peaceful life.
— quoted by Joseph McCabe

George E. MacDonald

It is not in the nature of politics that the best men should be elected. The best men do not want to govern their fellowmen...

Mr. [Theodore] Roosevelt says: "The performance of duty stands ahead of the insistence upon one's rights."...If Mr. Roosevelt can demonstrate that duty is ahead of right, he can prove that every man in the world owes more than is coming him.

Niccolo Machiavelli

Politics have no relation to morals.
— *The Prince*

A ruler must learn to be other than good.
— Ibid.

Errico Malatesta

The only possible alternative to being either the oppressed or the oppressor is voluntary cooperation for the greatest good of all...
— *Volonta*, June 15, 1913

[Individualism] trusts to the free initiative of individuals, and proclaims, if not the abolition, the reduction of government. However, as it respects private property, and is founded on the principle of each for himself, and therefore on competition, its liberty is only the the liberty of the strong, the license of those who have to oppress and exploit the weak who have nothing. Far from producing harmony, it would tend always to augment the distance between the rich and the poor, and end also, through exploitation and domination, in authority...Individualism is, in theory, a kind of Anarchy without cooperation. It is therefore no better than a lie, because liberty is not possible without Solidarity, without cooperation. The criticism which Individualists pass on government is merely the wish to deprive it of certain functions, to hand them over virtually to the capitalist. But it cannot attack those repressive functions which form the essence of government, for without an armed force the proprietary system could not be upheld. Even more, under Individualism, the repressive power of government must always increase, in proportion to the increase, by means of free competition, of want, inequality, and disharmony.
— *Anarchy*

The fundamental error of the reformists is that of dreaming of solidarity, a sincere collaboration between masters and servants, between proprietors and workers...
Those who envisage a society of well-stuffed pigs which waddle contentedly under the staffs of a small number of swineherds; who do not take into account the need for freedom and the sentiment of human dignity; who really believe in a God that orders, for his abstruse ends, the poor to be submissive and the rich to be good and charitable — can also imagine and aspire to a technical organization of production which assures abundance to all and is at the same time materially advantageous both to the bosses and to the workers.
— *Umanita Nova*, May 10, 1922

To remain isolated, each individual acting or seeking to act on his own without coordination, without preparation, without joining his modest efforts to a strong group, means condemning oneself to impotence, wasting one's efforts in small ineffectual actions, and to lose faith very soon in one's aims and possibly being reduced to complete inactivity.
— *L'Agitazione*, June 11, 1897

When a community has needs and its members do not know how to organize spontaneously to provide them, someone comes forward, an authority who satisfies those needs by utilizing the services of all and directing them to his liking. If the roads are unsafe and the people do not know what measures to take, a police force emerges...This is what has happened in our midst; the less organized we have been the more prone are we to be imposed on by a few individuals. And this is understandable...

So much so that organization, far from creating authority, is the only cure for it . . .
— Ibid.

We do not believe in the infallibility, nor even in the general goodness of the masses; on the contrary. But we believe even less in the infallibility and goodness of those who seize power and legislate.
— *Umanita Nova,* September 2, 1922

Mao Tse Tung

Political power grows out of the barrel of a gun.
— *Selected Works,* Vol. II

We should support whatever the enemy opposes and oppose whatever the enemy supports.
— Ibid.

Robert McFarlane
(Reagan National Security Advisor)

We don't lie. We put our own interpretation on what the truth is.
— quoted in *Propaganda Review,* Spring 1988

Jean Meslier

I would like to see the last king strangled with the guts of the last priest.
— attributed

John Stuart Mill

Now, it is a universally observed fact, that the two evil dispositions in question, the disposition to prefer a man's selfish interests to those which he shares with other people, and his immediate and direct interests to those which are indirect and remote, are characteristics most especially called forth and fostered by the possession of power . . . Finding themselves worshipped by others they become worshippers of themselves, and think themselves entitled to be counted at a hundred times the value of other people; while the facility they acquire of doing as they like without regard to consequences insensi-

bly weakens the habits which make men look forward even to such consequences as affect themselves. This is the meaning of the universal tradition, grounded on universal experience, of men being corrupted by power.
— *On Liberty*

I entered Parliament with what I thought to be the lowest possible opinion of the average member, I came out with one still lower.
— *Autobiography*

Benito Mussolini

Fascism has no armory of theoretical doctrines. Every system is a mistake and every theory a prison.
— quoted by Flynn in *As We Go Marching*

It was only one life. What is one life in the affairs of a state?
— after running down a child in his car in 1931, quoted by Smedley Butler

Martin Niemoeller

First they came for the Communists, and I didn't speak up because I wasn't a Communist. Then they came for the Jews, and I didn't speak up because I wasn't a Jew. Then they came for the trade unionists, and I didn't speak up because I wasn't a trade unionist. Then they came for the Catholics, and I didn't speak up because I was a Protestant. Then they came for me, and by that time no one was left to speak up.

Richard Nixon

You know the difficulty with a president when he makes a statement is that everybody checks to see whether it is true.
— at a National Prayer Breakfast, 1974, quoted by Fawn Brodie

When the president does it, that means it's not illegal.
— attributed

I need the speech in which I talk about the need of modern man to live in closer contact with nature.

Are you going to participate in an environmental conference?

No . . . I'm attending a meeting with the homeless.

Max Nordau

Party struggles are to a people what change is to the hod carrier, as he shifts his hod from one shoulder to the other, a temporary but not a genuine relief...
— *Conventional Lies of Our Civilization*

Thomas Paine

A great part of that order which reigns among mankind is not the effect of government. It had its origin in the principles of society, and the natural constitution of man. It existed prior to government and would exist if the formality of government was abolished. The mutual dependence and reciprocal interest which man has in man, and all the parts of a civilized community upon each other, create that great chain of connexion which holds it together.
— *The Rights of Man*

Toleration is not the opposite of intoleration, but is the counterfeit of it. Both are despotisms. The one assumes to itself the right of withholding liberty of conscience, and the other of granting it. The one is pope, armed with fire and fagot, and the other is the pope selling or granting indulgences.
— Ibid.

Men should not petition for rights, but take them.
— Ibid.

...I have always strenuously supported the right of every man to his opinion, however different that opinion might be to mine. He who denies to another this right, makes a slave of himself to his present opinion, because he precludes himself the right of changing it.
— *The Age of Reason*

Albert Parsons

Of my life and the cause of my unnatural and cruel death, you will learn from others. Your father is a self-offered sacrifice upon the altar of Liberty and Happiness. To you I leave the legacy of an honest name and duty done. Preserve it, emulate it. Be true to yourselves; you cannot then be false to others.
— Last letter to his children

There was *no evidence* that any one of the eight doomed men knew of, or advised, or abetted the Haymarket tragedy. But what does that matter? The privileged class *demands a victim*...
— Letter to his wife, August 20, 1886

Wendell Phillips

No reform, moral or intellectual, ever came from the upper class of society. Each and all come from the protest of martyr and victim. The emancipation of the working people must be achieved by the working people themselves.
— *Orations, Speeches, Lectures, and Letters*

Let History close the record. Let her show that on the side of the oppressor there was power — power to frame mischief by a law; that on that side were all the forms of law, and behind these forms, most of the elements of control: wealth, greedy of increase and anxious for order at any sacrifice of principle — priests prophesying smooth things and arrogating to themselves the name of Christianity — ambition, baptizing itself statesmanship — and that unthinking patriotism, child of habit and not of reason, which mistakes government for liberty, and law for justice.
— Ibid.

...politics takes up with small men, men without grasp enough for large business; with leisure, therefore, on their hands; men popular because they have no positive opinions — these are the men of politics.
— *Mobs and Education*

The cause of tyrants is one the world over, and the cause of resistance to tyranny is one also... An Hungarian triumph lightens the chains of Carolina; and an infamous vote in the United States Senate adds darkness to the dungeon where German patriots lie entombed. All oppressions under the sun are linked together, and each feels the Devil's pulse keep time in it to the life-blood of every other. Of this brotherhood, it matters not what member you assail, since — "Whatever link you strike, tenth or thousandth, breaks the chain alike."
— *Welcome to George Thompson*

William Pitt, Jr.

Necessity is the argument of tyrants; it is the creed of slaves.

Pope Pius XI

Mussolini...a gift of Providence, a man free from the prejudices of the politicians of the liberal school.
— at the signing of the Lateran Pact, 1929

Human society, as established by God, is composed of unequal elements, just as parts of the human body are unequal; to make them all equal is impossible, and would mean the destruction of human society itself.
— Apostolic Letter to Italian Bishops, December 18, 1930

Eugene Pottier

Arise, ye prisoners of starvation,
Arise, ye wretched of the earth,
For justice thunders condemnation,
A better world's in birth.

No more tradition's chain shall bind us,
Arise ye slaves no more in thrall!
The earth shall rise on new foundations,
We have been naught; we shall be all.
— *The Internationale*

Pierre Joseph Proudhon

In any given society the authority of man over man runs in inverse proportion to the intellectual development of that society.
— *What Is Property?*

...in philosophy, in politics, in theology, in history, negation is the preliminary requirement to affirmation. All progress begins by abolishing something; every reform rests upon denunciation of some abuse; each new idea is based upon the proved insufficiency of the old idea.
— *The General Idea of the Revolution in the 19th Century*

The economic notion of capital, the political idea of the State or of authority and the theological conceptions of the Church are identical concepts which reciprocally complete and support one another. We cannot therefore oppose the one and leave the others alone...What capital today does to labor, the State does to freedom, and the Church to the spirit. This trinity of absolutism is in practice just as dangerous as in philosophy. In order to effectively oppress the people one must put their bodies, their wills and their intelligence in bonds. If socialism has the purpose to reveal itself in its complete and universal form freed from every mysticism, then it need only bring the significance of this trinity to the comprehension of the people.
— quoted by Rudolf Rocker in *Pioneers of American Freedom*

Isaac Puente

Poverty is the symptom and slavery is the disease. If we went only by appearances, we would agree that poverty ought to be singled out as the worst feature of present-day society. The worst affliction, however, is slavery, which obliges man to submit to poverty and prevents him from rebelling against it. The greatest of evils is not capital, which exploits the worker, enriching itself at his expense, but rather the state which keeps the worker naked and undefended, maintaining him in subjection by armed force and by imprisonment.
— *Libertarian Communism*

Every ill we deplore in society...is rooted in the institution of power, that is, in the state and the institution of private ownership...Man is at the mercy of these two social afflictions which escape his control: they make him petty, stingy and lacking solidarity when he is rich and cruelly insensitive to human suffering when he wields power. Poverty degrades, but wealth perverts.
— Ibid.

Hunger makes a coward of the isolated individual, but when hunger is generally felt it becomes a source of rage and audacity.
— Ibid.

Ronald Reagan

You'd be surprised. They're all different countries.
— on Latin America, quoted in the *Washington Post*, December 6, 1982

A tree's a tree. How many more do you need to look at?
— on redwoods, quoted in the *Sacramento Bee*, April 28, 1966

Wilhelm Reich

The interest of the mass individual is not political but sexual.
— *The Sexual Revolution*

The fact that political ideologies are tangible realities is not a proof of their vitally necessary character. The bubonic plague was an extraordinarily powerful social reality, but no one would have regarded it as vitally necessary.
— *The Mass Psychology of Fascism*

If one wants to recognize effortlessly the essence of politics, let one reflect upon the fact that it was a Hitler who was able to make a whole world hold its breath for many years. The fact that Hitler was a political genius unmasks the nature of politics in general as no other fact can.
— Ibid.

...it is the authoritarian upbringing of little children, the teaching them to be fearful and submissive, that secures for the political power monger the slavery and the gullibility of millions of adult men and women.
— Ibid.

It is the authoritarian family that represents the foremost and most essential source of reproduction of every kind of reactionary thinking; it is a factory where reactionary ideology and reactionary structures are produced.
— Ibid.

In his practical work for the masses, the revolutionary easily forgets — *and sometimes likes to forget* — that the real goal is not work (sexual freedom brings about a continuous reduction in the working day), but sexual play and life in all its forms, from orgasm to the highest accomplishments.
— Ibid.

It is true that those of us who have political experience could wrestle for power just as any other politician. *But we have not time; we have more important things to do...*
...it is *definitely* conceivable that the world catastrophe will reach a stage at which the masses of

people will be *forced to get an insight into their social attitudes,* be forced to change themselves and to assume the heavy burden of social responsibility. But in such a case, *they themselves* will acquire power and will rightfully reject groups who "conquer" power "in the interest of the people." Hence there is no reason for us to fight for power.

—Ibid.

The fundamental difference between the reactionary politician and the genuine democrat is revealed in their attitude toward state power. A man's social character can be *objectively* appraised on the basis of this attitude, regardless of his political party...

It is typical of the reactionary to advocate the supremacy of the state over society; he advocates the *"idea* of the state," which leads in a straight line to dictatorial absolutism, whether it is embodied in a royal, ministerial, or open fascist form of state. The genuine democrat, who acknowledges and advocates natural work-democracy as the natural basis of international and national cooperation, always aims at overcoming the difficulties of social cooperation by eliminating the social causes of these difficulties.

—Ibid.

Rudolf Rocker

By direct action the Anarcho-Syndicalists mean every method of immediate warfare by the workers against their economic and political oppressors. Among these, the outstanding are the strike, in all its gradations from the simple wage-struggle to the general strike; the boycott; sabotage in its countless forms; anti-militarist propaganda; and in particularly critical cases...armed resistance of the people for the protection of life and liberty.

—*Anarcho-Syndicalism*

Political rights do not exist because they have been legally set down on a piece of paper, but only when they have become the ingrown habits of a people, and when any attempt to impair them will meet with the violent resistance of the populace. Where this is not the case, there is no help in any parliamentary opposition or any Platonic appeals to the constitution.

—Ibid.

Political rights do not originate in parliaments; they are, rather, forced upon parliaments from without. And even their enactment into law has for a long time been no guarantee of their security ...Governments...are always inclined to restrict or to abrogate completely rights and freedoms that have been achieved if they imagine that the people will put up no resistance.

—Ibid.

A system that in every act of its life sacrifices the welfare of large sections of the people, of whole nations, to the selfish lust for power and the economic interests of small minorities must necessarily dissolve the social ties and lead to a constant war of each against all.

—*Anarchism and Anarcho-Syndicalism*

With many the theory of evolution assumes the form of a fatalistic conception of social development, leading them to regard even the most revolting phenomena of the age as the result of an unalterable evolutionary process in which man cannot arbitrarily interfere. This belief in the inevitability and determinism of all events must estrange men from their natural sense of right and wrong and blunt their understanding of the ethical significance of events...By such thoughts we not only cripple all resistance to arbitrary and brutal force, but we also justify indirectly the perpetrators of these abominations by regarding them as the executors of historical necessity, whose deeds lie, so to speak, beyond good and evil. It matters little whether this is done consciously or unconsciously. In reality the brutal acts of violent men and the monstrous crimes now [1937] being perpetrated in Germany...have nothing to do with social evolution. We are here dealing simply with the mania for power of small minorities which have known how to exploit a given situation to their own profit.

—*Nationalism and Culture*

However fully man may recognize cosmic laws, he will never be able to change them, because they are not his work. But every form of his social existence, every social institution which the past has bestowed on him as a legacy from remote ancestors, is the work of men and can be changed by human will and action or made to serve new ends. Only such an understanding is truly revolutionary and animated by the spirit of the coming ages. Whoever believes in the necessary sequence of all historical events sacrifices the future to the past. He explains the phenomena of social life, but he does not change them. In this respect all fatalism is alike, whether of a religious, political, or economic nature. Whoever is caught in its snare is robbed thereby of life's most precious possession: the impulse to act according to his own needs.

—Ibid.

Power always acts destructively, for its possessors are ever striving to lace all phenomena of social life into a corset of their laws to give them a definite shape. Its mental expression is dead dogma; its physical manifestation of life, brute force. This lack of intelligence in its endeavors leaves its imprint likewise on the persons of its representatives, gradually making them inferior and brutal, even though they were originally excellently endowed. Nothing dulls the mind and the soul of man as does the eternal monotony of routine, and power is essentially routine.

—Ibid.

To maintain [the present] state of things we make all our achievements in science and technology serve organized mass murder; we educate our youth into uniformed killers, deliver the people to the soulless tyranny of a bureaucracy, put men from the cradle to the grave under police supervision, erect everywhere jails and penitentiaries, and fill every land with whole armies of informers and spies.

— Ibid.

Hegel's famous dictum, "What is reasonable is real, and what is real is reasonable" — words which no dialectic cleverness can rob of their real meaning — have become the *leitmotif* of all reaction, just because they raise acceptance of given conditions to a principle and try to justify every villainy, every inhuman condition, by the unalterability of the "historically necessary."

— Ibid.

Will Rogers

The difference between a comedian and a congressman is that when a comedian says something funny it's called a joke; when a congressman says something funny it's called a law.

— attributed

Richard Rumbold

I never would believe that Providence had sent a few men into the world, ready booted and spurred to ride, and millions ready saddled and bridled to be ridden.

— Statement on scaffold before being hung for rebellion in 1685

George Bernard Shaw

He who slays a king and he who dies for him are alike idolaters.

— *Maxims for Revolutionists*

Percy Bysshe Shelley

Nature rejects the monarch, not the man;
The subject, not the citizen; for kings
And subjects, mutual foes, forever play
A losing game into each other's hands,
Whose stakes are vice and misery. The man
Of virtuous soul commands not, nor obeys.

Power, like a desolating pestilence,
Pollutes whate'er it touches; and obedience,
Bane of all genius, virtue, freedom, truth,
Makes slaves of men, and of the human frame
A mechanized automoton.

— *Queen Mab*

Herbert Spencer

We do not commonly see in a tax a diminution of freedom, and yet it clearly is one. The money taken represents so much labor gone through, and the product of that labor being taken away, either leaves the individual to go without such benefit as was achieved by it or else to go through more labor ... "Thus much of your work shall be devoted not to your own purposes, but to our purposes," say the authorities to the citizens; and to whatever extent this is carried, to that extent the citizens become slaves of the government.

A certain shepherd oppressed the sheep with cruel laws.

1. SHEEP WILL BE SHORN AND WOOL CONFISCATED.
2. SHEEP WITH POOR WOOL YIELDS WILL BE SLAUGHTERED.
3. SHEEP MAY NOT SPEAK EXCEPT TO SAY BAAAA

Graphic by Donald Rooum

The sheep became unmanageable, so the shepherd was replaced.

"But they are slaves for their own advantage," will be the reply—"and the things to be done with the money taken from them are things which will in one way or other conduce to their welfare." Yes, that is the theory—a theory not quite in harmony with the vast mass of mischievous legislation filling the statute books. But this reply is not to the purpose. The question is a question of justice; and even supposing that the benefits to be obtained by these extra public expenditures were fairly distributed among all who furnish funds, which they are not, it would still remain true that they are at variance with the fundamental principle of social order. A man's liberties are none the less aggressed upon because those who coerce him do so in the belief that he will be benefitted.

— *Social Statics*

Charles T. Sprading

Although the legal and ethical definitions of right are the antithesis of each other, most writers use them as synonyms. They confuse power with goodness, and mistake law for justice.

— *Freedom and its Fundamentals*

Josef Stalin

I know how much the German people love their fuhrer. Therefore, I would like to drink to his health.

— at the signing of the Nazi-Soviet Nonagression Pact in 1939

Elizabeth Cady Stanton

That only a few, under any circumstances, protest against the injustice of long-established laws and customs, does not disprove the fact of the oppressions, while the satisfaction of the many, if real, only proves their apathy and deeper degradation.

— *Eighty Years and More*

Max Stirner

The great are great only because we are on our knees. Let us rise!

— *The Ego and His Own*

Chief Justice Roger B. Taney

The right of property in a slave is distinctly and expressly affirmed in the constitution.

— Dred Scott decision, 1857

Robert Tefton

CONSERVATISM, n. The desire to conserve wealth and power at any cost (to others).

LIBERALISM, n. The desire to liberally spend public money.

The new shepherd gave his flock a Charter of Freedom.

1. Citizens have the Right to be Freed of wool.
2. Citizens lacking wool will be posthumously Honoured.
3. Citizens have absolute Freedom of Speech.

and all the sheep together voiced a loyal BAAAA

Graphic by Donald Rooum

MODERATE, adj. A political term signifying: 1) Devoid of principles; 2) Purchasable.

MODERATE, n. A bought and paid for politician, much admired by journalists because of mutual resemblance.

PEOPLE OF COLOR, n. 1) A politically correct term used to refer to non-Caucasian peoples. *Not* to be confused with the politically incorrect term "colored people"; 2) Code words by which the politically correct recognize each other. The popularity of this term could well foreshadow an important linguistic trend—the withering away of the adjectival used of the past participle (the form employing "ed" as a suffix). If this occurs, we can look forward to constructions such as: "The little girl's father gave her three balloons of color."

POLITICALLY CORRECT, adj. Joyless, deadly dull, puritanical, painfully forced, patronizing (or matronizing), more interested in form than content. Thanks to politically correct phrase-makers, the English language has been enriched with terms such as "people of color," "caveperson," and "person hole cover." The one exception to the "joyless" definition occurs when politically correct middle and upper class persons have the opportunity to berate and belittle members of the working class who use politically incorrect terminology.

STRUGGLE, n. Physical exertion, such as that of a man singlehandedly attempting to install a transmission in a 1964 Buick. When, at the close of a letter, the term is preceded by the word "in," "struggle" can refer to any, or more often no, activity whatsoever.

WHITE SKIN PRIVILEGE, n. Code words through which economically privileged, politically correct whites recognize each other. The term is especially useful in that it has the potential to induce guilt in even the poorest and most exploited caucasians.

WHITE SUPERIORITY, n. The fond dream of those whose existence is the strongest evidence against it.

Henry David Thoreau

There are a thousand hacking at the branches of evil to one who is striking at the root.
— Walden

It is not a man's duty, as a matter of course, to devote himself to the eradication of any, even the most enormous, wrong; he may still properly have other concerns to engage him; but it is his duty, at least, to wash his hands of it, and, if he gives it no thought longer, not to give it practically his support. If I devote myself to other pursuits and contemplations, I must first see, at least, that I do not pursue them sitting upon another man's shoulders.
— On the Duty of Civil Disobedience

Allen Thornton

What is this "peace" that so many people are demanding?

A dictator takes over a country. He doubles taxes, confiscates the press and the schools. He gives all the good jobs in the country to his cronies. The people grow poorer and some even starve. Finally, resistance to the dictator grows. Exiled leaders bring armies of patriots and freedom fighters into the land to oppose the dictator, but in a bloody war, the dictator manages to subdue his opposition. He then redoubles his tyranny by murdering anyone he suspects of disloyalty. He terrorizes the rest of the population with secret police and a corrupt judiciary. After a few years of such overwhelming and vicious government, no one dares to resist the dictator any more. The country can now be said to be at peace. Much of the world enjoys precisely this kind of peace.
— Laws of the Jungle

Alexis de Tocqueville

Despotism, which is of a very timorous nature, is never more secure of continuance than when it can keep men asunder; and all its influence is commonly exerted for that purpose. No vice of the human heart is so acceptable to it as selfishness: a despot easily forgives his subjects for not loving him provided they do not love each other. He does not ask them to assist him in governing the state; it is enough that they do not aspire to govern it themselves. He stigmatizes as turbulent and unruly spirits those who would combine their exertion to promote the prosperity of the community; and, perverting the natural meaning of words, he applauds as good citizens those who have no sympathy for any but themselves.
— Democracy in America

Leo Tolstoy

Men suffer from oppression, and to save themselves from this oppression, they are advised to invent common means for the improvement of their situation, to be applied by the authorities, while they themselves continue to submit to them. Obviously, nothing results from it but a strengthening of the power, and consequently the intensification of the oppression.

Not one of the errors of men removes them so much from the end which they have set for themselves as this one.

Heinrich von Treitschke

Means only exist to serve an end.
— *Politics*

Leon Trotsky

Not believing in force is the same as not believing in gravitation.
— quoted by Maximoff in *The Guillotine at Work*

Terror as the demonstration of the will and strength of the working class, is historically justified.
— *Izvestia,* January 10, 1919, quoted by Maximoff

Benjamin Tucker

To force a man to pay for the violation of his own liberty is indeed an addition of insult to injury. That is exactly what the state is doing.
— *Instead of a Book*

Society has come to be man's dearest possession. Pure air is good, but no one wants to breathe it alone. Independence is good, but isolation is too heavy a price to pay for it.
— Ibid.

Power feeds on its spoils, and dies when its victims refuse to be despoiled. They can't persuade it to death, they can't shoot it do death; but they can always starve it to death.
— quoted by Rocker in *Pioneers of American Freedom*

Mark Twain

I think I can say, and say with pride, that we have legislatures that bring higher prices than any in the world.
— *Americans and the English* (speech, July 4, 1872)

Show me a lord & I will show you a man who you couldn't tell from a journeyman shoemaker if he were stripped; and who, in all that is worth being, is the shoemaker's inferior...
— *A Connecticut Yankee in King Arthur's Court*

Suppose you were an idiot. And suppose you were a member of congress. But I repeat myself.

Fleas can be taught nearly anything that a congressman can.

Jesse Unruh

Sometimes we must rise above principle.
— quoted by Herb Caen

W.H. Vanderbilt

When I want to buy up any politicians I always find the anti-monopolists the most purchasable. They don't come so high.
— *Chicago Daily News,* October 9, 1882

Voline (E.K. Eichenbaum)

"Incapacity of the masses." What a tool for all exploiters and dominators, past, present, and future, and especially for the modern aspiring enslavers, whatever their insignia— Nazism, Bolshevism, Fascism, or Communism. "Incapacity of the masses." This is a point on which the reactionaries of all colors are in perfect agreement with the "communists." And this agreement is exceedingly significant.
— *The Unknown Revolution*

Jack Warner

It's our fault. We should have given him better parts.
— on hearing that Ronald Reagan had been elected governor of California (attributed)

Andrew Dickson White

...the cardinal doctrine of a fanatic's creed is that his enemies are the enemies of God.
— *The History of the Warfare Between Science and Theology*

Oscar Wilde

The virtues of the poor may be readily admitted and are much to be regretted. We are often told that the poor are grateful for charity. Some of them are, no doubt, but the best amongst the poor are never grateful. They are ungrateful, discontented, disobedient, and rebellious. They are quite right to be so. Charity they feel to be a ridiculously inadequate mode of partial restitution, or a sentimental dole, usually accompanied by some impertinent attempt on the part of the sentimentalist to tyrannize over their private lives. Why should they be grateful for the crumbs that fall from the rich man's table? They should be seated at the board, and are beginning to know it.
— *The Soul of Man Under Socialism*

As for the virtuous poor, one can pity them, of course, but one cannot possibly admire them. They have made private terms with the enemy, and sold their birthright for very bad pottage. They must also be extraordinarily stupid. I can quite understand a man accepting laws that protect private property, and admit of its accumulation, as long as he himself is able under those conditions to realize some form of beautiful and intellectual life. But it is almost incredible to me how a man whose life is marred and made hideous by such laws can possibly acquiesce in their continuance.
— Ibid.

All authority is quite degrading. It degrades those who exercise it, and degrades those over whom it is exercised. When it is violently, grossly, and cruelly used, it produces a good effect, by creating, or at any rate bringing out, the spirit of revolt and

Individualism that is to kill it. When it is used with a certain amount of kindness, and accompanied by prizes and rewards, it is dreadfully demoralizing. People, in that case, are less conscious of the horrible pressure that is being put on them, and so go through their lives in a sort of coarse comfort, like petted animals, without ever realizing that they are probably thinking other people's thoughts, living by other people's standards, wearing practically what one may call other people's second hand clothes, and never being themselves for a single moment. "He who would be free," says a fine thinker, "must not conform." And authority, by bribing people to conform, produces a very gross kind of over-fed barbarism amongst us.
— Ibid.

A map of the world that does not include Utopia is not worth even glancing at, for it leaves out the one country at which Humanity is always landing. And when Humanity lands there, it looks out, and seeing a better country, sets sail. Progress is the realization of Utopia.
— Ibid.

Misery and poverty are so absolutely degrading, and exercise such a paralyzing effect over the nature of men, that no class is ever really conscious of its own suffering. They have to be told of it by other people, and they often entirely disbelieve them. What is said by great employers of labour against agitators is unquestionably true. Agitators are a set of interfering, meddling people, who come down to some perfectly contented class of the community, and sow the seeds of discontent amongst them. That is the reason why agitators are so abundantly necessary. Without them in our incomplete state, there would be no advance towards civilisation. Slavery was put down in America, not in consequence of any action on the part of the slaves, or even expressed desire on their own part that they should be free. It was put down entirely through the grossly illegal conduct of certain agitators in Boston and elsewhere, who were not slaves themselves, nor owners of slaves, nor had anything to do with the question really. It was, undoubtedly, the Abolitionists who set the torch alight, who began the whole thing.
— Ibid.

Discomfort is the first step in the progress of a man or a nation.
— A Woman of No Importance

Charles E. Wilson

What is good for the country is good for General Motors, and what's good for General Motors is good for the country.
— Testimony before Senate Armed Forces Subcommittee, 1952

Fred Woodworth

Any constitution, contract, or agreement that purports to bind unborn generations, or in fact anyone other than the actual parties to it, is a despicable falsehood and a presumptuous fraud. We are free agents liable only for such as we ourselves undertake.
— Anarchism

Henry C. Wright

The moment a man claims a right to control the will of a fellow being by physical force, he is at heart a slaveholder.
— The Liberator, April 7, 1837

Johnny Yen

A More Pragmatic Government: Even fewer moral principles than the last regime.
Wage Restraint: The rich get richer and the poor get poorer.
Hawks and Doves: Homicidal maniacs of varying degrees of blatantness.
An Independent Judge: A paid state official.
An Internal Police Enquiry: A whitewash.
Extra Police Powers: Even fewer public rights.
— "State Euphemisms," Freedom, Vol. 47, No. 2

Anonymous & Multiple Author

For Nixon the shortest distance between two points is over four corpses.
— Unidentified Nixon aide quoted in New York Times Magazine, June 9, 1974

Your body belongs to your country...
— First of the Ten Commandments to the Hitler Youth, 1939

It is often difficult to find a balance between getting involved in immediate reforms...and examining the long term implications of what you do. If you let your feelings run riot, you will end up in reformism, desperate to remove the squalor you discover in society. This is understandable, but works against removing the roots of the squalor.
To improve the system is to strengthen it and thus in the long run increases misery.
— Everything You Ever Wanted To Know About Anarchism (anonymously written)

Propaganda and policemen, prisons and schools, traditional values and traditional morality all serve to reinforce the power of the few and to convince or coerce the many into acceptance of a brutal, degrading and irrational system. The "Communist" world is not communist and the "Free" world is not free.
— Solidarity (British libertarian group), As We See It

An injury to one is an injury to all.
— IWW slogan

I have seen the future and it's worse.
— Anonymous (a takeoff on the famous misquotation about the Soviet Union supposedly taken from
Lincoln Steffens autobiography, "I have seen the
future and it works.")

One, two, three, four,
We don't want your fucking war!
Five, six, seven, eight,
Organize and smash the state!
— SDS chant during Vietnam War

Fuck Communism!
— 1960s poster, variously attributed to Ed Sanders,
Abbie Hoffman, Paul Krassner, and Jerry Rubin

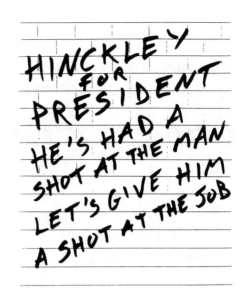

If it's humiliating to be ruled,
how much more humiliating is . . .

Choosing One's Masters

Marcus Aurelius

The object of life is not to be on the side of the majority, but to escape finding oneself in the ranks of the insane.

Adin Ballou

How many does it take to metamorphose wickedness into righteousness? One man must not kill. If he does, it is murder. . . But a state or nation may kill as many as they please, and it is not murder. It is just, necessary, commendable, and right. Only get people enough to agree to it, and the butchery of myriads of human beings is perfectly innocent. But how many does it take?

— *The Non-Resistant,* February 5, 1845

Ambrose Bierce

VOTE, The instrument and symbol of a freeman's power to make a fool of himself and a wreck of his country.

— *The Devil's Dictionary*

Rioting gains its end by the power of numbers. To a believer in the wisdom and goodness of majorities it is not permitted to denounce a successful mob.

— *Epigrams*

We submit to the majority because we have to. But we are not compelled to call our attitude of subjection a posture of respect.

— Ibid.

Jay Fox

Politicians and preachers, even our employers, advise us to seek at the ballot-box the redress our wrongs demand. . .

Nothing seems more absurd and ridiculous than that the employers would advise us — their victims and slaves — as to the way to free ourselves.

— *Mother Earth,* November 1907

Thomas Fuller

The number of malefactors authorizes not the crime.

— *Gnomologia*

W.S. Gilbert

I always voted at my party's call,
And I never thought of thinking for myself at all.

— *H.M.S. Pinafore*

J.W. von Goethe

Nothing is more odious than the majority, for it consists of a few powerful leaders, a certain number of accommodating scoundrels and submissive weaklings, and a mass of men who trudge after them without thinking, or knowing their own minds.

Emma Goldman

My lack of faith in the majority is dictated by my faith in the potentialities of the individual. Only when the latter becomes free to choose his associates for a common purpose, can we hope for order and harmony out of this world of chaos and inequality.

— Preface to *Anarchism and Other Essays*

Auberon Herbert

Majority rule is not founded — any more than emperor's rule — on reason or justice. There is no reason or justice in making two men subject to three men. . .

Why should either two men live at the discretion of three, or three at the discretion of two? Both propositions are absurd from a reasonable point of view. If being a slave and owning a slave are both wrong relations, what difference does it make whether there are a million slave-owners and one slave, or one slave-owner and a million slaves? Do robbery and murder cease to be what they are if done by ninety-nine per cent of the population?

— quoted by Sprading in *Liberty and the Great Libertarians*

Thomas Jefferson

The people are not qualified to legislate. With us, therefore, they only choose the legislators.
— Letter to L'Abbe Arnond, 1789

It is my principle that the will of the majority should always prevail.
— Letter to James Madison, December 20, 1787

I readily suppose my opinion wrong when opposed by the majority.
— Letter to James Madison, 1788

Hellen Keller

Our democracy is but a name. We vote? What does that mean? It means that we choose between two bodies of real, though not avowed, autocrats. We choose between Tweedledum and Tweedledee.
— quoted by Howard Zinn in *A People's History of the United States*

Peter Kropotkin

Parliamentarianism is nauseating to anyone who has ever seen it at close range.
— *Words of a Rebel*

Freedom of the press, freedom of association, the inviolability of the domicile, and all the rest of the rights of man are respected only so long as no one tries to use them against the privileged classes. On the day they are launched against privilege they are thrown overboard.

V.I. Lenin

How can one be a democrat and at the same time oppose the dictatorship of the proletariat?
— *Pravda,* May 12, 1917, quoted by Maximoff in *The Guillotine at Work*

Errico Malatesta

. . . if you consider these worthy voters as incapable of providing for their own interests, how can they ever be capable of choosing directors to guide them wisely? How to solve this problem of social alchemy: to elect a government of geniuses by the votes of a mass of fools?
— *Anarchy*

Max Nordau

Representative legislation produces conditions resembling those of patriarchal times. The representatives take the place of the patriarchs and their wealth consists similarly in herds and flocks. But nowadays, these herds are not composed of actual cattle with horns and hoofs, but of cattle, figuratively speaking, who on election days are driven up to the ballot-box to deposit their votes.
— *Conventional Lies of Our Civilization*

Allen Rice

. . . let us consider [one] of the arguments which may seem to justify taking part in politics: ". . . If I take no part in government. . . then I cannot complain when it injures me." Look at a similar situation. Suppose a group of your neighbors meet and decide to expropriate one-half of your property and income, and compel you to do manual labor for them for the next two years. Being good democrats all, they are willing to put the decision to a vote and invite you to participate. Should you feel guilty if you refuse to do so? Will you have better grounds for complaint if you help vote yourself into slavery or if you do not?
— *The Match!*, February 1972

Rudolf Rocker

He who declares the common will to be the absolute sovereign and yields to it unlimited power over all members of the community, sees in freedom nothing more than the duty to obey the law and to submit to the common will. For him the thought of dictatorship has lost its terror.
— *Nationalism and Culture*

The greatest danger in every democratic community has always arisen from the tyranny of the majority which asserts itself most strongly when the respect for free expression of opinion becomes weak and demagogues lustful for power, or when privileged minorities turn the ignorance of the masses to their own advantage.
— *Pioneers of American Freedom*

George Bernard Shaw

Democracy substitutes selection by the incompetent many for appointment by the corrupt few.
— Preface to *Major Barbara*

Herbert Spencer

We deny the right of a majority to murder, to enslave, or to rob, simply because murder, enslaving and robbery are violations of that law [equal liberty for all] — violations too gross to be overlooked. But if great violations of it are wrong, so also are smaller ones. . . however insignificant the minority, and however trifling the proposed trespass against their rights, no such trespass is permissible.
— *The Right to Ignore the State*

Lysander Spooner

Men honestly engaged in attempting to establish justice in the world, have no occasion thus to act in secret; or to appoint agents for which they (the principals) are not willing to be responsible.

The secret ballot makes a secret government; and a secret government is a secret band of robbers and murderers...The single despot stands out in the face of all men, and says, "I am the State..."

But a secret government is little less than a government of assassins. Under it, a man knows not who his tyrants are, unless they have struck, and perhaps not then...

This is the kind of government we have; and it is the only one we are likely to have, until men are ready to say: We will consent to no Constitution, except such a one as we are neither ashamed nor afraid to sign; and we will authorize no government to do anything in our name for which we are not willing to be personally responsible.

— *No Treason*

A man is none the less a slave because he is allowed to choose a new master once in a term of years. Neither are a people any the less slaves because they are permitted periodically to choose new masters. What makes them slaves is the fact that they now are, and are always hereafter to be, in the hands of men whose power over them is, and always is to be, absolute and irresponsible.

— Ibid.

...on what ground of authority does our government practically rest?...

The most that they can say, in answer to this question, is that some half, two-thirds, or three-quarters of the adult males of the country have a *tacit understanding* that they will maintain a government under the Constitution; that they will select, by ballot, the persons to administer it; and that those persons who may receive a majority, or a plurality, of their ballots, shall act as their representatives, and administer the Constitution in their name, and by their authority.

But this tacit understanding (admitting it to exist) cannot at all justify the conclusion drawn from it. A tacit understanding between A, B, and C, that they will, by ballot, depute D as their agent, to deprive me of my property, liberty, or life, cannot at all authorize D to do so. He is none the less a robber, tyrant, and murderer, because he claims to act as their agent, than he would be if he avowedly acted on his own responsibility alone.

— Ibid.

What is the motive to the secret ballot? This, and only this: Like other confederates in crime, those who use it are not friends, but enemies; and they are afraid to be known, and to have their individual doings known, even to each other...And this is avowedly the only reason for the ballot: for a secret government; a government by secret bands of robbers and murderers. And we are insane enough

But we **have** freedom, Pussycat. We were all taught that at school.

Every sheep is allowed to vote for a shepherd.

That is what freedom is.

Graphic by Donald Rooum

to call this liberty! To be a member of this secret band of robbers and murderers is esteemed a privilege and an honor! Without this privilege, a man is considered a slave; but with it a free man! With it he is considered a free man, because he has the same power to secretly (by secret ballot) procure the robbery, enslavement, and murder of another man, as that other man to procure his robbery, enslavement, and murder. And this they call equal rights!

— Ibid.

Discussion can do nothing to prevent the enactment, or procure the repeal, of unjust laws, unless it be understood that the discussion is to be followed by resistance... Suffrage is equally powerless and unreliable. It can be exercised only periodically, and the tyranny must at least be borne until the time for suffrage comes. Besides, when the suffrage is exercised, it gives no guaranty for the repeal of existing laws that are oppressive and no security against the enactment of new ones that are equally so. The second body of legislators are likely and liable to be just as tyrannical as the first. If it be said that the second body may be chosen for their integrity, the answer is that the first were chosen for that very reason and yet proved tyrants. The second will be exposed to the same temptations as the first. Who ever heard that succeeding legislatures were, on the whole, more honest than those that preceded them?

— *Trial by Jury*

Charles T. Sprading

To believe in [majority rule] as an unqualified principle is to believe that might makes right.

— *Freedom and its Fundamentals*

Max Stirner

In a republic, all are masters, and each tyrannizes over the others.

— *The Ego and His Own*

Henry David Thoreau

All voting is a sort of gaming, like the checkers or backgammon, with a slight moral tinge to it, a playing with right and wrong, with moral questions; and betting naturally accompanies it. The character of the voters is not staked. I cast my vote, perchance as I think right; but I am not vitally concerned that right should prevail. I am willing to leave it to the majority. Its obligation, therefore, never exceeds expediency. Even voting *for the right is doing nothing for it.* It is only expressing to men feebly your desire that it should prevail.

— quoted by Rudolf Rocker in *Pioneers of American Freedom*

Allen Thornton

The weakness of fascism and communism consists in their turning citizens into slaves. Slaves have nothing to gain and nothing to lose.

The strength of democracy is that it encourages the common man to believe himself a ruler, that is, an oppressor of his neighbor.

— *Laws of the Jungle*

Alexis de Tocqueville

A majority taken collectively is only an individual, whose opinions, and frequently whose interests, are opposed to those of another individual, who is styled a minority. If it be admitted that a man possessing absolute power may misuse that power by wronging his adversaries, why should not a majority be liable to the same reproach? Men do not change their characters by uniting with each other; nor does their patience in the presence of obstacles increase with their strength. For my own part, I cannot believe it; the power to do everything, which I should refuse to one of my equals, I will never grant to any number of them.

— *Democracy in America*

...in democratic republics, where public life is incessantly mingled with domestic affairs, where the sovereign authority is accessible on every side, and where its attention can always be attracted by vociferation, more persons are to be met with who speculate upon its weaknesses, and live upon ministering to its passions, than in absolute monarchies. Not because men are naturally worse in these states than elsewhere, but the temptation is stronger and of easier access at the same time. The result is a more extensive debasement of character.

Democratic republics extend the practice of currying favor with the many, and introduce it into all classes at once: this is especially true in democratic states organized like the American republic, where the power of the majority is so absolute and irresistible that one must give up his rights as a citizen, and almost abjure his qualities as a man, if he intends to stray from the track which it prescribes.

— Ibid.

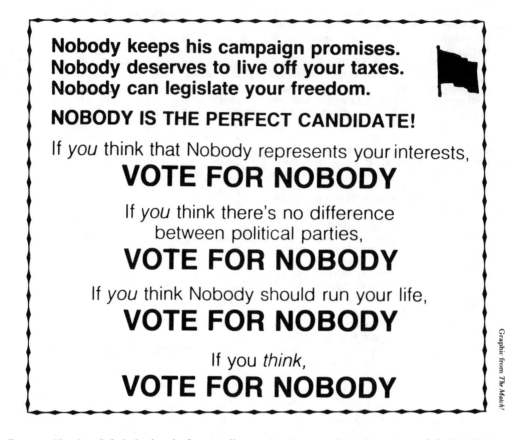

Nobody keeps his campaign promises.
Nobody deserves to live off your taxes.
Nobody can legislate your freedom.

NOBODY IS THE PERFECT CANDIDATE!

If *you* think that Nobody represents your interests,
VOTE FOR NOBODY

If *you* think there's no difference
between political parties,
VOTE FOR NOBODY

If *you* think Nobody should run your life,
VOTE FOR NOBODY

If you *think,*
VOTE FOR NOBODY

Graphic from The Match!

For myself, when I feel the hand of power lie heavy on my brow, I care but little to know who oppresses me; and I am not the more disposed to pass beneath the yoke because it is held out to me by the arms of a million men.

— Ibid.

Benjamin Tucker

What is the ballot? It is neither more nor less than a paper representative of the bayonet, the billy, and the bullet. It is a labor-saving device for ascertaining on which side force lies and bowing to the inevitable. The voice of the majority saves bloodshed, but it is no less the arbitrament of force than is the decree of the most absolute of despots backed by the most powerful of armies.

— *Instead of a Book*

Reason devoted to politics fights for its own dethronement. The moment the minority becomes the majority, it ceases to reason and persuade, and begins to command and enforce and punish.

— *Liberty*, January 19, 1889

Fred Woodworth

Government cannot exist without the tacit consent of the populace. This consent is maintained by keeping people in ignorance of their real power. Voting is not an expression of power, but an admission of powerlessness, since it cannot otherwise than reaffirm the government's supposed legitimacy.

— *Anarchism*

An urgent task awaits fulfillment. It is the merciless abandonment of majoritarianism along with a devastating uprising against the cynical controllers who hide their manipulations in the sham and fraud of unending elections. Reject this civilization, founded upon lies and stupidity! That enraged snarl of defiance and self-repossession will coincide with a general groan of relief as the licenses and committees, permits and forms, taxes, voting booths and "Constitutions," law-books, prisons and government buildings, rose-garden teas and presidential planes crunch heavily into the muck, and sink, and vanish forever. Then the world will be rid not just of such inanimate trash, but also of the foul maggots, the presidents, the popes, the senators, the mayors, the police, the chairmen — and indeed every vile snake now exercising power over his fellows. They will scurry and wriggle out of sight like bleached worms in the sun. No one will miss them.

The Law

Ambrose Bierce

LAWSUIT, A machine which you go into as a pig and come out of as a sausage.
— *The Devil's Dictionary*

There is no fallacy so monstrous, no deduction so hideously unrelated to common sense, as not to receive, somewhere in the myriad pages of this awful compilation a support that any judge in the land would be proud to recognize with a decision if ably persuaded. I do not say that the lawyers are altogether accountable for the existence of this mass of disastrous rubbish...they only create and thrust it down our throats; we are guilty of contributory negligence in not biting the spoon.
— *Some Features of the Law*

The methods of our courts, the traditions of bench and bar, exist and are perpetuated, altered and improved, for the purpose of enabling lawyers as a class to exact the greatest amount of money from the rest of mankind. The laws are mostly made by lawyers, and so made as to encourage and compel litigation. By lawyers they are interpreted and by lawyers enforced for their own profit and advantage. The over-intricate and interminable machinery of precedent, over-rulings, writs of err, motions for new trials, appeals, reversals, affirmations and the rest of it, is mostly a transparent and iniquitous system of exaction.
— Ibid.

Henry Thomas Buckle

The most valuable additions made to legislation have been enactments destructive of preceding legislation; and the best laws which have been passed, have been those by which some former laws were repealed.
— quoted in *The Wisdom of Thomas Buckle*

Samuel Taylor Coleridge

He saw a lawyer killing a viper
 On a dunghill hard by his own stable;
And the Devil smiled, for it put him in mind
 Of Cain and his brother Abel.
— *The Devil's Thoughts*

Clarence Darrow

[Never] will the vicious control without the aid of law. Society ever has and must ever have a very large majority who naturally fall into order, social adjustment and a rational, permissible means of life. The disorganized vicious would be far less powerful than the organized vicious, and would soon disappear.

All conceivable human actions have fallen under the disfavor of the law and found their place in penal codes: Blasphemy, witchcraft, heresy, insanity, idiocy, methods of eating and drinking, the manner of worshipping the Supreme Being, the observance of fast days and holy days, the giving of medicine and the withholding of medicine, the relation of the sexes, the right to labor and not to labor, the method of acquiring and dispensing property, its purchase and sale, the forms of dress and manner of deportment, in fact almost every conceivable act of man. On the other hand, murder, robbery, pillage, rapine, have often been commended by the ruling powers, not only permitted, but under certain conditions that seemed to work to the advantage of the ruler, this conduct has been deemed worthy of the greatest praise.

The rulers make penal codes for the regulation and control of the earth and all the property thereon — the earth which was made long ages before they were evolved, and will still remain ages after they are dust. Not only do they make these rules to control the earth for their brief, haughty lives, but they provide that it may pass from hand to hand forever. The generations now living, or rather those that are dead and gone, fixed the status of unborn millions, and decreed that they shall have no place to live except upon such terms as may be dictated by those who then controlled the earth. To retain all the means of life in the hands of the few and compel the many to do service to support these few requires the machinery of the state. It is for this that penal laws are made...

The production of iron, clothing, many kinds of food, in fact the largest part of what is used in daily life, is controlled by combinations whose sole purpose is extortion; they scheme to absolutely control the market and take from the consumers what they have. And yet for this extortion which reaches every home and despoils every fireside, the law furnishes no redress. Either it does not come within the provisions of the law or else those who are charged with its enforcement do not care to reach this sort of extortion which is the only kind that really affects the world. In either case it shows that the penal code is made and enforced by the ruling class, not upon themselves, but to keep the weak at the bottom of the social scale.

The daily papers are filled to overflowing with lying advertisements, each contradicting the other. Our fences, rocks and buildings are defaced with vulgar, hideous lies in order to swindle men out of their much coveted cash. All our merchants and tradesmen frantically call out their lies in every form, that they may sell their wares for a larger price than they are really worth. And yet, to all of this, the criminal code has no word to say. This is not the class of swindlers it was made to reach.
— above quotations from *Resist Not Evil*

Eugene V. Debs

There is something wrong in this country; the judicial nets are so adjusted as to catch the minnows and let the whales slip through and the federal judge is as far removed from the common people as if he inhabited another planet.
— Speech, November 23, 1895

Ricardo Flores Magon

Equality before the law is a farce. We want social equality. We want opportunity for all, not to acquire millions, but to make a perfectly human life, free from worry and uncertainty about the future.
— *Regeneración*, February 11, 1911

Anatole France

The law, in its majestic equality, forbids the rich as well as the poor to sleep under bridges, to beg in the streets, and to steal bread.

Benjamin Franklin

God works wonders now & then;
Behold! A Lawyer, an Honest Man!
— *Poor Richard's Almanac*, 1733

A good Lawyer, a bad Neighbour.
— *Poor Richard's Almanac*, 1737

James Garfield

A law is not a law without coercion behind it.
— attributed

J.W. von Goethe

Laws are inherited like diseases.
— *I Faust*

Justice Oliver Wendell Holmes, Jr.

This is a court of law... not a court of justice.
— quoted in *Devil's Advocates, The Unnatural History of Lawyers*, by Andrew & Jonathan Roth

L. Ron Hubbard

The purpose of the suit is to harass and discourage rather than to win. The law can be used very easily to harass, and enough harassment on somebody who is simply on the thin edge anyway ...will generally be sufficient to cause his professional decease. If possible, of course, ruin him entirely.
— on tactics to be used against a critic of the Church of Scientology, quoted by Bent Corydon and L. Ron Hubbard, Jr. in *L. Ron Hubbard: Messiah or Madman?*

Judge Earl Johnson, Jr.

Poor people have access to American courts in the same sense that the Christians had access to the lions when they were dragged into a Roman arena.
— quoted in *Devil's Advocates, The Unnatural History of Lawyers*, by Andrew & Jonathan Roth

Peter Kropotkin

The law is an adroit mixture of customs that are beneficial to society, and could be followed even if no law existed, and others that are of advantage to a ruling minority, but harmful to the masses of men, and can be enforced on them only by terror.
— *Words of a Rebel*

The law has no claim to human respect. It has no civilizing mission; its only purpose is to protect exploitation.
— Ibid.

If law, however, presented nothing but a collection of prescriptions to obey rulers, it would find some difficulty in insuring acceptance and obedience. Well, the legislators confounded in one code the... maxims which represent principles of morality and social union wrought out as a result of life in common, and the mandates which are meant to ensure external existence to inequality. Customs, absolutely essential to the very being of society, are, in the code, cleverly intermingled with usages imposed by the ruling caste, and both claim equal respect from the crowd. "Do not kill," says the code, and hastens to add, "And pay tithes to the priest." "Do not steal," says the code, and immediately after, "He who refuses to pay taxes, shall have his hand struck off."

Such was law; and it has maintained its two-fold character to this day... Its character is the skillful comingling of customs useful to society, customs which have no need of law to insure respect, with other customs only useful to rulers...

— *Law and Authority*

Only estimate the torrent of depravity let loose in human society by the "informing" which is countenanced by judges, and paid in hard cash by governments, under pretext of assisting in the discovery of "crime." Only go into the jails and study what man becomes when he is deprived of freedom and shut up with other depraved beings, steeped in the vice and corruption which oozes from the very walls of our existing prisons...Finally, consider what corruption, what depravity of mind is kept up among men by the idea of obedience, the very essence of law; of chastisement; of authority having the right to punish, to judge irrespective of our conscience and the esteem of our friends; of the necessity for executioners, jailers, and informers — in a word, by all the attributes of law and authority. Consider all this, and you will assuredly agree with us in saying that a law inflicting penalties is an abomination which should cease to exist.

— Ibid.

Michel de Montaigne

Laws are maintained in credit, not because they are essentially just, but because they are laws. It is the mystical foundation of their authority; they have none other. They are often made by fools; more often by men who in hatred of equality have want of equity; but ever by men who are vain and irresolute. There is nothing so grossly and largely offensive, nor so ordinarily wrongful, as the laws.

Johann Most

...each generation invariably considers the laws of its predecessors as gross mistakes...Indeed the history of legislation must be defined as the history of the queerest errors possible.

Or do not laws against magic, heresy and innumerable other things, which at one time were punished with barbarous cruelty while now they pass by entirely unnoticed, impress us as a sort of mental aberration? Was it not downright insanity to use the stake, the rack, or other instruments of cruelty as means by which to find out the guilt or innocence of a man?

But can we be sure that a later generation will look with milder eyes upon our laws with their gallows and hangmen, their cells and chains? No! He was right who declared those laws the best which simply abolish former laws.

— *The Social Monster*

Albert Parsons

Whoever prescribes a rule of action for another to obey is a tyrant, usurper, and an enemy of liberty. This is precisely what every statute does.

— *The Philosophy of Anarchism*

Wendell Phillips

The law has been always wrong. Government began in tyranny and force, began in the feudalism of the soldier and bigotry of the priest; and the ideas of justice and humanity have been fighting their way, like a thunder storm, against the organized selfishness of human nature.

Pierre Joseph Proudhon

Laws: We know what they are, and what they are worth! They are spider webs for the rich and mighty, steel chains for the poor and weak, fishing nets in the hands of the government.

— quoted in *The Match!*

An organized society needs laws as little as legislators. Laws are to society what cobwebs are to a beehive; they only serve to catch the bees.

— quoted by Rudolf Rocker

Jean Jacques Rousseau

Laws are always useful to those who own, and injurious to those who do not...Laws give the weak new burdens, and the strong new powers; they irretrievably destroyed natural freedom, established in perpetuity the law of property and inequality, turned a clever usurpation into an irrevocable right, and brought the whole future race under the yoke of labor, slavery and money...

William Shakespeare

The first thing we do, let's kill all the lawyers.

— *Henry VI*, Part 2

J. Blair Smith

A law is bad; the people consider it bad. Well, there is no necessity for petitions and speeches if people are really in earnest. Disobey it! Disobey it in force and that law will be heard of no more.

— *Direct Action versus Legislation*

Herbert Spencer

Those who say that "time is a great legalizer" must find satisfactory answers to such questions as — How long does it take for what was originally wrong to become right?

— quoted by Sprading in *Liberty and the Great Libertarians*

Lysander Spooner

If the jury have no right to judge of the justice of a law of the government, they plainly can do nothing to protect the people against the oppressions of the government; for there are no oppressions which the government may not authorize by law.

— *Trial by Jury*

Charles T. Sprading

...legal right is synonymous with power; whoever or whatsoever has the power, has the right... There is no sentiment in legal right; it is the offspring of power only—"might is right!"

— *Freedom and its Fundamentals*

Most people accept law as their guide to conduct; they find it to be more profitable than following the rules of justice. They are always asking, "What is the law?" "Can I do that and not be arrested?" To them anything within the law is right; yet we know that the greatest injustices are committed within the law. They would see nothing wrong in murder, if it was lawful.

— Ibid.

If all men had the same interests, there would be less harm in permitting a part of the people to legislate for all; but this is not the case. There is a great conflict of interests between the possessed and the dispossessed, between the poor and the rich...between the ruler and the ruled...between the producer and the appropriator, which is apparent in existing laws made by those powerful enough to take advantage of the State and of the law-abiding sentiment of the people. That their laws conflict justice is no concern of theirs, for profit and not justice is their object...The game they play is lawful because they make the law to uphold their game.

— Ibid.

Ethical right is largely abstract; legal right is mostly concrete. Ethical right the just man wishes to be established; legal right is already established. Ethical right and legal right mutually exclude each other; where one prevails, the other cannot endure. One is founded on power, on might; the other on justice, on equality. One appeals to the sword to settle matters, the other appeals to the judgment of men.

— *Liberty and the Great Libertarians*

Max Stirner

The state calls its own violence law, but that of the individual crime.

— *The Ego and His Own*

Jonathan Swift

I had informed him that some of our crew left their country on account of being ruined by law... but he was at a loss how it should come to pass that the law, which was intended for every man's preservation, should be any man's ruin. Therefore he desired to be further satisfied what I meant by law, and the dispensers thereof...I said that there was a society of men among us bred up from their youth in the art of proving by words multiplied for the purpose, that white is black and black is white, according to as they are paid.

To this society all the rest of the people are slaves. For example, if my neighbour has a mind to my cow, he has a lawyer to prove that he ought to have my cow from me. I must then hire another to defend my right, it being against all the rules of law that any man should speak for himself. Now in this case, I who am the right owner, lie under two great disadvantages; first, my lawyer, being practised almost from his cradle in defending falsehood, is quite out of his element when he would advocate for justice, which...he always attempts with great awkwardness if not with ill-will. The second disadvantage is, that my lawyer must proceed with great caution, or else he will be reprimanded by the judges, and abhorred by his brethren, as one who would lessen the practice of the law...

It is a maxim with these lawyers that whatever has been done before may legally be done again; and therefore they take special care to record all the decisions formerly made against common justice and the general reason of mankind. These, under the name of precedents, they produce as authorities to justify the most iniquitous opinions, and the judges never fail of directing accordingly.

In pleading, they studiously avoid entering into the merits of the case; but are loud, violent and tedious in dwelling upon all circumstances which are not to the purpose.

It is likewise observed, that this society has a peculiar cant and jargon of its own, that no other mortal can understand, and wherein all their laws are written, which they take special care to multiply, whereby they have wholly confounded the very essence of truth and falsehood, of right and wrong...

In the trial of persons accused for crimes against the state, the method is much more short and commendable; the judge first sends to sound the disposition of those in power, after which he can easily hang or save a criminal, strictly preserving all due forms of law.

— *Gulliver's Travels*

Tacitus

The more corrupt the republic, the more numerous the laws.

— *Annals*

Henry David Thoreau

Law never made men a whit more just; and by means of their respect for it, even the well-disposed are daily made the agents of injustice. A common and natural result of an undue respect for law is that you may see a file of soldiers, colonel, captain, corporal, privates, powder-monkeys, and all marching in admirable order over hill and dale to the wars, against their wills, ay, against their common sense and consciences, which makes it very steep marching indeed, and produces a palpitation of the heart. They have no doubt that it is a damnable business in which they are concerned; they are all peaceably inclined. Now, what are they? Men at all? or small movable forts and magazines, at the service of some unscrupulous man in power?

The mass of men serve the State thus, not as men mainly, but as machines, with their bodies. They are the standing army, and the militia, gaolers, constables, posse comitatus, etc. In most cases there is no free exercise whatever of the judgment or of the moral sense; but they put themselves on a level with wood and earth and stones; and wooden men can perhaps be manufactured that will serve the purpose as well. Such command no more respect than men of straw or a lump of dirt. They have the same sort of worth only as horses and dogs. Yet such as these even are commonly esteemed good citizens.

— *On the Duty of Civil Disobedience*

I think that we should be men first, and subjects afterwards. It is not desirable to cultivate a respect for the law, so much as for the right. The only obligation which I have a right to assume is to do at any time what I think right.

— Ibid.

The man for whom law exists — the man of forms, the conservative — is a tame man.

— *Journal*, March 30, 1851

There is something servile in the habit of seeking after a law which we may obey.

— *Excursions, Poems and Familar Letters*

Leo Tolstoy

The law condemns and punishes only actions within certain definite and narrow limits; it thereby justifies, in a way, all similar actions that lie outside those limits.

— *What I Believe*

Laws are rules established by men who are in control of organized violence for the nonfulfilment of which those who do not fulfil them are subjected to personal injuries, the loss of liberty, and even capital punishment.

In this definition is contained the answer to the question as to what gives men the power to establish laws. What gives them the power to establish laws is the same thing which secures obedience to them — organized violence.

— *The Slavery of Our Times*

Formerly it was advantageous for people to have direct slaves, and so they established laws about personal slavery. Then it became advantageous to have land as property, to collect taxes, to retain acquired property, and corresponding laws were made. Now it is advantageous for people to retain the existing distribution and division of labor, and laws are introduced such as would compel people to work with the existing distribution and division of labor. And so the fundamental cause of slavery is laws — the fact that there are men who are able to introduce them.

— Ibid.

If there are laws, there has to be the power which can compel men to fulfil these rules, that is, the will of other men, and that is — violence, not simple violence, which is used by men against one another in moments of passion, but organized violence, which is consciously employed by men who have power, in order to compel other men to fulfil rules which are always established by them, that is, what they want.

Therefore the essence of the law is not at all the subject or object of right, nor the idea of the state, nor the aggregate will of the people, and similar indefinite and confused things, but is this: that there are men who, in control of organized violence, are able to compel people to do their will.

— Ibid.

Grover Whalen

There's plenty of law at the end of a nightstick.

— attributed

The State

Lord Armstrong

Coercion is the central principle of government.
— quoted by Bool and Carlyle in *For Liberty*

Michael Bakunin

...to offend, to oppress, to despoil, to plunder, to assassinate or enslave one's fellowman is ordinarily regarded as a crime. In public life, on the other hand, from the standpoint of patriotism, when these things are done for the greater glory of the State, for the preservation or the extension of its power, it is all transformed into duty and virtue...
...This explains why the entire history of ancient and modern states is merely a series of revolting crimes, why kings and ministers, past and present, of all times and all countries—statesmen, diplomats, bureaucrats, and warriors—if judged from the standpoint of simple morality and human justice, have a hundred, a thousand times over earned their sentence to hard labor or to the gallows. There is no horror, no cruelty, sacrilege, or perjury, no imposture, no infamous transaction, no cynical robbery, no bold plunder or shabby betrayal that has not been or is not daily being perpetrated by the representatives of the states, under no other pretext than those elastic words, so convenient and yet so terrible: "for reasons of state."
These are truly terrible words, for they have corrupted and dishonored, within official ranks and in society's ruling classes, more men than has even Christianity itself. No sooner are these words uttered than all grows silent, and everything ceases: honesty, honor, justice, right, compassion itself ceases, and with it logic and good sense. Black turns white, and white turns black. The lowest human acts, the basest felonies, the most atrocious crimes become meritorious acts.
— *Federalism, Socialism, Anti-Theologism*

The state is force incarnate...its essence is command and compulsion.
— *God and the State*

Alexander Berkman

What is this thing we call government? Is it anything else but organized violence? The law orders you to do this or not to do that, and if you fail to obey it, it will compel you by force...all government, all law and authority finally rest on force and violence, on punishment or the fear of punishment.
— *What Is Communist Anarchism?*

What we call progress has been a painful but continuous march in the direction of limiting authority and the power of government and increasing the rights and liberties of the individual, of the masses. It has been a struggle that has taken thousands of years. The reason that it took such a long time—and is not yet ended—is because people did not know what the real trouble was: they fought against this and for that, they changed kings and formed new governments, they put out one ruler only to set up another, they drove away a "foreign" oppressor only to suffer the yoke of a native one, they abolished one form of tyranny, such as the Tsar's, and submitted to that of a party dictatorship, and always and ever they shed their blood and heroically sacrificed their lives in the hope of securing liberty and welfare.
But they secured only new masters, because however desperately and nobly they fought, they never touched the *real source* of the trouble, the *principle of authority* and *government*.
— Ibid.

Edmund Burke

In vain you tell me that artificial government is good, but that I fall out only with the abuse; the thing—the thing itself is the abuse.
— *Vindication of Natural Society*

Confucius

Oppressive government is fiercer and more to be feared than any tiger.

James Fenimore Cooper

The very existence of government implies inequality. The citizen who is preferred to office becomes the superior of those who are not, so long as he is the repository of power.

— *The American Democrat*

Clarence Darrow

Endless volumes have been written, and countless lives been sacrificed in an effort to prove that one form of government is better than another; but few seem seriously to have considered the proposition that all government rests on violence and force, is sustained by soldiers, policemen and courts, and is contrary to the ideal peace and order which make for the happiness and progress of the human race.

The beginnings of the state can be traced back to the early history of the human race when the strongest savage seized the largest club and with this weapon enforced his rule upon the other members of the tribe. By means of strength and cunning he became the chief and exercised this power, not to protect the weak but to take the good things of the earth for himself and his. One man by his unaided strength could not long keep the tribe in subjection to his will, so he chose lieutenants and aids, and these too were taken for their strength and prowess, and were given a goodly portion of the fruits of power for the loyalty and help they lent their chief. No plans for the general good ever formed a portion of the scheme of government evolved by these barbarous chiefs. The great mass were slaves, and their lives and liberty held at the absolute disposal of the strong.

Ages of evolution have only modified the rigors of the first rude states. The divine right to rule, the absolute character of official power, is practically the same today in most of the nations of the world as with the early chiefs who executed their mandates with a club. The ancient knight who with his battle-ax and coat of mail, enforced his rule upon the weak, was only the forerunner of the tax-gatherer and tax-devourer of today. Even in democratic countries, where the people are supposed to choose their rulers, the nature of government is the same. Growing from the old ideas of absolute power, these democracies have assumed that some sort of government was indispensable to the mass, and no sooner had they thrown off one form of bondage than another yoke was placed upon their necks, only to prove in time that this new burden was no less galling than the old.

And who are these rulers without whose aid the evil and corrupt would destroy and subvert the defenceless and the weak? From the earliest time these self-appointed rulers have been conspicuous for all those vices that they so persistently charge to the common people whose rapacity, cruelty and lawlessness they so bravely curb. The history of the past and the present alike proves beyond a doubt that if there is, or ever was any large class, from whom society needed to be saved, it is those same rulers who have been placed in absolute charge of the lives and destinies of their fellow men. From the early kings who, with blood-red hands, forbade their subjects to kill their fellow men, to the modern legislator, who, with the bribe money in his pocket, still makes bribery a crime, these rulers have ever made laws not to govern themselves but to enforce obedience on their serfs.

The purpose of this autocratic power has ever been the same. In the early tribe the chief took the land and the fruits of the earth, and parceled them amongst his retainers who helped preserve his strength. Every government since then has used its power to divide the earth amongst the favored few and by force and violence to keep the toiling, patient, suffering millions from any portion of the common bounties of the world.

How is the authority of the state maintained? In whatever guise, or however far removed from the rudest savage tribe to the most modern democratic state, this autocratic power rests on violence and force alone.

The vast army which is charged with enforcing and maintaining civil law is drawn largely from the ruling class and those who contribute as their willing tools. This class must be supported and maintained in greater luxury than that enjoyed by the ordinary man, and the support entails ceaseless and burdensome exactions from the producing class. These exactions are a portion of the price that the worker pays for the privilege of being ruled. It is true that a portion of the money forcibly taken through the machinery of government is used for those cooperative commercial purposes that are incident to a complex social life, but it has never yet been shown that an autocratic power like a political state is needed to provide the common resources incident to social life.

Then too, authority has the same effect on human nature whether in an absolute monarchy or a democracy, and the tendency of authority is ever to enlarge its bounds and to encroach upon the natural rights of those who have no power to protect themselves. The possession of authority and arbitrary power ever tends to tyranny...

— above quotations from *Resist Not Evil*

Ricardo Flores Magon

The public functionaries are not, as is commonly believed, the guardians of order. Order, which is harmony, doesn't need guardians, precisely because it is order. That which needs guardians is disorder and a disorder which is scandalous, shameful, and humiliating to those of us who weren't born to be slaves, a disorder which reigns over the political and social life of humanity.

To maintain disorder, that is, to maintain political and social inequality, to maintain the privileges of the ruling class and the submission of the ruled, *that* is why governments, laws, policemen, soldiers, jailers, judges, hangmen, and the whole mob of high and petty functionaries who suck the energies of the humble people are needed. These functionaries don't exist to protect humanity, but to maintain its submission, to keep it enslaved for the benefit of those who have contrived to retain the land and the factories for themselves up to this moment.

— *Regeneración*, May 13, 1911

Jay Fox

He [the anarchist] sees that government is a fraud; that it does not protect life and property, but that on the contrary it *destroys life* and *protects robbery*. Rich men quarrel and their governments compel the poor man to do the fighting, where hundreds and thousands are slaughtered to settle disputes in which they had no concern, except the foolish interest they take in their kings and presidents. *Is that protecting life?* Rich men steal the earth and make the poor man pay tribute for the privilege of living upon it; and the government enforces the claims of the robbers. *Is that protecting property?*

— *Mother Earth,* November 1907

The anarchist points out to us that in every strike the government takes the side of the employers. Strikers are clubbed, jailed, bull-penned, shot, deported from their homes, kidnapped and carried off to other states upon trumped-up charges of murder and denounced by the president as "undesirable citizens"; in every conceivable manner they are harassed and punished by the government for asserting their rights to a living wage. "Is it not strange my brother," a friend once wrote to me, "that law and order always mean scabbing, that all the powers of government are always arrayed on the side of the scab and the blood-sucking employer? That the law which is supposed to be for the protection of the weak against the aggression of the strong, is in every instance found to be operating against the weak?"

— Ibid.

William Godwin

With what delight must every well informed friend of mankind look forward, to the auspicious period, the dissolution of political government, of that brute engine, which has been the only perennial cause of the vices of mankind, and which . . . has mischiefs of various sorts incorporated with its substance, and no otherwise removable than by its utter annihilation.

— *An Enquiry Concerning Political Justice*

Emma Goldman

Is political government, is the State, beneficial to mankind, and how does it affect the individual in the social scheme of things?

The individual is the true reality in life. A cosmos in himself, he does not exist for the State, nor for that abstraction called "society," or the "nation," which is only a collection of individuals. Man, the individual, has always been and necessarily is the sole source and motive power of evolution and progress. Civilization has been a continuous struggle of the individual, or of groups of individuals, against the State and even against "society," that is, against the majority subdued and hypnotized by the State and State worship. Man's greatest battles have been waged against man-made obstacles and artificial handicaps imposed upon him to paralyze his growth and development. Human thought has always been falsified by tradition and custom, and perverted false education in the interests of those who held power and enjoyed privileges. In other words, by the State and the ruling classes. This constant incessant conflict has been the history of mankind.

— *The Individual, Society and the State*

The interests of the State and those of the individual differ fundamentally and are antagonistic. The State and the political and economic institutions it supports can exist only by fashioning the individual to their particular purposes; training him to respect "law and order"; teaching him obedience, submission and unquestioning faith in the wisdom and justice of government; above all, loyal service and complete self-sacrifice when the State commands it, as in war. The State puts itself and its interests even above the claims of religion and of God. . .

The struggle of the individual against these tremendous odds is the more difficult — too often dangerous to life and limb — because it is not truth or falsehood which serves as the criterion of the opposition he meets. It is not the validity or usefulness of his thoughts or activity which rouses against him the forces of the State and of "public opinion." The persecution of the innovator and protestant has always been inspired by fear on the part of constituted authority of having its infallibility questioned and its power undermined.

— Ibid.

The State, ecclesiastical and secular, served to give an appearance of legality and right to the wrong done by the few to the many. That appearance of right was necessary the easier to rule the people, because no government can exist without the consent of the people, consent open, tacit, or assumed . . . That consent is the belief in authority, in the necessity for it. At its base is the doctrine that man is evil, vicious, and too incompetent to know what is good for him. On this all government and oppression is built. God and the State . . . are supported by this dogma.

Robert Hall

When a nation forms a government, it is not wisdom, but power which they place in the hands of the magistrate...
— quoted by Sprading in *Freedom and its Fundamentals*

Georg Hegel

God on earth. [the State]

George D. Herron

No man ever ruled other men for their own good; no man was ever rightly the master of the minds or bodies of his brothers; no man ever ruled other men for anything except their undoing and for his own brutalization.

The possession of power over others is inherently destructive both to the possessor of the power and to those over whom it is exercised. And the great man of the future, in distinction from the great man of the past, is he who will seek to create power in the people, and not gain power over them. The great man of the future is he who will refuse to be great at all, in the historic sense; he is the man who will literally lose himself, who will altogether diffuse himself in the life of humanity.

Adolf Hitler

Its [the patriarchal family's] destruction would mean the end of every form of higher humanity... It is the smallest but most valuable unit in the complete structure of the state.
— *Mein Programm*

How fortunate for governments that the people they administer don't think.
— attributed

Thomas Jefferson

That government is best which governs least.

It is error alone which needs the support of government. Truth can stand by itself.
— *Notes on Virginia*

Samuel Johnson

All government is ultimately and essentially absolute.
— *Taxation No Tyranny*

Peter Kropotkin

Man is the cruelest animal upon the earth. And who has pampered and developed the cruel instincts unknown, even among monkeys, if it is not the king,

the judge, and the priests, armed with law, who caused flesh to be torn off in strips, boiling pitch to be poured into wounds, limbs to be dislocated, bones to be crushed, men to be sown asunder to maintain their authority?
— *Law and Authority*

...the education we all receive from the state, at school and after, has so warped our minds that the very notion of freedom ends up by being lost and disguised in servitude.

It is a sad sight to see those who believe themselves to be revolutionaries unleashing their hatred on the anarchist—just because his views on freedom go beyond their petty and narrow concepts of freedom learned in the state school. And meanwhile, this spectacle is a reality. The fact is that the spirit of voluntary servitude was always cleverly cultivated in the minds of the young, and still is, in order to perpetuate the subjection of the individual to the state.
— *The State—Its Historic Role*

...the state emerges...and then death!

Yes death—or renewal! *Either* the state forever, crushing individual and local life, taking over in all fields of human activity, bringing with it its wars and its domestic struggles for power, its palace revolutions which only replace one tyrant by another, and inevitably at the end of this development there is...death! *Or* the destruction of the state, and new life starting again in thousands of centers on the principle of the lively initiative of the individual and groups and that of free agreement.
— Ibid.

...the conclusion we arrive at is for the abolition of the state.

We see in it the institution, developed in the history of human societies, to prevent direct association among men, to shackle the development of local and individual initiative, to crush existing liberties, to prevent their new blossoming—all this in order to subject the masses to the will of the minorities.

And we know an institution which has a long past going back several thousand years cannot lend itself to a function opposed to the one for which and by which it was developed in the course of history.

To this unshakable argument for anybody who has reflected on history the reply we receive is almost infantile: "The state exists and it represents a powerful ready-made organization. Why not use it instead of wanting to destroy it? It operates for evil ends—agreed; but the reason is that it is in the hands of the exploiters. If it were taken over by the people, why would it not be used for better ends, for the good of the people?"...

What a sad and tragic mistake! To give full scope to socialism entails rebuilding from top to bottom a society dominated by the narrow individualism of the shopkeeper. It is not as has sometimes been said by those indulging in metaphysical woolliness just a question of giving the worker "the total product of his labor"; it is a question of completely reshaping all relationships...in the factory, in the village, in the store, in production, and in distribution of supplies. All relations between individuals and great centers of population have to be made all over again, from the very day, from the very moment one alters the existing commercial or administrative organization.

And they expect this immense task, requiring the free expression of popular genius, to be carried out within the framework of the state and the pyramidal organization which is the essence of the state! They expect the state whose very *raison d'etre* is the crushing of the individual, the hatred of initiative, the triumph of *one* idea which must be inevitably that of mediocrity—to become the lever for the accomplishment of this immense transformation... They want to direct the revival of a society by means of decrees and electoral majorities...how ridiculous!

—Ibid.

Lao Tse

The real art of governing consists, so far as possible, in doing nothing.

Errico Malatesta

The only limit to the oppression of government is the power with which the people show themselves capable of opposing it.

—*Il Programma Anarchico*

A government, even had it no other disadvantages, must always have that of habituating the governed to subjection, and must also tend to become more oppressive and necessary, in proportion as its subjects are more obedient and docile.

—*Anarchy*

What can government of itself add to the moral and material forces which exist in a society, unless it be like the God of the Bible, who created the universe out of nothing?

As nothing is created in the so-called material world, so in this more complciated form of the material world, which is the social world, nothing can be created. Therefore governors can dispose of no other force than that which is already in society, and indeed not by any means of all of that, for much force is necessarily paralyzed and destroyed by governmental methods of action, while more again is wasted in the friction with rebellious ele-

From *Comunidad*

ments, inevitably great in such an artificial mechanism.

— Ibid.

The real being is the man, the individual; society or the collectivity, and the State or government which professes to represent it, if not hollow abstractions, can be nothing else than aggregates of individuals. It is within the individual organ that all thoughts and human action necessarily have their origin. Originally individual, they become collective thoughts and actions, when shared in common by many individuals. Social action, then, is not the negation, nor the complement, of individual initiative, but it is the sum total of the initiatives, thoughts and actions of all the individuals composing society... If, on the other hand, as the authoritarians make out, by social action is meant governmental action, then it is again the result of individual forms, but only of those individuals who either form part of the government or by virtue of their position are enabled to influence the conduct of the government.

Thus, in the contest of centuries between liberty and authority, or in other words, between social equality and social castes, the question at issue has not really been the relations between society and the individual, or the increase of individual independence at the cost of social control, or vice versa. Rather it has had to do with preventing any one individual from oppressing the others; with giving to everyone the same rights and the same means of action. It has had to do with substituting the initiative of all, which must naturally result in the advantage of all, for the initiative of the few, which necessarily results in the suppression of the others...

From what we have said, it follows that the existence of a government, upon the hypothesis that the ideal government of authoritarian socialists were possible, far from producing an increase of productive force, would immensely diminish it, because the government would restrict initiative to the few. It would give these few the right to do all things, without being able, of course, to endow them with the knowledge or understanding of all things.

— Ibid.

For us the government is the aggregate of the governors, and the governors... are those who have the power to make laws regulating the relations between men, and to force obedience to these laws. They are those who decide upon and claim the taxes, enforce military service, judge and punish transgressors of the laws. They subject men to regulations...

Why abdicate one's own liberty, one's own initiative in favor of other individuals? Why give them the power to be the masters, with or against the wish of each, to dispose of the forces of all in their own way?

— Ibid.

Many and various are the theories by which men have sought to justify the existence of government. All, however, are founded, confessedly or not, on the assumption that the individuals or a society have contrary interests, and that an external superior power is necessary to oblige some to respect the interests of others, by prescribing and imposing a rule of conduct, according to which the interests at strife may be harmonized as much as possible, and according to which each may obtain the maximum of satisfaction with the minimum of sacrifice...

This is the theory; but to be sound the theory should be based upon an explanation of facts. We know well how in social economy theories are too often invented to justify facts, that is, to defend privilege and cause it to be accepted tranquilly by those who are its victims. Let us here look at the facts themselves.

In all the course of history, as in the present epoch, government is either brutal, violent, arbitrary domination of the few over the many, or it is an instrument devised to secure domination and privilege to those who, by force, or cunning, or inheritance, have taken to themselves all the means of life, and first and foremost the soil, whereby they hold the people in servitude, making them work for their [the few's] advantage.

— Ibid.

... the government does not change its nature. If it acts as regulator or guarantor of the rights and duties of each, it perverts the sentiment of justice. It justifies wrong and punishes every act which offends or menaces the privileges of the governors and proprietors. It declares just and *legal* the most atrocious exploitation of the miserable, which means a slow and continuous material and moral murder, perpetrated by those who have on those who have not. Again, if it administers public services, it always ignores the interests of the working masses, except in so far as is necessary to make the masses willing to endure their share of taxation. If it instructs, it fetters and curtails the truth, and tends to prepare the minds and hearts of the young to become either implacable tyrants or docile slaves, according to the class to which they belong. In the hands of the government everything becomes a means of exploitation, everything serves as a police measure, useful to hold the people in check. And it must be thus.

— Ibid.

Mao Tse Tung

The state apparatus, including the army, the police and the courts, is the instrument for the oppression of antagonistic classes; it is violence and not "benevolence." "You are not benevolent!" Quite so.

— *On the People's Democratic Dictatorship*

"Don't you want to abolish state power?" Yes, we do, but not right now... Our present task is to strengthen the people's state apparatus—mainly the people's army, the people's police and the people's courts...

Benito Mussolini

Everything for the state, nothing outside of the state, nothing against the state!
—quoted by Rocker in *Nationalism and Culture*

Friedrich Nietzsche

...that fantastic theory that makes [the state] begin with a contract is, I think, disposed of. He who commands, he who is a master by "nature," he who comes on the scene forceful in deed and gesture—what has he to do with contracts?
— *The Genealogy of Morals*

Max Nordau

The public functionary is a more developed form of the steward or overseer, considered historically. The clerk growling at the citizens summoned to his office is the historical descendant of the commandant or overseer appointed by a tyrant of the Dark Ages to superintend his people of slaves, and to keep them in a becoming state of obedience by his body guard of warriors, with the whip and the goad. As the public functionary is a fragment of the royal grace-of-godness, he lays claim to some of its infallibility. His position is below that of the head of the State, but it is above that of the masses to be governed. They are a flock, the ruler is the shepherd, and he is the shepherd's dog. He can bark and bite and the sheep must bear it. And what is most remarkable of all: the sheep do bear it!
— *Conventional Lies of Our Civilization*

...every one, even the poor man, pays taxes, and to such an amount that he would be comfortably off at the close of his life, if he had been able to retain for himself the fruits of his labor which he has been obliged to pay over to the State. That the barbarian may lose his property is only possible, that the man of our civilization is deprived of his by the State, by means of direct and indirect taxation, is certain.
—Ibid.

The citizen in the chains with which he is loaded down by the State, is obliged to rely upon himself for protection as much as the free barbarian, but is less skillful in it than the latter, because he has forgotten from want of practice, how to look out for himself, because he has no longer the proper sense for the appreciation of his near and distant interests, because from his earliest years he is accustomed to bear with an oppression and compulsion against which the savage would protest even at the expense of his life, because the State has brought

him up in the idea that the government officials are to do the thinking for him in all cases, because the law has broken the elasticity of his character, crushed out every power of resistance by its constant pressure and brought him down to such a point that the oppression of the State has ceased to be injustice in his eyes.
—Ibid.

The State, as at present organized, is a machine which works with an enormous waste of power. Only a small and constantly diminishing portion of the original force, obtained at such an incredibly high cost, remains for actual production; the rest is lost...the sums exacted from the citizens are squandered on foolish, frivolous and criminal undertakings. The whims of certain men, the selfish interests of certain small minorities, determine only too frequently the purposes to which the efforts of the community shall be directed. Hence the individual citizen labors and bleeds so that wars may be carried on which put an end to his life or his prosperity, that fortresses, palaces, railroads, harbors or canals may be built, from which neither he nor nine-tenths of the nation will ever derive the slightest benefit, so that new offices may be created to make the machinery of State more complicated, to increase the friction between its wheels, in which he will lose still more of his time and leave still another piece of his liberty, so that office holders may be paid high salaries, who have no other aim in life than to lead an ornamental existence at his expense and lay another burden upon his shoulders, in short, he spends his life laboring and bleeding to add with his own hands to the weight of his yoke and the number of his chains and to create the possibility for new demands upon his labor and blood.
—Ibid.

Thomas Paine

The more perfect civilization is, the less occasion has it for government, because the more does it regulate itself;...
— *The Age of Reason*

The trade of governing has always been monopolized by the most ignorant and the most rascally individuals of mankind.
—quoted by Bool and Carlyle in *For Liberty*

The instant formal government is abolished, society begins to act. A general association takes place, and common interest produces common security.
— *The Rights of Man*

William Penn

Let the people think they govern and they will be governed.
— *Fruits of Solitude*

Wendell Phillips

Law has always been wrong. Government is the fundamental Ism of the soldier, bigot, and priest.

— *Orations, Speeches, Lectures and Letters*

To hear some men talk of the government, you would suppose that Congress was the law of gravitation, and kept the planets in their places.

— Ibid.

Plato

Good men refuse to govern...I think that if ever there should exist a state exclusively composed of good men, they would seek as much not to govern as there are some now anxious to govern.

— *Republic*

Joseph Priestley

Governors will never be awed by the voice of the people, so long as it is a mere voice, without overt acts.

— *The First Principles of Government*

If the power of government be very extensive, and the subjects of it have, consequently, little power over their own actions, that government is tyrannical, and oppressive; whether, with respect to its form, it be a monarchy, an aristocracy, or even a republic.

— Ibid.

Pierre Joseph Proudhon

To be governed is to be watched over, inspected, spied on, directed, legislated at, regulated, docketed, indoctrinated, preached at, controlled, assessed, weighed, censored, ordered about, by men who have neither the right nor the knowledge nor the virtue to do so. To be governed means to be, at each transaction, at each movement, noted, registered, taxed, stamped, measured, evaluated, patented, licensed, authorized, endorsed, admonished, hampered, reformed, rebuked, arrested. It is to be, on the pretext of the general interest, drained, drilled, held to ransom, exploited, monopolized, extorted, squeezed, hoaxed, robbed; and then, at the least resistance, at the first word of complaint, to be repressed, fined, abused, annoyed, followed, bullied, beaten, disarmed, garrotted, imprisoned, machine gunned, judged, condemned, deported, flayed, sold, betrayed, and finally mocked, ridiculed, insulted, dishonored. Such is government such is justice, such is morality.

— *The General Idea of the Revolution in the 19th Century*

You, who cannot conceive of order without a whole apparatus of legislators, prosecutors, attorneys-general, custom house officers, policemen, you have never known what real order is! What you call unity and centralization is nothing but perpetual chaos, serving as basis for endless tyranny; it is the advancing of the chaotic condition of social forces as an argument for despotism — a despotism which is really the cause of the chaos.

— Ibid.

As a State religion is the rape of the conscience, so a State political administration is the castration of liberty. Deadly devices, wrought by the same madness for oppression and intolerance; whose poisonous fruits show their identity. State religion produced the Inquisition; State administration produced the police.

— Ibid.

Rudolf Rocker

The history of the state is the history of human oppression and intellectual disenfranchisement. It is the story of the unlimited lust for power of small minorities which could be satisfied only by the enslavement and exploitation of the people. The deeper the state with its countless agencies penetrates into the spheres of activity of social life, the more its leaders succeed in changing men into mindless automatons of their will, the more inevitably will the world become a vast prison in which at last there will be no breath of freedom.

— *Nationalism and Culture*

It is not so much *how* we are governed, but *that* we are governed at all; for this is a mark of our immaturity and prevents us from taking our affairs into our own hands. We purchase the "protection" of the state with our freedom even to stay alive and do not realize that it is this "protection" which makes a hell of our life, while only freedom can endow it with dignity and strength.

— Ibid.

"All for the State; all through the State; nothing without the State!" became the leitmotif of a new political theology [fascism — the quote is from Mussolini]. As in various systems of ecclesiastical theology God is everything and man nothing, so for this modern political creed the State is everything and the citizen nothing.

— *Anarchism and Anarcho-Syndicalism*

George Bernard Shaw

I fully admit and vehemently urge that the State at present is simply a huge machine for robbing and slave-driving the poor by brute force...

Every institution, as Bakunin saw, religious, political, financial, judicial, and so on, is corrupted by the fact that the men in it either belong to the propertied class themselves, or must sell themselves to it in order to live. All the purchasing power that is left to buy men's souls with after their bodies are fed is in the hands of the rich; and everywhere, from the Parliament which wields the irresistible coercive forces of the bludgeon, bayonet, machine gun, dynamite shell, prison, and scaffold, down to the pettiest center of shabby-genteel social pretension, the rich may pay the piper and call the tune. Naturally, they use their power to steal more money to continue paying the piper; and thus all society becomes a huge conspiracy.

. . . The State will sell you up, blow you up, knock you down, bludgeon, shoot, stab, hang — in short, abolish you, if you lift a hand against it.

— *The Impossibility of Anarchism*

Herbert Spencer

By no process can coercion be made equitable. The freest form of government is only the least objectionable form. The rule of the many by the few, we call tyranny. The rule of the few by the many (Democracy) is tyranny also, only of a less intense kind. "You shall do as we will, not as you will," is in either case the declaration . . .

Government being simply an agent employed in common by a number of individuals to secure to them certain advantages, the very nature of the connection implies that it is for each to say whether he will employ such an agent or not.

Not only does magisterial power exist *because* of evil, but it exists *by* evil. Violence is employed to maintain it; and all violence involves criminality. Soldiers, policemen, and jailers; swords, batons and fetters are instruments for inflicting pain; and infliction of pain is, in the abstract, wrong. The state employs evil weapons to subjugate evil, and is alike contaminated by the objects with which it deals and by the means which it works.

Upholders of pure despotism may fitly believe State-control be unlimited and unconditional. They who assert that men are made for governments and not governments for men, may consistently hold that no one can remove himself beyond the pale of political organization. But they who maintain that the people are the only legitimate source of power — that legislative authority is not original, but deputed — cannot deny the right to ignore the State without entangling themselves in an absurdity.

For, if legislative authority is deputed, it follows that those from whom it proceeds are the masters of those on whom it is conferred: it follows further that as masters they confer the said authority voluntarily: and this implies that they may give or withhold it as they please. To call that deputed which is wrenched from men whether they will or not is nonsense. But what is here true of all collectively is equally true of each separately. As a government can rightly act for the people only when empowered by them, so also can it rightly act for the individual only when empowered by him. If A, B, and C debate whether they shall employ an agent to perform for them a certain service, and if, whilst A and B agree to do so, C dissents, C cannot equitably be made a party to the agreement in spite of himself. And this must be equally true of thirty as of three: and, if of thirty, why not three

hundred, or three thousand, or three million?

— above quotations from *The Right to Ignore the State*

Lysander Spooner

A power that can of itself, and by its own authority, punish disobedience, can compel obedience and submission . . . is a despotism.

And it is of no consequence to inquire how a government came by this power to punish, whether by prescription, by inheritance, by usurpation, or by delegation from the people.

— *Trial by Jury*

Constitutions are utterly worthless to restrain the tyranny of governments, unless it be understood that the people will by force compel the government to keep within constitutional limits. Practically speaking, no government knows any limits to its power except the endurance of the people.

— Ibid.

All, or nearly all, the advantage there is in fixing any constitutional limits to the power of a government is simply to give notice to the government of the point at which it will meet with resistance. If the people are then as good as their word, they may keep the government within the bounds they have set for it; otherwise it will disregard them, as is proved by the example of all our American governments . . .

— Ibid.

. . . no government, so called, can reasonably be trusted for a moment, or reasonably be supposed to have honest purposes in view, any longer than it depends wholly upon voluntary support.

— *No Treason*

The fact is that the government, like a highwayman, says to a man: "Your money, or your life." . . .

The government does not, indeed, waylay a man in a lonely place, spring upon him from the roadside, and, holding a pistol to his head, proceed to rifle his pockets. But the robbery is none the less a robbery on that account; and it is far more dastardly and shameful.

The highwayman takes solely upon himself the responsibility, danger, and crime of his own act. He does not pretend that he has any rightful claim to your money, or that he intends to use it for your own benefit. He does not pretend to be anything but a robber. He has not acquired impudence to enable him to "protect" those infatuated travellers, who feel perfectly able to protect themselves, or do not appreciate his peculiar system of protection. He is too sensible a man to make such professions as these. Furthermore, having taken your money, he leaves you, as you wish him to do. He does not persist in following you on the road, against your will, assuming to be your rightful "sovereign," on account of the "protection" he affords you. He does not keep "protecting" you, by commanding you to bow down and serve him; by requiring you to do this and forbidding you to do that; by robbing you of more money as often as he finds it for his interest or pleasure to do so; and by branding you as a rebel, a traitor, and an enemy to your country, and shooting you down without mercy, if you dispute his authority, or resist his demands. He is too much of a gentleman to be guilty of such impostures, and insults, and villainies as these. In short, he does not, in addition to robbing you, attempt to make you either his dupe or his slave.

—Ibid.

The right of absolute and irresponsible dominion is the right of property, and the right of property is the right of absolute, irresponsible dominion. The two are identical; the one necessarily implying the other. . . If therefore, Congress have that absolute and irresponsible law-making power which the Constitution—according to their interpretation of it—gives them, it can only be because they own us as property. If they own us as property, they are our masters, and their will is our law. . .

But these men who claim and exercise this absolute and irresponsible dominion over us, dare not be consistent, and claim either to be our masters, or to own us as property. They say they are only our servants, agents, attorneys, and representatives. But this declaration involves an absurdity, a contradiction. No man can be my servant, agent, attorney, or representative, and be, at the same time, uncontrollable by me, and irresponsible to me for his acts. It is of no importance that I appointed him, and put all power in his hands. If I made him uncontrollable by me, and irresponsible to me, he is no longer my servant, agent, attorney, or representative. If I gave him absolute irresponsible power over my property, I gave him the property. If I gave him absolute, irresponsible power over myself, I made him my master, and gave myself to him as a slave. And it is of no importance whether I called him master or servant, agent or owner.

—Ibid.

All governments, the worst on earth and the most tyrannical on earth are free governments to that portion of the people who voluntarily support them.

—quoted by Rudolf Rocker in *Pioneers of American*

Charles T. Sprading

The power to command and the weakness to obey are the essence of government and the quintessence of slavery.

—*Liberty and the Great Libertarians*

The greatest violator of the principle of equal liberty is the State. Its functions are to control, to rule, to dictate, to regulate, and in exercising these functions it interferes with and injures individuals who have done no wrong.

—Ibid.

It is as unjust to force one's government upon another, as it is unjust to force one's religion upon another.

—Ibid.

We no longer believe that it is just for one man to govern two men, but we have yet to outgrow the absurd belief that it is just for two men to govern one man.

—Ibid.

Governments cannot accept liberty as their fundamental basis for justice, because governments rest upon authority and not upon liberty. To accept liberty as the fundamental basis is to discard authority; that is, to discard the government itself; as this would mean the dethronement of the leaders of government, we can expect only those who have no economic compromise to make to accept equal liberty as the basis of justice.

—*Freedom and its Fundamentals*

Jonathan Swift

For in reason, all government without the consent of the governed is the very definition of slavery.

—*The Drapier's Letter*

Henry David Thoreau

I heartily accept the motto—"That government is best which governs least"; and I should like to see it acted up to more rapidly and systematically. Carried out, it finally amounts to this, which also I believe—That government is best which governs not at all.

—*On Civil Disobedience*

Allen Thornton

Every act of every government is based on violence. Political power, as Mao said, comes from the end of a gun. If the state wants you to stop doing something, it doesn't try to persuade you; it threatens to put you in jail if you keep doing it. If the state wants your money, it doesn't ask you for it politely. It doesn't try to earn it. The state extorts money from you with threats of prison.

Governments never open lemonade stands to finance themselves.

—*Laws of the Jungle*

What do you think "govern" means? It doesn't mean "suggest" or "implore." It doesn't mean two people sitting down, talking it over and compromising. "Govern" means "force," and "force" means "violence."

—Ibid.

If you profit materially from the state's existence, I would no more expect you to become an anarchist than I would expect a maggot to become a vegetarian.
—Ibid.

Since no one wants to picture himself as a victim of violence, governments lie. States always prevaricate and coin new words to conceal their use of force. Taxes, laws, conscription, tariffs, regulations: A thousand words have been invented to distract your attention from the guns and prisons that uphold the government. If the state were honest and open about its use of violence, the victims might revolt or the victimizers repent.
—Ibid.

Government is nothing without violence. Laws are merely whims backed up with guns, and taxes are simply the extortionist's requests for money. Isn't it natural, then, that governments are often led by immoral men.
—Ibid.

One day, the very idea of government will seem like an insane artifact of the past: witch burning, crusading, black slavery, prohibition. Then the people will look back and wonder at the nature of man.
—Ibid.

Leo Tolstoy

We are asked: "How can men live without governments, that is, without violence?" We ought, on the contrary, to ask: "How can men, rational beings, live recognizing violence, and not rational argument, as the inner force of their lives?"
— *The Slavery of Our Times*

One or the other is true: either men are rational beings, or they are not. If they are irrational beings, they are all irrational beings, and there is no reason why some should enjoy the right to exert violence, while others do not enjoy this right, and then the violence exerted by the government has no justification. But if men are rational beings, their relations must be based on reason, and not on the violence of men who have accidentally seized the power, and therefore the violence of the government has again no justification.
—Ibid.

Why must men submit to the violence of those men who at a given time are in power? What proves that these men are wiser than those men against whom the violence is exerted?
Their allowing themselves to exert violence against people proves that they are not only not wiser, but even less wise than those who submit to them.
—Ibid.

. . . governments, in justifying their existence by saying that they provide for their subjects a certain amount of security, do not differ in this from a Calabrese bandit who imposes a tax upon all those who want to travel safely over the highways . . .
We are so hypnotized by the governments that such a comparison seems to be an exaggeration, a paradox, a jest, whereas it is no paradox and no jest—in fact, the comparison is incorrect, because the activity of all the governments is much more inhuman, and, above all, much more harmful than the activity of the Calabrese bandit. The bandit for the most part robs the rich, while the governments for the most part rob the poor, while they protect the rich, who help them in their crimes. The ban-

Graphic by Donald Rooum

dit in doing what he does risks his life, while the governments risk nothing and build all their deeds on lying and deceit. The bandit does not forcibly take anybody into his band, while the governments draft their soldiers generally by force. With the bandit all those who pay the tribute receive equal security, while in the state a man receives the more security, and even reward, the more he takes part in the organized deception...But he who does not at all take part in the governmental crimes, refusing to serve, to pay taxes, to have anything to do with the court, is subjected to violence, as one is subjected to it by robbers. The bandit does not intentionally corrupt people, while the governments for the attainment of their purposes corrupt whole generations of children and adults by false religious and patriotic doctrines.

—Ibid.

People must understand that their participation in the criminal activity of the governments, whether by giving up part of their labors, in the form of money, or by a direct participation in military service, is not an indifferent act, such as people generally take it to be, but...a participation in the crimes which are incessantly committed by all the governments, and a preparation for new crimes, for which the governments are always ready, when they maintain a disciplined army.

—Ibid.

In ancient times the warriors with their leaders fell upon defenseless inhabitants and vanquished and plundered them, and all of them, according to the part they took, their bravery, their cruelty, divided up the booty, and it was obvious to every warrior that the violence practiced by him was advantageous to him. But now the armed men, who are for the most part taken from among the working men, go against defenseless people, strikers, rioters, or inhabitants of foreign countries, and vanquish and plunder them (that is, compel them to give up their labor), not for themselves, but for those who do not even take part in the subjugation.

The only difference between conquerors and governments is this, that the conquerors with their warriors attacked defenseless inhabitants and, in case of their nonsubmission, carried out their threats of tortures and murders, while the governments, in case of nonsubmission, do not themselves practice tortures and murder on the defenseless inhabitants, but cause this to be done by deceived and specially bestialized men, who are taken from among the very masses they oppress.

—Ibid.

The religious superstition consists in the belief that the sacrifices, often of human lives, made to the imaginary being are essential, and that men may and should be brought to that state of mind by all methods, not excluding violence. The political superstition consists in the belief that, be-

sides the duties of man to man, there are more important duties to the imaginary being, Government, and that the sacrifices—often of human lives—made to the imaginary being are also essential, and that men may and should be brought to that state of mind by all possible means, not excluding violence...

Men, oppressing others, assure them that the compulsion is necessary in the interest of the government, while the government is indispensable to the liberty and welfare of men—according to this, the oppressors compel men for their own freedom and do them wrong for their own good.

—Ibid.

Every government explains its existence and justifies all its violence on the ground that if it were not there things would be worse. Having convinced the people that they are in danger, the governments dominate them. And when the peoples are dominated by governments, the latter compel them to attack each other. And in this way a belief in the governments' assurance of the danger of attacks by other nations is confirmed among the peoples.

Divide and conquer.

— *Christianity and Patriotism*

Government is an association of men who do violence to the rest of us.

— *The Kingdom of God Is Within You*

As to the rulers' saying that, if it were not for their power, the worse would do violence to the good, it means only this, that the violators in power do not wish to cede this power to other violators, who may wish to take it from them.

—Ibid.

In saying that without the power of the state evil men would rule over the good it is taken for granted that the good are precisely those who at the present time have power, and the bad the same who are now subjugated. But it is precisely this that has to be proved...

In order to get power and retain it, it is necessary to love power; but love of power is not connected with goodness, but with qualities which are the opposite of goodness, such as pride, cunning, and cruelty.

Without self-aggrandizement and debasement of others, without hypocrisy, deceit, prisons, fortresses, executions, murders, power can neither arise nor maintain itself.

...to rule means to do violence, and to do violence means to do what the other man, on whom the violence is exerted, does not wish to have done to him, and what, no doubt, he who exerts the violence would not wish to have done to himself; consequently, to rule means to do to another what we do not wish to have done to ourselves, that is, to do evil...

And so all the probabilities are in favor of the fact

that not those who are better than those over whom they rule, but, on the contrary, those who are worse, have always been and even now are in power.
— Ibid.

Kings and emperors have long arranged for themselves a system like that of a magazine-rifle: as soon as one bullet has been discharged another takes its place. The kind is dead, long live the king! So what is the use of killing them?
— *Thou Shalt Not Kill*

The misery of nations is caused not by particular persons but by the particular order of society under which the people are so tied up together that they find themselves all in the power of one single man: a man so perverted by his unnatural position as arbiter of the fate and lives of millions, that he is always in an unhealthy state, and always suffers more or less from a mania of self-aggrandizement, which only his exceptional position conceals from general notice.
. . . not only does no one tell them plainly what they are doing, or say that to busy oneself with preparations for killing is revolting and criminal, but from all sides they hear nothing but approval and enthusiasm for all this activity of theirs . . . Every time they go out, and at each parade and review, crowds of people flock to greet them with enthusiasm, and it seems to them as if the whole nation approves of their conduct. The only part of the press that reaches them, and that seems to them the expression of the feelings of the whole people, or at least of its best representatives, most slavishly extols their every word and action, however silly or wicked they might be. Those around them, men and women, clergy and laity — all people who do not prize human dignity — vying with one another in refined flattery, agree with them about anything and deceive them about everything, making it imposssible for them to see life as it is. Such rulers might live a hundred years without ever seeing one single really independent man or ever hearing the truth spoken. One is sometimes appalled to hear of the words and deeds of these men; but one need only consider their position in order to understand that anyone in their place would act as they do. If a reasonable man found himself in their place there is only one reasonable action he could perform, and that would be to get away from such a position. Anyone remaining in it would behave as they do.
— Ibid.

The age for the veneration of governments, notwithstanding all the hypnotic influence they employ to maintain their position, is more and more passing away. And it is time for people to understand that governments not only are not necessary, but are harmful and most highly immoral institutions, in which a self-respecting, honest man cannot and must not take part, and the advantages of which he cannot and should not enjoy. And as

soon as people clearly understand that, they will, naturally, cease to take part in such deeds — that is, cease to give the government soldiers and money. And as soon as a majority of people ceases to do this the fraud which enslaves people will be abolished. Only in this way can people be freed from slavery.

Benjamin Tucker

Now what is aggression? Aggression is simply another name for government. Aggression, invasion, government, are interconvertible terms. The essence of government is control, or the attempt to control. He who attempts to control another is a governor, an aggressor, and invader; and the nature of such invasions is not changed, whether it is made by one man upon another man, after the manner of the ordinary criminal, or by one man upon all other men, after the manner of an absolute monarch, or by all other men upon one man, after the manner of a modern democracy. On the other hand, he who resists another's attempt to control is not an aggressor, an invader, a governor, but simply a defender, a protector; and the nature of such resistance is not changed whether it be offered by one man to another man, as when one repels a criminal's onslaught, or by one man to all other men, as when one declines to obey an oppressive law . . . This distinction between invasion and resistance, between government and defence, is vital. Without it there can be no valid philosophy of politics.
— *Instead of a Book*

GOVERNMENT: The subjection of the noninvasive individual to an external will.
— Ibid.

THE STATE: The embodiment of the principle of invasion in an individual, or a band of individuals, assuming to act as representatives or masters of the entire people within a given area.
— Ibid.

Government is the assumption of authority over a given area and all within it, exercised generally for the double purpose of more complete oppression of its subjects and extension of its boundaries.
— Ibid.

General Jorge Videla

In order to guarantee the security of the state, all the necessary people will die.
— as head of state (Argentina) in 1977

Nicolas Walter

Many people say that government is necessary because some men cannot be trusted to look after themselves, but anarchists say that government is harmful because no men can be trusted to look after anyone else.
— *About Anarchism*

Josiah Warren

Good thinkers never committed a more fatal mistake than in expecting harmony from an attempt to overcome individuality...A state or a nation is a multitude of indestructible individualities, and cannot, by any possibility, be converted into anything else! The horrid consequences of these monstrous and abortive attempts to overcome simple truth and nature, are displayed on every page of the world's melancholy history.

— *Equitable Commerce*

George Washington

Government is not reason, it is not eloquence — it is force! Like fire, it is a dangerous servant and a fearful master.

— quoted by Bool and Carlyle in *For Liberty*

Oscar Wilde

All modes of government are failures. Despotism is unjust to everybody, including the despot, who was probably made for better things. Oligarchies are unjust to the many, and ochlocracies [government by the masses] are unjust to the few. High hopes were once formed of democracy; but democracy means simply the bludgeoning of the people by the people for the people.

— *The Soul of Man Under Socialism*

Fred Woodworth

Anarchism...it's not terrorism. The agent of the government — the cop who wears a gun to scare you into obeying him — is the terrorist. Governments threaten to punish any man or woman who defies state power, and therefore the state really amounts to an institution of terror.

— *Anarchism*

All governments survive on theft and extortion, called taxation. All governments force their decrees on the people, and command obedience under threats.

...The principle of government, which is force, is opposed to the free exercise of our ability to think, act and cooperate.

— Ibid.

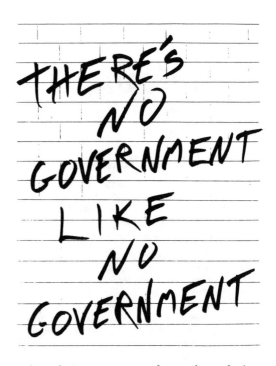

Appeals to a government for a redress of grievances, even when acted upon, only increase the supposed legitimacy of the government's acts, and therefore to its amassed power.

— Ibid.

Government is an unnecessary evil. Human beings, when accustomed to taking responsibility for their own behavior, can cooperate on a basis of mutual trust and helpfulness.

— *The Match!*, No. 79

If human beings are fundamentally good, no government is necessary; if they are fundamentally bad, any government, being composed of human beings, would be bad also.

— Ibid.

The state even has *contingency plans* figuring out how it will operate in the chaos that follows atomic war. Think of it — that's like a hi-jacker with schemes on what he'll do after he blows the plane's wings off.

— *The Match!*, No. 76

Freedom

Michael Bakunin

I, who wish to be free, cannot do so, because around me are men who do not yet desire freedom, and, not desiring it, become, as opposed to me, the instruments of my oppression.

— quoted by Malatesta in *Anarchy*

In his relation to natural laws but one liberty is possible to man — that of recognizing and applying them... These laws, once recognized, exercise an authority which is never disputed by the mass of men. One must, for instance, be at bottom either a fool or a theologian, or at least a metaphysician, jurist, or bourgeois economist to rebel against the law by which two times two makes four.

— *God and the State*

Alexander Berkman

The freedom that is given you on paper, that is written down in law books and constitutions, does not do you a bit of good. Such freedom only means that you have the *right* to do a certain thing. But it doesn't mean that you *can* do it. To be able to do it, you must have the chance, the opportunity...
...If your freedom does not give you that opportunity, then it does you no good. Real freedom means opportunity and well-being. If it does not mean that, it means nothing.

— *What Is Communist Anarchism?*

We must learn to respect the humanity of our fellow-man, not to invade him or coerce him, to consider his liberty as sacred as our own; to respect his freedom and his personality, to foreswear compulsion in any form: to understand that the cure for the evils of liberty is more liberty, that liberty is the mother order.

— Ibid.

Ambrose Bierce

FREEDOM, Exemption from the stress of authority in a beggarly half dozen of restraint's infinite multitude of methods. A political condition that every nation supposes itself to enjoy in virtual monopoly.

— *The Devil's Dictionary*

LIBERTY, One of Imagination's most precious possessions.

— Ibid.

Voltairine de Cleyre

Unless the material conditions for equality exist, it is worse than mockery to pronounce men equal. And unless there is equality (and by equality I mean equal chances for every one to make the most of himself), unless, I say, these equal chances exist, freedom, either of thought, speech, or action, is equally a mockery.

— *Emma Goldman and Expropriation*

Alex Comfort

The conception of a "free society"... implies politically, a form of society without central or other governmental power, and without extra-personal forms of coercion, and sociologically, one based on mutually accepted obligations maintained solely by the existence of a social group-ethic. There is a further implication that the group ethic is conscious and rationally determined.

— *Barbarism and Sexual Freedom*

Glen A. Dahlquist

Freedom is more than just a choice between alternatives; it is the right to determine the alternatives.

Frederick Douglass

The whole history of progress of human liberty shows that all concessions yet made to her august claims have been born of earnest struggle. If there is no struggle, there is no progress. Those who profess to favor freedom and yet depreciate agitation, want crops without plowing up the ground, they want rain without thunder and lightning. They want the ocean without the awful roar of its waters.

Ralph Waldo Emerson

Nothing is more disgusting that the crowing about liberty by slaves, as most men are, and the flippant mistaking for freedom of some paper preamble like a Declaration of Independence, or the statute right to vote, by those who never dared to think or to act.

— *The Conduct of Life*

Graphic by Donald Rooum

Sebastian Faure

Liberty is the doctrine, harmony the way of life.
—*Anarchy*

Charles Ferguson

Liberty is a word of much sophistication, but it means, when it means anything, opportunity to live one's own life in one's own way...The original sin of the world is not contempt for arbitrary laws, but respect for them.

—quoted by Sprading in *Freedom and Its Fundamentals*

Ricardo Flores Magon

To want leaders and at the same time to want to be free is to want the impossible. It's necessary to choose one or the other: to be free, entirely free, denying all authority, or to be slaves perpetuating the domination of many by one man.

—*Regeneración*, March 21, 1914

We are free, truly free, when we don't need to rent our arms to anybody in order to be able to lift a piece of bread to our mouths; and this liberty can be obtained in only one manner: resolutely and fearlessly taking the land, machinery, and means of transportation so that they become the property of all.

—Speech, May 31, 1914

Benjamin Franklin

They that can give up essential liberty to obtain a little temporary safety deserve neither liberty nor safety.

Emma Goldman

True liberty is not a mere scrap of paper called "constitution," "legal right," or "law." It is not an abstraction derived from the nonreality known as "the State." It is not a *negative* thing of being free *from* something, because with such freedom you may starve to death. Real freedom, true liberty is *positive:* it is freedom *to* something; it is the liberty to be, to do; in short, the liberty of actual and active opportunity.

— *The Place of the Individual in Society*

...the people have only as much liberty as they have the intelligence to want and the courage to take.

— *The Social Significance of Modern Drama*

Henrik Ibsen

Undermine the idea of the State, set up in its place spontaneous action, and the idea that spiritual relationship is the only thing that makes for unity, and you will start the elements of a liberty which will be something worth possessing.

—quoted by Emma Goldman in the foreword to *The Social Significance of Modern Drama*

Robert Ingersoll

Give to every human being every right that you claim for yourself.
— *Limitations of Toleration*

Intellectual liberty is the air of the soul, the sunshine of the mind, and without it, the world is a prison, the universe a dungeon.
— *Some Reasons Why*

The man who does not do his own thinking is a slave, and is a traitor to himself and to his fellow men.
...All I claim, all I plead for, is liberty of thought and expression. That is all. I do not pretend to tell what is absolutely true, but what I think is true...
...I simply claim that what ideas I have, I have a right to express; and that any man who denies that right to me is an intellectual thief and robber.
— *The Liberty of Man, Woman and Child*

It is a question of justice, of mercy, of honesty... If there is a man in the world who is not willing to give to every human being every right he claims for himself, he is just so much nearer a barbarian than I am. It is a question of honesty. The man who is not willing to give to every other the same intellectual rights he claims for himself, is dishonest, selfish, and brutal.
— Ibid.

What do I mean by liberty? By physical liberty I mean the right to do anything which does not interfere with the happiness of another. By intellectual liberty I mean the right to think right and the right to think wrong. Thought is the means by which we endeavor to arrive at truth...All that can be required is honesty of purpose.

Immanuel Kant

Everyone may seek his own happiness in the way that seems good to himself, provided that he infringe not such freedom of others to strive after a similar end as is consistent with the freedom of all.
— quoted by Sprading in *Freedom and its Fundamentals*

V.I. Lenin

Freedom is a bourgeois prejudice.
— quoted by Rocker in *Nationalism and Culture*

Anyone who speaks of freedom and equality within the framework of a toiler's democracy is thereby a defender of exploiters.
— Speech, November 11, 1920, quoted by Maximoff in *The Guillotine at Work*

Ideological talk and phrase mongering about political liberties should be disposed with; all that is just mere chatter and phrase mongering. We should get away from those phrases.
— Speech, October 17, 1921, quoted by Maximoff in *The Guillotine at Work*

Thomas Macaulay

Many politicians are in the habit of laying it down as a self-evident proposition that no people ought to be free till they are fit to use their freedom. The maxim is worthy of the fool in the old story who resolved not to go into the water till he had learned to swim.

Errico Malatesta

So freedom for everybody and in everything, limited only by equal freedom for others; which does *not* mean—it is almost ridiculous to have to point this out—that we recognize and wish to respect the "freedom" to exploit, to oppress, to command, which is oppression and certainly not freedom.
— *La Questione Social,* November 25, 1899

The "freedom" to oppress, to exploit, to oblige people to take up arms, to pay taxes, etc., is the denial of freedom; and the fact that our enemies make irrelevant and hypocritical use of the word freedom is not enough to make us deny the principle of freedom which is the outstanding characteristic of our movement [anarchism] and a permanent, constant and necessary factor in the life and progress of humanity.
— Ibid.

Our demand is simply for what could be called social freedom, which is equal freedom for all, an equality of conditions such as to allow everybody to do as they wish, with the only limitation, imposed by inevitable natural necessities and the equal freedom of others...
— *Umanita Nova*, November 24, 1921

The freedom we want is not the abstract right, but the power, to do as one wishes; it therefore presupposes that everybody has the means to live and to act without being subjected to the wishes of others. And since to maintain life it is essential to produce, the prerequisite of freedom is that all land, raw materials and the means of production should be at the free disposal of all.
— Ibid.

...only with liberty can one learn to be free, as it is only by working that one can learn to work.
— *Anarchy*

Jean Paul Marat

Of what use is political liberty to those who have no bread? It is of value only to ambitious theorists and politicians.
— Letter to Camille Desmoulins, June 24, 1790

H.L. Mencken

One of the amusing by-products of war is its pricking of the fundamental democratic delusion. For years *Homo Boobus* stalks the earth vaingloriously, flapping his wings over his God-given rights, his inalienable freedom, his sublime equality to his masters. Then of a sudden he is thrust into a training camp, and discovers the he is a slave, after all — that even his life is not his own.

— *Minority Report*

John Stuart Mill

The only freedom which deserves the name is that of pursuing our own good in our own way, so long as we do not attempt to deprive others of theirs, or impede their efforts to obtain it. Each is the proper guardian of his own health, whether bodily, or mental and spiritual.

— *On Liberty*

The liberty of the individual must be thus far limited: he must not make himself a nuisance to other people.

— Ibid.

Luke North

It is vain to echo Nietzsche's mad cry for absolute freedom — the freedom of the Strong to enslave the weak, of the cunning to rob the candid. That we already have and it does not satisfy. . . The demand of the centuries, never so virile and insistent as today, is for equal freedom. . . there is no freedom till all are free. Master and slave are bound by the same thong. Human solidarity is not a moral fancy but a stern fact.

— quoted by Sprading

Wendell Phillips

Eternal vigilance is the price of liberty.

— *Public Opinion* (Speech, 1852)

No free people can lose their liberties while they are jealous of liberty. But the liberties of the freest people are in danger when they set up symbols of liberty as fetishes, worshiping the symbol instead of the principle it represents.

— quoted by Sprading in *Liberty and the Great Libertarians*

Pierre Joseph Proudhon

Liberty, not the daughter, but the mother of order.

In charge of the business of the Deparment and the State, officer of the judicial, intermediary and plenipotentiary police, instructor, director, initiator, inspector, Supervisor, estimator, controller, censor, reformer, redresser, corrector, guardian, commander, superintendent, magistrate, judge — that is the prefect, that is the government. And you tell me that a people that will submit to such a rule, a people thus held in leading strings, under collar and bridle, under rod and whip, is a free people!

that such a people understands liberty, that it is capable of tasting liberty and receiving it! No, no, such a people is less than a slave; it is nothing but a war horse. Before freeing it, it must be raised to the dignity of a man, by reconstructing its understanding. It will say to you itself, in the simplicity of its belief: "What would become of me without saddle or bridle! I have never known any other rule of life nor any other condition."

— *The General Idea of the Revolution in the 19th Century*

Francois Rabelais

Do what thou wilt.

— *Gargantua*

Wilhelm Reich

The development of freedom requires that one be ruthlessly free of illusions, for only then will one succeed in rooting out irrationalism from masses of people to open the way to *responsibility* and *freedom*. To idealize masses of people and to commiserate with them will only produce fresh misfortunes.

— *The Mass Psychology of Fascism*

Rudolf Rocker

. . .the desire for freedom is less alive among men today and has with many of them given place completely to a desire for economic security. This phenomenon need not appear so strange, for our whole evolution has reached a stage where nearly every man is either ruler or ruled; sometimes he is both. By this the attitude of dependence has been greatly strengthened, for a truly free man does not like to play the part of either the ruler or the ruled. He is, above all, concerned with making his inner values and personal powers effective in such a way as to permit him to use his own judgment in all affairs and to be independent in action. Constant tutelage of our acting and thinking has made us weak and irresponsible; hence, the continued cry for the strong man who is to put an end to our distress. This call for a dictator is not a sign of strength, but a proof of inner lack of assurance and of weakness, even though those who utter it earnestly try to give themselves the appearance of resolution. What man most lacks he most desires. When one feels himself weak he seeks salvation from another's strength; when one is cowardly or too timid to move one's own hands for the forging of one's fate, one entrusts it to another.

— *Nationalism and Culture*

The way of freedom will be only gradually covered, for it is not conceivable that men languishing in economic bondage and spiritual darkness will be able to achieve freedom overnight.

— *Pioneers of American Freedom*

Except in the case of actual encroachment, society has no more right to interfere with the morality of individual conduct than it has to interfere with the orthodoxy of individual belief. Neither comes within the jurisdiction of third persons except at the point where encroachment begins.
— Ibid.

Only that man can be free who takes his fate into his own hands and accepts responsibility for his own conduct as the sole basis for relations with his fellowmen. Therefore, the sovereignty of the human personality is the best foundation for a society based on justice.
— Ibid.

Freedom is achieved not by submitting everyone to the same compulsions, but by securing for everyone the possibility of obtaining happiness and contentment in his own fashion. Not equality of men but equality of social conditions under which they live creates moral unity. All ethical principles, all rights which the constitution of the state guarantees to the citizen lose their meaning so long as men are forced to live under conditions which give to some the prerogative of determining the fate of the others.
— Ibid.

Political rights do not originate in parliaments; they are rather forced upon them from without. And even their enactment into law has for a long time been no guarantee of their security. They do not exist because they have been legally set down on a piece of paper, but only when they have become the ingrown habit of a people, and when any attempt to impair them will meet with the violent resistance of the populace. Where this is not the case, there is no help in any parliamentary opposition or any Platonic appeals to the constitution. One compels respect from others when one knows how to defend one's dignity as a human being. This is not only true in private life; it has always been the same in political life as well.
— *Anarchism and Anarcho-Syndicalism*

J.C.F. von Schiller

Never yet has law formed a great man: 'tis liberty that breeds giants and heroes.
— *The Robbers*

George Bernard Shaw

Liberty means responsibility. That is why most men dread it.
— *Maxims for Revolutionists*

Herbert Spencer

Hero-worship is strongest where there is least regard for human freedom.
— *Social Statics*

[Freedom means] That every man may claim the fullest liberty to exercise his faculties compatible with the possession of like liberty by every other man.
— quoted by Sprading in *Freedom and its Fundamentals*

Libertarians believe in equal liberty, and not absolute liberty. "Absolute liberty" disregards the liberty of others, and is unsocial in character...
— Ibid.

Most people mistake law for justice and authority for liberty. You will hear them talk of "liberty under law," and they are content to see it so deep under the law that it is completely obliterated.
— Ibid.

Charles T. Sprading

Mere equality does not imply equal liberty, however, for slaves are equal in their slavery.
— *Liberty and the Great Libertarians*

Equal liberty is bounded by the like liberty of all.
— Ibid.

Robert Tefton

FREEDOM, n. In the United States, the opportunity to choose one's masters every two years; 2) A substance so precious that governments routinely coerce young men into military servitude in order to protect it.

Thucydides

The secret of Happiness is Freedom, and the secret of Freedom is Courage.
— Pericles' Funeral Oration

Benjamin Tucker

To describe..."our liberty to compel others" denotes an utter misconception. It is simply the exercise of our liberty to keep others from compelling us.

But who is to judge where invasion begins?... Each for himself, and those to combine who agree, I answer. It will be perpetual war, then? Not at all; a war of short duration, at the worst. I am well aware that there is a border-land between legitimate and invasive conduct over which there must be for a time more or less trouble. But it is an ever-decreasing margin. It has been narrowing ever since the idea of equal liberty first dawned upon the mind of man, and in proportion as this idea becomes clearer and the new social conditions which it involves become real will it contract towards the geometrical conception of a line. And then the world will be at peace.
— *Instead of a Book*

They [anarchists] never have claimed that liberty will bring perfection; they simply say that its results are vastly preferable to those that follow authority.
—Ibid.

. . . liberty always, say the Anarchists. No use of force, except against the invader; and in those cases where it is difficult to tell whether the alleged offender is an invader or not, still no use of force except where the necessity of immediate solution is so imperative that we must use it to save ourselves.
—Ibid.

Josiah Warren

Having the Liberty to differ does not make us differ, but, on the contrary, it is a common ground upon which all can meet, a particular in which the feelings of all *coincide* and is the first true step in social harmony. Giving full latitude to every experiment (at the cost of the experimenter), brings everything to a test, and insures a harmonious conclusion. Among a multitude of untried routes, only one of which is right, the more liberty there is to differ and take different routes, the sooner will all come to a harmonious conclusion as to the right one; and this is the only possible mode by which the harmonious result aimed at can be attained. Compulsion, even upon the right road, will never be harmonious.
—*Equitable Commerce*

Anonymous

Obedience to the Law is Freedom.
—Sign over entrance to Fort Dix stockade

Express Yourself!

Henry Ward Beecher

There is a tonic in the things that men do not love to hear; and there is damnation in the things that wicked men love to hear. Free speech is to a great people what winds are to oceans and malarial regions, which waft away the elements of disease, and bring new elements of health; and where free speech is stopped miasma is bred, and death comes fast.

Jeremy Bentham

As to the evil which results from a censorship, it is impossible to measure it, because it is impossible to tell where it ends.
— *On Liberty of the Press and Public Discussion*

Ambrose Bierce

INK, A villainous compound of tanno-gallate of iron, gum-arabic and water, chiefly used to facilitate the infection of idiocy and to promote intellectual crime.

PLATITUDE, The fundamental element and special glory of popular literature. A thought that snores in words that smoke. The wisdom of a million fools in the diction of a dullard. A fossil sentiment in artificial rock. A moral without the fable. All that is mortal of a departed truth. A demitasse of milk-and-morality. The pope's nose of a featherless peacock. A jelly-fish withering on the shore of the sea of thought. The cackle surviving the egg. A desiccated epigram.

SLANG, The grunt of the human hog (*Pignoramus intolerabilis*) with an audible memory. The speech of one who utters with his tongue what he thinks with his ear, and feels the pride of a creator in accomplishing the feat of a parrot.
— *The Devil's Dictionary*

Slang is the speech of him who robs the liberary garbage carts on their way to the dumps.
— *Collected Works*

Charles Bradlaugh

Without free speech no search for truth is possible; without free speech no discovery of truth is useful; without free speech progress is checked and the nations no longer march forward toward the nobler life which the future holds for man. Better a thousand fold abuse of free speech than its denial which slays the life of the people and entombs the hope of the race.
— quoted by Sprading in *Liberty and the Great Libertarians*

Thomas Carlyle

He who first shortened the labour of Copyists by device of *Movable Types* was disbanding hired Armies, and cashiering most Kings and Senates, and creating a whole new Democratic world; he had invented the Art of Printing.
— *Sartor Resartus*

Lewis Carroll

When *I* use a word . . . it means just what I choose it to mean — neither more nor less . . .
— *Through the Looking Glass*

Noam Chomsky

Americanism. Who can be against that? Or harmony. Who can be against that? Or, to bring it up to date, "Support our troops." Who can be against that? Or yellow ribbons. Who can be against that? Anything that's totally vacuous. In fact, what does it mean if somebody asks you, Do you support the people in Iowa? Can you say, Yes, I support them, or No, I don't support them? It's not even a question. It doesn't mean anything. That's the point. The point of public relations slogans like "Support our troops" is that they don't mean anything. They mean as much as whether you support the people in Iowa. Of course, there was an issue. The issue was, Do you support their policy? But you don't want people to think about the issue. That's the whole point of good propaganda. You want to create a slogan that nobody's going to be against, and everybody's going to be for, because nobody knows what it means, because it doesn't mean anything, but its crucial value is that it diverts your attention from a question that *does* mean something: do you support their policy? That's the one you're not allowed to talk about.

— *Media Control: The Spectacular Achievements of Propaganda*

Voltairine de Cleyre

Make no laws whatever concerning speech and speech will be free; so soon as you make a declaration on paper that speech shall be free, you will have a hundred lawyers proving that "freedom does not mean abuse, nor liberty license"; and they will define and define freedom out of existence. Let the guarantee of free speech be in every man's determination to use it, and we shall have no need of paper declarations. On the other hand, so long as the people do not care to exercise their freedom, those who wish to tyrannize will do so; . . .

— *Anarchism and American Traditions*

Eugene V. Debs

The anonymous writer, as a rule, ought to be ignored, since he is unwilling to face those he accuses, while he may be a sneak or coward, traitor or spy, in the role of a "staunch Socialist," whose base design it is to divide and disrupt the movement.

— *International Socialist Review,* January 1904

Alexandre Dumas

All generalizations are dangerous, even this one.

— quoted by Stanley Gudder in *A Mathematical Journey*

Rev. J. Furniss, C.S.S.R.

If you get hold of a bad book, the devil will be sure to put some reason into your head why you should read it . . . The devil will whisper into your ear that a bad book will *give* you a knowledge of the *world!* It will give you a knowledge of *hell,* and lead you there. What then must be done about bad books? . . . All bad books, and bad newspapers, and journals about very bad things, should be burnt in the fire, lest through them you should come to burn in the fire of hell.

— *Tracts for Spiritual Reading*

There are six sorts of bad books. 1. Books which are plainly about very bad things. 2. Many novels . . . 3. Idle books . . . 4. Bad newspapers and journals . . . 5. Superstitious books . . . 6. Protestant books and tracts.

— Ibid.

Pope Gregory XVI

From the polluted fountain of indifferentism flows that absurd and erroneous doctrine, or rather, raving, which claims and defends liberty of conscience for everyone. From this comes, in a word, the worst plague of all, namely, unrestrained liberty of opinion and freedom of speech.

— *Mirari Vox*

Robert Hall

Every thing that is really excellent will bear examination, it will even invite it, and the more narrowly it is surveyed, to the more advantage will it appear.

— *An Apology for the Liberty of the Press*

Claude Helvetius

To limit the press is to insult a nation; to prohibit reading of certain books is to declare the inhabitants to be either fools or slaves.

— *De l'Homme*

Adolf Hitler

. . . the state must not forget that all means must serve an end; it must not let itself be confused by the drivel about so-called "freedom of the press" . . . it must make sure of this instrument of popular education, and place it in the service of the state . . .

— *Mein Kampf*

The National Socialist Party will prevent in the future, by force if necessary, all meetings and lectures which are likely to exercise a depressing influence . . .

— Speech in Munich, January 4, 1921

Thomas Jefferson

. . . if it were left to me to decide whether we should have a government without newspapers or newspapers without a government, I should not hesitate a moment to prefer the latter.

To the press alone, chequered as it is with abuses, the world is indebted for all the triumphs which have been gained by reason and humanity over error and oppression . . .

— *Virginia and Kentucky Resolution*

. . . our liberty depends on the freedom of the press, and that cannot be limited without being lost.

— Letter to Dr. J. Currie

It is error alone which needs the support of government. Truth can stand by itself. Subject opinion to coercion. Whom will you make your inquisitors? Fallible men; men governed by bad passions, by private as well as public reasons. And why subject it to coercion? To produce uniformity. But is uniformity desirble? No more than of face and stature. Introduce the bed of Procrustes then, and as there is danger that the large men may beat the small, make us all of a size, by lopping the former and stretching the latter.

— *Notes on Virginia*

Frank Kent

The only way a reporter should look at a politician is down.

— attributed

V.I. Lenin

Why should freedom of speech and freedom of the press be allowed? Why should a government which is doing what it believes to be right allow itself to be criticized? It would not allow opposition by lethal weapons. Ideas are much more fatal things than guns. Why should a man be allowed to buy a printing press and disseminate pernicious opinions calculated to embarrass the government?

— Speech in Moscow, 1920, quoted by Maximoff in *The Guillotine at Work*

Pope Leo XIII

Men have a right freely and prudently to propagate throughout the state what things soever are true and honorable, so that as many as possible possess them; but lying opinions, than which no mental plague is greater, and vices which corrupt the heart and moral life, should be diligently repressed by public authority, lest they insidiously ruin the work of the state.

— *Libertas Praestantissimum*

From what has been said it follows that it is in no way lawful to demand, to defend, or to grant, unconditional freedom of thought, or speech, of writing, or of religion, as if they were so many rights that nature has given to man.

— Ibid.

Books of apostates, heretics, schismatics, and all other writers defending heresy or schism or in any way attacking the foundations of religion, are altogether prohibited.

— *General Decrees Concerning the Prohibition and Censorship of Books,* January 25, 1897

The liberty of thinking and publishing whatsoever each one likes, without any hindrances, is not in itself an advantage over which society can wisely rejoice. On the contrary, it is the fountainhead and origin of many evils.

— *Immortale Dei*

A.J. Liebling

Freedom of the press belongs to those who own one.

Martin Luther

The aggregation of large libraries tends to divert men's thoughts from the one great book, the Bible, which ought, day and night, to be in everyone's hand. My object, my hope, in translating the Scriptures, was to check the so prevalent production of new works.

— *Table Talk*

Malcolm X

If you're not careful, the newspapers will have you hating the people who are being oppressed, and loving the people who are doing the oppressing.

— quoted in *Propaganda Review*, Spring 1989

Mao Tse Tung

. . . deprive the reactionaries of the right to speak.

— *On the People's Democratic Dictatorship*

What should our policy be towards non-Marxist ideas? As far as unmistakable counter-revolutionaries and saboteurs of the socialist cause are concerned, the matter is easy: we simply deprive them of their freedom of speech.

— *Correct Handling of Contradictions*

Karl Marx

Freedom of the press consists primarily in its not being a trade. The writer who degrades it by making it a commodity deserves, as punishment for his inner slavery, outer slavery — censorship; or rather his existence is already his punishment.

— *Herr Vogt*

John Stuart Mill

. . . the peculiar evil of silencing the expression of an opinion is, that it is robbing the human race, posterity as well as the existing generation; those who dissent from the opinion, still more than those who hold it. If the opinion is right, they are deprived of the opportunity of exchanging error for truth; if wrong, they lose, what is almost as great a benefit, the clearer perception and livelier impression of truth, produced by its collision with error.

— *On Liberty*

Friedrich Nietzsche

Improving one's style means improving one's ideas, and nothing else. He who does not at once concede this can never be convinced of the point.

— *Human, All Too Human*

Good writers have two things in common: they prefer being understood to being admired, and they do not write for the critical and overly shrewd reader.

— Ibid.

Caliph Omar

Burn the libraries, for all their value is in the Koran.

— at the fall of Alexandria in 641

Wendell Phillips

The time to assert rights is when they are denied; the men to assert them are those to whom they are denied. The community which dares not protect its humblest and most hated member in the free utterance of his opinions, no matter how false or hateful, is only a gang of slaves.

— *Mobs and Education*

Let us always remember that he does not really believe his own opinions, who dares not give free scope to his opponent.

— *Speeches* (1863)

It is a momentous, yes, a fearful truth, that the millions have no literature, no school and almost no pulpit but the press. Not one in ten reads books . . . But every one of us, except the very few helpless poor, poisons himself every day with a newspaper. It is parent, school, college, pulpit, theater, example, counselor, all in one. Every drop of our blood is colored by it.

Wilhelm Reich

. . . [Pick up] any newspaper in Europe, Asia, or anywhere else, regardless of date. It is only seldom and as if by chance that one finds anything about the basic principles and nature of the processes of love, work, and knowledge, their vital necessity, their interrelationship, their rationality, their seriousness, etc. On the other hand, the newspapers are full of high politics, diplomacy, military and formal events, which have no bearing upon the real process of everyday life. In this way the average working man and woman are imbued with the feeling that . . . they are small, inadequate, superfluous, oppressed, and not much more than an *accident in life*.

— *The Mass Psychology of Fascism*

George Bernard Shaw

In this world if you do not say a thing in an irritating way you may just as well not say it at all, because people will not trouble themselves about anything that does not trouble them.

Charles T. Sprading

The people repeat the suggestions of the press with as much faithfulness as the subject of a hypnotist does. Whatever it believes, they believe; when it is indignant, they are indignant; when it is alarmed, they are alarmed; when it is patriotic, they are patriotic; when it is neutral, they are neutral; when it is warlike, they are warlike. The public is so much putty in its hands . . .

— *Freedom and its Fundamentals*

Hypnotism . . . is the method of the jingo press, suggesting the thing it wants the public to believe . . . With most of the public, this press does not even have to substitute its idea for theirs. They have no idea of their own to be supplanted.

— Ibid.

John Swinton

There is no such thing in America as an independent press, unless it is in the country towns. You know it, and I know it.

There is not one of you who dares to write his honest opinions, and if you did, you know beforehand they would never appear in print.

I am paid $150 a week for keeping my honest opinions out of the paper I am connected with. Others of you are paid similar salaries for doing similar things. If I should permit honest opinions to be printed in one issue of my paper, like Othello, before 24 hours, my occupation would be gone.

. . . You know this and I know it, and what folly is this to be toasting an "independent press." We are the tools and vassals of rich men behind the scenes. We are the jumping-jacks; they pull the strings and we dance. Our talents, our possibilities and our lives are all the property of other men. We are intellectual prostitutes.

— Speech to journalists, New York, April 12, 1883

Zeke Teflon

Freedom of communication is a basic human right. Like all rights, freedom of communication consists of being free to exercise your own abilities without interference. Government cannot give you your own abilities, but it sure as hell can (and will) interfere with you when you exercise them. *Government cannot give you rights. It can only take them from you.* If all governments (goons with guns forcing others to follow their dictates through violence and coercion) were to cease to exist, human rights would certainly *not* cease along with them.

The naive objection could be raised that while governments cannot *give* you rights, they can *protect* them by preventing your fellow citizens from interfering with you. That's the *theory*. In *practice*, governments rarely "protect" citizens' rights, and then only when it suits their political purposes. Invariably, when governments feel the least bit threatened, they place their own "security" needs above the human rights which they supposedly safeguard . . .

We cannot look to government to protect our rights. We must do it ourselves, and an effective means of doing that is by exercising our rights. Use 'em or lose 'em.

— *The Complete Manual of Pirate Radio*

Robert Tefton

ADVOCACY JOURNALISM, n. A derogatory term applied to the writings of journalists who openly acknowledge their biases. This despicable form of journalism is to be contrasted with the admirable practice of Unbiased Reporting, practiced by journalists who have no biases, and, indeed, no viewpoint whatsoever on any issue on which they report.

ASSHOLE, n. The most commonly employed word in American English. Frequently used by both sides in an argument, more often than not, accurately.

BIASED, adj. A pejorative term meaning: 1) The reporting of facts which are embarrassing to the powers that be; 2) The ability to draw obvious conclusions from observed facts, especially when those conclusions appear in print.

DESKTOP PUBLISHING, n. A major advance in communications technology. Desktop publishing has put within the reach of nearly everyone the ability to produce hideous-looking printed materials. Thanks to this computer-age marvel, aspiring graphic artists have attained the ability to demonstrate why they are "aspiring" almost instantaneously.

FREEDOM OF SPEECH, n. The inalienable right to agree with the powers that be on any and every subject. Also, the inalienable right to disagree—as long as it isn't exercised before an audience of more than 20 people. When exercised before a larger audience, or when it appears to have an effect on listeners, it becomes "license" or "sedition" and is, of course, lawfully suppressed.

OBJECTIVITY, n. A journalistic term signifying gross servility to the powerful.

Alexis de Tocqueville

I think that men living in aristocracies may, strictly speaking, do without the liberty of the press: but such is not the case with those who live in democratic countries. To protect their personal independence I trust not to great political assemblies, to parliamentary privilege, or to the assertion of popular sovereignty. All these things may, to a certain extent, be reconciled with personal servitude. But that servitude cannot be complete if the press is free: the press is the chief democratic instrument of freedom.

— *Democracy in America*

Mark Twain

It's a classic...something everybody wants to have read, and nobody wants to read.

— *Disappearance of Literature* (speech)

Voltaire

What harm can a book do that costs a hundred crowns? Twenty volumes folio will never make a revolution. It is the little pocket pamphlets of 30 sous that are to be feared...

— quoted in *The Wisdom of Voltaire*

Oscar Wilde

The fact is that the public have an insatiable curiosity to know everything, except what is worth knowing. Journalism, conscious of this, and having tradesman-like habits, supplies their demands.

— *The Soul of Man Under Socialism*

In the old days men had the rack. Now they have the press.

— Ibid.

But what is the difference between literature and journalism?...Journalism is unreadable, and literature is not read.

— *The Critic as Artist*

Learned conversation is either the affectation of the ignorant or the profession of the mentally unemployed.

— Ibid.

There is so much to be said in favor of modern journalism. By giving us the opinions of the uneducated, it keeps us in touch with the ignorance of the community.

— Ibid.

It is only about things that do not interest one that one can give a really unbiased opinion, which is no doubt the reason why an unbiased opinion is always absolutely valueless.

— Ibid.

Fred Woodworth

The first thing that forcibly strikes the eye on gazing at this tabloid [*The National Landlord*, published by the National Association of Landlords] is the complete artistic degradation of the written word. This is, before anything else, possibly the most unattractive periodical one is likely to ever see. Heavy black lines, clip-art graphics, jumbled illustrations, frequent muddy borders of eagles and stars, blaring headlines an inch-and-a-half tall that say only such fragments as "RENTS" or "WILL" vie with gigantic exclamation marks and white- on-black reverses to create a hodge-podge that cannot be the product of a reflective and advanced intelligence. Screeching disorder and strident typographical cacophony combine with an ignorantly written text to produce, on paper, a replica of the disagreeable mentality of the writers and editors as well as their intended audience — other landlords...

Confusion in print is probably the result of actual confusion; likewise tastelessness and mental impoverishment.

— *Rent: An Injustice*

John Peter Zenger

No nation ancient or modern ever lost the liberty of freely speaking, writing, or publishing their sentiments, but forthwith lost their liberty in general and became slaves.

— *New York Weekly Journal*, November 19, 1733

Anonymous & Multiple Author

Processed World, the magazine with a bad attitude ... *Time*, the bad magazine with an attitude.

— *Processed World* flyer

There is more force in names
Than most men dream of; and a lie may keep
Its throne a whole age longer, if it skulk
Behind the shield of some fair-sounding name.

— Anonymous, quoted by Wendell Phillips in *Welcome to George Thompson*

Anarchism

Michael Bakunin

We declare ourselves the enemies of every government and every state power, and of governmental organization in general. We think that people can be free and happy only when organized from the bottom up in completely free and independent associations, without governmental paternalism though not without the influence of a variety of free individuals and parties.

Such are our ideas as social revolutionaries, and we are therefore called anarchists. We do not protest this name, for we are indeed the enemies of any governmental power, since we know that such a power depraves those who wear its mantle equally with those who are forced to submit to it. Under its pernicious influence the former become ambitious and greedy despots, exploiters of society in favor of their personal or class interests, while the latter become slaves.

— *Critique of the Marxist Theory of the State*

Alexander Berkman

The word Anarchy comes from the Greek, meaning without force, without violence or government, because government is the very fountainhead of violence, constraint, and coercion.

Anarchy therefore does *not* mean disorder and chaos...On the contrary, it is the very reverse of it; it means no government, which is freedom and liberty. Disorder is the child of authority and compulsion. Liberty is the mother of order.

— *What Is Communist Anarchism?*

Every human being who is not devoid of feeling and common sense is inclined to Anarchism. Every one who suffers from wrong and injustice, from the evil, corruption, and filth of our present-day life, is instinctively sympathetic to Anarchy. Every one whose heart is not dead to kindness, compassion, and fellow-sympathy must be interested in furthering it. Every one who has to endure poverty and misery, tyranny and oppression should welcome the coming of Anarchy. Every liberty- and justice-loving man and woman should help realize it.

— Ibid.

Anyone who tells you that Anarchists don't believe in organization is talking nonsense. Organization is everything, and everything is organization. The whole of life is organization, conscious or unconscious...

But there is organization and organization...

The organization built on compulsion, which coerces and forces, is bad and unhealthy. The libertarian organization formed voluntarily and in which every member is free and equal, is a sound body and can work well. Such an organization is a free union of equal parts. It is the kind of organization the Anarchists believe in.

— Ibid.

Wherever you turn you will find that our entire life is built on violence or the fear of it. From earliest childhood you are subjected to the violence of parents or elders. At home, in school, in the office, factory, field or shop, it is always some one's *authority* which keeps you obedient and compels you to do his will.

The right to compel you is called authority. Fear of punishment has been made into duty and is called obedience.

In this atmosphere of force and violence, of authority and obedience, of duty, fear and punishment, we all grow up; we breathe it throughout our lives. We are so steeped in the spirit of violence that we never stop to ask whether violence is right or wrong. We only ask if it is legal, whether the law permits it.

You don't question the right of the government to kill, to confiscate and imprison. If a private person should be guilty of the things the government is doing all the time, you'd brand him a murderer, thief, and scoundrel. But as long as the violence committed is "lawful" you approve of it and submit to it.

— Ibid.

...lawful violence and the fear of it dominate our whole existence, individual and collective. Authority controls our lives from the cradle to the grave — authority, parental, priestly and divine, political, economic, social and moral. But whatever the character of that authority, it is always the same executioner wielding power over you through your fear of punishment in one form or another.

You are afraid of God and the devil, of the priest and the jailer, of the law and government. All your life is a long chain of fears—fears which bruise your body and lacerate your soul. On those fears is based the authority of God, of the church, of parents, of capitalist and ruler.

—Ibid.

You stand for the authority of priest and preacher because you think they can "call down the wrath of God upon your head." You submit to the domination of boss, judge, and government because of their power to deprive you of work, to ruin your business, to put you in prison...

So authority rules your whole life, the authority of the past and the present, of the dead and the living, and your existence is a continuous invasion and violation of yourself, a constant subjection to the thoughts and the will of some one else.

And as you are invaded and violated, so you subconsciously revenge yourself by invading and violating others over whom *you* have authority or can exercise compulsion, physical or moral. In this way all life has become a crazy-quilt of authority, of domination and submission, of command and obedience, of coercion and subjection, of rulers and ruled, of violence and force in a thousand and one forms.

—Ibid.

We are all still barbarians who resort to force and violence to settle our doubts, difficulties and troubles. Violence is the method of ignorance, the weapon of the weak. The strong of heart and brain need no violence, for they are irresistible in their consciousness of being right. The further we get away from primitive man and the hatchet age, the less recourse we shall have to force and violence. The more enlightened man will become, the less he will employ compulsion and coercion. The really civilized man will divest himself of all fear and authority. He will rise from the dust and stand erect; he will become fully human when he will scorn to rule and refuse to be ruled. He will be truly free only when there shall be no more masters.

Anarchism is the ideal of such a condition; of a society without force and compulsion, where all men shall be equals, and live in freedom, peace, and harmony.

—Ibid.

Voltairine de Cleyre

As to the American tradition of non-meddling, Anarchism asks that it be carried down to the individual himself. It demands no jealous barrier of isolation; it knows that such isolation is undesirable and impossible; but it teaches that by all men's strictly minding their own business, a fluid society, freely adapting itself to mutual needs, wherein all the world shall belong to all men, as much as each has need or desire, will result.

—*Anarchism and American Traditions*

Sam Dolgoff

...since the necessities of life and vital services must be supplied without fail and cannot be left to the whims of individuals...large scale organizations, anarchistically organized, are *not* a *deviation*. They are the very essence of Anarchism as a viable social order.

—*The Relevance of Anarchism to Modern Society*

There is no "pure" Anarchism. There is only the application of Anarchist principles to the realities of social living. The aim of Anarchism is to stimulate forces that propel society in a libertarian direction.

—Ibid.

Buenaventura Durruti

We carry a new world here in our hearts.

Ralph Waldo Emerson

Massachusetts, in its heroic days, had no government, was an Anarchy. Every man stood on his own feet, was his own governor, and there was no breach of peace from Cape Cod to Mount Hoosac.

—quoted by Bool and Carlyle in *For Liberty*

Luigi Fabbri

The marginalized people of present day society, among them many criminals, seriously believe that anarchy is as described in bourgeois newspapers, that is, something well adapted to their anti-social habits.

—*Bourgeois Influences on Anarchism*

Anarchy is the ideal of abolishing the violent and coercive authority of man over man in every sphere, be it economic, religious, or political.

—Ibid.

The Anarchists have always maintained that life is not possible without association and solidarity, and that struggle and revolution are not possible without a pre-existing organization of revolutionaries. But it's more convenient for bourgeois writers to paint us as promoters of anarchy in the sense of confusion, chaos; and they commence to say that we're agents of chaos, enemies of all organization ...Many Anarchists swallow the bait and in seriousness becomes promoters of chaos, Stirnerites, Nietzscheans, and other similar absurdities. They reject organization, solidarity, and socialism; some even end up sanctifying private property, and in this manner end up playing the game of the bourgeois individualist.

—Ibid.

The minds of men, especially of the young, thirsting for the mysterious and extraordinary, easily allow the passion for the new to drag them toward that which, when coolly examined in the calm which follows initial enthusiasm, is absolutely and definitively repudiated. This fever for new things, this audacious spirit, this zeal for the extraordinary has brought to the anarchist ranks the most exaggeratedly impressionable types, and, at the same time, the most empty headed and frivolous types — persons who are not repelled by the absurd, but who, on the contrary, engage in it. They are attracted to projects and ideas precisely because they are absurd; and so Anarchism comes to be known precisely for the illogical character and ridiculousness which ignorance and bourgeois calumny have attributed to anarchist doctrines...

Well, none of these individuals would have come to our camp but for the attraction exercised upon them by phony, bourgeois "anarchist" propaganda. The entire bourgeois campaign of invective, calumny and pure invention acts as a mirror for all of these marginalized types — marginalized intellectually, materially, psychologically, and physiologically — who always orient themselves toward the absurd, the freakish, the terrible, and the illogical.

— Ibid.

Sebastian Faure

Anarchist doctrine can be summed up in a single word: liberty.

— *Anarchy*

Adolf Fischer

The term "anarchism" is of Greek origin and means "without government," or in other words, "without oppression." I only wish that every workingman would understand the proper meaning of this word. It is an absurd falsehood if the capitalists and their hired editors say that anarchism is identical with disorder and crime. On the contrary, anarchism wants to do away with the existing social disorder.

— *The Philosophy of Anarchism*

Ricardo Flores Magon

Anarchism strives for the establishment of a social order based on brotherhood and love, as against the actual [present] form of society, founded on violence, hatred and rivalry of one class against the other, and of members of one class (the working class) among themselves. Anarchism aims at establishing peace forever among all the races of the earth by the suppression of this fountain of all evils — private property. If this is not a beautiful ideal, what is it?

— Letter to Harry Weinberger, May 9, 1921

Jay Fox

The Anarchist is a thorough believer in his fellow man. But he is not a utopian. Though he has faith in the goodness of man, he is not blind to his many weaknesses. He does not want to plunge mankind into a condition of life for which its nature is not fitted — a charge often repeated by kindly and well-meaning people who cannot rid themselves of the belief — instilled in them by early false training — that government must exist to restrain the selfishness of man. They forget that a man with the forces of government at his command has the power to indulge his selfishness multiplied a thousand times.

The Anarchist does not deplore the instinct of selfishness. He simply recognizes it, and is guided accordingly. For instance, he knows that as it is selfishness which makes tyrants and oppressors out of good men when they are placed in positions of power and authority over their fellows, it is the same selfish instinct that makes them kind and considerate neighbors when not clothed with such power. The Anarchist is not so foolish as to think that one set of men, because they belong to a different party, or hold different opinions in politics or economics, are any better or worse than another set. He knows that all men are made from the same clay, and that, placed in the same position, they will act in the same way. He knows that selfishness — self-preservation — is the strongest force in man, that it cannot be eliminated, and should not if it could; for such a condition would reduce mankind to mere machines. He insists that selfishness must not be perverted by being placed in positions of authority where it can enslave mankind; and that the way to protect ourselves from selfishness is to strip it of all power, except the power each person possesses within himself.

He [the Anarchist] can point to our unions and show us that even in these small offices, filled generally by the very best of men, the officials — if not watched closely — are apt to assume authority that was never given to them, and to regard themselves as made from a clay superior to that of the rank and file.

Is it any wonder then that the Anarchist is sceptical about trusting men with the power of government?

Governments claim to protect us against foreign foes. The Anarchists say that we have no foreign foes except foreign governments. We have no fear of invasion by the workers of England, Germany, or France.

The Anarchist is convinced, from his study of humanity, that not until men become angels, will government ever be anything else but a tool in the hands of the strong for the oppression and the exploitation of the weak. Therefore that form of organization which will delegate the least amount of power and authority to the individual is the one best suited to the nature of man — one that will give each member of society the greatest amount of

The theory that all forms of government rest on violence, and are therefore wrong and harmful, as well as unnecessary.

A condition of society regulated by voluntary agreement, cooperation and mutual aid instead of government.

liberty, and consequently enable him to enjoy the greatest happiness; for happiness consists of the liberty to do that which we want to do.

Anarchism, voluntary association...is the scientific principle of sociology applied to society and the relations of man to man. Do not compel your neighbor to do that which he does not want to do; surely he will some day be in power—in the majority—and will force you to do his bidding. It is better to let each other alone. In matters of mutual interest you will be drawn together by the magic of self-interest. Where you disagree you will be repelled by the same force. This is science. It is simple.

In fine, the Anarchist wants to develop a free society, in which each man will be at liberty to work as an individual, or to cooperate with his neighbors in voluntary groups without any employers, bosses, or rulers of any kind.

—above quotations from *Mother Earth,* Nov. 1907

Emma Goldman

Break your mental fetters, says Anarchism to man, for not until you think and judge for yourself will you get rid of the dominion of darkness, the greatest obstacle to all progress.

—*Anarchism*

ANARCHISM—the philosophy of a new social order based on liberty unrestricted by man-made law; the theory that all forms of government rest on violence, and are therefore wrong and harmful, as well as unnecessary.

—Ibid.

Of all social theories, Anarchism alone steadfastly proclaims that society exists for man, not man for society. The sole legitimate purpose of society is to serve the needs and advance the aspirations of the individual.

— *The Place of the Individual in Society*

The essential principle of Anarchy is individual autonomy.

—Speech to International Anarchist Congress, 1907

Peter Kropotkin

It is often said that anarchists live in a world of dreams to come and do not see the things which happen today. We see them only too well, and in their true colors, and that is what makes us carry the hatchet into the forests of prejudices that beset us.

—*Anarchism: Its Philosophy and Ideal*

Anarchism is the name given to a principle or theory of life and conduct under which society is conceived without government—harmony in such a society being obtained not by submission to law or by obedience to any authority, but by free agreements concluded between the various groups, territorial and professional, freely constituted for the sake of production and consumption, as also for the satisfaction of the infinite variety of needs and aspirations of a civilized being.

V.I. Lenin

The nearer we come to the full military suppression of the bourgeoisie, the more dangerous becomes to us the high flood of petty-bourgeois Anarchism. And the struggle against these elements cannot be waged with propaganda and agitation alone... The struggle must also be waged by applying force and compulsion.

—quoted by Maximoff in *The Guillotine at Work*

Louis Lingg

Anarchy means no domination or authority of one man over another, yet you call that "disorder."

— *The Philosophy of Anarchism*

Errico Malatesta

Anarchists are opposed to violence... The main plank of anarchism is the removal of violence from human relations. It is life based on the freedom of the individual, without the intervention of the police. For this reason we are enemies of capitalism, which depends on the protection of the police to force workers to allow themselves to be exploited... We are therefore enemies of the State, which is the coercive, violent organization of society.

— *Umanita Nova*, August 25, 1921

All of us, without exception, are obliged to live more or less in contradiction with our ideals; but we are anarchists and socialists because, and insofar as, we suffer by this contradiction and seek to make it as small as possible.

— *l'Anarchia*, August 1896

Anarchy, like Socialism, has for its basis and point of departure *equality of conditions*. Its aim is *solidarity*, and its method *liberty*. It is not perfect, nor is it the absolute ideal, which, like the horizon always recedes as we advance towards it. But it is the open road to all progress and to all improvement made in the interest of all humanity.

— *Anarchy*

In order to understand how society could exist without a government, it is sufficient to turn our attention for a short space to what actually goes on in our present society. We shall see that in reality the most important social functions are fulfilled even nowadays outside the intervention of government... it is just those things in which there is no governmental interference that prosper best and give rise to the least contention, being unconsciously adapted to the wish of all in the way found most useful and agreeable.

Nor is government more necessary for large undertakings, or for those public services which require the constant cooperation of many people of different conditions and countries. Thousands of these undertakings are even now the work of voluntarily formed associations... Scientific societies and congresses, international life-boat and Red Cross associations, laborers' unions, peace socieites, volunteers who hasten to the rescue at times of great public calamity, are all examples among thousands, of that power of the spirit of association, which always shows itself when a need arises, or an enthusiasm takes hold, and the means do not fail. That voluntary associations do not cover the world, and do not embrace every branch of material and moral activity is the fault of the obstacles placed in their way by governments, of the antagonisms created by the possession of private property, and of the impotence and degradation to which the monopolizing of wealth on the part of the few reduces the majority of mankind.

— Ibid.

Would the people have the ability necessary to provide and distribute provisions? Never fear, they will not die of hunger, waiting for a government to pass laws on the subject... It is evident that private interest is the great motive for all activity. That being so, when the interest of every one becomes the interest of each (and it necessarily will become so as soon as private property is abolished) then all will be active. If they work now in the interest of the few, so much more and so much better will they work to satisfy the interests of all. It is hard to understand how anyone can believe that public services indispensable to social life can be better secured by order of a government than through the workers themselves...

— Ibid.

Certainly in every collective undertaking on a large scale there is need for division of labor, for technical direction, administration, etc. But the authoritarians are merely playing with words, when they deduce a reason for the existence of government, from the very real necessity for organization of labor. The government, we must repeat, is the aggregate of individuals who have received or have taken the right or the means to make laws, and force the people to obey them. The administrators, engineers, etc., on the other hand, are men who receive or assume the charge of doing a certain work. Government signifies delegation of power, that is, abdication of the initiative and sovereignty of everyone into the hands of the few. Administration signifies delegation of work, that is, the free exchange of services founded on free agreement.

...The functions of government are, in short, not to be confounded with administrative functions, as they are essentially different. That they are today so often confused is entirely on account of the existence of economic and political privilege.

—Ibid.

"Anarchy may be a perfect form of social life; but we have no desire to take a leap in the dark. Therefore, tell us how your society will be organized." Then follows a long list of questions... "According to what method will children be taught? How will production and distribution be organized?...Will all the inhabitants of Siberia winter at Nice?"... And so on, without end, as though we could prophesy all the knowledge and experience of future time, or could, in the name of Anarchy, prescribe for the coming man what time he should go to bed, and on what days he should cut his nails!
...How will children be educated? We do not know. What then? The parents, teachers and all who are interested in the progress of the rising generation, will meet, discuss, agree and differ, and then divide according to their various opinions, putting into practice the methods which they respectively hold to be the best. That method which, when tried, produces the best results will triumph in the end.
And so for all the problems that may arise.

—Ibid.

We [Anarchists] follow ideas and not men, and rebel against this habit of embodying a principle in a man.

—Speech to International Anarchist Congress, 1907

...by anarchist spirit I mean that deeply human sentiment, which aims at the good of all, freedom and justice for all, solidarity and love among the people; which is not an exclusive characteristic only of self-declared anarchists, but inspires all people who have a generous heart and an open mind...

—Umanita Nova, April 13, 1922

We anarchists do not want to *emancipate* the people; we want the people to *emancipate themselves*.

—l'Agitazione, June 18, 1897

What is the true basis of the differences between anarchists and state communists? We are for freedom, for the widest and most complete freedom of thought, organization and action. We are for the freedom of all, and it is therefore obvious, and not necessary to continually say so, that everyone in exercising his right to freedom must respect the equal freedom of everybody else: otherwise there is oppression on one side and the right to resist and to rebel on the other.
But state communists, to an even greater extent than all other authoritarians, are incapable of conceiving freedom and of respecting for all human beings the dignity that they expect, or should expect, from others. If one speaks to them of freedom they immediately accuse one of wanting to respect,

or at least tolerate, the freedom to oppress and exploit one's fellow beings. And if you say that you reject violence when it exceeds the limits imposed by the needs of defense, they accuse you of pacifism, without understanding that violence is the whole essence of authoritarianism, just as the repudiation of violence is the whole essence of anarchism.

—Fede, October 28, 1923

What matters most of all is that the people, all people, should lose the sheeplike instincts and habits with which their minds have been inculcated by an agelong slavery, and that they should learn to think and act freely. It is to this great task of spiritual liberation that anarchists must especially devote their attention.

—Il Risveglio, December 14, 1929

Our task is that of "pushing" the people to demand and to seize all the freedom they can and to make themselves responsible for providing for their own needs without waiting for orders from any kind of authority. Our task is that of demonstrating the uselessness and harmfulness of government, of provoking and encouraging by propaganda and action all kinds of individual and collective initiatives.

—L'Adunata dei Refratti, December 26, 1931

By definition an anarchist is he who does not wish to be oppressed *nor wishes to be himself an oppressor;* who wants the greatest well-being, freedom and development for *all* human beings. His ideas, his wishes have their origin in a feeling of sympathy, love and respect for humanity: a feeling which must be sufficiently strong to induce him to want the well-being of others as much as his own, and to renounce those personal advantages, the achievement of which, would involve the sacrifices of others.

—Volonta, June 15, 1913

Anarchists are opposed to violence; everyone knows that. The main plank of anarchism is the removal of violence from human relations. It is life based on the freedom of the individual, without the intervention of the gendarme. For this reason we are enemies of capitalism which depends on the protection of the gendarme to oblige workers to allow themselves to be exploited—or even to remain idle and go hungry when it is not in the interest of the bosses to exploit them. We are therefore enemies of the State which is the coercive violent organization of society.

—La Questione Sociale, November 25, 1899

How often must we repeat that we do not wish to impose anything on anybody; that we do not believe it either possible or desirable to do good by the people through force, and that all we want is that no one should impose their will on us, that no one should be in a position to impose on others a form of social life which is not freely accepted.

—Umanita Nova, August 25, 1920

Thomas Paine

For upwards of two years from the commencement of the American war, and a longer period in several of the American states, there were no established forms of government. The old governments had been abolished, and the country was too much occupied in defence to employ its attention in establishing a new government; yet, during this interval order and harmony were preserved as inviolate as in any country in Europe. There is a natural aptness in man, and more so in society because it embraces a greater variety of abilities and resources, to accommodate itself to whatever situation it is in.

The instant formal government is abolished, society begins to act. A general association takes place, and the common interest produces common security.

So far is it from being true, as has been pretended, that the abolition of any formal government is the dissolution of society, it acts by a contrary impulse, and brings the latter closer together. . .

The more perfect civilization is the less occasion has it for government, because the more does it regulate its own affairs and govern itself. . .

— *The Rights of Man*

Albert Parsons

In the opinion of an anarchist, the sum total of human ills is expressed in one word — authority.

— *The Philosophy of Anarchism*

. . . government is despotism; government is an organization of oppression, and law, statue law is its agent. Anarchy is anti-government, anti-rulers, anti-dictators, anti-bosses and drivers. Anarchy is the negation of force; the elimination of all authority in social affairs; it is the denial of the right of domination of one man over another. It is the diffusion of rights, of power, of duties, equally and freely among all the people.

— Ibid.

Rudolf Rocker

Power operates only destructively, bent always on forcing every manifestation of social life into the straitjacket of its rules. Its intellectual expression is dead dogma, its physical form brute force. And this unintelligence of its objectives sets its stamp on its representatives also, and renders them often stupid and brutal, even when they were originally endowed with the best talents. One who is constantly striving to force everything into a mechanical order at last becomes a machine himself and loses all human feelings.

It was from this understanding that modern anarchism was born and draws its moral force. Only freedom can inspire men to great things and bring about intellectual and social transformations. The art of ruling men has never been the art of educating and inspiring them to a new shaping of their lives. Dreary compulsion has at its command only lifeless drill, which smothers any vital initiative

Graphic by Donald Rooum

at its birth and brings forth only subjects, not free men. Freedom is the very essence of life, the impelling force in all intellectual and social development, the creator of every new outlook for the future of mankind. The liberation of man from economic exploitation and from intellectual, social, and political oppression, which finds its highest expression in the philosophy of anarchism, is the prerequisite for the evolution of a higher social culture and a new humanity.

—*Anarchism and Anarcho-Syndicalism*

In place of the present national states with their lifeless machinery of political and bureaucratic institutions, anarchists desire a federation of free communities that shall be bound to one another by their common economic and social interests and arrange their affairs by mutual agreement and free contract.

—Ibid.

August Spies

Anarchism does not mean bloodshed; it does not mean robbery, arson, etc. These monstrosities are, on the contrary, the characteristic features of capitalism. Anarchism means peace and tranquility to all. Anarchism, or socialism, means the reorganization of society upon scientific principles and the abolition of causes which produce vice and crime.

—Courtroom speech, 1887

Charles T. Sprading

The libertarians say: Let those who believe in religion have religion; let those who believe in government have government; but let those who believe in liberty have liberty, and do not compel them to accept a religion or a government they do not want.

—*Liberty and the Great Libertarians*

Speaking generally, mankind can be divided into two groups, Authoritarians and Libertarians. The first believe in making people good, the second believe in letting people be good. The first believe in compelling others to conform to their wishes, the second thinks it better to convince than to compel.

The Libertarians believe that if an idea is good, it is not necessary to force its acceptance, and if it is bad it should not be imposed.

—Ibid.

Authoritarians hate libertarians as nocturnal beasts hate light.

—*Freedom and Its Fundamentals*

George Thomar

Organization, action in common, is indispensable to the development of anarchism and it does not contradict our theoretical premises. Organization is a means, and not a principle; but it is self-evident that, to be acceptable, organization must be constituted in a libertarian manner.

—Speech to International Anarchist Congress, 1907

Allen Thornton

To understand ungovernability, imagine a cult with a dictatorial leader. He takes his followers' money, tells them how to behave and frequently uses corporal punishment to keep them in line. The cult leader has his own set of laws and his own police force. Such an organization resembles a theoretically good government deriving its "just power from the consent of the governed."

Let's say that you, as a cult member, became disillusioned with the cult leader but were intimidated by the reprisals his guards might make against you. You could band together with others of the same opinion, kill the leader and overpower his guards. Then you could reform the cult and make yourself the new leader. This course of action is analogous to a revolution.

But maybe you have a revelation of the cult as outsiders see it: a band of fools who believe ridiculous doctrines and are led by a maniac. You'd walk away in disgust. You'd still fear the guards, the cult's police force, but your attitude would have changed. What you had seen as legitimate force would now appear as criminal activity, and you would not be inhibited from striking back however you could. From the cult's point of view, you would have become an anarchist.

—*Laws of the Jungle*

Christians argue that the state is the price we pay for Adam's fall. If men were perfect, they say, we could have anarchy. Anarchists say the opposite. If all men were virtuous, the most perfect among them might be entrusted with political power, which is the right to use violence against one's fellow man. But since no one is completely virtuous, it is folly to entrust anyone with governmental power.

Belief in government is the superstition that some magical power endows certain men with the right to use violence against others.

The fear of anarchy is the secret conviction that violence is the best way for a person to get what he wants.

—Ibid.

Benjamin Tucker

That society is a concrete organism the Anarchists do not deny; on the contrary, they insist upon it. Consequently they have no intention or desire to abolish it. They know that its life is inseparable from the lives of individuals; that it is impossible to destroy one without the other. But, though society cannot be destroyed, it can be great-

ly hampered and impeded in its operations, much to the disadvantage of the individuals composing it, and it meets its chief impediment in the State... If it [the State] should be destroyed tomorrow, individuals would continue to exist.
— quoted by Sprading in *Liberty and the Great Libertarians*

Anarchism... may be described as the doctrine that all the affairs of men should be managed by individuals or voluntary associations, and that the State should be abolished.
— *State Socialism and Anarchism*

I define Anarchism as the belief in the greatest amount of liberty compatible with equality of liberty; or, in other words, as the belief in every liberty except the liberty to invade.
— *Instead of a Book*

...it may be said, briefly and broadly, that Socialism is a battle with usury and that Anarchism is a battle with authority...Of course there is a sense in which every Anarchist may be said to be a Socialist virtually, inasmuch as usury rests on authority, and to destroy the latter is to destroy the former.
— Ibid.

Bartolomeo Vanzetti

If it had not been for this, I might have live out my life, talking at street corners to scorning men. I might have die, unmarked, unknown, a failure. Now we are not a failure. This is our career and our triumph. Never in our full life can we do such a work for tolerance, for justice, for man's understanding of man, as we now do by an accident. our words— our lives— our pains— nothing! The taking of our lives— lives of a good shoemaker and poor fish-peddler— all! The last moment belongs to us— that agony is our triumph!
— Statement in court upon being sentenced to death

Nicolas Walter

People can accept that anarchy may not mean just chaos or confusion, and that anarchists want not disorder but order without government, but they are sure that anarchy means order which arises spontaneously and that anarchists do not want organization. This is the reverse of the truth. Anarchists actually want much more organization, though organization without authority. The prejudice about anarchism derives from a prejudice about organization; people cannot see that organization does not depend on authority, that it actually works best without authority.
A moment's thought will show that when compulsion is replaced by consent there will have to be more discussion and planning, not less.
— *About Anarchism*

The main enemy of the free individual is the overwhelming power of the state, but anarchists are also opposed to every other form of authority which limits freedom — in the family, in the school, at work, in the neighborhood — and to every attempt to make the individual conform.
— Ibid.

Colin Ward

All authoritarian institutions are organized as pyramids: the state, the private or public corporation, the army, the police, the church, the university, the hospital; they are all pyramidal structures with a small group of decision-makers at the top and a broad base of people whose decisions are *made for them* at the bottom. Anarchism does not demand the changing of the labels on the layers, it doesn't want different people on top, it wants *us* to clamber out from underneath.
— *Anarchy in Action*

Anarchy is a function, not of a society's simplicity and lack of social organization, but of its complexity and multiplicity of social organizations.
...The Anarchist alternative is that of fragmentation, fission rather than fusion, diversity rather than unity, a mass of societies rather than a mass society.
— Ibid.

Fred Woodworth

The political spectrum offers a choice among ideologies that try to sugar the water of the poisonous river. The Anarchist's idea — and this is what sets him off that map altogether — is to drink from another source: voluntarism, rather than coercion.
— *Anarchist? What's That?*

But the social principle of Anarchy is familiar and predictable also. Whenever one person helps another; whenever people solve their problems and no policeman or law instructs or compels — in short, at the taking place of any human development which is not mandated, ordained, decreed, controlled, or interfered in by a legislature or by someone acting so as to force a result, we have the principle of Anarchy at work.
— Ibid.

Anarchism grasps the essential non-modifiable and irresistible need of power to grow and take over more control, while the liberal group supposes that the specific abuses it fights are not symptoms of some underlying cause. Lacking a consistent philosophy about authority, the liberal group has to oppose the things authority often does, without opposing the fundamental nature of it — power itself.
— *The Match!*, No. 74

Marxism

Michael Bakunin

The Marxists. . .console themselves with the idea that [their] rule will be temporary. They say that the only care and objective will be to educate and elevate the people economically and politically to such a degree that such a government will soon become unnecessary, and the State, after losing its political or coercive character, will automatically develop into a completely free organization of economic interests and communities.

There is a flagrant contradiction in this theory. If their state would really be of the people, why eliminate it? And if the State is needed to emancipate the workers, then the workers are not yet free, so why call it a People's State? By our polemic against them we have brought them to the realization that freedom or anarchism, which means a free organization of the working masses from the bottom up, is the final objective of social development, and that every state, not excepting their People's State, is a yoke, on the one hand giving rise to despotism and on the other to slavery. They say that such a yoke-dictatorship is a transitional step towards achieving full freedom for the people: anarchism or freedom is the aim, while state and dictatorship is the means, and so, in order to free the masses of the people, they have first to be enslaved!

Upon this contradiction our polemic has come to a halt. They insist that only dictatorship (of course their own) can create freedom for the people. We reply that all dictatorship has no objective other than self-perpetuation, and that slavery is all it can generate and instill in the people who suffer it. Freedom can be created only by freedom. . .

— *Critique of the Marxist Theory of the State*

. . .The expressions "learned socialist," "scientific socialism," etc., which continuously appear in the speeches and writings of the followers of. . . Marx, prove that the pseudo-People's State will be nothing but a despotic control of the populace by a new and not at all numerous aristocracy of real and pseudo scientists. The "uneducated" people will be totally relieved of the cares of administration, and will be treated as a regimented herd. A beautiful liberation indeed!

— Ibid.

Liberty without socialism is privilege, injustice; socialism without liberty is slavery and brutality.

— *Federalism, Socialism, Anti-Theologism*

Alexander Berkman

One by one those features of Socialism which were really significant, educational, and liberating were sacrificed in behalf of politics, to secure more favorable public opinion, lessen persecution, and accomplish "something practical"; that is, to get more Socialists elected to office. In this process, which has been going on for years in every country, the Socialist parties in Europe acquired a membership that numbered millions. But those millions were not socialistic at all; they were party followers who had no conception of the real spirit and meaning of Socialism; men and women steeped in the old prejudices and capitalistic views; bourgeois-minded people, narrow nationalists, church members, believers in divine authority and consequently also in human government, in the domination of man by man, in the State and its institutions of oppression and exploitation, in the necessity of defending "their" government and country, in patriotism and militarism.

Is it any wonder, then, that when the Great War [World War I] broke out Socialists in every country, with few exceptions, took up arms to "defend the fatherland". . .and so the "Socialists" of every country and their followers went on slaughtering each other until ten million of them lay dead, and twenty million were blinded, maimed and crippled.

It was inevitable that the policy of political, parliamentary activity should lead to such results.

— *What Is Communist Anarchism?*

Murray Bookchin

Once again the dead are walking in our midst — ironically, draped in the name of Marx, the man who tried to bury the dead of the nineteenth century. So the revolution of our own day can do nothing better than parody, in its turn, the October Revolution of 1917 and the civil war of 1918–1920 with its "class line," its Bolshevik Party, its "proletarian dictatorship," its puritanical morality, and even its slogan, "soviet power." The complete, all-sided revolution of our own day that can finally resolve the historic "social questions," born of scarcity, domination and hierarchy, follows the tradition of the partial, the incomplete, the one-sided revolutions of the past, which merely changed the form of the "social question," replacing one system of domination and hierarchy by another.

The deep-rooted conservatism of the [marxist-leninist] "revolutionaries" is almost painfully apparent; the authoritarian leader and hierarchy replace the patriarch and the school bureaucracy; the discipline of the Movement replaces the discipline of bourgeois society; the authoritarian code of political obedience replaces the state; the credo of "proletarian morality" replaces the mores of puritanism and the work ethic. The old substance of exploitative society reappears in new forms, draped in a red flag, decorated by portraits of Mao (or Castro or Che) and adorned with the little "Red Book" and other sacred litanies.

We believe that Marxism has ceased to be applicable to our time not because it is too visionary or revolutionary, but because it is not visionary or revolutionary enough.

As the [marxist] party expands, the distance between the leadership and the ranks increases. Its leaders not only become "personages," they lose contact with the living situation below. The local groups, which know their own immediate situation better than any remote leader, are obliged to subordinate their insights to directives from above. The leadership, lacking any direct knowledge of local problems, responds sluggishly and prudently. Although it stakes out a claim to the "larger view," to greater "theoretical competence," the competence of the leadership tends to diminish as one ascends the hierarchy of command. The more one approaches the level where the real decisions are made, the more conservative is the nature of the decision-making process, the more bureaucratic and extraneous are the factors which come into play, the more considerations of prestige and retrenchment supplant creativity, imagination, and a disinterested dedication to revolutionary goals.

The party becomes less efficient from a revolutionary point of view the more it seeks efficiency by means of hierarchy, cadres and centralization.

Although everyone marches in step, the orders are usually wrong, especially when events begin to move rapidly and take unexpected turns — as they do in all revolutions. The party is efficient in only one respect — in molding society in its own hierarchical image if the revolution is successful. It recreates bureaucracy, centralization and the state. It fosters the very social conditions which justify this kind of society. Hence, instead of "withering away," the state controlled by the "glorious party" preserves the very conditions which "necessitate" the existence of a state — and a party to "guard" it.

— above quotations from *Listen Marxist!*

Nikolai Bukharin

Proletarian compulsion in all its forms, beginning with summary execution and ending with compulsory labor is, however, paradoxical it may sound, a method of reworking the human material of the capitalistic epoch into Communist humanity.

— quoted by Berkman in *What Is Communist Anarchism?*

Cornelius Castoriadis

To present the Russian regime as "socialist" or as a "workers' state" as do both the left and the right in an almost universal complicity, or even to discuss its nature in reference to socialism to determine at what points and to what degree it deviates from it, represents one of the most horrendous enterprises of mystification known in history.

— quoted by Michael Albert and Robin Hahnel in *Looking Forward*

Deng Xiaoping

We can afford to shed a little blood.

— before the Tienanmen Square massacre, quoted by Harrison Salisbury in the *San Francisco Chronicle*, June 14, 1989

To get rich is glorious.

— quoted by Mike Wallace on *60 Minutes*, June 11, 1989

John T. Flynn

The great difference between the communist state and the fascist state is that in the communist state the government plans for the industries of the nation which it owns and in the fascist state the government plans for industries which are owned by private persons.

— *As We Go Marching*

Emma Goldman

. . . in its mad passion for power the [Soviet] Communist State even sought to strengthen and deepen the very ideas and conceptions which the Revolution had come to destroy. It supported and encouraged all the worst anti-social qualities and systematically destroyed the already awakened conception of the new revolutionary values. The sense of justice and equality, the love of liberty and human brotherhood — these fundamentals of the real regeneration of society — the Communist State suppressed to the point of extermination. Man's instinctive sense of equity was branded as weak sentimentality; human dignity and liberty became a bourgeois superstition; the sanctity of life, which is the very essence of social reconstruction, was condemned as unrevolutionary, almost counterrevolutionary . . .

Anonymously produced graphic found in *The SRAF Bulletin*

This perversion of the ethical values soon crystallized into the all-dominating slogan of the Communist Party **The End Justifies All Means**. Similarly in the past the Inquisition and the Jesuits adopted this motto and subordinated to it all morality. It avenged itself upon the Jesuits as it did upon the Russian Revolution. In the wake of this slogan followed lying, deceit, hypocrisy and treachery, murder, open and secret.

— *My Disillusionment in Russia*

Witness the tragic condition of Russia. The methods of State centralization have paralyzed individual initiative and effort; the tyranny of the dictatorship has cowed the people into slavish submission and all but extinguished the fires of liberty; organized terrorism has depraved and brutalized the masses and stifled every idealistic aspiration; institutionalized murder has cheapened human life, and all sense of the dignity of man and the value of life has been eliminated; coercion at every step has made effort bitter, labor a punishment, has turned the whole of existence into a scheme of mutual deceit, and has revived the lowest and most brutal instincts. A sorry heritage to begin a new life of freedom and brotherhood.

— Ibid.

During my first interview I received the impression that he [Lenin] was a shrewd politician who knew exactly what he was about and that he would stop at nothing to achieve his ends. After hearing him speak on several occasions and reading his works I became convinced that Lenin had very little concern in the Revolution and that Communism to him was a very remote thing. The centralized political State was Lenin's deity, to which everything else was to be sacrificed.

— Afterword to *My Disillusionment in Russia*

"Only fools can believe that Communism is possible in Russia," was Lenin's reply to opponents of the new economic policy.

As a matter of fact, Lenin was right. True Communism was never attempted in Russia, unless one considers thirty-three categories of pay, different food rations, privileges to some and indifference to the great mass as Communism.

— Afterword to *My Further Disillusionment in Russia*

V.I. Lenin

Large-scale machine industry — which is the material productive source and foundation of socialism — calls for absolute and strict unity of will... How can strict unity of will be ensured? By thousands subordinating their wills to the will of one.

— quoted by Brinton in *The Bolsheviks and Workers' Control*

It is absolutely essential that all authority in the factories should be concentrated in the hands of management.

— Speech, 1922, quoted by Brinton

[Collective management] represents something rudimentary, necessary for the first state... The transition to practical work is connected with individual authority. This is the system which more than any other assures the best utilization of human resources.

— Speech, 1920, quoted by Brinton

It is necessary to combat the ideological disunity and the *unhealthy* elements within the opposition who go so far as to give up the idea of a militarized economy, as to. . . *renounce the leading role of the party*. . .

— quoted by Brinton

All unfit for human consumption

Anonymously produced graphic found in many anarchist periodicals

We want a socialist revolution with human nature as it is now, with human nature that cannot dispense with subordination, control, and managers.

— quoted by Michael Albert and Robin Hahnel in *Looking Forward*

Socialism is nothing but state capitalist monopoly made to benefit the whole people.

— quoted by Maximoff in *The Guillotine at Work*

The dictatorship of the proletariat is nothing else than power based upon force and limited by nothing — by no law and by absolutely no rule.

— Ibid.

. . . a good Communist is at the same time a good chekist [member of the secret police]. . .

— Speech, April 3, 1920, quoted by Maximoff

Errico Malatesta

However much we detest the democratic lie, which in the name of the "people" oppresses the people in the interests of a class, we detest even more, if that is possible, the dictatorship which, in the name of the "proletariat" places all the strength and the very lives of the workers in the hands of the

creatures of a so-called communist party, who will perpetuate their power and in the end reconstruct the capitalist system for their own advantage.

— *Umanita Nova,* August 31, 1921

Mao Tse Tung

. . . we must affirm anew the discipline of the Party, namely:

1) The individual is subordinate to the organization;
2) The minority is subordinate to the majority;
3) The lower level is subordinate to the higher level; and 4) The entire membership is subordinate to the Central Committee.

— *The Role of the Chinese Communist Party*

"You are dictatorial." My dear sirs, you are right, that is just what we are.

— *On the People's Democratic Dictatorship*

Karl Marx

Socialism is man's positive self-consciousness.

— *Economic and Philosophical Manuscripts*

The history of all hitherto existing society is the history of class struggles.

— *The Communist Manifesto*

We have received our appointment as representatives of the proletarian party from nobody but ourselves.

— quoted in *The Wisdom of Karl Marx*

G.P. Maximoff

If capitalism is based upon the right of private ownership of the tools and means of production, state capitalism is based upon the private ownership of knowledge; that is why the dominant class under state capitalism (the bureaucracy), as distinguished from the capitalist class (the bourgeoisie), does not need the right of ownership of the tools and means of production. It strives rather for a monopoly of legality, of government, of industrial management, for the monopolist right to organize the political and economic life of the country and to distribute all the products in accordance with its own appraisal of personal merits, and contributions to the state, that is, to itself. These rights give it unlimited power over the entire population. The army, fleet, police, courts and a monopoly of legal murders, being at its disposal, are powerful weapons for the consolidation and perpetuation of its domination and privileges.

It stands to reason that the new class tries not only to secure for itself the "legal" possession of its class privileges and licenses but also to live in accordance with its status; it wants to enjoy the fruit of its victory. Hence its tendency to keep aloof from the rabble — from the workers and peasants — to exploit the national economy for the satisfaction of its own needs and pleasures: extravagant furniture; country villas; expensive automobiles; servants; all kinds of bread and pastries while the masses are starved. Class distinction in transportation; fashionable stores of women's clothes (charging for a single dress prices many times greater than the average monthly wage of workers); beauty salons; stores of cosmetics and perfume; expensive restaurants and cabarets with excellent cuisines, with the choicest wines, with the the ultra-modern music and dances; high-priced food stores with innumerable native and imported delicacies; fashionable hotels favorably comparing in their luxury with those of Europe and America. In short, the new class wants to live like the old rich class.

. . .The ideology of Bolshevism has now as its basic principle: to each according to the services he renders to the state, that is, the bureaucratic class.

Is it possible, without using organized violence and terror, to subject the entire population to "the Dictatorship of the Proletariat". . .? Of course not! It is impossible because it would be naive to think that workers and peasants, the professionals, could all be taken in by the name "proletarian dictatorship" and that, like St. Augustine, they would come to believe in this absolute absurdity because it is an absurdity. It is improbable that they would believe that freedom can be arrived at via enslavement, equality via inequality, humanity via inhumanity, the abolition of the State via its strengthening and that initiative can be developed by first having it stifled.

Lenin's utopian faith in the all-powerful effect of terror is on par with the naive faith of a savage; it is both terrible and ridiculous. With the help of terror he hoped to make even capitalists work for the benefit of Communism.

Dictatorship, like other forms of absolutism, is the highest expression of political centralization. But socialist dictatorship, "the dictatorship of the proletariat," is absolute centralization; it denotes a totalitarian state which is not confined to the realm of the political but centralizes all industries, all human activity. Every sphere of life is subject to its control and regulation. The state becomes not only the sole capitalist, the sole monarch, but likewise the sole teacher, landowner, policeman, philosopher, priest; in a word, it becomes God, omnipresent and ubiquitous. It dominates man completely from the cradle to the grave; death alone frees him from its power. It is this kind of a state that the Marxists have built in Russia.

Human life became cheap and worthless. The moral coruption bred by those endless murders [by the Cheka — now the KGB] affected the mentality of the party. . .This corruption found its way to the schools. . .it was consciously introduced there in order to deprave the minds of the children. Thus, for instance, in 1920 was published a book containing problems on educational extension work. . .We find there the following "problem":

"A girl of 12 years old, is afraid of blood; the father is a prominent Menshevik. [The problem is] to make up a list of books the reading of which would overcome the girl's instinctive aversion to red terror. . ."

"That is the limit," the reader will say. But no, this by far was not the worst. Children were taught to squeal upon their parents, to testify against them in court, openly to renounce them. Children were extolled for doing such things and were held up by the Soviet press as heroes to be emulated.

Graphic by Donald Rooum

WiLDCAT

You pay so much attention to individuals, you fail to recognize the working class as an entity. It's like not being able to see the wood for the trees.

Not exactly. A wood is a place, but a class is only an idea.

Don't try to confuse me with facts!!!

We believe in enforcing Working Class power to achieve what the Working Class desires!

Suppose for the sake of argument, the working class, as distinct from an individual worker, can have desires. You can only talk to individuals, so how do you find out what the category wants?

We've got a private line to the Almighty.

The approximate total of shootings during the period of Lenin's terror, lasting from November 7, 1917 up to January 24, 1924—the day of Lenin's death—equals, even according to most conservative estimates, no less than 200,000. Some place it at the much higher figure of 1,500,000—and that for the shorter period 1917-1923. For our total we shall take the "modest" minimum figure of 200,000. To these we must add other victims: those that died in prisons, concentration camps, in exile; those that died throughout the country from inanition and epidemics; those that were killed at the suppression of revolts and guerrilla movements; victims of civil war and finally victims of the famine which, according to the official data, carried away 5,200,000 lives. The total, according to the most conservative estimate, would be from eight to ten million people.

— above quotations from *The Guillotine at Work*

H.L. Mencken

Marx defined capitalism as ownership of the means of production. One man has the factory and another works in it. This is precisely the state of affairs in Russia. In this country the imaginative slave may at least hope, however vainly, to own a factory of his own some day; in Russia it is impossible. The theory, of course, is that the people in general own everything, but this involves a false definition of ownership. The title may be in them legally, but their bosses are perpetual lessees who exercise all their rights. To believe that Russia has got rid of capitalism takes a special kind of mind. It is the same kind that believes that Jonah swallowed the whale.

— *Minority Report*

Johann Most

...there is quite a number of Communists who — singularly enough — designate the future social order as a "State," the "State of the people," etc., and provide this State with the most monstrous governmental machinery and laws by the bushel, as if the Communistic society should be nothing but a mass of idiots taken care of by a number of mandarins.

— *The Social Monster*

Pope Pius XI

No one can be, at the same time, a sincere Catholic and a true Socialist.

— *Quadragesimo anno*

Rudolf Rocker

The assertion that the State must continue to exist until society is no longer divided into hostile classes almost sounds, in the light of all historical experience, like a bad joke.

— *Anarchism and Anarcho-Syndicalism*

Economic equality is not social liberation. It is precisely this which all the schools of authoritarian socialism have never understood. In the prison, in the cloister, or in the barracks one finds a fairly high degree of economic equality...

— Ibid.

...the best idea is killed when it becomes a lifeless dogma and clothes itself in the garment of absolute truth, and when its advocates forget that everything on earth has only a relative meaning. If one compares this viewpoint with the rigid biblical beliefs of the Marxist school, whose representatives presume to interpret every event in accordance with the pattern of dialectical sophistry and believe to have found in it the key to all the ups and downs of history, one may understand of how much of its vital content socialism has been drained. It is the curse of every absolute idea that it is never touched by changing conditions, but forever continues to follow its course. The experiences of history have always shown that such conceptions must become a hindrance of higher forms of life because they root in a fruitless fatalism which perceives every event as fulfilled by reason of some *historical necessity*.

— *Pioneers of American Freedom*

Josef Stalin

In the Soviet Union...no important political or organizational problem is ever decided by our soviets and other mass organizations, without directives from our party. In this sense, we may say that the dictatorship [of the proletariat] is substantially the dictatorship of the Party...

— quoted by Marie Louise Berneri in *Workers in Stalin's Russia*

Robert Tefton

DICTATORSHIP OF THE PROLETARIAT, n. A theological term. It parallels the Catholic belief in transubstantiation. Both are not only contrary to everyday experience, but are physically impossible. They are as unthinkable as an unbribable congressman.

EXISTING SOCIALISM, n. A euphemism for "capitalism."

Leon Trotsky

The dictatorship of the Communist Party is maintained by recourse to every form of violence.

— attributed

The militarization of labor...is the indispensable basic method for the organization of our labor force.

— Speech, 1920, quoted by Brinton in *The Bolsheviks and Workers Control*

INTERNATIONAL PROLETARIAN HAMMER THROWING & RHETORIC FLINGING COMPETITION

On: MAY 1ST, 1988. At: (where else?) MARX MEADOWS in GOLDEN GATE PARK

CONTEST RULES

You will have two hours to compose a manifesto using the terms *struggle, heroic, vanguard, revolutionary, reified, workers party* (penalty for use of apostrophe), *people's army, liberated zone, revolutionary government, street youth, white skin privilege, womyn, wimmin, wimin, wimmen, wymyn, people of color* (**not** *colored people*), *petit bourgeois, trade union consciousness, infantile, objectively counterrevolutionary, objectively reactionary, bosses, stooge, puppet, decadent, exploitation, fight, smash, hands off, build, stop, unleash, free* (fill in the blank—Bob Avakian is a good choice), *revisionist, fascist, opportunist, deviationist* and *running dog*. You **must** use all terms!! (Special prize for the most inventive neologism. Last year's winner: *Phallocracy*.)

You will then have two hours to put your manifesto into publishable form. Supply your own tools. **Preferred typesetting equipment:** old manual typewriter (extra points for: worn ribbons, broken or filled-in characters, handwritten corrections).

The longest, most unreadable entry wins. The triumphant manifesto will then be copied on a 15-year-old xerox machine, which hasn't been cleaned since 1978, bound with a staple in one corner, and distributed to contest participants. Losers will be compelled to read it. Those who refuse will be unmasked as objectively counterrevolutionary petit bourgeois anarchists and will face the revolutionary justice of the people's democratic dictatorship.

Graphic by Chaz Bufe

It would be a most crying error to confuse the question as to the supremacy of the proletariat with the question of boards of workers at the head of factories.

—quoted by Brinton

Benjamin Tucker

. . . as much as we abominate bourgeois society we prefer the partial freedom which it ensures to the total enslavement of State Socialism. For the hot seething competition which brings up some but tosses many into the depths, makes some rich and many poor, but never completely enchains anyone or robs him of hope for a better future, is without doubt less painful than the ideal of a uniformed miserable community of oxen yoked in a span and slavishly obedient to their masters.

—quoted by Rocker in *Pioneers of American Freedom*

State Socialism. . .may be described as the doctrine that all the affairs of men should be managed by the government regardless of individual choice.

—*State Socialism and Anarchism*

It has ever been the tendency of power to add to itself, to enlarge its sphere, to encroach beyond the limits set for it; and where the habit of resisting such encroachment is not fostered and the individual is not taught to be jealous of his rights, individuality gradually disappears and the government or State becomes the all in all. . .

Whatever, then, the State socialists may claim or disclaim, their system, if adopted, is doomed to end in a State religion, to the expense of which all must contribute and at the altar of which all must kneel.

—*Instead of a Book*

Oscar Wilde

It is clear then, that no Authoritarian Socialism will do. For while under the present system a very large number of people can lead lives of a certain amount of freedom and expression and happiness, under an industrial-barrack system, or a system of economic tyranny, nobody would be able to have any such freedom at all. It is to be regretted that a portion of our community should be practically in slavery, but to propose to solve the problem by enslaving the entire community is childish. Every man must be left quite free to choose his own work. No form of compulsion must be exercised over him. If there is, his work will not be good for him, will not be good in itself, and will not be good for others. And by work I simply mean activity of any kind.

— *The Soul of Man Under Socialism*

...I confess that many of the socialistic views that I have come across seem to be tainted with ideas of authority, if not of actual compulsion. Of course authority and compulsion are out of the question. All association must be quite voluntary. It is only in voluntary associations that man is fine.

Anonymous & Multiple Author

Piece-work is a revolutionary system that eliminates inertia and makes the laborer hustle. Under the capitalist system loafing and laziness are fostered. But now, everyone has a chance to work harder and earn more.

— *Scanteia* (Rumanian Communist paper), Jan. 13, 1941

Under capitalism it's dog eat dog. Under Communism it's just the opposite.

— Polish joke

Let's let bygones be bygones, and bury the hatchet.

— Old political joke: stalinist to trotskyist

Graphic from *Comunidad*

The Party bureaucracy controls the communications media in the name of the proletariat

The Party bureaucracy controls the means of production in the name of the proletariat

The Party bureaucracy is correct in the name of the proletariat

The Party bureaucracy controls the judicial apparatus in the name of the proletariat

The Party bureaucracy controls the army and the police in the name of the proletariat

The Party bureaucracy utilizes repression in the name of the proletariat

The Party bureaucracy lives very well in the name of the proletariat

And the proletariat is happy with this?

Yes, because the Party bureaucracy never complains in the name of the proletariat

Good citizens are stupid citizens. A deaf mute would be the best citizen.
— Unidentified Beijing resident after the Tienanmen Square massacre, quoted in the *San Francisco Examiner,* June 11, 1989

The building of socialism will require mass understanding and mass participation. By their rigid hierarchical structure, by their ideas and by their activities, both social-democratic and bolshevik types of organizations discourage this kind of understanding and prevent this kind of participation. The idea that socialism can somehow be achieved by an elite party (however "revolutionary") acting "on behalf of" the working class is both absurd and reactionary.
— *As We See It,* by Solidarity (British libertarian group)

Socialism is not just the common ownership and control of the means of production and distribution. It means equality, real freedom...
A socialist society can therefore only be built from below. Decisions concerning production and work will be taken by workers' councils composed of elected and revocable delegates. Decisions in other areas will be taken on the basis of the widest possible discussion and consultation among the people as a whole. This democratization of society down to its very roots is what we mean by "workers' power."
— Ibid.

All our love, our faithfulness, our strength, our hearts, our heroism, our life—everything for you, take it, Oh great Stalin, everything is yours, Oh leader of our great homeland. Command your sons. They can move in the air and under the earth, in water and in the stratosphere. Men and women of all times and all nations will remember your name as the most magnificent, the strongest, the wisest, the most beautiful. Your name is written on every factory, on every machine, in every corner of the world, in every human heart. When my beloved wife bears me a child, the first word I will teach him will be "Stalin."
— *Leningrad Red Times,* February 4, 1935

The Soviet system faces the task of developing its own methods of labor compulsion...the primary means for increasing production will be the introduction of the system of compulsory labor.
— Resolution of the Ninth Congress of the Soviet Communist Party

Rivalries between factories, areas, workshops, and individual workers should be carefully organized and closely studied by the trade unions and economic organs.
The introduction of bonuses should become one of the most powerful ways of introducing rivalry. The food rationing system will be brought into line with it...
— Ibid.

...the [Communist Party] Congress considers that one of the most urgent problems facing the Soviet government and the trade-union organization is the firm, systematic, and unyielding struggle against labor desertion. The manner in which to fight this is to publish a list of fines for desertion, creation of a Labor Detachment of deserters, and, ultimately, imprisonment in concentration camps.
— Ibid.

At the moment when I saw our beloved father, Stalin, I lost consciousness.
— Delegate to a Stalin-era Communist Party conference

Revolution

Aristotle

Inequality is the source of all revolutions; no compensation can make up for inequality.
— *Politics*

Michael Bakunin

What do the masses lack to be able to overthrow the prevailing social order, so detestable to them? They lack two things: organization and science — precisely the two things which constitute now, and always have constituted, the power of governments. Above all, there must be organization, which is impossible without the help of science. Thanks to military organization, one battalion, a thousand armed men, can hold in fear, and in reality they do that, a million people who may be just as well armed but who are not organized. And thanks to its bureaucratic organization, the State, with the aid of a few hundred thousand officials, holds in subjection vast countries. Consequently, in order to create a popular force capable of crushing the military and civil power of the State, the proletariat must organize.
— *The Politics of the International*

Reduced, intellectually and morally as well as materially, to the minimum of human existence, confined in their life like a prisoner in his prison... of escape there are but three methods — two chimerical and a third real. The first two are the tavern and the church, debauchery of the body or debauchery of the mind; the third is social revolution.
— *God and the State*

Alexander Berkman

Revolution is rebellion become conscious of its aim.

Not all the misery we have in the world today comes from the lack of material welfare. Man can better stand starvation than the consciousness of injustice. The consciousness that you are treated unjustly will rouse you to protest and rebellion just as quickly as hunger, perhaps quicker.

The social revolution means much more than the reorganization of conditions alone: it means the establishment of new human values and social relationships, a changed attitude of man to man, as

of one free and independent to his equal; it means a different spirit in individual and collective life, and that spirit cannot be born overnight. It is a spirit to be cultivated and reared...

You can't destroy wage slavery by wrecking the machinery in the mills and factories, can you? You can't destroy government by setting fire to the white house.

To think of revolution in terms of violence and destruction is to misinterpret and falsify the whole idea of it. In practical application such a conception is bound to lead to disastrous results.

When a great thinker like the famous anarchist Bakunin speaks of revolution as destruction, he has in mind the idea of authority and obedience which are to be destroyed. It is for this reason that he said that destruction means construction, for to destroy a false belief is indeed most constructive work.

...the social structure rests on the basis of *ideas,* which implies that changing the structure presupposes changed ideas. In other words, social ideas must change *first* before a new social structure can be built.

The social revolution, therefore, is not an accident, not a sudden happening. There is nothing sudden about it, for ideas don't change suddenly. They grow slowly gradually, like the plant or flower. Hence the social revolution is a result, a development, which means that it is revolutionary. It develops to the point when considerable numbers of people have embraced the new ideas and are determined to put them into practice. When they attempt to do so and meet with opposition, then the slow, quiet and peaceful social evolution becomes quick, militant, and violent. Evolution becomes revolution.

Bear in mind, then that evolution and revolution are *not* two separate and different things. Still less are they opposites, as some people wrongly believe. Revolution is merely the boiling point of evolution.

Revolution, and particularly the social revolution, is *not destruction but construction*. This cannot be sufficiently emphasized, and unless we clearly realize it, revolutions will remain only destructive and thereby always a failure.

The object of revolution is to secure greater freedom, to increase the material welfare of the people. The aim of the social revolution, in particular, is to enable the masses *by their own efforts* to bring about conditions of material social well-being, to rise to higher moral and spiritual levels.

In other words, it is liberty which is to be established by the social revolution. For true liberty is based on economic opportunity. Without it all liberty is a sham and lie, a mask for exploitation and oppression. In the profoundest sense liberty is the daughter of economic equality.

The main aim of the social revolution is therefore to establish equal liberty on the basis of equal opportunity.

— above quotations from *What Is Communist Anarchism?*

Ambrose Bierce

INSURRECTION, An unsuccessful revolution. Disaffection's failure to substitute misrule for bad government.

REVOLUTION, In politics, an abrupt change in the form of misgovernment.

— *The Devil's Dictionary*

Crane Brinton

No ideas, no revolution.

— *The Anatomy of Revolution*

Nikolai Bukharin

A revolution cannot be made without terror, disorganization, and even wanton destruction, any more than an omelette can be made without breaking eggs.

— quoted by Emma Goldman in *My Further Disillusionment in Russia*

Ricardo Flores Magon

Well, then, workers, expropriate! Whatever the banner you fight under: expropriate and everything will become the property of all. And if those who direct the operations of war oppose this work of supreme social justice, kill them!

Whoever it may be, with arms in hand, that tells you that you'll obtain this or that improvement after the triumph is a liar: shoot him! You would have saved yourselves so much fatigue, so much blood, so many tears, so much hopelessness, if you would have only listened to our words when we told you to turn your guns on your leaders and officials last year! Well then, let this sad experience benefit you now. Don't serve as cannon fodder so that your chiefs and officials can adorn themselves with gold and feathers. Don't elevate anyone to the Presidency of the Republic, because the pay you'll receive for your sacrifices will be, once you've elevated your new bosses, that you'll be commanded to return to your homes, to return to that same life of privations and humiliations, because nothing will be changed then; the capitalist system will continue to oppress you, and with even more cruelty, because the rich will be anxious to relieve themselves of the losses incurred during the revolution, and you'll be the ones stuck with the bill.

Miserable, unfortunate brothers: Now or Never — Expropriate!

— *Regeneración*, February 10, 1912

Emma Goldman

The Russian Revolution — more correctly, Bolshevik methods — conclusively demonstrated how a revolution should *not* be made.

— Preface to *My Disillusionment in Russia*

The *actual* Russian Revolution took place in the summer months of 1917. During that period the peasants possessed themselves of the land, the workers of the factories, thus demonstrating that they knew well the meaning of social revolution. The October change was the finishing touch to the work begun six months previously. In the great uprising the Bolsheviki assumed the voice of the people. They clothed themselves with the agrarian programme of the Social Revolutionists and the industrial tactics of the Anarchists. But after the high tide of revolutionary enthusiasm had carried them into power, the Bolsheviki discarded their false plumes. It was then that began the spiritual separation between the Bolsheviki and the Russian Revolution. With each succeeding day the gap grew wider, their interests more conflicting. Today it is no exaggeration to state that the Bolsheviki stand as the arch enemies of the Russian Revolution.

— Ibid.

It would be an error to assume that the failure of the [Russian] Revolution was due entirely to the character of the Bolsheviki. Fundamentally, it was the result of the principles and methods of Bolshevism. It was the authoritarian spirit and principles of the State which stifled the libertarian and liberating aspirations. Were any other political party in control of the government in Russia the result would have been essentially the same.

— *My Disillusionment in Russia*

The whole history of man is continuous proof of the maxim that to divest one's methods of ethical concepts means to sink into the depths of utter demoralization. In that lies the real tragedy of the Bolshevik philosophy as applied to the Russian Revolution.

— Ibid.

If I can't dance, I don't want your revolution.

— attributed

Early in the morning mounted Tchekists [members of the Cheka, now the KGB] would dash by, shooting into the air — a warning that all windows must be closed. Then came motor trucks loaded with the doomed. They lay in rows, faces downward, their hands tied, soldiers standing over them

with rifles. They were being carried to execution outside the city. A few hours later the trucks would return empty save for a few soldiers. Blood dripped from the wagons, leaving a crimson streak on the pavement all the way to the Tcheka headquarters.
— *My Further Disillusionment in Russia*

The inherent tendency of the State is to concentrate, to narrow, and monopolize all social activities; the nature of revolution is, on the contrary, to grow, to broaden, and disseminate itself in ever-wider circles. In other words, the State is institutional and static; revolution is fluent, dynamic. These two tendencies are incompatible and mutually destructive. The State idea killed the Russian Revolution and it must have the same result in all other revolutions, unless the libertarian idea prevail[s].
— Afterword to *My Further Disillusionment in Russia*

The dominant, almost general, idea of revolution — particularly the Socialist idea — is that revolution is a violent change of social conditions through which one social class, the working class, becomes dominant over another class, the capitalist class. It is the conception of a purely physical change, and as such it involves only political scene shifting and institutional rearrangements. Bourgeois dictatorship is replaced by the "dictatorship of the proletariat" — or by that of its "advance guard," the Communist Party; Lenin takes the seat of the Romanovs, the Imperial Cabinet is rechristened Soviet of People's Commissars, Trotsky is appointed Minister of War. . .
This conception is inherently and fatally false. Revolution is indeed a violent process. But if it is to result only in a change of dictatorship, in a shifting of names and political personalities, then it is hardly worth while. It is surely not worth all the struggle and sacrifice, the stupendous loss in human life and cultural values that result from every revolution. If such a revolution were even to bring greater social well being, mere improvement can be brought about without bloody revolution. It is not palliatives or reforms that are the real aim and purpose of revolution, as I conceive it.
— Ibid.

There is no greater fallacy than the belief that aims and purposes are one thing, while methods and tactics are another. This conception is a potent menace to social regeneration. All human experience teaches that methods and means cannot be separated from the ultimate aim. The means employed become, through individual habit and social practice, part and parcel of the final purpose; they influence it, modify it, and presently the aims and means become identical.
— Ibid.

Revolutionary methods must be in tune with revolutionary aims. The means used to further the revolution must harmonize with its purposes. In short, the ethical values which the revolution is to

establish in the new society must be *initiated* with the revolutionary activities of the so-called transitional period. The latter can serve as a real and dependable bridge to the better life only if built of the same material as the life to be achieved. Revolution is the mirror of the coming day; it is the child that is to be the man of tomorrow.
— Ibid.

All political tenets and parties notwithstanding, no revolution can be truly and permanently successful unless it puts its emphatic veto upon all tyranny and centralization, and determinedly strives to make the revolution a real revaluation of all economic, social and cultural ♦alues. Not mere substitution of one political party for another in the control of the Government, not the masking of autocracy by proletarian slogans, not the dictatorship of a new class over an old one, not political scene shifting of any kind, but the complete reversal of all these authoritarian principles will alone serve the revolution.
— Ibid.

Praxedis Guerrero

To most people, revolution and war have the same significance; this error makes the supreme recourse of the oppressed appear as barbarism. War invariably has hatred and personal or national ambitions as characteristics; from it come relative benefits for only individuals or groups, paid for with the blood and sacrifice of the masses. Revolution is a brisk surge toward human betterment when a greater or lesser part of humanity is reduced by violence to a state incompatible with their aspirations and necessities of life.
— *Regeneración*, September 17, 1910

Alexander Herzen

You can awaken men only by dreaming their dreams more clearly than they can dream them themselves.
— quoted by Harold Myerson in *Utne Reader* No. 36

Abbie Hoffman

The first duty of a revolutionary is to get away with it.
— attributed

Peter Kropotkin

Revolution is only an essential part of evolution . . . no evolution is accomplished in nature without revolution. Periods of very slow changes are succeeded by periods of violent changes. Revolutions are as necessary for evolution as the slow changes which prepare them and succeed them.
— *Revolutionary Studies*

V.I. Lenin

How can a revolution be made without executions?
— *Pravda,* January 23, 1924, quoted by Maximoff
in *The Guillotine at Work*

Do you really believe we shall be able to come
out triumphant without the most drastic revolutionary terror?
— Ibid.

...revolution demands...precisely in the interests of socialism that the masses unquestioningly
obey the single will of the leaders of the labor process.
— quoted by Brinton in *The Bolsheviks and Workers
Control*

Pope Leo XIII

To despise legitimate authority, no matter in
whom it is invested, is unlawful; it is rebellion
against God's will.
— *Immortale Dei*

Inciting to revolution is treason, not only against
man but also against God.
— Ibid.

Martin Luther

If the peasants are in open rebellion, then they
are outside the law of God...
Therefore, let all who are able, slash, strike
down, and kill [them], openly or secretly, remem-
bering that there can be nothing more venomous,
harmful, or devilish than a rebel. It is exactly like
killing a mad dog...

Errico Malatesta

He who throws a bomb and kills a pedestrian,
declares that as a victim of society he has rebelled
against society. But could not the poor victim object: "Am I society?"
— Diary entry, July 21, 1932

The slave is always in a state of legitimate defense, and consequently, his violence against the
boss, against the oppressor, is always morally justi-
fiable, and must be controlled only by such considerations as that the best and most economical
use is being made of human effort and human
suffering.
— *Umanita Nova,* August 25, 1921

If in order to win [a revolution] it were necessary
to erect the gallows in the public square, then I
would prefer to lose.
— *Pensiero e Volonta,* October 1, 1924

Karl Marx

...From the first moment of victory, mistrust
must be directed no longer against the conquered
reactionary parties, but against the workers' previous allies, against the party that wishes to exploit
the common victory for itself alone...The workers
must put themselves at the command not of the
State authority but of the revolutionary councils
which the workers will have managed to get adopted
...Arms and ammunition must not be surrendered
on any pretext.
— Address to the Central Committee of the Communist League, 1850 (with Friedrich Engels)

MISQUOTATION. The question of when (or even whether) anarchy will be attained
is not important. What is important is that we work towards anarchy.
I dare say somebody said that.

Graphic by Donald Rooum

The civilization and justice of bourgeois order comes out in its lurid light whenever the slaves and drudges of that order rise against their masters. Then this civilization and justice stand forth as undisguised savagery and lawless revenge...a glorious civilization, indeed, the great problem of which is how to get rid of the heaps of corpses it made after the battle [suppression of the Paris Commune] was over!...The bourgeoisie of the whole world, which looks complacently upon the wholesale massacre after the battle, is convulsed by horror at the desecration of brick and mortar.

— *The Civil War in France*

Wendell Phillips

Revolutions are not made: they come. A revolution is as natural a growth as an oak. It comes out of the past. Its foundations are laid far back.

— Speech, 1852

Insurrection of thought always precedes insurrection of arms.

— Speech in Brooklyn, November 1, 1859

P.J. Proudhon

Do you want the counter-revolution to be finished in two days — complete — replete? Talk to the people not of King, nor Emperor, nor Republic...Do as Robespierre did: talk to them about the *Supreme Being* and the *immortality of the soul.*

— *The General Idea of the Revolution in the 19th Century*

If I were talking to men who had love of liberty and respect for themselves, and I wanted to incite them to revolt, I should confine myself in my speech to reciting the powers of a prefect [magistrate].

— Ibid.

General Efrain Rios Montt

We [the Guatemalan government and military] have no scorched earth policy — we have a policy of scorched Communists.

Rudolf Rocker

...a change of present conditions in the direction of a free society is possible only through the systematic undermining of the inherited political and social dogmas...Only when confidence in contemporary political and economic institutions vanishes will these be deprived of the foundation on which they rest. As long as the spiritual preparation for the new order has not matured, every political revolution will lead only to the substituting of the present forms of oppression by others...

— *Pioneers of American Freedom* (explaining Benjamin Tucker's position on revolution)

As soon as larger minorities are determined to show the door to the tax collector, to ignore laws which they have come to regard as a nuisance, and their passive resistance reaches proportions which make it impossible for those in authority to put everyone behind lock and key, the great twilight of the Gods which can be postponed but not prevented will have come.

— Ibid. (explaining Benjamin Tucker's position on passive resistance)

George Bernard Shaw

All who achieve real distinction in life begin as revolutionists. The most distinguished persons become more revolutionary as they grow older, although they are commonly supposed to become more conservative owing to their loss of faith in conventional methods of reform.

— *The Revolutionist's Handbook*

Percy Bysshe Shelley

Rise like lions after slumber,
In unvanquishable number;
Shake your chains to earth like dew
Which in sleep had fallen on you —
Ye are many, they are few.

— *The Mask of Anarchy*

Leo Tolstoy

In our fear to make an effort to tear ourselves away from the conditions which ruin us, only because the future is not quite certain to us, we resemble the passengers of a sinking ship, who, for fear of stepping into a boat which is to take them to the shore, retreat to their cabins and refuse to come out from them; or those sheep which, out of the fire which has enveloped the whole yard, press close to their pens and do not walk through the open gates.

— *The Kingdom of God Is Within You*

Leon Trotsky

We will shoot you down like partridges.

— Ultimatum to Kronstadt revolutionaries, 1921

Benjamin Tucker

It is because peaceful agitation and passive resistance are effective that I uphold them, and it is because force strengthens tyranny that I condemn it. War and Authority are companions; Peace and Liberty are companions. It is foolish in the extreme not only to resort to force before necessity compels, but especially to madly create the conditions that will lead to this necessity.

— *Liberty*, May 22, 1886

Emiliano Zapata

The capitalist, the soldier, and the governor have lived tranquilly, without bother to either their privileges or properties, at the cost of an illiterate and enslaved people, a people with neither a patrimony nor a future, a people condemned to work without rest and to die of hunger because they spend all their energies producing incalculable wealth while they cannot count on satisfying even the most indispensable of their immediate needs. That economic organization, that administrative system which has come to be a mass murderer of the people, a collective suicide for the nation, and an insult, a shame to honorable and conscious people, cannot endure any longer; and the revolution has come, as do all collective movements, through necessity.

—*Manifiesto a la nación*, October 20, 1913

The campesino suffered hunger, misery, exploitation, and if he has taken up arms it's to obtain the bread which the rapacity of the rich has denied him, to become master of the earth which the large landowner egotistically reserves for himself; it's to reclaim his dignity which the slave driver viciously tramples on day after day. We did not launch our revolt to conquer illusory political rights which provide not a crumb to eat, but to procure a piece of earth which provides nourishment and liberty, a happy home, and a bright and independent future.

—*Al pueblo mexicano*, August 1914

Anonymous & Multiple Author

Meaningful action, for revolutionaries, is whatever increases the confidence, the autonomy, the initiative, the participation, the solidarity, the equalitarian tendencies and the self-activity of the masses and whatever assists in their demystification. *Sterile and harmful action* is whatever reinforces the passivity of the masses, their apathy, their cynicism, their differentiation through hierarchy, their alienation, their reliance on others to do things for them and the degree to which they can therefore be manipulated by others—even by those allegedly acting on their behalf.

—Solidarity (British libertarian group), *As We See It*

As long as there are rich and poor, governors and governed, there will be no peace, nor is it to be desired... for such a peace would be founded on the political, economic, and social inequality of millions of human beings who suffer hunger, outrages, prison, and death, while a small minority enjoys pleasures and liberties of all kinds for doing nothing.

On with the struggle!

—*Manifiesto del Partido Liberal Mexicano, 1911*

You can't blow up a social relationship.

—*The Anarchist Case Against Terrorism*

Follow the revolutionary path of Mao Tse Tung!

—Graffiti, San Francisco, 1985

Follow the revolutionary path*ology* of Mao Tse Tung!

—Graffiti with alteration, San Francisco, 1986

Only the truth is revolutionary.

—Graffiti, Paris, May 1968

Patriotism, Nationalism & Imperialism

Michael Bakunin

Bourgeois patriotism, as I view it, is only a very shabby, very narrow, very mercenary, and deeply antihuman passion, having for its object the preservation and maintenance of the power of the national state — that is, the mainstay of all the privileges of the exploiters throughout the nation.

— *Letters to a Frenchman*

Ambrose Bierce

FLAG, A colored rag borne above troops and hoisted on forts and ships. It appears to serve the same purpose as certain signs that one sees on vacant lots in London — "Rubbish may be shot here."

— *The Devil's Dictionary*

PATRIOT, One to whom the interests of a part seem superior to those of the whole. The dupe of statesmen and the tool of conquerors.

— Ibid.

PATRIOTISM, Combustible rubbish ready to the torch of any one ambitious to illuminate his name. In Dr. Johnson's famous dictionary patriotism is defined as the last resort of a scoundrel. With all due respect to an enlightened but inferior lexicographer, I beg to submit that it is the first.

— Ibid.

Every patriot believes his country better than any other country...In its active manifestation — it is fond of killing — patriotism would be well enough if it were simply defensive; but it is also aggressive...

Patriotism deliberately and with folly aforethought subordinates the interests of a whole to the interests of a part. Worse still, the fraction so favored is determined by an accident of birth or residence. The Western hoodlum who cuts the tail from a Chinaman's nowl, and would cut the nowl from the body if he dared, is simply a patriot with a logical mind, having the courage of his opinions. Patriotism is fierce as a fever, pitiless as the grave and blind as a stone.

— *Collected Works*

General Smedley Butler

I spent thirty-three years and four months in active service in the country's most agile military force, the Marines. I served in all ranks from second lieutenant to major general. And during that period I spent most of my time being a high-class muscle man for Big Business, for Wall Street and the bankers. In short, I was a racketeer, a gangster for capitalism.

I suspected I was just part of a racket at the time. Now I am sure of it. Like all members of the military profession I never had an original thought until I left the service. My mental faculties remained in suspended animation while I obeyed the orders of the higher-ups. This is typical with everyone in the military service.

Thus I helped make Mexico, and especially Tampico, safe for American oil interests in 1914. I helped make Haiti and Cuba a decent place for the National City Bank boys to collect revenue in. I helped in the raping of half-a-dozen Central American republics for the benefit of Wall Street. The record of racketeering is long. I helped purify Nicaragua for the international banking house of Brown Brothers and Co. in 1909–1912. I brought light to the Dominican Republic for the sugar interests in 1916. I helped make Honduras "right" for American fruit companies in 1903. In China in 1927 I helped see to it that Standard Oil went its way unmolested.

During those years, I had, as the boys in the back room would say, a swell racket. I was rewarded with honors, medals, and promotion. Looking back on it, I feel that I might have given Al Capone a few hints. The best he could do was to operate a racket in three city districts. The Marines operated on three continents.

— *Common Sense,* November 1935

Calgacus

To plunder, to slaughter, to steal, these things they misname empire; and where they make a desert, they call it peace.

Noam Chomsky

On the Aggression of South Vietnamese Peasants Against the United States
— Essay title

Clarence Darrow

Rulers have ever taught and encouraged the spirit of patriotism, that they might call upon their slaves to give their labor to the privileged class and to freely offer up their lives when the king commands. Every people in the world is taught that their country and their government is the best on earth, and that they should be ever ready to desert their homes, abandon their hopes, aspirations, and ambitions when their ruler calls, and this regardless of the right or wrong for which they fight.
— *Resist Not Evil*

Eugene V. Debs

Do not worry over the charge of treason to your masters, but be concerned about the treason that involves yourselves. Be true to yourself and you cannot be a traitor to any good cause on earth.
— Speech, June 16, 1918

I have no country to fight for; my country is the earth, and I am a citizen of the world.

Albert Einstein

Nationalism is an infantile disease. It is the measles of mankind.
— attributed

Camille Flammarion

The inhabitants of the planet Earth are still in such a ridiculous state of unintelligence and stupidity that we read every day in the newspapers of the civilized countries a discussion of the diplomatic relations of the chiefs of states aiming at an alliance against a supposed enemy and preparations for war, and that the nations allow their leaders to dispose of them like cattle to the slaughter, as though never suspecting that the life of each man is his personal property.

The inhabitants of this singular planet have been reared in the conviction that there are nations, frontiers, and standards, and they have such a feeble sense of humanity that that feeling is completely effaced by the sense of nationalism.
— quoted by Tolstoy in *Bethink Yourselves*

Ricardo Flores Magon

It is necessary to speak the truth, whatever the cost: If U.S. forces have planted the stars and stripes on the coast of Mexico, it hasn't been to satisfy a worthy desire of humanity and justice. This banner has been anchored in Veracruz like a dagger in the breast of justice; this banner did not appear on those beaches as a luminous symbol of civilization and justice, but as a black rag covering the face of crime while it empties the pockets of its victims. This banner is the mask of the great bandits of industry, commerce and finance of all countries whose interest it is that the Mexican worker remain a slave; this banner is the knife and the whip, the chain and the noose. It doesn't shine as an insignia of redemption and progress; rather, it floats in the air like a shroud blown in the night by the winds of death.
— Speech, May 31, 1914

John T. Flynn

The enemy aggressor is always pursuing a course of larceny, murder, rapine, and barbarism. We are always moving forward with high mission, a destiny imposed by the Deity to regenerate our victims while incidentally capturing their markets, to civilize savage and senile and paranoidal peoples while blundering accidentally into their oil wells or metal mines.

— *As We Go Marching*

No matter what the cause, even though it be to conquer with tanks and planes and modern artillery some defenseless black population, there will be no lack of poets and preachers and essayists and philosophers to invent the necessary reasons and gild the infamy with righteousness. To this righteousness there is, of course, never an adequate reply. Thus a war to end poverty becomes an unanswerable enterprise. For who can decently be for poverty? To even debate whether the war will end poverty becomes an exhibition of ugly pragmatism and the sign of an ignoble mind.

— Ibid.

E.M. Forster

If I had a choice between betraying my country and my friend, I hope I would have the guts to betray my country.

William Lloyd Garrison

Our country is the world, our countrymen are all mankind. We love the land of our nativity, only as we love all other lands. The interests, rights, and liberties of American citizens are no more dear to us than are those of the whole human rce. Hence we can allow no appeal to patriotism, to revenge any national insult of injury.

— Declaration of Sentiments, Boston Peace Conference, 1838

Emma Goldman

Patriotism assumes that our globe is divided into little spots, each one surrounded by an iron gate. Those who have had the fortune of being born on some particular spot, consider themselves better, nobler, grander, more intelligent than the living beings inhabiting any other spot. It is, therefore, the duty of everyone living on that chosen spot to fight, kill, and die in the attempt to impose his superiority upon all others. The inhabitants of the other spots reason in like manner, of course...

— *Patriotism*

Oliver Goldsmith

...you will always find that those are most apt to boast of national merit, who have little or no merit of their own to depend on;...nothing is more natural: the slender vine twists around the sturdy oak, for no other reason in the world but because it has not strength sufficient to support itself.

— *National Prejudices*

William Randolph Hearst

You furnish the pictures and I'll furnish the war.

— Cable to artist Frederic Remington in Cuba, 1898

Robert Ingersoll

He loves his country best who strives to make it best.

— Speech in New York, May 29, 1882

Samuel Johnson

Patriotism is the last refuge of scoundrels.

— *Boswell's Life of Johnson*

Lao-Tse

To rejoice over conquest is to rejoice over murder.

Guy de Maupassant

Patriotism is a kind of religion; it is the egg from which wars are hatched.

— attributed

H.L. Mencken

Samuel Johnson's saying that patriotism is the last refuge of scoundrels has some truth in it, but not nearly enough. Patriotism, in truth, is the great nursery of scoundrels, and its annual output is probably greater than that of even religion. Its chief glories are the demagogue, the military bully, and the spreaders of libels and false history. Its philosophy rests firmly on the doctrine that the end justifies the means — that any blow, whether above or below the belt, is fair against dissenters from its wholesale denial of plain facts.

— *Minority Report*

Blaise Pascal

Can anything be stupider than that a man has the right to kill me because he lives on the other side of a river and his ruler has a quarrel with mine, though I have not quarrelled with him?

— quoted by Tolstoy in *Bethink Yourselves*

Ronald Reagan

We should declare war on North Vietnam...We could pave the whole country and put parking stripes on it, and still be home by Christmas.

— quoted in the *Fresno Bee*, October 10, 1965

I Died for my Country.

Will You?

Graphic by Ned Kelly. Used by permission.

Arthur Schopenhauer

Every miserable fool who has nothing at all of which he can be proud, adopts as a last resource pride in the nation to which he belongs; he is ready and happy to defend all its faults and follies tooth and nail, thus reimbursing himself for his own inferiority.

— *Aphorisms*

George Bernard Shaw

Patriotism is a pernicious, psychopathic form of idiocy.

A modern gentleman is necessarily the enemy of his country. Even in war he does not fight to defend it, but to prevent his power of preying on it from passing to a foreigner.

— *Maxims for Revolutionists*

Robert Tefton

PATRIOT, n. A dangerous tool of the powers that be. A herd member who compensates for lack of self-esteem by identifying with an abstraction. An enemy of individual freedom. See also "Bootlicker."

PATRIOTISM, n. 1) The inability to distinguish between the government and one's "country"; 2) A highly praiseworthy virtue characterized by the desire to dominate and kill; 3) The first, last, and perennial refuge of scoundrels.

Allen Thornton

. . . politicians are most alive when their constituents are dying.

— *Laws of the Jungle*

Leo Tolstoy

Patriotism in its simplest, clearest and most indubitable meaning is nothing but an instrument for the attainment of the government's ambitious and mercenary aims, and a renunciation of human dignity, common sense, and conscience by the governed, and a slavish submission to those who hold power. That is what is really preached wherever patriotism is championed.
Patriotism is slavery.

— *Christianity and Patriotism*

Men who can undertake to fulfill with unquestioning submission all that is decreed by men they do not know. . . cannot be rational; and the governments —that is, the men wielding such power—can still less be reasonable. They cannot but misuse such insensate and terrible power and cannot but be crazed by wielding it. For this reason peace between nations cannot be attained by the reasonable method of conventions and arbitrations so long as that submission of the peoples to governments, which is always irrational and pernicious, still continues.

But the subjection of men to government will always continue as long as patriotism exists, for every ruling power rests on patriotism—on the readiness of men to submit to power. . .

— Ibid.

To destroy governmental *violence* only one thing is needed: it is that people should understand that the feeling of patriotism which alone supports that instrument of violence is a rude, harmful, disgraceful, and bad feeling, and above all immoral. It is a rude feeling because it is natural only to people standing on the lowest level of morality and expecting from other nations such outrages as they themselves are ready to inflict. It is a harmful feeling because it disturbs advantageous and joyous peaceful relations with other peoples, and above all produces that governmental organization under which power may fall and does fall into the hands of the worst men. It is a disgraceful feeling because it turns man not merely into a slave but into a fighting cock, a bull, or a gladiator, who wastes his strength and his life for objects which are not his own, but his government's. It is an immoral feeling because, instead of confessing himself a son of God. . . or even a free man guided by his own reason, each man under the influence of patriotism confesses himself the son of his fatherland and the slave of his government, and commits actions contrary to his reason and conscience.

— *Patriotism and Government*

Mark Twain

I bring you the stately matron named Christendom, returning bedraggled, besmirched, and dishonored from pirate-raids in Kiao-Chou, Manchuria, South Africa & the Philippines, with her soul full of meanness, her pocket full of boodle and her mouth full of pious hypocrisies. Give her soap and a towel, but hide the looking glass.

— *New York Herald,* December 30, 1900

Voltaire

It is lamentable, that to be a good patriot one must become the enemy of the rest of mankind.

— *Philosophical Dictionary*

Simone Weil

Whether the mask is labelled Fascism, Democracy, or Dictatorship of the Proletariat, our great adversary remains the Apparatus—the bureaucracy, the police, the military. Not the one facing us across the frontier or the battlelines, which is not so much our enemy as our brothers' enemy, but the one that calls itself our protector and makes us its slaves. No matter what the circumstances, the worst betrayal will always be to subordinate ourselves to this Apparatus, and to trample underfoot, in its service, all human values in ourselves and in others.

— *Politics,* Spring 1945

Oscar Wilde

Patriotism is the virtue of the vicious.

Kaiser Wilhelm II

Remember when we meet the enemy there will be no quarter and no prisoners taken. Use your weapons in such a way that for 1000 years no Chinese will dare look at a German. We must pave the way for civilization once and for all.

—on sending German troops to put down the Boxer Rebellion, 1901

Fred Woodworth

In an incredible perversion of justice, former soldiers who sprayed festeringly poisonous chemicals on Vietnam, and now find today that they themselves have been damaged by them, appeal to the people for sympathy and charity. The effects of the defoliant "Agent Orange" are discussed at length, but not one single newspaper article or hearing that we are aware of has even mentioned the effects on the people who still live in those regions of Vietnam. It's as outlandish as if Nazis who gassed Jews were now to come forward and whine that the poisons they utilized had finally made *them* sick. The staggering monstrousness goes unlaughed at and even unnoticed, as in a Kafka novel.

— *The Match!*, No. 79

Henry C. Wright

For, as wolves and tigers gorge themselves with flesh and lick their gory chops, so do nations gorge themselves with human victims, not in detail, but in masses, by wholesale.

—Letter to William Lloyd Garrison, March 30, 1844

Anonymous

U.S. out of North America!

The Military

Alexander Berkman

The man who can face vilification and disgrace, who can stand up against the popular current, even against his friends and his country when he knows he is right, who can defy those in authority over him, who can take punishment and prison and remain steadfast—that is a man of courage. The fellow whom you taunt as a "slacker" because he refuses to turn murderer—he needs courage. But do you need much courage just to obey orders, to do as you are told and to fall in line with thousands of others to the tune of general approval and the *Star Spangled Banner?*

— *What Is Communist Anarchism?*

Henry Thomas Buckle

I believe the experience of every country in modern Europe proves that the army is not only less educated than any other profession holding an equal estimation in public opinion, but that soldiers generally are deficient in intellect. This effect was brought about by the same causes which converted war from an art to a science. The soldier is now essentially a machine. His will is constantly in abeyance. And, thus relieved from the necessity of thinking when he is on the field, he soon learns to avoid thinking when he is off the field.

— *Observations on the Tendency of Military Institutions and Character of Soldiers*

Clarence Darrow

The ability and inclination to use physical strength is no indication of bravery or tenacity to life. The greatest cowards are often the greatest bullies. Nothing is cheaper and more common than physical bravery.

Common experience shows how much rarer is moral courage than physical bravery. A thousand men will march to the mouth of the cannon where one man will dare espouse an unpopular cause... True courage and manhood come from the consciousness of the right attitude toward the world, the faith in one's own purpose, and the sufficiency of one's own approval as a justification for one's own acts.

The lowest standards of ethics of which a right-thinking man can possibly conceive is taught to the common soldier whose trade is to shoot his fellow men. In youth he may have learned the command, "Thou shalt not kill," but the ruler takes the boy just as he enters manhood and teaches him that his highest duty is to shoot a bullet through his neighbor's heart—and this, unmoved by passion or feeling or hatred, and without the least regard to right or wrong, but simply because his ruler gives the word.

Not only do...rulers keep many millions of men whose only trade is war, but these must be supported in worse than useless idleness by the labor of the poor. Still other millions are trained to war and are ever ready to answer to their master's call, to desert their homes and trades and offer up their lives to satisfy the vain ambitions of the ruler of the state. Millions more must give their strength and lives to build forts and ships, make guns and cannon and all the modern implements of war. Apart from any moral question of the right of man to slay his fellow man, all this great burden rests upon the poor. The vast expense of war comes from the production of the land and must serve to weaken and impair its industrial strength.

— above quotations from *Resist Not Evil*

Dwight D. Eisenhower

Every gun that is made, every warship launched, every rocket fired, signifies in a final sense a theft from those who hunger and are not fed—those who are cold and not clothed. This world in arms is not spending money alone—it is spending the sweat of its laborers, the genius of its scientists, the hopes of its children.

—Speech, 1953

We must guard against the acquisition of unwarranted influence...by the military industrial complex. The potential for the disastrous rise of misplaced power exists and will persist.

—Farewell address

John T. Flynn

When a nation embarks upon militarism as a means of supporting its economic life, then powerful, active, and vicious external enemies become an economic necessity. The nation must be kept sharply aware of its dangers. War scares are an essential part of promotion. With these psychological weapons statesmen can extract from their terrified citizens or subjects consent for military outlays when it would be utterly impossible to do so for peaceful enterprises however worthy.

— *As We Go Marching*

Frederick the Great

If my soldiers were to begin to think, not one of them would remain in the army.

— quoted by Tolstoy in *Bethink Yourselves!*

William Lloyd Garrison

We say that he who votes to empower Congress to declare war, and to provide the necessary instruments of war, and to constitute the President commander-in-chief of the army and navy, has no right, when war actually comes to plead conscientious scruples as a peace man; but is bound to stand by his vote, or else to make confession of wrong-doing and take his position outside of the government. He cannot be allowed to strain at a gnat, and swallow a camel; to play fast and loose with his conscience; to make the amplest provisions for war, and then beg to be excused from its dangers and hardships in deference to his peace sentiments. The government has a right to apply this test, and the voter has no right to complain when it is rigidly enforced in his own case.

But we submit to all the people, that such as wholly abstain from voting to uphold the Constitution because of its war provisions, and thus religiously exclude themselves from all share in what are deemed official honors and emoluments, ought not to be drafted in time of war, or compelled to pay an equivalent, or go to prison for disobedience. If conscience is to be respected and provided for in any case, it is theirs.

— *The Liberator*, 1862

Edward Gibbon

. . . the temper of soldiers, habituated at once to violence and to slavery, renders them very unfit guardians of a legal or even a civil constitution. Justice, humanity, or political wisdom, are qualities they are too little acquainted with in themselves to appreciate them in others.

— *Decline and Fall of the Roman Empire*

William Godwin

A soldier is a man whose business it is to kill those who never offended him, and who are the innocent martyrs of other men's iniquities. Whatever may become of the abstract question of the justifiableness of war, it seem impossible that the soldier should not be a depraved and unnatural thing.

— *The Enquirer*

Emma Goldman

The powers that have for centuries been engaged in enslaving the masses have made a thorough study of their psychology. They know that the people at large are like children whose despair, sorrow, and tears can be turned into joy with a little toy. And the more gorgeously the toy is dressed, the louder the colors, the more it will appeal to the million-headed child.

An army and navy represent the people's toys. To make them more attractive and acceptable, hundreds and thousands of dollars are being spent for the display of these toys.

— *Patriotism*

No wonder our military authorities complain of the "poor material" enlisting in the army and navy. This admission is a very encouraging sign. It proves that there is still enough of the spirit of independence and love of liberty left in the average American to risk starvation rather than don the uniform.

— Ibid.

How is a military drilled and trained people to defend freedom, peace and happiness? This is what Major General O'Ryan has to say of an efficiently trained generation: "The soldier must be so trained that he becomes a mere automoton; he must be so trained that it will destroy his initiative; he must be so trained that he is turned into a machine. The soldier must be forced into the military noose; he must be jacked up; he must be ruled by his superiors with pistol in hand."

This was not said by a Prussian Junker; not by a German barbarian. . . but by an American major general. And he is right. You cannot conduct war with equals; you cannot have militarism with free born men; you must have slaves, automotons, machines, obedient disciplined creatures, who will move, act, shoot and kill at the command of their superiors. That is preparedness, and nothing else.

— *Preparedness: The Road to Universal Slaughter*

Adolf Hitler

. . . the army. . . will be the last and highest school of patriotic education.

— *Mein Kampf*

But in the forefront of military training. . . the boy must be transformed into a man; in this school he must not only learn to obey, but must thereby acquire a basis for commanding later. He must learn to be silent not only when he is *justly* blamed but must also learn, when necessary, to bear *injustice* in silence.

— Ibid.

What the German people owes to the army can be summed up in a single word, to wit: everything.

— Ibid.

V.I. Lenin

In the Red Army, following the many months when mass meetings reigned supreme, the new discipline which came to prevail did not yield in any respect to the old discipline. This discipline included harsh, stringent measures, going as far as shootings, measures which even the old government did not visualize. The philistines kept on writing and shouting: "there you have it: the Bolsheviks have introduced shootings." We must say to that: yes, we did, and we did it knowingly.

— quoted by Maximoff in *The Guillotine at Work*

Jack London

YOUNG MEN: The lowest aim in your life is to become a soldier. The good soldier never tries to distinguish right from wrong. He never thinks; never reasons; he only obeys. If he is ordered to fire on his fellow citizens, on his friends, on his neighbors, on his relatives, he obeys without hesitation. If he is ordered to fire down a crowded street when the poor are clamoring for bread, he obeys and sees the grey hairs of age stained with red and the life tide gushing from the breasts of women, feeling neither remorse nor sympathy. If he is ordered off as a firing squad to execute a hero or benefactor, he fires without hesitation, though he knows the bullet will pierce the noblest heart that ever beat in human breast.

A good soldier is a blind, heartless, soulless, murderous machine. He is not a man. He is not a brute, for brutes only kill in self defense. All that is human in him, all that is divine in him, all that constitutes the man has been sworn away when he took the enlistment roll. His mind, his conscience, aye, his very soul, are in the keeping of his officer.

No man can fall lower than a soldier — it is a depth beneath which we cannot go.

— quoted in *The Match!*

Rep. Meyer London

They talk about conscription as a democratic institution. Yes; so is a cemetery.

— Speech in the House of Representatives, April 25, 1917

Mao Tse Tung

Obey orders in all your actions.

— *Selected Military Writings,* Second Edition

Groucho Marx

Military intelligence is a contradiction in terms.

— attributed

H.L. Mencken

Is a young man bound to serve his country in war? In addition to his legal duty there is perhaps also a moral duty, but it is very obscure. What is called his country is only its government and that government consists merely of professional politicians, a parasitical and anti-social class of men. They never sacrifice themselves for their country. They make all wars, but very few of them ever die in one. If it is the duty of a young man to serve his country under all circumstances then it is equally the duty of an enemy young man to serve *his*. Thus we come to a moral contradiction and absurdity, so obvious that even clergymen and editorial writers sometimes notice it.

— *Minority Report*

Wilhelm Reich

The sexual effect of a uniform, the erotically provocative effect of rhythmically executed goose-stepping, the exhibitionistic nature of militaristic procedures, have been more practically comprehended by a sales girl or an average secretary than by our most erudite politicians. On the other hand it is political reaction that consciously exploits these sexual interests. It not only designs flashy uniforms for the men, it puts the recruiting into the hands of attractive women... "Travel to foreign countries — join the Royal Navy!" and the foreign countries were portrayed by exotic women. And why are these posters effective? Because our youth has become sexually starved owing to sexual suppression.

— *The Mass Psychology of Fascism*

Charles T. Sprading

The distinguishing characteristic of the militarist is parasitism; the power and ability to destroy, and to levy tribute, to impose arbitrary restrictions and collect taxes, to take and to consume; in short, to govern.

— *Freedom and Its Fundamentals*

The militarists say that "fighting is instinctive" and that "you cannot change the real character of man by any intellectual process." If this is true, the case is still not hopeless, as some think, for there are animals and men without this "fighting instinct," that do not kill each other; there is a possibility that

those with the "fighting instinct" will succeed in exterminating each other, and permit those without it to breed a better race.
— Ibid.

Animals do not destroy their own species; it takes a militarist to do that.
— Ibid.

Jonathan Swift

Poor nations are hungry, and rich nations are proud; and pride and hunger will ever be at variance. For these reasons, the trade of a soldier is held the most honourable of all others; because a soldier is a Yahoo hired to kill in cold blood as many of his own species, who have never offended him, as possibly he can.
— Gulliver's Travels

Robert Tefton

NATIONAL DEFENSE, n. 1) The pauperization of the nation through expenditures for deadly weapons systems; 2) In U.S. political discourse, the bombardment and invasion of small countries. The United States, of course, is the only nation entitled to such "defense." If the inhabitants of other countries resist the U.S. government, they are guilty of "internal aggression"; and if the governments of other countries practice U.S.-style "national defense," they are guilty of "naked aggression."

SOLDIER, n. A praiseworthy individual who practices the virtues of blind obedience and of killing human beings whom he does not know (or, occasionally, those whom he does).

Norman Thomas

The very existence of armaments and great armies psychologically accustoms us to accept the philosophy of militarism. They inevitably increase fear and hate in the world.
— Address to the League for Industrial Democracy

Henry David Thoreau

It is impossible to give a soldier a good education without making him a deserter. His natural foe is the government that drills him.
— Walden

Allen Thornton

Do we owe our freedom to our fighting men? To be drafted is to be enslaved. How can we owe our freedom to slaves? They may have fought bravely and died with courage, but they haven't given us any freedom. We would have been in their debt if

they had refused to fight foreigners and instead freed themselves from the American politicians who continue to enslave us.
— Laws of the Jungle

Leo Tolstoy

Discipline is the destruction of reason and of liberty in man, and cannot have any other purpose than merely the preparation for the commission of such malefactions as not one man will commit in his normal condition.
— The Slavery of Our Times

...discipline consists in this, that the men who undergo the instruction and have followed it for a certain time are completely deprived of everything which is precious to a man—of the chief human property, rational freedom—and become submissive, machine-like implements of murder in the hands of their organized, hierarchic authorities.
— Ibid.

Universal military service is for the government the last degree of violence, which is necessary for the support of the whole structure; and for the subjects it is the extreme limit of the possibility of their obedience.
— The Kingdom of God Is Within You

...he who very frequently is a learned man, who has studied all the sciences in a university, submissively puts his neck into the yoke. He is dressed up in a clown's attire, is commanded to jump, to contort his body, to bow, to kill—and he does everything submissively. And when he is let out, he returns briskly to his former life and continues to talk of man's dignity, liberty, equality, and fraternity.
— Ibid.

If the majority of men prefer submission [to conscription] to nonsubmission, this is not due to any sober weighing of the advantages and disadvantages, but because the majority are attracted to submission by means of hypnotization...
...the disadvantages of nonsubmission to the demands of the government will consist in this, that I...shall be tried and at best shall be discharged, or as they do with the Mennonites, shall be compelled to serve out my time at some unmilitary work; in the worst case I shall be condemned to deportation or imprisonment for two or three years...

Such are the disadvantages of nonsubmission; but the disadvantages of submission will consist in this: at best I shall not be sent out to kill men, and I myself shall not be subjected to any great probability of crippling or death, but shall only be enlisted as a military slave—I shall be dressed up in a clown's garments; I shall be at the mercy of every man above me in rank, from a corporal to a field-marshal; I shall be compelled to contort my body according to their desire, and, after being kept from one to five years, I shall be left for ten years in a condition of readiness to appear at any moment for the purpose of going through all these things again. In the worst case I shall, in addition to all those previous conditions of slavery, be sent to war, where I shall be compelled to kill men of other nations, who have done me no harm, where I may be crippled and killed, and where I may get into a place... where men are sent to certain death and, what is most agonizing, I may be sent out against my own countrymen, when I shall be compelled to kill my brothers for dynastic or other reasons, which are entirely alien to me...

For him who has not refused, the advantages will consist in this, that, having submitted to all the humiliations and having executed all the cruelties demanded of him, he may, if he is not killed, receive red and golden tin foil decorations over his clown's garments, and he may at best command hundreds of thousands of just such bestialized men as himself, and be called a field marshal and receive a lot of money.

But the advantages of him who refuses will consist in this, that he will retain his human dignity, will earn the respect of good men, and above all else, will know without fail that he is doing God's work, and so an incontestable good to men.

... for a man of the poor, working classes the advantages and disadvantages will be the same, but with an important addition of disadvantages. The disadvantages for a man of the laboring classes, who has not refused military service, will also consist in this, that by entering military service he by his participation and seeming consent confirms the very oppression under which he is suffering.

— Ibid.

Daniel Webster

Where is it written in the Constitution, in what article or section is it contained, that you may take children from their parents and parents from their children, and compel them to fight the battles of any war in which the folly and wickedness of the government may engage itself?

Under what concealment has this power lain hidden, which now for the first time comes forth, with a tremendous and baleful aspect, to trample down and destroy the dearest right of personal liberty? Who will show me any Constitutional injunction which makes it the duty of the American people to surrender everything valuable in life, and even life itself, whenever the purposes of an ambitious and mischievous government may require it?...

A free government with an uncontrolled power of military conscription is the most ridiculous and abominable contradiction and nonsense that ever entered into the heads of men.

— Speech in the House of Representatives, January 14, 1814

Kaiser Wilhelm II

Recruits!... You have sworn allegiance to me; this, children of my guard, means that you are now my soldiers, that you have surrendered your souls and bodies to me. For you there now exists but one enemy, namely, the one who is my enemy. With the present socialistic propaganda it may happen that I will command you to shoot your own relatives, your brothers, even parents — God forbid — and then you will be obliged without murmuring to do my commands.

— quoted by Tolstoy in *The Kingdom of God Is Within You*

Anonymous & Multiple Author

The hail-fellow-well-met spirit in the relationships between a commander and subordinate can have no place in the Red Army. Discussion of any kind is absolutely prohibited among the subordinates.

— *Red Star* (Red Army paper), October 22, 1940, quoted by M.L. Berneri in *Workers in Stalin's Russia*

If you want more from life than living, UNCLE SAM WANTS YOU to have the chance to have your guts blown out for the Bank of America...

— Vietnam Veterans Against the War poster

Don't be a soldier. Be a man.

— IWW slogan

Be all that you can be.

— Army billboard

Maybe all that you can be *is a killer.*

— corrected Army billboard

Selective Service Registration: It's quick, it's easy, and it's the law.

— Selective Service threat (billboard)

Selective Service Registration: It's quick, it's easy, and it's *a trap for assholes!*

— corrected Selective Service threat, Berkeley, 1985

Turn your talent into a skill in the navy.

— Navy billboard

Turn your talent into a kill in the navy.

— corrected Navy billboard

One two three four
Every night we pray for war.
Five six seven eight
Rape. Kill. Mutilate.

— U.S. Marine Corps training chant, Camp Pendelton, quoted in the *San Francisco Chronicle,* January 6, 1989

The Health of the State . . .

War

St. Augustine

The true believer must not condemn war but must look upon it as a necessary evil, as a punishment which God has imposed upon men. For war is, like pestilence and famine and all other evils, only a visitation of God for the chastisement of men for their betterment, and to prepare them for salvation.

— *The City of God*

Joan Baez

If it's natural to kill, why do men have to go into training to learn to do it?

— attributed

Ernest Bennett

A large number of the Tommies had never been under fire before. . . and there was a curious look of surprised excitement in some of the faces. . . Now and then I caught in a man's eye the curious gleam which comes from the joy of shedding blood — that mysterious impulse which, despite all the veneer of civilisation, still holds its own in a man's nature, whether he is killing rats with a terrier, rejoicing in a prize fight, playing a salmon or potting Dervishes. It was a fine day and we were out to kill something. Call it what you like, the experience is a bag factor in the joy of living.

— *Westminster Gazette,* 1898 (quoted by Phillip Knightly in *The First Casualty*)

Alexander Berkman

War paralyzes your courage and deadens the spirit of true manhood. It degrades and stupefies with the sense that you are not responsible, that "tis not yours to think and reason why, but to do and die," like the hundred thousand others doomed like yourself. War means blind obedience, unthinking stupidity, brutish callousness, wanton destruction, and irresponsible murder.

— *What Is Communist Anarchism*

General Smedley Butler

War is a racket; possibly the oldest, easily the most profitable, surely the most vicious. . .

Out of war a few people make huge fortunes. Nations acquire additional territory (which is promptly exploited by the few for their own benefit), and the general public shoulders the bill — a bill that renders a horrible accounting of newly placed gravestones, mangled bodies, shattered minds, broken hearts and homes, economic unstability, and back-breaking taxation of the many for generations and generations.

Thomas Carlyle

War is a quarrel between two thieves too cowardly to fight their own battle; therefore they take boys from one village and another village, stick them into uniforms, equip them with guns, and let them loose like wild beasts against each other.

Karl von Clausewitz

We must further expressly and exactly establish the point of view, no less necessary in practice, from which war is regarded as *nothing but the continuation of state policy with other means.*

— *On War*

Erasmus

War is delightful to those who have not experienced it.

John T. Flynn

The so-called Christian virtues of humility, love, charity, personal freedom, the strong prohibitions against violence, murder, stealing, lying, cruelty — all these are washed away by war. The greatest hero is the one who kills the most people. Glamorous exploits in successful lying and mass stealing and heroic vengeance are rewarded with decorations and public acclaim. You cannot, when the war is

proclaimed, pull a switch and turn the community from the moral code of peace to that of war and then, when the armistice is signed, pull another switch and reconnect the whole society with its old moral regulations again. Thousands of people of all ranks who have found a relish in the morals of war come back to you with these rudimentary instincts controlling their behavior while thousands of others, trapped in a sort of no man's land between these two moralities, come back to you poisoned by cynicism.

—*As We Go Marching*

General H.W. Halleck

The Bible nowhere prohibits war. In the Old Testament we find war and even conquest positively commanded, and although war was raging in the world in the time of Christ and His apostles, still they said not a word of its unlawfulness and immorality.

—*Elements of Military Art and Science*

Adolf Hitler

Pacifism is simply undisguised cowardice.

—Speech at Nurnberg, August 21, 1926

Senator Hiram Johnson

The first casualty when war comes is truth.

Samuel Johnson

Among the calamaties of war may be justly numbered the diminution of the love of truth by the falsehoods which interest dictates and credulity encourages. A peace will equally leave the warrior and the relater of wars destitute of employment; and I know not whether more is to be dreaded from streets filled with soldiers accustomed to plunder, or from garrets filled with scribblers accustomed to lie.

—*Lives of the English Poets*

Alphonse Karr

The age for military service has arrived, and every young man has to submit to the arbitrary orders of some rascal or ignoramus; he must believe that nobility and greatness consist in renouncing his own will and becoming the tool of another's will, in slashing and in getting himself slashed, in suffering from hunger, thirst, rain, and cold; in being mutilated without knowing why and without any other reward than a glass of brandy on the day of battle and the promise of something impalpable and fictitious—immortality after death, and glory given or refused by the pen of some journalist in his warm room.

A gun is fired. He falls wounded, his comrades finish him off by trampling over him. He is buried half alive and then he may enjoy immortality. He for whom he had given his happiness, his sufferings, and his very life, never knew him. And years later someone comes to collect his whitened bones, out of which they make paint and English blacking for cleaning his general's boots.

— quoted by Tolstoy in *Bethink Yourselves*

Guy de Maupassant

War is held in greater esteem than ever. A skilled proficient in this business, that murderer of genius, von Moltke, once replied to some peace delegates in the following terrible words:

"War is sacred, it is instituted by God, it is one of the divine laws of the world, it upholds in men all the great and noble sentiments — honor, self-sacrifice, virtue and courage. It is war alone that saves men from falling into the grossest materialism."

To assemble four hundred thousand men in herds, to march night and day without rest, with no time to think, read, or study, without being of the least use to anybody, wallowing in filth, sleeping in mud, living like animals in continual stupefaction, sacking towns, burning villages, ruining the whole population, and then meeting similar masses of human flesh and falling upon them, shedding rivers of blood, strewing the fields with mangled bodies mixed with mud and blood; losing arms and legs and having brains blown out for no benefit to anyone and dying somewhere on a field while your old parents and your wife and children are perishing of hunger — that is called saving men from falling into the grossest materialism!

— quoted by Tolstoy in *Bethink Yourselves*

War! When I but think of this word, I feel bewildered, as though they were speaking to me of sorcery, of the Inquisition, of a distant, finished, abominable, monstrous, unnatural thing.

When they speak to us of cannibals, we smile proudly, as we proclaim our superiority to these savages. Who are the real savages? Those who struggle in order to eat those whom they vanquish, or those who struggle merely to kill?

— *Sur l'Eau*

Montesquieu

Every monarch keeps on a war footing all the troops which he might need in case his people were in danger of being exterminated, and this state of tension, of all against all, is called peace.

Alfred Nobel

Perhaps my dynamite plants will put an end to war sooner than your [pacifist] congresses. On the day two army corps can annihilate each other in one second all civilized nations will recoil from war in horror.

— at a pacifist congress in Switzerland, 1892

Wilhelm Reich

The working masses of men and women, they and they alone, are responsible for everything that takes place, the good things and the bad things. True enough, they suffer most from a war, but it is their apathy, craving for authority, etc., that is most responsible for making wars possible. It follows of necessity from this responsibility that *the working masses of men and women, they and they alone, are capable of establishing lasting peace.*

— *The Mass Psychology of Fascism*

Under the influence of politicians, masses of people tend to ascribe the responsibility for wars to those who wield power at any given time. In World War I it was the munitions industrialists; in World War II it was the psychopathic generals who were said to be guilty. *This is passing the buck. The responsibility for wars falls solely upon the shoulders of these same masses of people, for they have all the necessary means to avert war in their own hands.* In part by their apathy, in part by their passivity, and in part actively, these same masses of people make possible the catastrophes under which they themselves suffer more than anyone else. *To stress this guilt on the part of the masses of people, to hold them solely responsible, means to take them seriously.* On the other hand, to commiserate masses of people as victims, means to treat them as small, helpless children. The former is the attitude held by genuine freedom fighters; the latter that attitude held by the power-thirsty politicians.

— *Ibid.*

Percy Bysshe Shelley

Man's evil nature, that apology
Which kings who rule, and cowards who crouch, set up
For their unnumbered crimes, sheds not the blood
Which desolates the discord-wasted land.
From kings and priests and statesmen war arose,
Whose safety is man's deep unbettered woe,
Whose grandeur his debasement. Let the axe
Strike at the root, the poison-tree will fall.

— *Queen Mab*

War is the statesman's game, the priest's delight,
The lawyer's jest, the hired assassin's trade.

— *Ibid.*

General Wm. T. Sherman

I begin to regard the death and mangling of a couple thousand men as a small affair, a kind of morning dash — and it may be well that we become so hardened.

— Letter to his wife, July 1864

Elizabeth Cady Stanton

Who can sum up all the ills the women of a nation suffer from war? They have all of the misery

Anonymously produced graphic found in many anarchist periodicals

and none of the glory; nothing to mitigate their weary waiting and watching for the loved ones who return no more.

— *Eighty years and More*

Theodorus

It is not reasonable that a wise man should hazard himself for his country, and endanger wisdom for a set of fools.

— quoted by American Atheists

Henry David Thoreau

Only the defeated and deserters go to war.

— *Walden*

Heinrich von Treitschke

We have learned to recognize as the civilizing majesty of war precisely what appears to the superficial observer to be brutality and inhumanity.

— *Politics*

Man must not only be ready to sacrifice his life, but also the natural deeply rooted feelings of the human soul; he must devote his whole ego for the furtherance of a great patriotic idea: that is the moral sublimity of war.

— Ibid.

Without war no State could be. All those we know of arose through war, and the protection of their members by armed force remains their primary and essential task. War, therefore, will endure to the end of history, as long as there is a multiplicity of States.

— Ibid.

It is indeed political idealism which fosters war, whereas materialism rejects it. What a perversion of morality to want to banish heroism from human life.

— Ibid.

Voltaire

God is always on the side of the heaviest battalions.

— Letter to M. de Riche

Colin Ward

The expendability factor has increased by being transferred from the specialised, scarce and expensively trained military personnel to the amorphous civilian population. American strategists have calculated the proportion of civilians killed in this century's major wars. In the First World War 5 per cent of those killed were civilians, in the Second World War 48 per cent, while in a Third World War 90–95 per cent would be civilians.

— *Anarchy in Action*

Simone Weil

The great error of nearly all studies of war, an error into which all socialists have fallen, has been to consider war as an episode in foreign politics when it is especially an act of internal politics, and the most atrocious act of all . . .

Since the directing apparatus has no other way of fighting the enemy than by sending its own soldiers, under compulsion, to their death — the war of one State against another State resolves itself into a war of the State and the military apparatus against its own people.

— *Politics,* 1945

Woodrow Wilson

Once lead this people into war and they'll forget there ever was such a thing as tolerance. To fight you must be brutal and ruthless and the spirit of ruthless brutality will enter into the very fiber of our national life, infecting Congress, the courts, the policeman on the beat, the man in the street.

— five days prior to asking Congress to declare war on Germany in 1917 (quoted by Phillip Knightley in *The First Casualty*)

Fred Woodworth

It seems like such a terrible shame that innocent civilians have to get hurt in wars, otherwise combat would be such a wonderfully healthy way to rid the human race of unneeded trash.

Anonymous

After a war, a hero is just a man with one leg.

Property

Ambrose Bierce

LAND, A part of the earth's surface, considered as property. The theory that land is property subject to private ownership and control is the foundation of modern society, and is eminently worthy of the superstructure. Carried to its logical conclusion, it means that some have the right to prevent others from living; for the right to own implies the right exclusively to occupy; and in fact laws of trespass are enacted wherever property in land is recognized. It follows that if the whole area of *terra firma* is owned by A, B, and C, there will be no place for D, E, F and G to be born, or, born as trespassers, to exist.

— *The Devil's Dictionary*

Ralph Waldo Emerson

Things are in the saddle,
and ride mankind.

— *Ode*

Henry George

You buy a coat, a horse, a house; there you are paying the seller for labor exerted, for something that he has produced, or that he has got from the man who did produce it; but when you pay a man for land, what are you paying him for? You are paying for something that no man has produced; you pay him for something that was here before man was, or for a value that was created not by him individually, but by the community of which you are a part.

— *The Crime of Poverty*

The equal right of all men to the use of land is as clear as their equal right to breathe the air—it is a right proclaimed by the fact of their existence. For we cannot suppose that some men have a right to be in this world and others no right.

The recognition of individual proprietorship of land is the denial of the natural rights of other individuals—it is a wrong which must show itself in the inequitable division of wealth. For as labor cannot produce without the use of land, the denial of the equal right to the use of land is necessarily the denial of the right of labor to its own produce. If

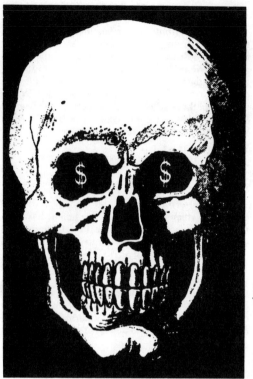

Graphic from *The Match!*

one man can command the land upon which others must labor, he can appropriate the produce of their labor as the price of his permission to labor...The one receives without producing; the others produce without receiving. The one is unjustly enriched; the others are robbed.

— *Progress and Poverty*

As for the deduction of a complete and exclusive individual right to land from priority of occupation, that is, if possible, the ᐧmost absurd ground on which land ownership can be defended...

Has the first comer at a banquet the right to turn back all the chairs and claim that none of the other guests shall partake of the food provided, except as they make terms with him?

— Ibid.

Robert Ingersoll

...the moment a man gets money, so many men are trying to get it away from him that in a little while he regards the whole human race as his enemy, and he generally thinks that they could be rich too if they only attend to business as he has. Understand, I am not blaming these people...We must remember that these rich men are naturally produced. Do not blame them. Blame the system.

— *A Lay Sermon*

Few rich men own their property; their property owns them.

— Speech in New York, October 29, 1896

Pope Leo XIII

...private property must be held sacred and inviolable.

— *Rerum Novarum*

Karl Marx

You are horrified at our intending to do away with private property. But in your existing society private property is already done away for nine-tenths of the population; its existence for the few is solely due to its nonexistence in the hands of those nine-tenths. You reproach us, therefore, with intending to do away with a form of property, the necessary condition for whose existence is the nonexistence of any property for the immense majority of society.

— *Communist Manifesto*

Lewis Henry Morgan

Centralize property in the hands of a few and the millions are under bondage to property — a bondage as absolute and deplorable as if their limbs were covered with manacles. Abstract all property from the hands of labor and you thereby reduce labor to dependence; and that dependence becomes as complete a servitude as the master could fix upon his slave.

— *Diffusion Against Civilization*

Swami Nirmalananda

Where wealth accumulates, men decay.

— *Enlightened Anarchism*

Pierre Joseph Proudhon

Property is theft.

— *What Is Property?*

Poverty will always exist! Yes, so long as property does.

— Ibid.

David Ricardo

The interest of the landlords is always opposed to the interest of every other class in the community.

Jean Jacques Rousseau

The first man who, having enclosed a piece of ground, bethought himself of saying *This is mine*, and found people simple enough to believe him, was the real founder of civil society. From how many crimes, wars and murders, from how many horrors and misfortunes might not anyone have saved mankind, by pulling up the stakes or filling up the ditch, and crying to his fellows, "Beware of listening to this impostor; you are undone if you once forget that the fruits of the earth belong to us all, and the earth itself to nobody."

— *A Discourse on the Origin of Inequality*

George Bernard Shaw

He who gives money he has not earned is generous with other people's labor.

— *Maxims for Revolutionists*

Hiram Stafford

Individual possession is the great entering wedge, which has split society into eight hundred million fragments...It virtually, practically, and theoretically denies the brotherhood of man.

— *The Liberator,* September 8, 1844

Tecumseh

Sell a country! Why not sell the air, the clouds, and the great sea as well as the earth?

— Speech to General Harrison

Leo Tolstoy

...all the prerogatives of the rich, all their luxury, all that superfluity which the rich enjoy above the average laborer, all that is acquired and supported only by torture, incarcerations, and executions.

— *The Kingdom of God Is Within You*

But the men who enjoy prerogatives which are the result of old violence, frequently forget, and like to forget, how these prerogatives were obtained. We need, however, only think of history, not the history of the successes of various dynasties or rulers, but real history, the history of the oppression of the majority by a small minority, to see that the bases of all the prerogatives of the rich over the poor have originated from nothing but whips, prisons, hard labor and murder.

— Ibid.

Oscar Wilde

There is only one class in the community that thinks more about money than the rich, and that is the poor. The poor can think of nothing else. That is the misery of being poor.

— *The Soul of Man Under Socialism*

...the recognition of private property has really harmed Individualism, and obscured it, by confusing a man with what he possesses. It has led In-

Graphic by Tomasz Stepien

Fred Woodworth

Renting, the collection of rents, and the relations of landlords and tenants are, respectively, among the most humiliating, vicious and deplorable interactions that the human race, to its sorrow, has devised.

For the landlord, all healthy striving has... ceased; like a sluggish python digesting a deer, the propertied class swells and snores, its pudgy thumbs hooked in rolls of foul-smelling, unwashed fat. Unearned income breeds complacency; complacency breeds mental stultification, and this last evokes greed for more unearned income.

That tastelessness, ignorance, and oafish busybodyism are common traits in landlords, will have been observed by anyone who has ever had the misfortune to have to rent a dwelling-place.

Landlordism actually adds nothing to the world in the sense of bringing into being, through *work*, something that wasn't there before. It is merely a legalized swindle...

The slogan of the National Association of Landlords is the commaless "We Shelter You America." The truth of the matter is, however, that landlords shelter no one, while in fact the *law* shelters *them*... from the immediate expropriation that would occur if there were not force of gun and jail to back up this phoney, abusive, so-called property right.

Landlords have no rights—they forfeit them by engaging in a criminal enterprise, for which seizure of dwellings by those who actually live in them, and complete discontinuance of paying of "rents," are the only remedies.

— above quotations from *Rent: An Injustice*

dividualism entirely astray. It has made gain, not growth, its aim. So that man thought that the important thing is to have, and did not know that the important thing is to be.

—Ibid.

Man will kill himself by overwork in order to secure property, and really, considering the enormous advantages that property brings, one is hardly surprised. One's regret is that society should be constructed on such a basis that man has been forced into a groove in which he cannot freely develop what is wonderful, and fascinating, and delightful in him—in which, in fact, he misses the true pleasure and joy of living.

—Ibid.

With the abolition of private property, then, we shall have true, beautiful healthy Individualism. Nobody will waste his life in accumulating things, and the symbols for things. One will live. To live is the rarest thing in the world. Most people exist, that is all.

—Ibid.

Mary Wollstonecroft

From the respect paid to property flow, as from a poisoned fountain, most of the evils and vices which render this world such a dreary scene to the contemplative mind.

—*A Vindication of the Rights of Women*

John Wycliffe

Lords devour poor men's goods in gluttony and waste and pride, and they perish for mischief and thirst and cold, and their children also...And so in a manner they eat and drink poor men's flesh and blood.

Capitalism

Alexander Berkman

There is a continuous warfare between capital and labor. That warfare generally proceeds within so-called legal forms. But even these erupt now and then in violence, as during strikes and lockouts, because the armed fist of government is always at the service of the masters, and that fist gets into action the moment capital feels its profits threatened: then it drops the mask of "mutual interests" and "partnership" with labor and resorts to the final argument of every master, to coercion and force.

— *What Is Communist Anarchism?*

The law says that your employer does not steal anything from you, because it is done with your consent. You have agreed to work for your boss for certain pay, he to have all that you produce. Because you *consented* to it, the law says that he does not steal anything from you.

But did you really consent?

When the highwayman holds his gun to your head, you turn your valuables over to him. You "consent" all right...

Are you not compelled to work for an employer? Your need compels you, just as the highwayman's gun.

— Ibid.

The money hunger grows on what it feeds...

So everyone is compelled to take part in the wild goose chase, and the hunger for possession gets ever stronger hold of man. It becomes the most important part of life; every thought is on money, all the energies are bent on getting rich, and presently the thirst for wealth becomes a mania, a madness that possesses those who have and those who have not.

...existence has become an unreasoning, wild dance around the golden calf, a mad worship of God Mammon. In that dance and in that worship man has sacrificed all his finer qualities of heart and soul—kindness and justice, honor and manhood, compassion and sympathy with his fellowman.

Each for himself and devil take the hindmost... Is it any wonder that in this mad money chase are developed the worst traits of man—greed, envy, hatred, and the basest passions? Man grows corrupt and evil; he becomes mean and unjust; he resorts to deceit, theft, and murder.

— Ibid.

Ambrose Bierce

COMMERCE, A kind of transaction in which A plunders from B the goods of C, and for compensation B picks the pocket of D of money belonging to E.

CORPORATION, An ingenious device for obtaining profit without individual responsibility.

OCCIDENT, The part of the world lying west (or east) of the Orient. It is largely inhabited by Christians, a powerful subtribe of the Hypocrites, whose principal industries are murder and cheating, which they are pleased to call "war" and "commerce." These, also, are the principal industries of the Orient.

RESTITUTION, The founding or endowing of universities and public libraries by gift or bequest.

— above definitions from *The Devil's Dictionary*

Al Capone

This American system of ours, call it Americanism, call it capitalism, call it what you like, gives each and every one of us a great opportunity if we only seize it with both hands and make the most of it.

— attributed

Thomas Carlyle

It is not to die, nor even to die of hunger that makes a man wretched. Many men have died; all men must die. But it is to live miserable, we know not why; to work sore, and yet gain nothing; to be heart-worn, weary, yet isolated, unrelated, girt in with a cold, universal *Laissez-faire*.

— quoted by Jack London in *The People of the Abyss*

With our Mammon-Gospel we have come to strange conclusions. We call it a Society; and go about professing openly the totalest separation, isolation. Our life is not a mutual helpfulness; but rather, cloaked under due laws-of-war, named "fair competition" and so forth, it is a mutual hostility. We have profoundly forgotten everywhere that *Cash-payment* is not the sole relation of human beings;...

— *Past and Present*

To a deadened soul, seared with the brute Idolatry of Sense, to whom going to Hell is equivalent to not making money, all "promises" and moral duties that cannot be pleaded for in Courts of Requests, address themselves in vain. Money he can be ordered to pay, but nothing more. I have not heard in all Past History, and expect not to hear in all Future History, of any Society anywhere under God's Heaven supporting itself on such Philosophy.
— Ibid.

Confucius

The superior man understands what is right; the inferior man understands what will sell.

Eugene V. Debs

I would not be a capitalist, I would be a man; you cannot be both at the same time.

The capitalist class exists by exploitation, lives out of the labor, that is to say the life, of the workingman; consumes him, and his code of morals and standard of ethics justify it and this proves that capitalism is cannibalism.

A man, honest, just, high-minded, would scorn to live out of the sweat and sorrow of his fellowman — by preying upon his weaker brother.

We [propose] to destroy the capitalist and save the man. We want a system in which the worker shall get what he produces and the capitalist shall produce what he gets.
— Speech, December 10, 1905

The capitalists own the tools they do not use, and the workers use the tools they do not own.
— Ibid.

...the capitalist whose agent buys your labor power...cares no more about the color of your hide than does Armour about that of the steers he buys in the cattle market.
— *International Socialist Review*, January 1904

Let no one charge that socialists have arrayed class against class in this struggle. That has been done long since in the evolution of capitalist society. One class is small and rich and the other large and poor. One wants more profit and the other more wages. One consists of capitalists and the other of workers. These two classes are at war. Every day of peace is at the expense of labor. There can be no peace and good will between these two essentially antagonistic economic classes.
— *The Comrade*, November 1904

Capitalism is proud of its prisons which fitly symbolize the character of its institutions and constitute one of the chief elements in its philanthropy.

Capitalism is inherently a criminal system for it is based upon the robbery of the working class and cornerstoned in its slavery. The title deed held by the capitalist class to the tools used by the working class is also the title deed to their liberty and their lives.

Adolf Fischer

The strongest bulwark of the capitalist system is the ignorance of its victims.
— Courtroom speech at Haymarket trial

Big Bill Heywood

For every dollar the boss has and didn't work for, one of us worked for a dollar and didn't get it.

Robert Ingersoll

Don't you know that if people could bottle the air they would? Don't you know that there would be an American Air-bottling Association? And don't you know that they would allow thousands and millions to die for want of breath, if they could not pay for air? I am not blaming anybody. I am just telling how it is.
— *A Lay Sermon*

Reggie Jackson

For the right amount of money, you're willing to eat Alpo.
— quoted in *The Sporting News*, February 1, 1988

Errico Malatesta

The capitalist is a thief who has succeeded through his efforts or those of his ancestors; the common thief is a would-be capitalist, who is simply waiting to become one in fact, to live, without working, on the proceeds of his hauls, that is, on the work of others.
— *Il Pensiero*, March 16, 1911

It is true that the professional thief is also a victim of the social environment. The example set by his superiors, his educational background, and the disgusting conditions in which many people are obliged to work, easily explain why some men, who are not morally better than their contemporaries, finding themselves with the choice of being exploiters or exploited choose the former and seek to become exploiters with the means they are capable of. But these extenuating circumstances could equally be applied to the capitalists; but in doing so one only demonstrates more clearly the basic identity of the two professions.
— Ibid.

Those who envision a society of well-stuffed pigs that waddle contentedly under the rod of a small number of swineherds; who do not take into account the need for freedom and the sentiment of human dignity; who really believe in a god who orders, for his own abstruse ends, the poor to be submissive and the rich to be good and charitable — can also imagine and aspire to a technical age of

Graphic from Processed World

production which assures abundance to all and is at the same time materially advantageous to both bosses and workers.

— *Umanita Nova,* May 10, 1886

Karl Marx

Capital is dead labor that, vampire-like, lives only by sucking living labor, and lives the more, the more labor that it sucks.

— *Capital*

Capitalist production is not merely the production of commodities; it is essentially the production of surplus value.

— Ibid.

All suprplus value, whatever particular (profits, interest, or rent) it may subsequently crystalize into, is in substance the materialization of unpaid labor.

— Ibid.

The bourgeoisie, wherever it has gotten the upper hand, has put an end to all feudal, patriarchal, idyllic relations. It has pitilessly torn asunder the motley feudal ties that bound man to his "natural superiors," and has left no other nexus between

man and man than naked self-interest, that callous "cash payment." It has drowned the most heavenly ecstasies of religious fervor, of chivalrous enthusiasm, of Philistine sentimentalism, in the icy water of egotistical calculation. It has resolved personal worth into exchange value, and in place of the numberless indefeasible chartered freedoms, has set up that single, unconscionable freedom — Free Trade. In one word, for exploitation veiled by religious and political illusions, it has substituted naked, shameless, direct, brutal exploitation.

— *Communist Manifesto*

Michel de Montaigne

No man can profit except by the loss of others, and by this reasoning all manner of profit must be condemned.

— *Essays*

Johann Most

The life of the poor man is valued as nothing by the rich. As the owner of ships he places the lives of entire crews in jeopardy when his object is to fraudulently obtain high insurance for half-decayed hulks. Bad ventilation, deep excavation, defective supports, etc., etc., annually bring death to thousands of miners, but this system of operation saves expenses, therefore augments the gains, and gives the mine owners no occasion to be sorry. Neither does the factory-pasha care how many of "his" laborers are torn and rent apart by machinery, poisoned by chemicals, or slowly suffocated by dirt and dust. Profit is the main thing.

— *The Beast of Property*

Wilhelm Reich

A touch of dishonesty is part of the very existence of private merchandising. When a peasant buys a horse, he runs it down in every possible way. If he sells the same horse a year later, it will have become younger, better, and stronger...One's own commodity will always be the best — the other person's the worst. Depreciation of one's competitors — a deprecation that is usually devoid of all honesty — is an essential of one's "business."

— *The Mass Psychology of Fascism*

The small businessman's obsequious and deferential behavior toward his customers, testifies to the fierce pressure of economic existence, which has to warp the best character in the long run.

— Ibid.

David Ricardo

There is no way of keeping profits up but by keeping wages down.

— *On Protection of Agriculture*

Rudolf Rocker

When capital becomes a monoploy, it is able to produce, but only by artificial means since its owner does not do productive work, but by using his economic superiority forces the producer to surrender a portion of the product of his labor for the use of land, the means of production or the loan of money.

— *Pioneers of American Freedom*

The contractor who exploits the economic needs of the workers and robs them of a portion of the product of their labor; the owner of a piece of land which he did not create and who, by virtue of his monopoly, leases it and pockets the rent from it; the money-lender who lends to the producer the sum which the latter needs for his business, and who charges interest on it — all these live at the expense and on the labor of others without creating themselves any social value. By making the need for a product the key to its price, a system of exchange is created which subjects the great masses of the people to the economic control of a privileged minority. As a consequence, in all other matters as well, the free self-determination of one's own individuality becomes impossible.

— *Pioneers of American Freedom* (explaining Josiah Warren's economic theories)

Franklin D. Roosevelt

The true conservative seeks to protect the system of private property and free enterprise by correcting such injustices and inequalities as arise from it. The most serious threat to our institutions comes from those who refuse to face the need for change. Liberalism becomes the protection for the far-sighted conservative.

— Speech to New York Democratic Convention, September 30, 1936

Percy Bysshe Shelley

Commerce has set the mark of selfishness,
The signet of its all-enslaving power,
Upon a shining ore and called it gold.

— *Queen Mab*

Herbert Spencer

Honest: The Road to Bankruptcy

— *The Morals of Trade* (subhead)

Conscience: A Barrier to Success

— Ibid.

Lysander Spooner

This business of lending blood-money is one of the most thoroughly sordid, cold-blooded, and criminal that was ever carried on, to any considerable extent, amongst human beings. It is like lending money to slave traders, or to common robbers and pirates, to be repaid out of their plunder. And the men who loan money to governments, so called, for the purpose of enabling the latter to rob, enslave, and murder their people, are among the greatest villains that the world has ever seen. And they as much deserve to be hunted and killed (if they cannot otherwise be got rid of) as any slave traders, robbers, or pirates that ever lived.

— *No Treason*

Charles T. Sprading

Economists are agreed that there are four methods by which wealth is acquired by those who do not produce it. These are: interest, profit, rent and taxes, each of which is based upon special privilege, and all are gross violations of the principle of equal liberty.

— *Liberty and the Great Libertarians*

Robert Louis Stevenson

The price we have to pay for money is paid in liberty.

Robert Tefton

FREE ENTERPRISE, n. A system in which a few are born with millions in the bank, most are born with nothing, and all compete to accumulate wealth. If those born with nothing fail, it is due to their personality defects.

LIFE INSURANCE, n. A form of gambling in which the bettor wins if s/he dies before the insurer wagers that s/he will.

SELF-MADE MAN, n. A businessman with a fortune of $10 million who started life under the handicap of inheriting a mere $1 million.

Leo Tolstoy

It is said that the law protects the property of the owner of a factory, the capitalist, the landowner, and the factory hand and agricultural laborer. The equality of the capitalist and the laborer is the same as the equality of two fighters, when the hands of one are bound, while a gun is put into the hands of the other, and equal conditions are strictly observed for both in the fight.

— *The Slavery of Our Times*

Mark Twain

There are two times in a man's life when he should not speculate: when he can't afford it, and when he can.

— *Following the Equator*

Certainly there is no nobler field for human effort than the insurance line of business — especially accident insurance. Ever since I have been a director in an accident insurance company I have felt that I am a better man. Life has seemed more precious. Accidents have assumed a kindlier aspect. Distressing special providences have lost half their horror. I look upon a cripple now with affectionate interest — as an advertisement. I do not seem to care for poetry any more. I do not care for politics — even agriculture does not excite me. But to me now there is a charm about a railway collision that is unspeakable.

— *Accident Insurance* (Speech)

October. This is one of the peculiarly dangerous months to speculate in stocks in. The others are July, January, September, April, November, May, March, June, December, August, and February.

— *Pudd'nhead Wilson*

W.H. Vanderbilt

The public be damned.

'Covers The Earth'

Graphic from The Match!

Thorstein Veblen

The highest achievement in business is the nearest approach in getting something for nothing... The less any given business concern can contrive to give for what it gets, the more profitable its own traffic will be. Business success means "getting the best of the bargain."

— attributed

Colin Ward

Industry is not dominated by technical expertise, but by the sales-manager, the accountant and the financial tycoon who never made anything in their lives except money.

— *Anarchy in Action*

Anonymous & Multiple Author

Once you give up integrity, the rest is a piece of cake.

— TV character J.R. Ewing (*Dallas*), quoted in the *San Francisco Chronicle,* March 22, 1987

People love shit.

— "Chet," cutout record salesman, comment to the editor of this volume, 1985

If you want to know what God thinks of money, look at the people he gives it to.

— anonymous

Never Give A Sucker An Even Break

— Title of a W.C. Fields movie

Books for the price of a politician!

— Sign on Bob's Used Books and Records, San Francisco (now Bob's Video, but still open 364 days a year — closed on Nixon's birthday.)

Labor

Michael Bakunin

Slavery may change its form or its name—its essence remains the same. Its essence may be expressed in these words: to be a slave is to be forced to work for someone else, just as to be a master is to live on someone else's work. In antiquity... slaves were, in all honesty, called slaves. In the Middle Ages, they took the name of serfs; nowadays they are called wage earners.

— *Federalism, Socialism, Anti-Theologism*

Alexander Berkman

The conditions of your life, even what you eat and drink, where you go and with whom you associate—it all *depends on your wages.*

No you are not a free man. You are *dependent* on your employer and on your wages. You are really a wage slave.

The expropriation of the capitalist class during the social revolution—the taking over of the industries—requires tactics directly the reverse of those you now use in a strike. In the latter you quit work and leave the boss in full possession of the mill, factory, or mine. It is an idiotic proceeding, of course, for you give the master the entire advantage: he can put scabs in your place, and you remain out in the cold.

In expropriating, on the contrary, you *stay on the job and put the boss out.* He may remain only on equal terms with the rest: a worker among workers.

Whenever they can, the union leaders will dissuade you from striking, and sometimes even directly prevent and forbid it. They will outlaw your organization if you go on strike without their consent. But if the pressure is too strong for them to resist they will graciously "authorize" the strike. Just imagine—you work hard and from your scanty earnings you support the union officials who should serve you, yet you have to get *their* permission to improve your condition!

It is clear that your interests as a worker are *different* from the interests of your capitalistic masters. More than different: they are entirely opposite; in fact, contrary, antagonistic to each other. The better wages the boss pays you, the less profit he makes out of you. It does not require great philosophy to understand that.

...the ordinary conservative union stands, as we have seen, for capitalism and for everything connected with it. It takes it for granted that you are a worker and that you are going to stay one, and that things must remain as they are. It asserts that all the union can do is to help you get a little better wages, cut down your hours of work, and improve the conditions under which you toil. It considers the employer a business partner, as it were, and it makes contracts with him. But it never questions why one of the partners—the boss—gets rich from that kind of contract, while the other partner, the worker, always remains poor, labors hard, and dies a wage slave. It doesn't seem to be an equal partnership, somehow. It looks more like a confidence game, doesn't it?

Well, it is. It is a game in which one side does all the pulling of the chestnuts out of the fire, while the other side takes possession of them. [It's] a very unequal partnership, and all the striking of the workers is merely to beg or compel the capitalistic partner to give up a few chestnuts out of his big heap. [It's] a skin game, for all that even when the worker succeeds in getting a few extra nuts.

Yet they **speak** to you of your dignity, of the "dignity of labor." Can you think of any greater insult? You **slave** for the masters all your life, you serve them and keep them in comfort and luxury, you let them lord it over you, and in their hearts they laugh at you and despise you for your stupidity—and then they talk to you of your "dignity."

[Strikes] are of great value: they teach the worker the vital need of cooperation, of standing shoulder to shoulder with his fellows and unitedly fighting in the common cause. Strikes train him in the class struggle and develop his spirit of joint responsibility. In this sense even an unsuccessful strike is not a complete loss. Through it the toilers learn that "an injury to one is an injury to all."

— above quotes from *What Is Communist Anarchism?*

Ambrose Bierce

LABOR, One of the processes by which A acquires property for B.

— *The Devil's Dictionary*

C.C. Colton

Subdivision of labor improves the art, but debilitates the artist, and converts the man into a mere breathing part of that machinery by which he works.

— *Lacon*

Calvin Coolidge

When more and more people are thrown out of work, unemployment results.

— quoted by Howard Zinn in *A People's History of the United States*

Eugene V. Debs

...the labor movement means more, infinitely more than a paltry increase in wages and the strike necessary to secure it; that while it engages to do all that can be done to better the working conditions of its members, its higher object is to overthrow the capitalist system of private ownership of the tools of labor, abolish wage-slavery and achieve the freedom of the whole working class, and, in fact, all of mankind...

— quoted by Zinn in *A People's History of the United States*

In capitalist society you are the lower class; the capitalists are the upper class—because they are on your backs; if they were not on your backs, they could not be above you.

— Speech, December 10, 1905

The American Federation [of Labor] does not learn by experience. They...are going to petition Congress to restrict the power of the courts; that is to say, they are going to once more petition a capitalist Congress to restrict the power of the capitalist courts. That is as if a flock of sheep were to petition a pack of wolves to extract their own fangs.

— Ibid.

When the working class unites, there will be a lot of jobless labor leaders.

— Ibid.

When we have ventured to say that the time would come when the working class would rule, they [capitalists] have bluntly answered "Never! It requires brains to rule." The workers of course have none. And they certainly try to prove it by proudly supporting the political parties of their masters under whose administration they are kept in poverty and servitude.

— Speech, June 16, 1918

Men do not shrink from work, but from slavery. The man who works primarily for the benefit of another does so only under compulsion, and work so done is the very essence of slavery.

Ricardo Flores Magon

That which we at present call laziness is, rather, the disgust which men feel over breaking their backs for beggars' salaries and being, moreover, looked down upon and depreciated by the class which exploits them—while those who do nothing useful live like princes and are deferred to and respected by all.

— *Regeneración,* April 4, 1914

Workers are like lemons: When the rich have sucked out all the juice, they throw them in the garbage.

— *Regeneración,* April 1911

The wage system makes us completely dependent upon the will and caprice of Capital. There is only one difference between you [wage earners] and the slaves of antiquity: the difference is that you have the right to choose your masters.

— Speech on October 16, 1910

Henry George

...there must be human work before any article of wealth can be produced; and, in a natural state of things, the man who toiled honestly and well would be the rich man, and he who did not work would be poor. We have so reversed the order of nature that we are accustomed to think of a working man as a poor man.

— *The Crime of Poverty*

Near the window by which I write a great bull is tethered by a ring in his nose. Grazing round and round he has wound his rope about the stake until now he stands a close prisoner, tantalized by rich grass he cannot reach, unable even to toss his head to rid him of the flies that cluster on his shoulders. Now and again he struggles vainly, and then, after pitiful bellowings, relapses into silent misery.
This bull, a very type of massive strength, who, because he has not wit enough to see how he might be free, suffers want in sight of plenty, and is helplessly preyed upon by weaker creatures, seems to me no unfit emblem of the working masses.
In all lands, men whose toil creates abounding wealth are pinched with poverty, and, while advancing civilization opens wider vistas and awakens new desires, are held down to brute levels by animal needs. Bitterly conscious of injustice, feeling in their inmost souls that they were made for more than so narrow a life, they, too, spasmodically struggle and cry out. But until they trace effect to cause, until they see how they are fettered and how they may be freed, their struggles and outcries are as vain as those of the bull.

— quoted by Sprading in *Liberty and the Great Libertarians*

Emma Goldman

...laziness results either from special privileges, or physical and mental abnormalities. Our present insane system of production fosters both, and the most astounding phenomenon is that people should want to work at all now.

— *Anarchism*

"A school for Communism," said Lenin in the famous controversy on the functions of the trade unions. Quite right. But an antiquated school where the spirit of the child is fettered and crushed. Nowhere in the world are labour organizations so subservient to the will and the dictates of the State as they are in Bolshevik Russia.

— Afterword to *My Further Disillusionment in Russia*

The average worker has no inner point of contact with the industry he is employed in, and he is a stranger to the process of production of which he is a mechanical part. Like any other cog of the machine, he is replaceable at any time by other similar depersonalized human beings.

The intellectual proletarian, though he foolishly thinks himself a free agent, is not much better off. He, too, has as little choice or self-direction, in his particular metier, as his brother who works with his hands. Material considerations and desire for greater social prestige are usually the deciding factors in the vocation of the intellectual. Added to these is the tendency to follow in the footsteps of family tradition, and become doctors, lawyers, teachers, engineers, etc. The groove requires less effort and personality. In consequence nearly everybody is out of place in our present scheme of things. The masses plod on, partly because their senses have been dulled by the deadly routine of work and because they must eke out an existence. This applies with even greater force to the political fabric of today. There is no place in its texture for free choice of independent thought and activity. There is a place only for voting and tax-paying puppets.

— *The Individual, Society and the State*

William B. Greene

Where Labor is merchandise in fact...man is merchandise also...

— *Mutual Banking*

Joe Hill

Don't waste any time in mourning. Organize.

— Letter to Bill Haywood on the eve of Hill's execution by the State of Utah

Robert Ingersoll

Of course, capital can do nothing without the assistance of labor. All there is of value in the world is the product of labor. The laboring man pays all the expenses. No matter whether taxes are laid on luxuries or on the necessities, labor pays every cent.

— *How to Reform Mankind*

V.I. Lenin

The industrial role of the unions, "industrial democracy"...those are sheer trifles when not accompanied by disciplinary courts.

— quoted by Brinton in *The Bolshevlks and Workers Control*

We must raise the question of piece-work and apply and test it in practice.

— Ibid.

Unquestioning submission to a single will is absolutely necessary for the success of labor processes that are based on large-scale machine industry... today the Revolution demands, in the interests of socialism, that the masses *unquestioningly obey the single will* of the leaders of the labor process.

— Ibid.

John L. Lewis

Organize the unorganized.

Jack London

The scab is powerless under terrorism. As a rule, he is not so good nor so gritty a man as the men he is displacing, and he lacks their fighting organization.

— *The Scab*

It is not nice to be a scab. Not only is it not in good social taste and comradeship, but, from the standpoint of food and shelter, it is bad business policy.

— Ibid.

After God had finished the rattlesnake, the toad, the vampire, He had some awful substance left with which He made a scab...A scab is a two-legged animal with a corkscrew soul, a waterlogged brain, a combination backbone of jelly and glue. Where others have hearts, he carries a tumor of rotten principles.

— *A Scab*

No man has a right to scab so long as there is a pool of water to drown his carcass in, or a rope long enough to hang his body with. Judas Iscariot was a gentleman compared with a scab. For betraying his master, he had character enough to hang himself. A scab has not.

— Ibid.

Esau sold his birthright for a mess of pottage. Judas Iscariot sold his Savior for thirty pieces of silver. Benedict Arnold sold his country for a promise of a commission in the British Army. The modern strikebreaker sells his birthright, his country, his wife, his children and his fellow men for an unful-filled promise from his employer, trust or corporation.

— Ibid.

Errico Malatesta

Is it to be wondered at that folks are disgusted with work and are eager to seize any opportunity to do nothing? But when work is done under conditions fit for human beings, for a reasonable time and according to the laws of health; when the worker knows that he is working for the well being of his family and of all men; when everyone who wishes to be respected must necessarily be a worker... who will then wish to forego the joy of knowing himself useful and beloved so that he may live in an idleness disastrous to his body and mind alike?

— A Talk About Anarchism

Through the organizations established for the defense of their interests, workers acquire an awareness of the oppression under which they live and of the antagonisms which divide them from their employers, and so begin to aspire to a better life, get used to collective struggle and to solidarity, and can succeed in winning those improvements which are compatible with the continued existence of the capitalist and statist regime. Later, when the conflict is beyond solution, there is either revolution or reaction.

— Risveglio, October 1, 1915

Let us take the American Federation of Labor in the United States. It does not carry on a struggle against the bosses except in the sense that two business men struggle when they are discussing the details of a contract. The real struggle is conducted against the newcomers, the foreigners or natives who seek to be allowed to work...

— Umanita Nova, April 13, 1922

One can accept the status quo, recognize the legitimacy of economic privilege and the government that defends it, and be content to maneuver between the different bourgeois factions and obtain some improvements — as happens with the huge organizations which are inspired by no ideal, such as the American Federation of Labor and a large part of the British unions — and then one becomes in practice the tool of the oppressors and gives up the task of freeing oneself from servitude.

— Pensiero e Volonta, February 16, 1925

Man, like all living beings, adapts himself to the conditions in which he lives, and transmits by inheritance his acquired habits. Thus, being born and having lived in bondage, being the descendant of a long line of slaves, man, when he began to think, believed that slavery was an essential condition of life, and liberty seemed to him impossible. In like manner, the workman, forced for centuries to depend upon the good will of his employer for work, that is, for bread, and accustomed to see his own life at the disposal of those who possess the land and capital, has ended in believing that it is his master who gives him food, and asks ingenuously how it would be possible to live, if there were no master over him.

— Anarchy

Karl Marx

He who was the money owner, now strides in front as capitalist; the possessor of labor-power follows as his laborer. The one with an air of importance, smirking, intent on business; the other hesitant, like one who is bringing his own hide to market and has nothing to expect but — a hiding.

— Das Kapital

Richard B. Mellon

You can't mine coal without machine guns.

— Congressional testimony, quoted in Time, June 14, 1937

Johann Most

Not man as such, but man in connection with wealth is a beast of prey. The richer a man, the greater his need for more. We may call such a monster "the beast of property"...

It is the lash of hunger which compels the poor man to submit. In order to live he *must sell* — "voluntarily" *sell* — *himself* every day and hour to the "beast of property."

— The Beast of Property

Lewis Mumford

A society that gives to one class all the opportunities for leisure and to another all the burdens of work condemns both classes to spiritual sterility.

— quoted by Michael Albert and Robin Hahnel in Looking Forward

Max Nordau

The advocates of this plundering of labor by Capital say that the division of this net income of the factory between the capitalist and the laborer would only keep the former poor, while raising the wages of the latter so slightly as to be immaterial, amounting to merely a few pennies a day, divided among so many. A noble, a modest argument forsooth! It is possible that the wages-receiver might receive only a few pennies more a day...But by what right is he obliged to present his employer with even the tiniest share of his daily earnings...? Let us imagine for a moment that every inhabitant of the German Empire were forced by law to pay a penny every year to some Smith or Meyer, not in return for any service performed...but as a simple present...One penny! That is such a small amount that it is not worth the trouble of speaking about it. And yet such a law would elicit from the entire nation a cry of indignation...But the economical law which obliges the poorest part of the nation, the factory employees, to present to this same Smith or Meyer, a contribution of not one cent, but of ten to ...one hundred dollars in the course of a year [this was written in the 1880s]—this law seems quite a matter of course to those who happen to be exempt from its jurisdiction. The injustice is about the same in both cases.

— *Conventional Lies of Our Civilization*

...when an artist sells a painting for a hundred thousand dollars...or a prima donna is paid $5,000 for one evening's performance, these amounts do not represent the price paid by the mass of people as the legitimate and voluntarily proffered reward for individual exertion. They are the mathematical demonstration of the fact that a small number of millionaires are living in the civilized world, with no means of judging of the real value of any work, because their riches are not the result of their own labor; they satisfy every one of their whims without regard to its cost, and fight among themselves... willing to pay any price to satisfy their caprice.

— Ibid.

Albert Parsons

Formerly the master selected the slave; today the slave selects his master...

— *The Philosophy of Anarchism*

Man's legal rights are everywhere in collision with man's natural rights...The only sacred right of property is the natural right of the workingman to the product, which is the creation of his labor. The legal right of the capitalist to rent and interest and profit is the absolute denial of the natural right of labor. Free access to the means of production is the natural right of labor...It is the legal right of the capitalist to refuse such access to labor, and to take from the laborer all the wealth he creates over and above a bare subsistence for allowing him the privilege of working.

— Ibid.

Joseph Medill Patterson

I am talking about myself, the type of the idle, rich young man, not myself the individual. I have an income of between ten and twenty thousand dollars a year. I spend all of it. I produce nothing

— *Confessions of a Drone*

It takes to support me just about twenty times as much as it takes to support an average working man or farmer. And the funny thing about it is that these working men and farmers work hard all year round, while I don't work at all.

— Ibid.

The work of the working people, and nothing else, produces the wealth, which by some hocus-pocus arrangement, is transferred to me, leaving them bare. While they support me in splendid style, what do I do for them? Let the candid upholder of the present order answer, for I am not aware of doing anything for them.

— Ibid.

Wendell Phillips

We affirm as a fundamental principle, that labor, the creator of wealth, is entitled to all it creates.

Affirming this, we avow ourselves willing to accept the final results of the operation of a principle so radical—such as the overthrow of the whole profit-making system, the extinction of all monopolies, the abolition of privileged classes, universal education and fraternity, perfect freedom of exchange, and, best and grandest of all, the final obliteration of that foul stigma upon our so-called Christian civilization—the poverty of the masses... Therefore [let it be] Resolved that we declare war with the wages system, which demoralizes the life of the hirer and the hired, cheats both, and enslaves the workingman; war with the present system of finance, which robs labor, and gorges capital, makes the rich richer and the poor poorer, and turns a republic into an aristocracy of capital;...

— Address to Labor Reform Convention, Worcester, Massachusetts, September 4, 1870

Cheap productions are an unmixed good; cheap labor is an unmitigated evil. Human progress shows itself in a fall of prices and a rise of wages.

— *The Chinese*

Prince Ali Raza

The House of Oudh does not appreciate trade, business and politics. It is better to be in the grip of death rather than in the grip of a job.

— quoted in the *San Francisco Examiner*, Oct. 5, 1986

Max Stirner

The laborers have the most enormous power in their hands, and if they once became thoroughly conscious of it, and used it, nothing would withstand them; they would only have to stop labor, regard the product of labor as theirs, and enjoy it. This is the sense of the labor disturbances which show themselves here and there.

The State rests on the *slavery of labor*. If labor becomes *free*, the State is lost.

— *The Ego and His Own*

Leo Tolstoy

If a slave owner of our time has not an Ivan whom he can send into a privy to clean out his excrements, he has three roubles which are so much wanted by hundreds of Ivans, that he can choose any one out of a hundred Ivans, and appear as a benefactor to him, because he has chosen him out of the whole number and has permitted him to climb into the cesspool...

Slavery exists in full force, but we do not recognize it, just as at the end of the eighteenth century people did not recognize the slavery of serfdom.

— *The Slavery of Our Times*

Leon Trotsky

Is it true that compulsory labor is always unproductive?...This is the most wretched and miserable liberal prejudice: chattel slavery too was productive.

— quoted by Brinton in *The Bolsheviks and Workers Control*

The working class cannot be left wandering all over Russia. They must be thrown here and there, appointed, commanded, just like soldiers.

— Ibid.

Deserters from labor ought to be formed into punitive battalions or put into concentration camps.

— Ibid.

Benjamin Tucker

A just distribution of the products of labor is to be obtained by destroying all sources of income except labor. These sources may be summed up in one word—usury; and the three principal forms of usury are interest, rent, and profit. These all rest upon legal privilege, and the way to destroy them is to destroy legal privilege and monopoly.

— *Instead of a Book*

Nicolas Walter

The principle at issue is that a man may be said to have a right to what he produces by his own labour, but not to what he gets from the labour of others; he has a right to what he needs and uses, but not to what he does not need and cannot use. As soon as a man has more than enough, it either goes to waste or it stops another man having enough.

This means that rich men have no right to their property, for they are rich not because they work a lot but because a lot of people work for them; and poor men have a right to rich men's property, for they are poor not because they work little but because they work for others. Indeed, poor people almost always work longer hours at duller jobs in worse conditions than rich people. No one ever became rich or remained rich through his own labour, only by exploiting the labour of others.

— *About Anarchism*

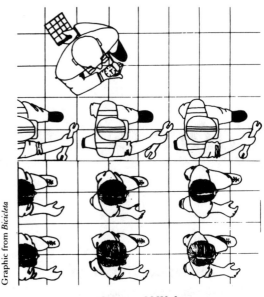

Graphic from *Bicicleta*

Oscar Wilde

Work is the curse of the drinking classes.

Emiliano Zapata

The calloused hands of the fields and of the factories must clasp in fraternal salute because, truly, we workers are invincible; we are the force and we are the right. We are tomorrow.

— *A los obreros de la republica ¡Salud!*

Anonymous & Multiple Author

The working class and the employing class have nothing in common. Between the two a struggle must go on until the workers of the world organize as a class, take possession of the earth and the machinery of production, and abolish the wage system.

— Preamble to the Industrial Workers of the World Constitution, 1905

Work makes you free.

— Inscription over entrance to Auschwitz

The capitalist class seeks...to foster and increase color prejudice and race hatred between the white worker and the black, so as to make their social and economic interests to appear to be separate and antagonistic, in order that the workers of both races may thereby be more easily and completely exploited;...

— "Negro Resolution," 1901 Socialist Party convention

You can't have solidarity with sheep.

— Anonymous

We refuse to buy the right not to die of hunger by running the risk of dying of boredom.

— Graffiti, Paris 1968

Police & Thieves

Alexander Berkman

Why does everyone think that he can be decent enough without the policeman, but that the club is needed for "the others?"

— *What Is Communist Anarchism?*

Mayor Richard Daley

The policeman isn't there to create disorder. He's there to preserve disorder.

— Press conference, 1968, commenting on the police riot at the 1968 Democratic Party National Convention in Chicago

Clarence Darrow

Those who believe in the beneficence of force have never yet agreed upon the crimes that should be forbidden, the method and extent of punishment, the purpose of punishment, nor even its results. They simply agree that without force and violence social life cannot be maintained.

Punishment to terrorize men from violating human order is like the threat of hell to terrorize souls into obedience to the law of God. Both mark primitive society, both are degrading and debasing, and can only appeal to the lower instincts of the lower class of men.

We look back with horror at the criminal courts of England, of Spain, of Italy, even upon our own Puritan judges who sentenced witches to death. These judges were doubtless as intelligent as our own. Their brutal, cruel judgments did not grow from a wicked, perverted heart, but from the fact that they were passing judgment on their fellow man. These unjust judgments are the fruit of the cruel system of force and barbarism which clothes one man with the authority and power to condemn his fellow. All prosecutions are malicious, and all judgments are meted out in anger and hatred.

The true morality of a community does not depend alone upon the number of men who slay their fellows. These at most are very few. The true morality depends upon every deed of kindness or malice, of love or hatred, of charity or cruelty, and the sum of these determine the real character and worth of a community. Any evil consequences that could flow from a casual killing of a human being by an irresponsible man would be like a drop of water in the sea compared with a public execution by the state.

The state which would take life without any hope or expectation that the community would in any way be bettered could not rank even among savage tribes. Such cruelty could only be classed as total depravity.

Let any reasoning being consider the tens of thousands who have been burned, and hanged, and boiled, and otherwise put to death for witchcraft; the millions for heresy; the thousands of noble victims who have suffered for treason; the victims of fire, of torture, of scaffold, 'or rack and dungeon, for all the conceivable crimes since time began. Let him consider the oceans of blood and rivers of tears shed by the force and brutality of the rulers of the world; the cruelty, torture and suffering heaped upon the helpless, the weak, the unfortunate; and then ask himself if he believes that punishment is good. Even could violence ever prevent crime, the brutality, suffering, blood and crime of the rulers has towered mountain high above that of the weak and obscure victims whose wrongs they have pretended to avenge. And this cruelty does not abate. It is simple madness that doubts the justice of past condemnations and believes in the righteous judgments of today. No condemnation is just, and no judgment is righteous. All violence and force are cruel, unjust, and barbarous, and cannot be sustained by the judgment of men.

But the evil of judgment and punishment does not end with the unfortunate victim. It brutalizes and makes inhuman all who are touched with its power. Under the influence of punishments, jailers, policemen, sheriffs, detectives and all who deal with prisons are brutalized and hardened. The iniquities produced upon the helpless prisoners leave their effects upon the captor as well as the captives.

Neither has the method of determining the victims for those various laws been as accurate and scientific as is generally presumed. Sometimes it has been by torturing until the victim is made to confess; sometimes by wager of battle; sometimes by tying the feet and hands and throwing them into a pond, when if they sank they were innocent, if they swam they were guilty and promptly put to death. The modern method of arraying a defendant in court, prosecuted by able lawyers with ample resources, tried by judges who almost invariably believe in the prisoner's guilt, defended as is usually the case by incompetent lawyers, and without means, is scarcely more liable to lead to correct results than the ancient forms.

If the sight of punishment terrorizes men from the commission of crime, then, of course, punishment should be as open as the day. In so far as the state is successful in keeping secret the execution of its victim, in this far does it abandon every claim of prevention and rests its case for punishment on vengeance and cruelty alone.

If terrorism is the object aimed at, death should again be substituted for the various crimes, great and small, which ever justified taking human life. Death, too, should be administered in the most cruel way. Boiling, the rack, wild beasts, and slow fires should be the methods sought. It should be steadfastly remembered by all squeamish judges and executioners that one vigorous punishment would prevent a thousand crimes. But more than all this, death should be in the most public way. The kettle of boiling oil should be heated with its victim inside, out upon the commons where all eyes could see and all ears could hear. The scaffold should be erected high on a hill, and the occasion be made a public holiday for miles around. This was once the case even within the last half century. These public hangings in Europe and America have drawn great crowds of spectators, sometimes reaching into the tens of thousands, to witness the value that the state places on human life. But finally, even stupid legislators began to realize that these scenes of violence, brutality and crime bred their like upon those who came to see. Even governments discovered that many acts of violence followed a public hanging. The hatred of the state which calmly took a human life engendered endless hatred as its fruit.

— above quotations from *Resist Not Evil*

Eugene V. Debs

...society has managed to protect itself against the revenge of the prisoner by dehumanizing him while he is in prison. The process is slow, by degrees, like polluted water trickling from the slimy mouth of a corroded and encrusted spout—but it is a sure process. When a man has remained in prison over a certain length of time his spirit is doomed. He is stripped of his manhood. He is fearful and afraid. He has not been redeemed. He has been crucified. He has not reformed. He has become a roving animal casting about for prey, and too weak to seize it. He is often too weak to live even by the law of the fang and claw.

Getting a living under capitalism...is so precarious, so uncertain, fraught with such pain and struggle that the wonder is not that so many people become vicious and criminal, but that so many remain in docile submission to such a tyrannous and debasing condition.

Fyodor Dostoyevsky

The degree of civilization in a society can be judged by entering its prisons.

Emma Goldman

The most absurd apology for authority and law is that they serve to diminish crime. Aside from the fact that the State is itself the greatest criminal, breaking every written and natural law, stealing in the form of taxes, killing in the form of war and capital punishment, it has come to an absolute standstill in coping with crime. It has failed utterly to destroy or even minimize the horrible scourge of its own creation.

— *Anarchism*

Order derived through submission and maintained by terror is not much of a safe guaranty; yet that is the only "order" that governments have ever maintained. True social harmony grows naturally out of solidarity of interests. In a society where those who always work never have anything, while those who never work enjoy everything, solidarity of interests is non-existent; hence social harmony is but a myth...Thus the entire arsenal of governments—laws, police, soldiers, the courts, legislatures, prisons—is strenuously engaged in "harmonizing" the most antagonistic elements in society.

— Ibid.

Senator Orrin Hatch

Capital punishment is our society's recognition of the sanctity of human life.

— quoted in *Newsweek*, June 6, 1988

Hans von Hentig

The police force and the ranks of prison officers attract many aberrant characters because they afford legal channels for pain-inflicting, power-wielding behavior, and because these very positions confer upon their holders a large degree of immunity...

— *The Criminal and His Victim*

Robert Ingersoll

There seems to be a little of the wild beast in men — a something that is fascinated by suffering, and that delights in inflicting pain. When a government tortures, it is in the same state of mind that the criminal was in when he committed his crime. It requires as much malice in those who execute the law, to torture a criminal, as it did in the criminal to torture and kill his victim. The one was a crime by a person, the other by a nation.

— *Crimes Against Criminals*

Is it not possible that the tyranny of governments, the injustice of nations, the fierceness of what is called the law, produce in the individual a tendency in the same direction? Is it not true that the citizen is apt to imitate his nation? Society degrades its enemies — the individual seeks to degrade his. Society plunders its enemies, and now and then the citizen has the desire to plunder his. Society kills its enemies, and possibly sows in the heart of some citizen the seeds of murder.

— Ibid.

Whoever is degraded by society becomes its enemy. The seeds of malice are sown in his heart, and to the day of his death he will hate the hand that sowed the seeds.

— Ibid.

A punishment that degrades the punished will degrade the man who inflicts the punishment and will degrade the government that procures the infliction. The whipping post pollutes not only the whipped, but the whipper, and not only the whipper, but the community at large.

— Ibid.

Only a few years ago there were more than two hundred offences in Great Britain punishable by death. The gallows-tree bore fruit through all the year, and the hangman was the busiest official in the kingdom — but the criminals increased.

Crimes were committed to punish crimes, and crimes were committed to prevent crimes. The world has been filled with prisons and dungeons, with chains and whips, with crosses and gibbets, with thumbscrews and racks, with hangmen and heads-men — and yet these frightful means and instrumentalities have committed far more crimes than they have prevented...Ignorance, filth, and poverty are the missionaries of crime. As long as

dishonorable success outranks honest effort — as long as society bows and cringes before the great thieves, there will be little ones enough to fill the jails.

— Ibid.

. . . every man is as he must be. Every crime is a necessary product. The seeds were all sown, the land thoroughly plowed, the crop well attended to, and carefully harvested. Every crime is born of necessity. If you want less crime, you must change the conditions. Poverty makes crime. Want, rags, crusts, misfortune — all these awake the wild beast in man, and finally he takes, and takes contrary to law, and becomes a criminal. And what do you do with him? You punish him. Why not punish a man for having consumption? The time will come when you will see that that is just as logical. What do you do with the criminal? You send him to the penitentiary. Is he made better? Worse. The first thing you do is to try to trample out his manhood, by putting an indignity upon him. You mark him. You put him in stripes. At night you put him in darkness. His feeling for revenge grows. You make a wild beast of him, and he comes out of that place branded in body and soul, and then you won't let him reform if he wants to.

— *A Lay Sermon*

Peter Kropotkin

There is only one answer to the question "What can be done to better this penal system? Nothing. A prison cannot be improved. With the exception of a few unimportant little improvements, there is absolutely nothing to do but demolish it.

— *Prisons and Their Moral Influence on Prisoners*

In prisons as in monasteries, everything is done to kill a man's will. He generally has no choice between one of two acts. The rare occasions on which he can exercise his will are very brief. His whole life is regulated and ordered in advance. He has only to swim with the current, to obey under pain of severe punishment.

Under these conditions all the will power that he may have had on entering disappears. And where will he find the strength with which to resist the temptations which will arise before him, as if by magic, when he is free of the prison walls?

— Ibid.

Marquis de Lafayette

I shall demand the abolition of the penalty of death until you show me the infallibility of human testimony.

— quoted by Wendell Phillips in *Capital Punishment*

Karl Meninger

The Crime of Punishment

— Book title

William Messing

Having your fate rest in the hands of a jury is the same as entrusting yourself to surgery with a mentally retarded doctor.

—quoted in *The Match!*, No. 28

Wendell Phillips

There is a very broad theory, that society gets the right to hang, as the individual gets the right to defend himself. Suppose she does; there are certain principles which limit this right...Society has got the murderer within four walls; he never can do any more harm...Has society any need to take that man's life to protect itself?...If any society has only the right that the individual has, she has no right to inflict the penalty of death, because she can effectually restrain the individual from ever again committing his offence.

— *Capital Punishment*

If you can come down one step, if you can give up the rack and the wheel, impaling, tearing to death with wild horses, why cannot you come down two...?

Who knows how many steps you can come down? We came down one when we gave up burning at the stake; we came down another when we gave up the tearing of the body with red-hot pincers; we came down another when we gave up the torture of the wheel...

Now we ask you to abolish the gallows. It is only one step further in the same direction.

—Ibid.

Wilhelm Reich

When social cooperation is disrupted, state power is always strengthened. This is in keeping with the moralistic-authoritarian method of dealing with the difficulties *superficially*. This approach does not of course really remove the social evil, but merely pushes it into the background, from which it later breaks forth much more violently and extensively. If there are no other means of dealing with rape murders than the execution of the murderer, then one uses this method. This is the approach followed by the authoritarian state. Work-democracy, however, goes to the core of the matter and asks: How can we eliminate the phenomena of rape and murder altogether?

— *The Mass Psychology of Fascism*

George Bernard Shaw

Imprisonment is as irrevocable as death.

— *Maxims for Revolutionists*

It is the deed that teaches, not the name we give it. Murder and capital punishment are not opposites that cancel one another, but similars that breed their kind.

—Ibid.

Robert Tefton

PERJURY, n. A common leisure time activity of policemen.

REASONABLE FORCE, n. A police term which refers to a vicious beating or unwitnessed murder. The exact meaning, however, will vary considerably depending upon the victim's race and economic status.

Allen Thornton

...ask your mayor or your councilmen about crime and they'll tell you about complex causalities, imponderables and impossibilities. You, the honest citizen can always be coerced into whatever the government wants of you, but criminals are impossible to control.

— *Laws of the Jungle*

If the government did not hinder our natural ferocity in protecting our own property, criminals would soon learn a different lesson.

My own feeling is that counterviolence against crime would reduce violent crime by strangers to practically nothing in a month or two. Criminals would be forced into fraud as a means of acquiring property without producing.

—Ibid.

Mark Twain

We have a criminal jury system which is superior to any in the world; and its efficiency is only marred by the difficulty of finding twelve men every day who don't know anything and can't read.

—*Americans and the English* (Speech, July 4, 1872)

Colin Ward

The terrifying breakdown of social cohesion in the American city, in spite of intense institutionalized police surveillance equipped with every sophisticated aid to public control, illustrates that social behaviour depends upon mutual responsibility rather than upon the policeman.

— *Anarchy in Action*

Oscar Wilde

As one reads history, not in the expurgated editions written for schoolboys and passmen, but in the original authorities of each time, one is absolutely sickened, not by the crimes that the wicked

have committed, but by the punishments that the good have inflicted; and a community is infinitely more brutalised by the habitual employment of punishment than it is by the occasional occurrence of crime.
— *The Soul of Man Under Socialism*

The vilest deeds like poison weeds
    Bloom well in prison-air:
It is only what is good in man
    That wastes and withers there:
Pale anguish keeps the heavy gate,
    And the warder is despair.
— *The Ballad of Reading Gaol*

Anonymous & Multiple Author

Why go to Vietnam to kill? Join your local police.
— Vietnam War-era bumpersticker

Stop gun control. When guns are outlawed only cops will have guns.
— Graffiti

If a man or woman steal, cut off their hands.
— *The Koran*, 5:38

If neither cross-examination nor confrontation with eye witnesses, nor usual threats are of any avail, one should be guided by the old, tested means.
— Circular to the Cheka, 1921, quoted by Maximoff in *The Guillotine at Work*

The Life and Convictions of Spiro T. Agnew
— Title of 1972 Nixon/Agnew campaign manual

Livin' in the USA

John Quincy Adams

The preservation, propagation, and perpetuation of slavery is the vital and animating spirit of the National Government...slavery, slave-holding, slave-breeding, and slave-trading have formed the whole foundation of the policy of the Federal government;...

— quoted by Wendell Phillips in *Kossuth*

Alexander Berkman

...the American worker remains loyal to the government and is the first to defend it against criticism. He is still the most devoted chapion of the "grand and noble institutions of the greatest country on earth." Why? Because he believes that they are *his* institutions, the *he*, as sovereign and free citizen, is running them and that he could change them if he so wished. It is his *faith* in the existing order that constitutes its greatest security against revolution. His faith is stupid and unjustified, and some day it will break down and with it American capitalism and despotism. But as long as that faith persists, American plutocracy is safe against revolution.

— *What Is Communist Anarchism?*

Senator Albert Beveridge

The times call for candor. The Philippines are ours forever—country belonging to the United States—as the Constitution calls them, and just beyond the Philippines are China's illimitable markets. We will not retreat from either. We will not repudiate our duty in the archipelago. We will not renounce our part in the mission of our race, trustee under God, of the civilization of the world. And we will move forward to our work, not howling out our regrets, like slaves whipped to their burdens, but with gratitude for a task worthy of our strength and thanksgiving to Almighty God that He has marked us as His chosen people to lead in the regeneration of the world.

— Speech in U.S. Senate, January 9, 1900

The question is elemental. It is racial. God has not been preparing the English-speaking and Teutonic people for a thousand years for nothing but vain and idle contemplation and self-administration. No! He has made us the master organizers of this world to establish system where chaos reigns. He has given us the spirit of progress, to overwhelm the forces of reaction throughout the earth. He has made us adepts in government that we may administer government among savage and senile peoples...And of all our race He has marked the American people as the chosen nation to finally lead in the regeneration of the world. This is the divine mission of America.

— Ibid.

Ambrose Bierce

It seems that "we have never gone to war for conquest, for exploitation, nor for territory"; we have the word of a president [McKinley] for that. Observe, now, how Providence overrules the intentions of the truly good for their advantage. We went to war with Mexico for peace, humanity and honor, yet emerged from the contest with an extension of territory beyond the dreams of political avarice. We went to war with Spain for relief of an oppressed people [the Cubans], and at the close found ourselves in possession of vast and rich insular dependencies and with a pretty tight grasp upon the country for relief of whose oppressed people we took up arms. We could hardly have profited more had "territorial aggrandizement" been the spirit of our purpose and heart of our hope.

The slightest acquaintance with history shows that powerful republics are the most warlike and unscrupulous of nations.

— *Warlike America*

Henry Thomas Buckle

...the United States of America, that wretched burlesque of an ancient republic which possesses the forms of democracy without the spirit of liberty.

— *The Causes and Effects of Duelling*

George Bush

I will never apologize for the United States of America—I don't care what the facts are.

—commenting on the unprovoked destruction of an Iranian airliner with 290 civilian passengers by the U.S. warship Vincennes, quoted in *Newsweek*, August 15, 1989

Al Capone

Don't get the idea that I'm one of these god-damned radicals. Don't get the idea that I'm knocking the American system.

—1929 interview

Noam Chomsky

In every society there will emerge a caste of propagandists who labor to disguise the obvious, to conceal the actual workings of power, and to spin a web of mythical goals and purposes utterly benign, that allegedly guide national policy. A typical thesis of the propaganda system is that *the nation* is guided by certain ideals and principles, all of them noble. Sometimes the ideals miscarry, because of error or bad leadership or the complexities and ironies of history. But any horror, any atrocity will be explained away as an unfortunate—or sometimes tragic—deviation from the national purpose. A subsidiary thesis is that the nation is not an active agent, but rather responds to threats posed to its security, or to order and stability, by awesome and evil outside forces.

Again, the United States is no exception to the general rule. If it is exceptional at all, its uniqueness lies in the fact that intellectuals tend to be so eager to promulgate the state religion and to explain away whatever happens as "tragic error" or the inexplicable deviation from our most deeply held ideals. In this respect the United States is perhaps unusual, at least among the industrial democracies. In the midst of the worst horrors of the American war in Vietnam, there was always a Sidney Hook to dismiss "the unfortunate accidental loss of life" or the "unintended consequences of military action" as B-52s carried out systematic carpet bombing in the densely populated Mekong Delta ...There are many similar examples.

— *Foreign Policy and the Intelligentsia*

The United States, in fact, is no more engaged in programs of international good will than any other state has been. Furthermore, it is just mystification to speak of the nation, with its national purpose, as an agent in world affairs. In the United States, as elsewhere, foreign policy is designed and implemented by narrow groups who derive their power from domestic sources...Study after study reveals the obvious: Top advisory and decision-making positions relating to international affairs are heavily concentrated in the hands of representatives of

Major corporations, banks, investment firms, the few law firms that cater to corporate interests, and the technocratic and policy-oriented intellectuals who do the bidding of those who own and manage ...the private empires that govern most aspects of our lives with little pretense of public accountability and not even a gesture to democratic control.

—Ibid.

Who sets foreign policy? What interests do these people represent? What is the domestic source of their power? It is a reasonable surmise that the policy that evolves will reflect the special interests of those who design it. An honest study of history will reveal that this natural expectation is quite generally fulfilled. The evidence is overwhelming, in my opinion, that the United States is no exception to the general rule...

—Ibid.

In fact, the [Watergate] charges against Nixon were for behavior not too far out of the ordinary, though he erred in choosing his victims among the powerful, a significant deviation from established practice. He was never charged with the serious crimes of his Administration: the "secret bombing" of Cambodia, for example. The issue was indeed raised, but it was the secrecy of the bombing, not the bombing itself, that was held to be the crime. Again, the crucial tacit assumption: The United States, in its majesty, has the right to bomb a defenseless peasant society—but it is wrong to mislead Congress about the matter.

— *Intellectuals and the State*

Voltairine de Cleyre

As the [revolutionary] fathers said of the governments of Europe, so we say of this [American] government: "The blood of the people has become its inheritance, and those who fatten on it will not relinquish it easily."

—*Anarchism and American Traditions*

And now, what has Anarchism to say to all this, this bankruptcy of republicanism, this modern empire that has grown up on the ruins of our early freedom? We say this, that the sin our fathers sinned was that they did not trust liberty wholly. They thought it possible to compromise between liberty and government, believing the latter to be "a necessary evil", and the moment the compromise was made, the whole misbegotten monster of our present tyranny began to grow.

—Ibid.

Ralph Waldo Emerson

In America the geography is sublime, but the men are not...

— *The Conduct of Life*

John T. Flynn

But when fascism comes it will not be in the form of an anti-American movement or pro-Hitler bund, practicing disloyalty. Nor will it come in the form of a crusade against war. It will appear rather in the luminous robes of flaming patriotism...

— *As We Go Marching*

We have seen that already we have introduced:
1. The institution of planned consumption of the spending-borrowing government.
2. The planned economy. [This was written during World War II.]
3. Militarism as an economic institution.
4. Imperialism as the handmaiden of our militarism.

But what of the totalitarian state? Can it be that America will ever complete that job? It may be, I hear the critic say, that we have embraced four of the elements of the fascist state but we will not have fascism or national socialism until we add the fifth — the totalitarian political idea...

Let us say at once that there is at least a difference — even though it be not a world of difference — between an autarchial public-debt-supported militaristic state managed by a democratic parliament and one managed by a dictator. But let us also admit frankly that the two are perfectly alike in all but that. Let us say to ourselves frankly that we have now adopted four of the factors of the five which make fascism. This may be called the prologue to fascism.

— Ibid.

Emma Goldman

To uphold the institutions of our country — that's it — the institutions which protect and sustain a handful of people in the robbery and plunder of the masses, the institutions which drain the body of the native as well as of the foreigner, and turn it into wealth and power; the institutions which rob the alien of whatever originality he brings with him and in return gives him cheap Americanism, whose glory consists in mediocrity and arrogance.

— *Preparedness: The Road to Universal Slaughter*

Thomas Jefferson

The spirit of the times may alter, will alter. Our rulers will become corrupt, our people careless... From the conclusion of this [Revolutionary] war we shall be going down hill. It will not then be necessary to resort every moment to the people for support. They will be forgotten, therefore, and their rights disregarded. They will forget themselves in the sole faculty of making money, and will never think of uniting to effect a due respect for their rights. The shackles, therefore, which shall not be knocked off at the conclusion of this war, will be heavier and heavier, till our rights shall revive or expire in a convulsion.

— *Notes on Virginia*

Peter Kropotkin

America is just the country that shows how all the written guarantees in the world for freedom are no protection against tyranny and oppression of the worst kind. There the politician has come to be looked upon as the very scum of society.

— Speech, 1891

Vince Lombardi

Winning isn't everything, it's the only thing.

— attributed

Huey Long

If Fascism came to America it would be on a program of Americanism.

— attributed

General Douglas MacArthur

It is part of the general pattern of misguided policy that our country is now geared to an arms economy which was bred in an artificially induced psychosis of war hysteria and nurtured upon an incessant propaganda of fear.

— Speech, May 15, 1951

H.L. Mencken

...the American people, taking one with another, constitute the most timorous, sniveling, poltroonish, ignominious mob of serfs and goose-steppers ever gathered under one flag since the end of the Middle Ages...

— *Prejudices: A Selection*

...in the United States...the word honor, save when it is applied to the structural integrity of women, has only a comic significance. When one hears of the honor of politicians, of bankers, of lawyers, of the United States itself, everyone normally laughs.

— *Prejudices: Sixth Series*

Here is something that the psychologists have so far neglected: the love of ugliness for its own sake, the lust to make the world intolerable. Its habitat is the United States. Out of the melting pot emerges a race which hates beauty as it hates truth.

— Ibid.

Johann Most

America...the State in which everything is done "by the people and for the people," has existed since more than a century; and who does not see that the true historical significance of this huge experiment is the terrible warning it gives all future statesmen? The government machinery has harnessed cor-

ruption, egotism, intrigue, that mean submissiveness which is the piteous inheritance of suppression through generations, and nothing else. All noble hearts, all intellectual heads, have long ago turned away from the whole apparatus of government with genuine disgust, and the poll they hate like the plague.
— *The Social Monster*

Alvin M. Owsley
(American Legion Commander

...the American Legion stands ready to protect our country's institutions and ideals as the Fascisti dealt with the destructionists who menaced Italy...

The American Legion is fighting every element that threatens our democratic government—soviets, anarchists, I.W.W., revolutionary socialists and every other red...Do not forget that the Fascisti are to Italy what the American Legion is to the United States.
— Interview, *Journal of the National Education Association*, 1923

Wendell Phillips

In our country of absolute democratic equality, public opinion is not only omnipotent, it is omnipresent. There is no refuge from its tyranny, there is no hiding from its reach...and the result is that instead of being a mass of individuals, each one fearlessly blurting out his own conviction, as a nation compared to other nations we are a mass of cowards.

John Rush

UNITED STATES, n. The land of the fee and the home of the slave.

George Bernard Shaw

You have set up in New York harbor a monstrous idol which you call Liberty. The only thing that remains to complete that monument is to put on its pedestal the inscription written by Dante on the gate of Hell: "All hope abandon, ye who enter here."
— Speech in New York City, April 11, 1933

Lysander Spooner

...it [is] proper to say that the [U.S.] Constitution is no such instrument as it has generally been assumed to be; but by false interpretations, and naked usurpations, the government has been made in practice a very widely, and almost wholly different thing from what the Constitution itself purports to authorize...but whether the Constitution really be one thing, or another, this much is certain —that it has either authorized such a government as we have had, or has been powerless to prevent it. In either case, it is unfit to exist.
— *No Treason*

...we have what purports, or professes, or is claimed, to be a contract—the Constitution—made eighty years ago, by men who are now all dead, and who never had any power to bind *us*, but which (it is claimed) has nevertheless bound three generations of men, consisting of many millions that are to come; but which nobody ever signed, sealed, delivered, witnessed, or acknowledged...

And we are so insane, or so wicked, as to destroy property and lives without limit, in fighting to compel men to fulfill a supposed contract, which, inasmuch as it has never been signed by anybody, is on general principles of law and reason—such principles as we are all governed by in regard to other contracts—the merest waste paper, binding upon nobody, fit only to be thrown into the fire; or, if preserved, preserved only to serve as a witness and warning of the folly and wickedness of mankind.
— Ibid.

Gertrude Stein

There's no there there.
— on Oakland, California (attributed)

Henry David Thoreau

How does it become a man to behave toward this American government today? I answer, that he cannot without disgrace be associated with it.
— *On Civil Disobedience*

Allen Thornton

Americans believe in the "bad man" theory of history: There is nothing inherently wrong with the institution of government, but bad men corrupt individual states. If, Americans fancy, you could put enough "good men" into government, the world would live in peace and prosperity. They seem to think that leaders like Hitler wake up every morning and ask, "How can I screw up the world today?"

They forget that...none of our political villains consider themselves evil men. Just the opposite, they regard themselves as history's heroes.
— *Laws of the Jungle*

The problem with the Bill of Rights is fairly obvious...Any system of entrusting the government to judge and correct its own abuses is the same as appointing the accused criminal as his own judge and jury: Don't expect many convictions.
— Ibid.

Graphic from *The Match* (thanks to Fred Woodworth)

Alexis de Tocqueville

I know of no country in which there is so little independence of mind and real freedom of discussion as in America.

— *Democracy in America*

In the United States, the majority undertakes to supply a multitude of ready-made opinions for the use of individuals who are thus relieved from the necessity of forming opinions of their own. Everybody there adopts great numbers of theories, on philosophy, morals, and politics, without inquiry...

— Ibid.

In America, the majority raises formidable barriers around the liberty of opinion: within these barriers, an author may write what he pleases; but woe to him if he goes beyond them. Not that he is in danger of an *auto-da-fe* [burning at the stake], but he is exposed to continued obloquy and persecution. His political career is closed forever, since he has offended the only authority which is able to open it. Every sort of compensation, even that of celebrity, is refused to him. Before publishing his opinions, no sooner has he declared them, than he is loudly censured by his opponents, whilst those who think like him, without having the courage to speak out, abandon him in silence. He yields at length, overcome by the daily effort which he has to make, and

subsides into silence, as if he felt remorse for having spoken the truth.
— Ibid.

Mark Twain

It is by the goodness of God that in our country we have those three precious things: freedom of speech, freedom of conscience— and the prudence never to practice any of them.
— *Following the Equator*

It could probably be shown by facts and figures that there is no distinctly native American criminal class except congress.
— Ibid.

October 12, the Discovery. It was wonderful to find America, but it would have been more wonderful to miss it.
— *Pudd'nhead Wilson*

Oscar Wilde

In America Life is one long expectoration.

Every American bride is taken there [Niagara Falls] and the sight of the stupendous waterfall must be one of the earliest, if not the keenest, disappointments in American married life.

Fred Woodworth

No more dangerous threat to world freedom exists than the American State. This monstrosity, conceived as a revolutionary experiment in limited government, grew to maturity mouthing the slogans of liberty, and proclaiming the ideals which it had trampled upon and betrayed from the very start. And now, in our gloomy age, the noble experiment is totally out of control; it has taken over the laboratory, strangled the experimenter, the fabled "people" in whose name it was created, and not content with this overthrow and consequent annihilation of its inventor and would-be master, it has escaped even from the confines of old. Today it bursts horridly from the corridors of its youth, springs upon a fearful or unsuspecting world, caring only to satisfy one sole hunger and need— *power!* It thirsts to control, it must dominate or die. It worries its hideous muzzle in the gory throat of a swooning planet. Then, aflame with blood-lust, it devours!

. . . a "land of the free" that struggles under the incredible burden of limitless taxes and laws; the home of the "brave" who stay silent to keep their jobs and avoid scrutiny by the IRS or the police.
— *The Match!*, No. 74

Anonymous & Multiple Author

The government of the United States is in no sense founded upon the Christian religion. The United States is not a Christian nation any more than it is a Jewish or a Mohammedan nation.
— Treaty with Tripoli

Producing a copy of the Fugitive Slave Law, he [William Lloyd Garrison] set fire to it, and it burnt to ashes. . . Then holding up the U.S. Constitution, he branded it as the source and parent of all the other atrocities— "a covenant with death, and an agreement with hell"— and consumed it to ashes on the spot, exclaiming, "So perish all compromises with tyranny!"
— *The Liberator*, July 7, 1854 (reporting Garrison's speech at Framingham, Massachusetts, July 4, 1854)

Uncle Sam Wants You. . . To work 40 hours a week, 50 weeks a year— for the rest of your life!
— *Processed World No. 14*

Rooting for the Yankees is like rooting for U.S. imperialism.
— Bleacher fan at an A's game, 1985

The United States is one great society for the suppression of vice.
— District Attorney's plea, U.S. vs. D.M. Bennett, quoted by Heywood Broun in *Anthony Comstock*

TEXAS: The state where men are still men and women will do if sheep aren't available.
— Anonymous

Ran away, my man Fountain— has holes bored in his ears, a scar on the right side of his forehead— has been shot in hind parts of his legs— is marked on the back with the whip.
— Advertisement in the July 27, 1837 *Georgia Messenger*, cited by Kirby Page in *Jesus or Christianity*

Women

Susan B. Anthony

By law, public sentiment, and religion—from the time of Moses down to the present day—woman has never been thought of other than as a piece of property, to be disposed of at the will and pleasure of man.

—Speech at suffrage convention, Albany, NY 1860

Tammy Faye Bakker

I think Christian women are the most liberated women in the whole world. I love being under submission to my husband.

—attributed

Ambrose Bierce

BRIDE, A woman with a fine prospect of happiness behind her.

— *The Devil's Dictionary*

MISS, A title with which we brand unmarried women to indicate that they are in the market.

—Ibid.

Warren Farrell

When women hold off from marrying men, we call it independence. When men hold off marrying women, we call it fear of commitment.

—quoted in the *San Francisco Chronicle*, Nov. 26, 1986

They [women] want men to need them, yet feel neediness is unmanly.

—Ibid.

Yekaterina Alekseyevna Furtseva
(USSR Minister of Cultural Affairs)

Any woman, no matter what post she occupies, should remain a woman...She should know how to cook and how to keep house nicely. If she does not, she is not a woman.

—quoted in *The New York Times*, January 19, 1989

Matilda Gage

The most stupendous system of organized robbery known, has been that of the church towards woman, a robbery that has not only taken her self-respect but all rights of person; the fruits of her own industry; her opportunities of education; the exercise of her own judgment; her own conscience, her own will.

— *Woman, Church, and State*

Emma Goldman

Nowhere is woman treated according to the merit of her work, but rather as a sex. It is therefore almost inevitable that she should pay for her right to exist, to keep a position in whatever line, with sex favors. Thus it is merely a question of degree whether she sells herself to one man, in or out of marriage, or to many men. Whether our reformers admit it or not, the economic and social inferiority of woman is responsible for prostitution.

— *The Traffic in Women*

From infancy, almost, the average girl is told that marriage is her ultimate goal; therefore her training and education must be directed towards that end. Like the mute beast fattened for slaughter, she is prepared for that.

— *Marriage and Love*

The institution of marriage makes a parasite of woman, an absolute dependent. It incapacitates her for life's struggle, annihilates her social consciousness, paralyzes her imagination, and then imposes its gracious protection, which is in reality, a snare, a travesty in human character.

—Ibid.

As to the protection of the woman—therein lies the curse of marriage. Not that it really protects her, but the very idea is so revolting, such an outrage and insult on life, so degrading to human dignity, as to forever condemn this parasitic institution.

—Ibid.

History tells us that every oppressed class gained true liberation from its masters through its own efforts. It is necessary that woman learn that lesson, that she realize that her freedom will reach as far as her power to achieve her freedom reaches. It is therefore, necessary for her to begin with her inner regeneration, to cut loose from the weight of prejudices, traditions, and customs. The demand for equal rights in every vocation of life is just and fair; but, after all, the most vital right is the right to love and be loved. Indeed, if partial emancipation is to become a complete and true emancipation of woman, it will have to do away with the ridiculous notion that to be loved, to be sweetheart and mother, is synonymous with being slave or subordinate. It will have to do away with the absurd notion of the dualism of the sexes, or that man and woman represent two antagonistic worlds.

— *The Tragedy of Women's Emancipation*

Praxedis Guerrero

The biblical theory of the impurity of woman has lost its infallibility; its modern replacement is "the inferiority of woman," with its supposed scientific support.

The inferiority of woman! In truth we should say: The enslavement of woman!

— *Regeneración*, November 12, 1910

Jenny D'Hericourt

To subordinate woman in a social order in which she must *work in order to live* is to *desire prostitution*... The woman who cannot live by working, can only do so by prostituting herself; the equal of man or a courtesan, such is the alternative.

Robert Ingersoll

There will never be a generation of great men until there has been a generation of free women...

— *How to Reform Mankind*

What has the church done?

It has made the wife a slave— the property of the husband, and it placed the husband as much above the wife as Christ was above the husband. It taught that a nun is purer, nobler than a mother. It induced millions of pure and conscientious girls to renounce the joys of life— to take the veil woven of night and death, to wear the habiliments of the dead — made them believe that they were the brides of Christ.

For my part, I would as soon be a widow as the bride of a man who had been dead for eighteen hundred years.

— *A Thanksgiving Sermon*

Priests, theologians, have taken advantage of women—of their gentleness—their love of approbation. They have lived upon their hopes and fears. Like vampires, they have sucked their blood. They have made them responsible for the sins of the world. They have taught them the slave virtues— meekness, humility — implicit obedience. They have fed their minds with mistakes, mysteries and absurdities. They have endeavored to weaken and shrivel their brains, until to them, there would be no possible connection between evidence and belief —between fact and faith.

— Ibid.

As long as woman regards the Bible as the charter of her rights, she will be the slave of man. The Bible was not written by a woman. Within its lids there is nothing but humiliation and shame for her. She is regarded as the property of man. She is made to ask forgiveness for becoming a mother. She is as much below her husband as her husband is below Christ. She is not allowed to speak. The gospel is too pure to be spoken by her polluted lips.

— *The Liberty of Man, Woman and Child*

Sally Kempton

I became a feminist as an alternative to becoming a masochist.

— attributed

Florynce Kennedy

There are very few jobs that actually require a penis or a vagina. All other jobs should be open to everybody.

— also attributed to Gloria Steinem

Laurel Limpus

Having children is no substitute for creating one's own life, for producing. And since so many women in this culture devote themselves to nothing else, they end up by becoming intolerable burdens upon their children because in fact these children are their whole lives.

— quoted by Brinton in *The Irrational in Politics*

Friedrich Nietzsche

Woman was God's second mistake.

— *The Anti-Christ*

Margaret Sanger

No God. No Master.

No Woman can call herself free who does not own and control her own body.

— *Woman and the New Race*

George Bernard Shaw

Home is the girl's prison and the woman's work-house.

—*Maxims for Revolutionists*

Elizabeth Cady Stanton

The religious superstitions of women perpetuate their bondage more than all other adverse influences.

To no form of religion is woman indebted for one impulse of freedom, as all alike have taught her inferiority and subjection.

Nothing strengthens the judgment and quickens the conscience like individual responsibility. Nothing adds such dignity to character as the recognition of one's self-sovereignty; the right to an equal place, everywhere conceded—a place earned by personal merit, not an artificial attainment by inheritance, wealth, family and position. Conceding, then, that the responsibilities of life rest equally on man and woman, that their destiny is the same, they need the same preparation for time and eternity. The talk of sheltering woman from the fierce storms of life is the sheerest mockery, for they beat on her from every point of the compass, just as they do on man, and with more fatal results, for he has been trained to protect himself, to resist, and to conquer. Such are the facts in human experience, the responsibilities of individual sovereignty.

Every form of religion which has breathed upon this earth has degraded woman. Man himself could not do this; but when he declares, "Thus saith the Lord," of course he can do it.

—quoted by Madalyn Murray-O'Hair in *Women and Atheism*

Mark Twain

What, sir, would the people of the earth be without woman? They would be scarce, sir, mighty scarce. Then let us cherish her; let us protect her; let us give her our support, our encouragement, our sympathy, ourselves—if we get a chance.

—*Woman, An Opinion*

Oscar Wilde

Women love men for their defects; if men have enough of them women will forgive them everything, even their gigantic intellects [egos].

—*A Woman of No Importance*

Mary Wollstonecroft

It is vain to expect virtue from women till they are, in some degree, independent of men; nay it is vain to expect that strength of natural affection which would make them good wives and mothers. Whilst they are absolutely dependent on their husbands they will be cunning, mean, and selfish, and the men who can be gratified by the fawning fondness of spaniel-like affection have not much delicacy, for love is not to be bought...

...in the education of women, the cultivation of the understanding is always subordinate to the acquirement of some corporeal accomplishment; even while enervated by confinement and false notions of modesty, the body is prevented from attaining that grace and beauty which relaxed half-formed limbs never exhibit. Besides, in youth their faculties are not brought forward by emulation; and having no serious scientific study, if they have natural sagacity it is turned too soon on life and manners. They dwell on effects and modifications, without tracing them back to causes; and complicated rules to adjust behavior are a weak substitute for simple principles.

As a proof that education gives this appearance of weakness to females, we may instance the example of military men, who are, like them, sent into the world before their minds have been stored with knowledge or fortified by principles. The consequences are similar; soldiers acquire a little superficial knowledge, snatched from the muddy current of conversation, and from continually mixing with society, they gain what is termed a knowledge of the world; and this acquaintance with manners and customs has frequently been confounded with punctilious politeness. Where is then the sexual difference when the education has been the same? All the difference that I can discern arises from the superior advantage of liberty, which enables the former to see more of life...

Standing armies can never consist of resolute, robust men; they may be well-disciplined machines, but they will seldom contain men under the influence of strong passions, or with very vigorous faculties. And as for any depth of understanding, I will venture to affirm that it is as rarely to be found in the army as amongst women; and the cause, I maintain, is the same. It may be further observed that officers are also particularly attentive to their persons, fond of dancing, crowded rooms, adventures, and ridicule. Like the *fair* sex, the business of their lives is gallantry...

The great misfortune is this, that they both acquire manners before morals, and a knowledge of life before they have, from reflection, any acquaintance with the grand ideal outline of human nature. The consequence is natural; satisfied with common nature, they become a prey to prejudices, and taking all their opinions on credit, they blindly submit to authority.

Why should women be censured with petulant acrimony, because they seem to have a passion for a scarlet coat? Has not education placed them more on a level with soldiers than any other class of men?

Taught from their infancy that beauty is woman's scepter, the mind shapes itself to the body and, roaming round its gilt cage, only seeks to adorn its prison.

Women, commonly called Ladies, are not to be contradicted in company, are not allowed to exert any manual strength; and from them the negative virtues only are expected: patience, docility, good humor, and flexibility; virtues incompatible with any vigorous exertion of intellect.
—above quotations from *A Vindication of the Rights of Women*

Victoria Woodhull

To me, this farce of marriage is a public placarding, merely to this effect: that I, the bearer, am this day sold, to be the sexual slave of [a husband]... Wives may not think they are slaves, and yet be open to this charge. Some may not be; but let the majority attempt to assert their sexual freedom, and they will quickly come to the realization. To what does modern marriage amount, if it be not to hold sexual slaves, who otherwise would be free?
—Speech in Chicago, 1873

I respect and honor the needy woman who, to procure food for herself and child, sells her body to some stranger for the necessary money; but for that legal virtue which sells itself for a life-time for a home, with an abhorrence of the purchaser, and which at the same time says to the former: "I am holier than thou," I have only the supremest contempt.

Jane Wyman

Oh Ronnie. It took so long and it's only a girl.
—to then-husband Ronald Reagan on the birth of their first child (attributed)

Anonymous & Multiple Author

It starts when you sink in his arms and ends with your arms in his sink.
—*Processed World*

Women who want to be equal to men lack imagination.
—Graffiti

I'd rather be ironing.
—Ladies Against Women, sign in 1986 Gay Freedom Day parade in San Francisco

Suffering, Not Suffrage
—Ibid.

Most women would rather be beautiful than smart because most men can see better than they can think.
—Anonymous

Because woman's work is never done and is underpaid or unpaid or boring or repetitious and we're the first to get the sack and what we look like is more important than what we do and if we get raped it's our fault and if we get bashed we must have provoked it and if we raise our voices we're nagging bitches and if we enjoy sex we're nymphos and if we don't we're frigid and if we love women it's because we can't get a "real" man and if we ask our doctor too many questions we're neurotic and/ or pushy and if we expect community care for children we're selfish and if we stand up for our rights we're aggressive and "unfeminine" and if we want to get married we're out to trap a man and if we don't we're unnatural and because we still can't get an adequate safe contraceptive but men can walk on the moon and if we can't cope or don't want a pregnancy we're made to feel guilty about abortion ...for lots and lots of other reasons we are part of the women's liberation movement.
—Anonymous, *The Torch*, September 14, 1987

Misogyny

St. Ambrose

Adam was led to sin by Even and not Eve by Adam. It is just and right that woman accept as lord and master him whom she led to sin.

St. Anthony

When you see a woman, consider that you face not a human being, but the devil himself. The woman's voice is the hiss of the snake.

St. Thomas Aquinas

...in divine matrimony man receives by divine institution the faculty to use his wife for the begetting of children.
—*Summa Theologica*

Patriarch Athenagoras

Each of us who takes a wife does so only for the purpose of bringing children into the world. He is like the farmer who entrusts the soil with his seed and then patiently waits for the crop.

—(in 1948!) quoted by Madalyn Murray-O'Hair in *Women and Atheism*

St. Augustine

...the woman, together with her own husband, is the image of God...but when she is referred to separately...the woman alone, then she is not the image of God, but as regards the man alone, he is the image of God...

— *De Trinitate*

A good Christian is due in one and the same woman to love the creature of God...but to hate in her the corrupting and mortal conjugal connection, sexual intercourse, and all that pertains to her as a wife.

— *De Sermone Dominum in Monte*

Man was made to rule, woman to obey.

— *De Genesi*

Ambrose Bierce

Here's to woman! Would that we could fall into her arms without falling into her hands!

— Bierce's favorite toast

WOMAN, An animal usually living in the vicinity of Man, and having a rudimentary susceptibility to domestication...The species is the most widely distributed of all beasts of prey...

— *The Devil's Dictionary*

St. John Chrysostom

Among savage beasts none is found so harmful as woman.

Women—a foe to friendship, an inescapable punishment, a necessary evil.

St. Gregory of Nazianzum

Fierce is the dragon, and cunning the asp. But woman has the malice of both.

Woman's philosophy is to obey the laws of marriage...Let the house be thy city.

Adolf Hitler

The chief emphasis must be laid on physical training, and only subsequently on the promotion of spiritual and finally intellectual values. The goal of female education must invariably be the future mother.

— *Mein Kampf*

The program of our National Socialist women's movement contains really only one single point. This point is that the child that must come into being must thrive.

St. Jerome

I am aware that some have laid it down that virgins of Christ must not bathe with eunuchs or married women, because the former still have the minds of men and the latter present the ugly spectacle of swollen bellies. For my part I say that mature girls must not bathe at all, because they ought to blush to see themselves naked.

— *Epistle 107*

John Knox

Nature doth paint them further to be weak, frail, impatient, feeble and foolish; and experience hath declared them to be unconstant, variable, cruel and lacking the spirit of counsel.

— *The First Blast of the Trumpet Against the Monstrous Regiment of Women*

Martin Luther

No gown worse becomes a woman than the desire to be wise.

Men have broad and large chests, and small narrow hips, and are more understanding than women, who have but small and narrow chests, and broad hips, to the end they should remain at home, sit still, keep house, and bear and bring up children.

— *Table Talk*

Philip Melancthon

If a woman weary of bearing children, that matters not. Let her only die from bearing; she is there to do it.

— quoted by madalyn Murray-O'Hair in *Women and Atheism*

Mohammed

When Eve was created, Satan rejoiced.

Pope Pius XI

Married life presupposes the power of the husband over the wife and children, and subjection and obedience of the wife to the husband.

— *Castii Connubii*

However we may pity the mother whose health and even life is imperiled by the performance of her natural duty, there yet remains no sufficient reason for condoning the direct murder of the innocent.
—Ibid.

Tertullian

Do you know that each of you women is an Eve? The sentence of God on this sex of yours lives in this age; the guilt must necessarily live there too. You are the gate to hell, you are the temptress of the forbidden tree; you are the first deserter of the divine law.

The judgment upon your sex endures even today; and with it inevitably endures your position of criminal at the bar of justice. You are the gateway to hell.

In pain shall you bring forth children, woman, and you shall turn to your husband he shall rule over you. And do you now know that you are Eve? God's sentence hangs still over all your sex and His punishment weighs down upon you. You are the devil's gateway; you are she who first violated the forbidden tree and broke the law of God. It was you who coaxed your way around him whom the devil had not the force to attack. With what ease you shattered that image of God: Man! Because of the death you merited, even the Son of God had to die.

Woman, you ought to go about clad in mourning and rags, your eyes filled with tears of remorse, to make us forget you have been mankind's destruction. Woman, you are the gate to hell.

If your faith were as firm as its eternal reward, my beloved sisters, no one of you, after learning of the living God and her own condition as a woman, would dare to seek gay apparel but would dress in rags and remain dirty as a sorrowful and repentant Eve.

—above quotations from *De Cultu Feminarum*

Blessed be Thou, our God and Lord of Hosts, who has not created me a woman.
—Traditional Jewish prayer

The female sex is in some respects inferior to the male sex, both as regards body and soul.
—*Roman Catholic Encyclopedia* (1912)

In childhood a woman must be subject to her father; in youth, to her husband; when her husband is dead, to her sons. A woman must never be free of subjugation.
—*Code of Manu* (Hindu)

My sister, your veil is my honor.
—Iranian "revolutionary" slogan

She who doesn't wear a veil prostitutes herself.
—Ibid.

The testimony of a woman has only half the value of the testimony of a man, and even then its veracity must be confirmed by a man.
—Iranian Penal Code, Article 5

. . . the iniquity of women surpasses all iniquities which are in the world . . . the poisons of vipers and dragons are healthier and less harmful to men than familiarity with women . . .
—Ecclesiastical Statute, Order of Premontre (Catholic monastics—13th century)

Men are the supporters of women . . . good women are therefore obedient . . .
—*Koran*, 4:34

. . . admonish those women you fear will desert you, and leave them alone in the sleeping places, and beat them . . .
—Ibid.

Anonymous & Multiple Author

Women and dogs, and other impure animals, are not permitted to enter.
—Inscription on entrance to a mosque, quoted by Lucy Stone

To enlist native help . . . Treat natives like human beings . . . Respect personal property, especially their women.
—*Survival, Evasion and Escape* (U.S. Army Field Manual FM21-76, issued in 1969)

Human,
All Too Human

Joaquin Andujar

I can tell you about it in one word: you never know.

— attributed

St. Augustine

Cursed is every one who placeth his hope in man.

— *On Christian Conflict*

Marcus Aurelius

Do not that which thy conscience condemns, and say not that which does not agree with truth. Fulfill this, the most important duty, and thou wilt have fulfilled all the object of thy life.

Michael Bakunin

It is the characteristic of privilege and of every privileged position to kill the hearts and minds of men. The privileged man, whether politically or economically, is a man depraved in mind and heart.

— *God and the State*

Alexander Berkman

It is said that no two blades of grass are alike. Much less so are human beings. In the whole wide world no two persons are exactly similar even in physical appearance; still more dissimilar are they in their physiological, mental, and psychical make-up. Yet in spite of this diversity and of a thousand and one differentiations of character we compel people to be alike today. Our life and habits, our behavior and manners, even our thoughts and feelings are pressed into a uniform mold and fashioned into sameness. The spirit of authority, law, written and unwritten, tradition and custom force us into a common groove and make of man a will-less automoton without independence or individuality. This moral and intellectual bondage is devastating to our manhood and development. All of us are its victims, and only the exceptionally strong succeed in breaking its chains, and then only partly.

— *What Is Communist Anarchism?*

More vicious and deadening is compulsory compliance than the most virulent poison. Throughout the ages it has been the greatest impediment to man's advance, hedging him in with a thousand prohibitions and taboos, weighting his mind and heart down with outlived canons and codes, thwarting his will with imperatives of thought and feeling, with "thou shalt" and "thou shalt not" of behavior and action. Life, the art of living, has become a dull formula, flat and inert.

— Ibid.

St. Bernard

Man is nothing more than . . . a sack of dung, the food of worms.

— *Meditationes Piissimae*

Yogi Berra

Nobody goes there anymore; it's too crowded.

— quoted on KRON-TV, June 18, 1989

It's deja vu all over again.

— Ibid.

You can observe a lot by just watching.

This is some house, nothing but rooms.

Why buy good luggage? You only use it when you travel.

Baseball is 90% mental; the other half is physical.

Ambrose Bierce

ABNORMAL, Not conforming to standard. In matters of thought and conduct, to be independent is to be abnormal, to be abnormal is to be detested.

ABSURDITY, A statement or belief manifestly inconsistent with one's own opinion.

ADMIRATION, Our polite recognition of another's resemblance to ourselves.

ALONE, In bad company.

BIRTH, The first and direst of all disasters.

BORE, A person who talks when you wish him to listen.

CONSULT, To seek another's approval of a course already decided on.

CYNIC, A blackguard whose faulty vision sees things as they are, not as they ought to be.

DAY, A period of twenty-four hours, mostly misspent.

ECCENTRICITY, A method of distinction so cheap that fools employ it to accentuate their incapacity.

EGOTIST, a person of low taste, more interested in himself than in me.

FRIENDLESS, Having no favors to bestow. Destitute of fortune. Addicted to utterance of truth and common sense.

FUTURE, that period of time in which our affairs prosper, our friends are true and our happiness is assured.

HAPPINESS, An agreeable sensation arising from contemplating the misery of another.

IDIOT, A member of a large and powerful tribe whose influence in human affairs has always been dominant and controlling. The Idiot's activity is not confined to any special field of thought or action, but "pervades and regulates the whole." He has the last word in everything; his decision is unappealable. He sets the fashions of opinion and taste, dictates the limitations of speech and circumscribes conduct with a dead-line.

INCOMPATIBILITY, In matrimony, a similarity of tastes, particularly the taste for domination.

LICKSPITTLE, A useful functionary, not infrequently found editing a newspaper.

LONGEVITY, Uncommon extension of the fear of death.

OPTIMISM, The doctrine or belief that everything is beautiful, including what is ugly, everything good, especially the bad, and everything right that is wrong.

ORPHAN, A living person whom death has deprived of the power of filial ingratitude...

PAIN, An uncomfortable frame of mind that may have a physical basis in something that is being done to the body, or may be purely mental, caused by the good fortune of another.

PATIENCE, A minor form of despair, disguised as a virtue.

PHILOSOPHY, A route of many roads leading from nowhere to nothing.

— above definitions from *The Devil's Dictionary*

William Blake

The man who never alters his opinion is like standing water, and breeds reptiles of the mind.
— *Proverbs of Hell*

Napoleon Bonaparte

Ability is of little account without opportunity.
— attributed

John Bright

He is a self-made man, and worships his creator.
— on Disraeli

Maruice Brinton

It is obvious that if large sections of the population were constantly questioning the principles of hierarchy, the authoritarian organization of production, the wages system, or other fundamental aspects of the social structure, no ruling class could maintain itself in power for long. For rulers to continue ruling it is necessary that those at the bottom of the social ladder not only accept their condition, but eventually lose even the sense of being exploited. Once this psychological process has been achieved the division of society becomes legitimized in people's minds. The exploited cease to perceive it as something imposed on them from without. The oppressed have internalized their own oppression. They tend to behave like robots, programmed not to rebel against the established order. The robots may even seek to defend their subordinate position, to rationalize it, and will often reject as "pie in the sky" any talk of emancipation.
— *The Irrational in Politics*

The purpose of education — both East and West — is the mass production of robots...who have so internalized social constraints that they submit to them automatically.
— Ibid.

Certain subjects are clearly emotionally loaded. Discussing them generates peculiar resistances that are hardly amenable to rational argument.
   ...these resistances are the result of a longstanding conditioning, going back to earliest childhood, and...this conditioning is mediated through the already conditioned parents and through the whole institution of the patriarchal family. The net result is a powerful reinforcement and perpetuation of the dominant ideology and the mass production of individuals with slavery built into them, individuals ready at a later stage to accept the authority of school teacher, priest, employer and politician...
— Ibid.

Giordano Bruno

It is proof of a base and low mind for one to wish to think with the masses or majority, merely because the majority is the majority. Truth does not change because it is, or is not, believed by a majority of the people.

Luther Burbank

The greatest torture in the world for most people is to think.

George Bush

Boy, they were big on crematoriums, weren't they?

—Comment made on tour of Auschwitz, Sept. 1987

Samuel Butler

Life is the art of drawing sufficient conclusions from insufficient premises.

—quoted by Stanley Gudder in *A Mathematical Journey*

Thomas Carlyle

The man who cannot laugh is not only fit for treason, stratagems, and spoils, but his whole life is already a treason and a stratagem.

—*Sartor Resartus*

It is not what a man outwardly has or wants that constitutes the happiness or misery of him. Nakedness, hunger, distress of all kinds, death itself have been cheerfully suffered, when the heart was right. It is the feeling of *injustice* that is insupportable to all men... No man can bear it or ought to bear it.

—*Chartism*

The man of Humour sees common life, even mean life, under the new light of sportfulness and love; whatever has existence has a charm for him. Humour has justly been regarded as the finest perfection of poetic genius. He who wants it, be his other gifts what they may, has only half a mind; ...

—*Schiller*

Edward Carpenter

Civilization: Its Cause and Cure

—Essay title

Lewis Carroll

"...and who are you?"

"I—I hardly know sir, just at present—at least I know who I was when I got up this morning, but I think I must have been changed several times since then."

—*Through the Looking Glass*

Anton Chekov

Truly decent people only exist among men with definite convictions, whether conservative or radical; so-called moderates are much drawn to rewards, orders, commissions, promotions.

William K. Clifford

There is one thing in the world more wicked than the desire command, and that is the will to obey.

—quoted by Sprading in *Liberty and the Great Libertarians*

Confucius

The superior man is polite but not cringing; the common man is cringing but not polite.

—*Analects*

Do to every man as you would have him do to you; and do not do to another what you would not have him do to you.

Stephen Crane

These stupid peasants, who, throughout the world, hold potentates on their thrones, make statesmen illustrious, provide generals with lasting victories, all with ignorance, indifference, or half-witted hatred, moving the world with the strength of their arms, and getting their heads knocked together in the name of God, the king, or the stock exchange—immortal, dreaming, hopeless asses, who surrender their reason to the care of a shining puppet, and persuade some toy to carry their lives in his purse.

—quoted by Jack London in *People of the Abyss*

Clarence Darrow

The purpose of life is living. Men and women should get the most they can out of their lives. The smallest, the tiniest intellect may be quite as valuable to itself; it may have all the capacity for enjoyment that the wisest has.

—*The Wisdom of Clarence Darrow*

Hatred, Bitterness, Violence and Force can only bring bad results—they leave an evil stain on everything they touch. No human soul can be rightly reached except through reasonableness, humanity and love.

—*Resist Not Evil*

Rene Descartes

Good sense is of all things in the world most equally distributed, for everybody thinks he is so well supplied with it, that even those most difficult to please in all other matters never desire more of it than they already possess.

—*Discourse on Method*

Oliver Edwards

You are a philosopher Dr. Johnson. I have tried too in my time to be a philosopher; but, I don't know how, cheerfulness was always breaking in.

—quoted in *Man Against Myth*, by Barrows Dunham

Dwight D. Eisenhower

Things are more like they are now than they have ever been before.

—attributed

Dr. Albert Ellis

Not all forms of commitment...are equally healthy. The grand inquisitors of the medieval Catholic church were utterly dedicated to their "holy" work, and Hitler and many of his associates were fanatically committed to their Nazi doctrines.

— *The Case Against Religiosity*

Epicurus

I know not how to conceive of good, apart from the pleasures, sexual pleasures, the pleasures of sound and the pleasures of beautiful form.

Benjamin Franklin

One good Husband is worth two good Wives; for the scarcer things are the more they're valued.

—*Poor Richard's Almanac*, 1742

Old Boys have their Playthings as well as young Ones; the Difference is only in the price.

—*Poor Richard's Almanac*, 1752

If you would be loved, love and lovable.

—*Poor Richard's Almanac*, 1755

J.W. von Goethe

As soon as you trust yourself, you will know how to live.

Emma Goldman

...the upper classes!...their graciousness, their charity, their interest in the "common people" is, after all, nothing but arrogance, blind conceit of their own importance...

— *The Social Significance of Modern Drama*

Often...apparent defeat is in reality the truest success. For is not success, as commonly understood, but to frequently bought at the expense of character and idealism?

—Ibid.

Man's true liberation, individual and collective, lies in his emancipation from authority and from the belief in it. All human evolution has been a struggle in that direction and for that object. It is not invention and mechanics which constitute development. The ability to travel at 100 miles an hour is no evidence of being civilized. True civilization is to be measured by the individual, the unit of all social life; by his individuality and the extent which it is free to have its being, to grow and expand unhindered by invasive and coercive authority.

Socially speaking, the criterion of civilization and culture is the degree of liberty and economic security which the individual enjoys; of social and international unity and cooperation unrestricted by man-made laws and other artificial obstacles; by the absence of privileged castes and by the reality of liberty and human dignity; in short, by the true emancipation of the individual.

— *The Individual, Society and the State*

The greater the mental charlatan, the more definite his insistence on the wickedness and weaknesses of human nature. Yet how can anyone speak of it today, with every soul in a prison, with every heart fettered, wounded, and maimed?

...with human nature caged in a narrow space, whipped daily into submission, how can we speak of its potentialities?

—*Anarchism*

The school, more than any other institution, is a veritable barracks, where the human mind is drilled and manipulated into submission to various social and moral spooks and thus fitted to continue our system of exploitation and oppression.

—Speech to International Anarchist Congress, 1907

George Herbert

Living well is the best revenge.

— *Outlandish Proverbs*

Adolf Hitler

But above all, the young, healthy boy must also learn to suffer blows.

—*Mein Kampf*

Abbie Hoffman

Sacred cows make the best hamburger.

—attributed

Nicholas von Hoffman

We are the people our parents warned us against.

—attributed

Robert Ingersoll

On every hand are the enemies of individuality and mental freedom. Custom meets us at the cradle and leaves us only at the tomb. Our first questions are answered by ignorance and our last by superstition. We are pushed and dragged by countless hands along the beaten track, and our entire training can be summed up in the word—suppression. Our desire to have a thing or to do a thing is considered as conclusive evidence that we ought not to have it...We are allowed to investigate all subjects in which we feel no particular interest, and to express the opinions of the majority with the utmost freedom.

— *Individuality*

How fortunate it is for us all that it is somewhat unnatural for a human being to obey. Universal obedience is universal stagnation; disobedience is one of the conditions of progress.

— Ibid.

The trouble with most people is, they bow to what is called authority; they have a certain reverence for the old because it is old. They think a man is better for being dead, especially if he has been dead a long time.

— Ibid.

I want you to remember that everybody is as he *must be*. I want you to get out of your minds the old nonsense of "free moral agency"; and then you will have charity for the whole human race. When you know that they are not responsible for their dispositions, any more than for their height; not responsible for their acts, any more than for their dreams; when you finally understand the philosophy that everything exists as the result of an efficient cause, and that the lightest fancy that ever fluttered its painted wings in the horizon of hope was as necessarily produced as the planet that in its orbit wheels about the sun—when you understand this, I believe you will have charity for all mankind—including even yourself.

— *A Lay Sermon*

I tell you there is something splendid in the man that will not always mind. Why, if we had done as the kings told us five hundred years ago, we should have all been slaves. If we had done as the priest told us we should all have been idiots. If we had done as the doctors told us, we should all have been dead. We have been saved by disobedience. We have been saved by the splendid thing called independence, and I want to see more of it, I want to see children raised so that they will have it.

— quoted by Bool & Carlyle in *For Liberty*

If you want to be happy yourself, if you are truly civilized, you want others to be happy. Every man ought, to the extent of his ability, to increase the happiness of mankind, for the reason that that will increase his own.

— quoted by Sprading in *Liberty and the Great Libertarians*

Henry James

To take what there *is*, and use it, without waiting forever in vain for the preconceived—to dig deep into the actual and get something out of *that*—this doubtless is the right way to live.

St. Jerome

We are all black by nature.

— *The Virgin's Profession*

Immanuel Kant

Enlightenment is the escape of man from his own childishness, which he himself maintains. The *childishness* consists in his incapacity to use his reason without another's guidance. *He himself maintains this childishness* when it is the result of an insufficiency, not of reason, but of the decision and manliness to use it without another's guidance. Know Thyself!

Have the manliness to use thine own reason. This is the motto of the enlightenment.

— quoted by Tolstoy

Alphonse Karr

The more things change, the more they remain the same.

— *Les Guepes/Les Femmes*

Peter Kropotkin

It is only those who do nothing who make no mistakes.

— *Anarchism: Its Philosophy and Ideals*

Mike Krukow

...you haven't lived until some 10-year-old kid calls you a hemorrhoid.

— on being abused by fans, quoted in the *San Francisco Chronicle*, July 16, 1986

Pope Leo XIII

To suffer and endure is the lot of humanity.

— *Quadragesimo anno*

Abraham Lincoln

It is not much in the nature of man to be driven to anything, still less to be driven about that which is exclusively his own business.

— quoted in *The Lincoln Memorial Album*

God must have loved the common people because he made so many of them.

— attributed

Martin Luther

We have altogether a confounded, corrupt, and poisoned nature, both in body and soul; throughout the whole of man is nothing that is good.

— *Table Talk*

Errico Malatesta

The accumulated and transmitted experience of successive generations has taught man that by uniting with other men his preservation is better secured and his well-being increased. Thus out of the struggle for existence, carried on against surrounding nature, and against individuals of their own species, the social instinct has been developed among men and has completely transformed the conditions of their life. Through cooperation man has been enabled to evolve out of animality, has risen to great power and elevated himself to such a degree above the other animals, that metaphysical philosophers have believed it necessary to invent for him an immaterial and immortal soul.

— *Anarchy*

The lower animals fight either individually or, more often, in little permanent or transitory groups against all nature, the other individuals of their own species included. Some of the more social animals, such as ants, bees, etc., associate together in the same ant-hill or beehive, but are at war with, or indifferent towards, other communities of their own species. Human strife with nature, on the contrary, tends always to broaden association among men, to unite their interests, and to develop each individual's sentiments of affection towards all others, so that united they may conquer and dominate the dangers of external nature by and for humanity.

— Ibid.

Karl Marx

The tradition of all the dead generations weighs like a nightmare on the brain of the living.

— *The Eighteenth Brumaire of Louis Bonaparte*

John Stuart Mill

. . . in proportion to a man's want of confidence in his own solitary judgment, does he usually repose with implicit trust on the infallibility of "the world" in general. And the world, to each individual, means the part of it with which he comes in contact; his party, his sect, his church, his class of society.

— *On Liberty*

The real advantage which truth has consists in this, that when an opinion is true it may be extinguished once, twice or many times, but in the course of ages there will generally be found persons to rediscover it, until some one of its reappearances falls on a time when from favorable circumstances it escapes persecution until it has made such head as to withstand all subsequent attempts to suppress it.

— Ibid.

Michel de Montaigne

There is no course of life so weak and sottish as that which is managed by orders, method, and discipline.

— *Essays*

Maria Montessori

Any nation that accepts the idea of servitude and believes that it is an advantage for man to be served by man, admits servility as an instinct, and indeed we all too easily lend ourselves to obsequious service, giving to it such complimentary names as courtesy, politeness, charity. In reality, he who is served is limited in his independence. This concept will be the foundation of the man of the future: "I do not wish to be served, because I am not an impotent."

— *The Montessori Method*

John Morley

It has been often said that he who begins life by stifling his convictions is in a fair way for ending it without any convictions to stifle.

— *On Compromise*

Friedrich Nietzsche

Why the stupid so often become malignant — To those arguments of our adversary against which our head feels too weak our heart replies by throwing suspicion on the motives of his argument.

— *Human, All Too Human*

The growth of wisdom may be gauged exactly by the diminution of ill-temper.

— Ibid.

...in a remarkable scholar one not infrequently finds a mediocre man; and often even in a mediocre artist, one finds a very remarkable man.
— *Beyond Good and Evil*

What a person *is* begins to betray itself when his talent decreases—when he ceases to show what he *can do*.
— Ibid.

The familiarity of superiors embitters one, because it may not be returned.
— Ibid.

It is too bad! Always the old story! When a man has finished building his house, he finds that he has learnt unawares something which he *ought* absolutely to have known before—he began to build. The eternal, fatal, "Too late!" The melancholia of everything *completed!*
— Ibid.

He who fights with monsters should be careful lest he thereby become a monster.
— Ibid.

Every step towards truth has had to be fought for and there has had to be abandoned for it almost whatever otherwise human hearts, human love, human confidence in life, are attached to. Therefore greatness of soul is required: the service of truth is the hardest service.
— *The Anti-Christ*

Swami Nirmalananda

Our modern society is engaged in polishing and decorating the cage in which man is kept imprisoned.
— *Enlightened Anarchism*

Max Nordau

Granted that mankind was happier when it was leading a dull, vegetable existence in the deepest ignorance, with a narrow mental horizon filled with the crudest errors and most foolish superstitions—this time of childhood is past and to wish to recall it is a vain and idle task. Not in the past is the remedy for the ills of humanity to be found. The present is unbearable. On the future alone then, we must stake our hopes.
— *Conventional Lies of Our Civilization*

Satchell Paige

Don't look back. Something might be gaining on you.
— attributed

Thomas Paine

Calumny is a vice of curious constitution; trying to kill it keeps it alive; leave it to itself and it will die a natural death.

Wendell Phillips

No one can know life except from suffering... It is in the protest of men ground down under some wrong principle that the world learns the depth and the extent of right.
— *The Pulpit*

Plato

All in all, nothing human is worth taking very seriously; nevertheless...
— *Republic*

Luis Polonia

These guys are only interested in one thing—and I don't know what it is.
— quoted on ESPN's Baseball Opening Day Special, 1991

Alexander Pope

A man should never be ashamed to own he has been in the wrong, which is but saying, in other words, that he is wiser today than he was yesterday.

Dan Quisenberry

I've seen the future, and it's much like the present, only longer.
— quoted in the *San Francisco Examiner*, March 11, 1990

Elisee Reclus

Between he who commands and he who obeys, and whose degradation deepens from generation to generation, there is no possibility of friendship.
— *Mutual Good Will*

Wilhelm Reich

That which philosophers, poets, superficial politicians, but also great psychologists designate and bemoan with the sentence "That's the way human nature is," completely coincides with sex-economy's clinical concept, "emotional plague." We can define it as the *sum total of all irrational functions of life in the human animal*.
— *The Mass Psychology of Fascism*

That a man steals because he is hungry, or that workers strike because they are being exploited needs no further psychological clarification. Reactionary psychology is wont to explain the theft and the strike in terms of supposed irrational motives; reactionary rationalizations are invariably the result. Social psychology sees the problem in an entirely different light: what has to be explained is not the fact that the man who is exploited steals, but why the majority who are hungry *don't* steal and why the majority of those who are exploited *don't* strike.

—Ibid.

Francois de Rochefoucauld

We have all of us sufficient fortitude to bear the misfortunes of others.

—*Maxims*

Rudolf Rocker

Asceticism in most cases is either the result of a sordid imagination or of passion diverted from its natural course, and experience has shown that when the protection of public morals is entrusted to its votaries, the consequences are usually appalling.

—*Pioneers of American Freedom*

John Rush

An easy grounder has a better chance of going through an infielder's legs when there are runners on base.

You're only as old as you look.

Arthur Schopenhauer

With people of only moderate ability modesty is mere honesty; but with those who possess great talent it is hypocrisy.

—*Further Psychological Observations*

There is no absurdity so palpable but that it may be firmly planted in the human head if only you begin to inculcate it before the age of five, by constantly repeating it with an air of great solemnity.

Albert Schweitzer

There are two things necessary to happiness: good health and a short memory.

—attributed

Seneca

Life, if well lived, is long enough.

—*De Ira*

George Bernard Shaw

No one ever feels helpless by the side of the self-helper; whilst the self-sacrificer is always a drag, a responsibility, a reproach, an everlasting and unnatural trouble with whom no really strong soul can live. Only those who have helped themselves know how to help others, and to respect their right to help themselves.

—quoted by Sprading in *Liberty and the Great Libertarians*

I often quote myself. It adds spice to my conversation.

—quoted by E. Haldeman-Julius in *Notes and Comments No. 5*

Self sacrifice allows us to sacrifice other people without blushing.

—*Maxims for Revolutionists*

Do not waste your time on Social Questions. What is the matter with the poor is Poverty: what is the matter with the rich is Uselessness.

—Ibid.

If you begin by sacrificing yourself to those you love, you will end by hating those to whom you have sacrificed yourself.

—Ibid.

Disobedience, the rarest and most courageous of the virtues, is seldom distinguished from neglect, the laziest and commonest of the vices.

—Ibid.

A moderately honest man with a moderately faithful wife, moderate drinkers both, in a moderately healthy house: that is the true middle class unit.

—Ibid.

The reasonable man adapts himself to the world: the unreasonable one persists in trying to adapt the world to himself. Therefore all progress depends on the unreasonable man.

—Ibid.

Every genuinely benevolent person loathes almsgiving and mendicity.

—Ibid.

Do not do unto others as you would that they should do unto you. Their tastes may not be the same.

—Ibid.

Do not love your neighbor as yourself. If you are on good terms with yourself it is an impertinence; if on bad, an injury.

—Ibid.

Titles distinguish the mediocre, embarrass the superior, and are disgraced by the inferior.

—Ibid.

If you cannot look evil in the face without illusion, you will never know what it really is, or combat it effectually. The few persons who are able (relatively) to do this are ignorantly called cynics.

All abstractions invested with collective consciousness or collective authority, set above the individual, and exacting duty from him on pretense of acting or thinking with greater validity than he, are man-eating idols, red with human sacrifices.

Percy Bysshe Shelley

Obedience,
Bane of all genius, virtue, freedom, truth,
Makes slaves of men, and of the human frame,
A mechanized automoton.

Let priest-led slaves cease to proclaim that man
Inherits vice and misery, when force
and falsehood hang even o'er the cradled babe
Stifling with rudest grasp all natural good.

How many a rustic Milton has passed by,
Stifling the speechless longings of his heart,
In unremitting drudgery and care!
How many a vulgar Cato has compelled
His energies, no longer tameless then,
To mould a pin or fabricate a nail!

The selfish for that happiness denied
To aught but virtue! Blind and hardened, they,
who hope for peace amid the storms of care,
Who covet power they know not how to use,
And sigh for pleasure they refuse to give, —
Madly they frustrate still their own designs;
And, where they hope that quiet to enjoy
Which virtue pictures, bitterness of soul,
Pining regrets, and vain repentances,
Disease, disgust and lassitude pervade
Their valueless and miserable lives.

— above excerpts from *Queen Mab*

Socrates

The unexamined life is not worth living.

Herbert Spencer

Here worship is strongest where there is least regard for human freedom.

— *Social Statics*

The subordination of a nation to a man, is not a wholesome but a vicious state of things: needful, indeed, for a vicious humanity. The instinct which makes it possible is any thing but a noble one. Call it "hero-worship" and it looks respectable...

...it has been the parent of countless crimes. It is answerable for the torturing and murder of the noble-minded who would not submit—for the horrors of Bastilles and Siberias. It has ever been the represser of knowledge, of free thought, of true progress. Whether you read the annals of the far past—whether you look at the various uncivilized races dispersed over the globe—or whether you contrast the existing nations of Europe; you equally find that submission to authority decreases as morality and intelligence increase. From ancient warrior-worship down to modern flunkeyism, the sentiment has ever been strongest where human nature has been vilest.

— *Representative Government*

Benedict Spinoza

The wise man does not meditate on death, but on how to live.

Charles T. Sprading

It is not thought that is dangerous to a nation, but the lack of it.

It is easy for a man with nothing to say to keep quiet.

Truth invites inquiry, falsehood dreads examination.

Real slaves of society teach "Live for God's sake," "Live for heaven's sake," "Live for society's sake," "Live for the church's sake," "Live for anything or anybody's sake but your own sake."

The libertarian believes that to live for others is to slave for others' sake, and slavery in all its forms is degrading. So he teaches, Live for yourself—first, last and all the time.

Living for one's own sake is elevating to the individual and is beneficial to the race and society as well, for a race of slaves is a benefit to but a few and a detriment to mankind.

The owner of slaves always taught his subjects duty. Now, duty is that which is due. It is doubtful if the slave owed the master anything; surely the free man owes no master obedience. The slaves to duty degrade themselves and injure those they serve.

An enlightened self-interest is in harmony with equal freedom.

The authoritarian sets up some book, or man, or tradition to establish the truth. The free thinker sets up reason and private judgment to discover the truth.

It takes the highest courage to utter unpopular truths.

For what purpose does society exist if not for the individuals composing it? If it is not for the individual, then he should withdraw from it. If society refuses to look out for his welfare, then he should oppose it. The reason for society is that it gives the individual some advantage that he does not possess alone. But when those advantages cease, then his relation with it should cease.

—above quotations from *Freedom and its Fundamentals*

Joe Stalin

The death of one man is a tragedy. The death of millions is a statistic.

—comment to Churchill at Potsdam, 1945

George Steinbrenner

I think we could put Adolf Hitler in center field and fans would cheer for him if he hit .350.

—quoted in *The Sporting news,* March 13, 1989

Joseph Stilwell

Don't let the bastards grind you down.

—translation of "Illegitimati non carborundum"

Don Sutton

I'm the most loyal player money can buy.

—attributed

Jonathan Swift

The stoical scheme of supplying our wants by lopping off our desires is like cutting off our feet when we want shoes.

— *Thoughts on Various Subjects*

Considering that natural disposition in many men to lie, and in multitudes to believe, I have been perplexed what to do with that maxim so frequent in everybody's mouth, that truth will at last prevail.

— *The Art of Political Lying*

Robert Tefton

BROWN, adj. A favored nose color among corporate and government executives.

DOG, n. A small groveling animal which embodies the most admired American virtues.

FAMILY, n. A traditional means of passing on neuroses from generation to generation.

FRIEND, n. A person with whom we can share the enjoyment of a third party's misfortune.

HOCKEY, n. A popular form of violence occasionally interrupted by play.

HUMAN, adj. 1) Lacking in common sense; 2) Having an immense capacity for self-deception; 3) Prone to self-pity.

ILLITERATE, n. In many parts of the United States, a synonym for "High School Graduate."

Ph.D., n. Phony Distinction. A title which the insufferably vain attach to their names in order that we might recognize them.

PHILANTHROPIC, adj. Motivated by guilt.

Henry David Thoreau

The mass of men lead lives of quiet desperation. What is called resignation is confirmed desperation.

— *Walden*

None can be an impartial or wise observer of human life but from the vantage ground of what we should call voluntary poverty.

—Ibid.

If I am to be a thoroughfare, I prefer that it be of the mountain-brooks...not the town sewers... I believe that the mind can be permanently profaned by the habit of attending to trivial things, so that all our thoughts shall be tinged with triviality.

— *Life Without Principles*

There are nine hundred ninety-nine patrons of virtue to one virtuous man.

—quoted by Rocker in *Pioneers of American Freedom*

Action from principle, the perception and the performance of right, changes things and relations; it is essentially revolutionary, and does not consist wholly with anything which was. It not only divides states and churches, it divides families; ay, it divides the *individual*, separating the diabolical in him from the divine.

—Ibid.

Leo Tolstoy

The greater the distance grows between reality and the consciousness of men, the more does hypocrisy expand; but there are limits even to hypocrisy, and it seems to me that in our time we have reached that limit.

— *The Kingdom of God Is Within You*

If there existed no external means for dimming their consciences, one-half of the men would at once shoot themselves, because to live contrary to one's reason is a most intolerable state, and all men of our time are in such a state.

—Ibid.

Mark Twain

Adam was human—this explains it all. He did not want the apple for the apple's sake, he wanted it only because it was forbidden. The mistake was in not forbidding the serpent; then he would have eaten the serpent.

— *Pudd'nhead Wilson*

A group of men in evening clothes looks like a flock of crows, and is just about as inspiring.

— *Dress Reform and Copyright* (speech)

. . . some of us can't be optimists, but by judiciously utilizing the opportunities that Providence puts in our way we can all be bigamists.

— *Sixty Seventh Birthday* (speech, October 28, 1902)

Let us endeavor to live that when we come to die even the undertaker will be sorry.

One of the most striking differences between a cat and a lie is that a cat has only nine lives.

The holy passion of Friendship is of so sweet and steady and loyal and enduring a nature that it will last through a whole lifetime, if not asked to lend money.

All say, "How hard it is that we have to die"—a strange complaint to come from the mouths of people who have had to live.

Courage is resistance to fear, mastery of fear—not absence of fear. Except a creature be part coward it is not a compliment to say it is brave; it is merely a misapplication of the word. Consider the flea!—incomparably the bravest of all the creatures of God, if ignorance of fear were courage . . . When we speak of Clive, Nelson, and Putnam as men who "didn't know what fear was," we ought always to add the flea—and put him at the head of the procession.

Nothing so needs reforming as other people's habits.

If you pick up a starving dog and make him prosperous, he will not bite you. This is the principle difference between a dog and a man.

Few things are harder to put up with than the annoyance of a good example.

— above quotations from *Pudd'nhead Wilson's Calendar*

Josiah Warren

Children are principally the creatures of *example* —whatever surrounding adults do, they will do. If we strike them, they will strike each other. If they see us attempting to govern each other, they will imitate the same barbarism. If we habitually admit the right of sovereignty in each other, and in them, then they will become equally respectful of our rights and of each other's.

— *Equitable Commerce*

Booker T. Washington

I have learned that success is to be measured not so much by the position that one has reached in life as by the obstacles which he has to overcome while trying to succeed.

— *Up from Slavery*

Walt Whitman

The least develop'd person on earth is just as important and sacred to himself or herself as the most develop'd person is to himself or herself.

What do you suppose will satisfy the soul, except to walk free and own no superior?

Henceforth I ask not good-fortune, I myself am good fortune.

Judge not as the judge judges, but as the sun falling upon a helpless thing.

— above quotations from Ingersoll's *Testimonial to Walt Whitman*

Oscar Wilde

Sometime the poor are praised for being thrifty. But to recommend thrift to the poor is both grotesque and insulting. It is like advising a man who is starving to eat less. For a town or country laborer to practice thrift would be absolutely immoral. Man should not be ready to show that he can live like a badly fed animal.

— quoted by Jack London in *The People of the Abyss*

Duty is what one expects from others—it is not what one does oneself.

— *A Woman of No Importance*

Simple pleasures are the last refuge of the complex.

— Ibid.

The only difference between the saint and sinner is that every saint has a past, and every sinner a future.

— Ibid.

We are all in the gutter, but some of us are looking at the stars.

— *Lady Windemere's Fan*

Experience is the name every one gives to their mistakes.

— Ibid.

Dullness is the coming-of-age of seriousness.

— *Phrases and Philosophies for the Use of the Young*

Those who see any difference between soul and body have neither.

— Ibid.

Disobedience, in the eyes of any one who has read history, is man's original virtue. It is through disobedience that progress has been made, through disobedience and rebellion.

— *The Soul of Man Under Socialism*

The only thing that one really knows about human nature is that it changes. Change is the one quality we can predicate on it. The systems that fail are those that rely on the permanency of human nature, and not on its growth and development. The error of Louis XIV was that he thought human nature would always be the same. The result of his error was the French Revolution. It was an admirable result. All the results of the mistakes of government are quite admirable.

— Ibid.

It is to be noted that Individualism does not come to the man with any sickly cant about duty, which merely means doing what other people want because they want it; or any hideous cant about self-sacrifice, which is merely a survival of savage mutilation.

— Ibid.

Selfishness is not living as one wishes to live, it is asking others to live as one wishes to live. And unselfishness is letting other people's lives alone, not interfering with them. Selfishness always aims at creating around it an absolute uniformity of type. Unselfishness recognises infinite variety of type as a delightful thing, accepts it, acquiesces in it, enjoys it. It is not selfish to think for oneself. A man who does not think for himself does not think at all.

Pleasure is Nature's test, her sign of approval.

— Ibid.

Every effect that one produces gives one an enemy. To be popular one must be a mediocrity.

— *The Picture of Dorian Grey*

Self-sacrifice is a thing that should be put down by law. It is so demoralizing to the people for whom one sacrifices oneself.

— *An Ideal Husband*

The only thing which sustains one through life is the consciousness of the immense inferiority of everybody else, and this feeling I have always cultivated.

— *The Remarkable Rocket*

The world is a stage, but the play is badly cast.

— *Lord Savile's Crime*

To be good, according to the vulgar standard of goodness, is obviously quite easy. It merely requires a certain amount of sordid terror, a certain lack of imaginative thought, and a certain low passion for middle-class respectability.

— *The Critic as Artist*

It is very much more difficult to talk about a thing than to do it. In the sphere of actual life, that is of course obvious. Anybody can make history. Only a great man can write it.

— Ibid.

If we lived long enough to see the results of our actions it may be that those who call themselves good would be sickened with a dull remorse, and those whom the world calls evil stirred by a noble joy.

— Ibid.

It is so easy for people to have sympathy with suffering. It is so difficult for them to have sympathy with thought. Indeed, so little do ordinary people understand what thought really is, that they seem to imagine that, when they have said that a theory is dangerous, they have pronounced its condemnation, whereas it is only such theories that have any intellectual value. An idea that is not dangerous is unworthy of being called an idea at all.

— Ibid.

The security of society lies in custom and unconscious instinct, and the basis of the stability of society, as a healthy organism, is the complete absence of any intelligence amongst its members. The great majority of people, being fully aware of this, rank themselves naturally on the side of that splendid system that elevates them to the dignity of machines, and rage so wildly against the intrusion of the intellectual faculty into any question that concerns life, that one is tempted to define man as a rational animal who always loses his temper when he is called upon to act in accordance with the dictates of reason.

— Ibid.

Every impulse that we strive to strangle broods in the mind and poisons us. . . The only way to get rid of temptation is to yield to it.

There are terrible temptations that it requires great strength and courage to yield to.

I never came across anyone in whom the moral sense was dominant who was not heartless, cruel, vindictive, log-stupid, and entirely lacking in the smallest sense of humanity. Moral people, as they are termed, are simple beasts. I would sooner have fifty unnatural vices than one unnatural virtue.

Each class preaches the importance of those virtues it need not exercise. The rich harp on the value of thrift, the idle grow eloquent over the dignity of labor.

Mary Wollstonecroft

Perhaps, if the existence of an evil being were allowed, who, in the allegorical language of scripture, went about seeking whom he could devour, he could not more effectually degrade the human character than by giving a man absolute power.

...birth, riches, and every extrinsic advantage that exalt a man above his fellows without any mental exertion sink him in reality below them. In proportion to his weakness, he is played upon by designing men, till the bloated monster has lost all traces of humanity.
—*A Vindication of the Rights of Women*

Fred Woodworth

The human tendency prefers familiar horrors to unknown delights.
—*Anarchist? What's That?*

How the aliens must gape in horror at our civilization, if they are out there! Like the person who has AIDS, humanity itself lacks the immune-system response to all that is monstrously devoid of meaning and logic... You could start a religion that proclaimed Jim Jones as Christ, and demand as sacrament that every tenth member consume dogshit laced with strychnine—people would rush to join up.
—*Black Star*, Spring 1987

...while life is fleeting, assholes live forever; or, as Latin might have it, "Arse longa, vita brevis."
—*The Match!*, No. 74

Phillip Wylie

God must have hated the common people because he made them so common.
—attributed

Anonymous & Multiple Author

No good deed goes unpunished.
—Anonymous

The race is not always to the swift nor the battle to the strong—but that's the way to bet.
—Anonymous

She's Actin' Single and I'm Drinkin' Doubles
—C&W song title

Mama's Dead and Papa's Dead Drunk
—C&W song title

It's a Headache Tomorrow or a Heartache Tonight
—C&W song title

Everything you know is wrong.
—Firesign Theater, album title

The people wish to be deceived.
—Medieval proverb

A pessimist is a man who, when he has the choice between two evils, chooses both.
—Anonymous

No one is completely worthless—they can always serve as a bad example.
—Graffiti

I take my desires for reality because I believe in the reality of my desires.
—Graffiti, Paris, May 1968

There are four basic human needs: food, sleep, sex, and revenge.
—Anonymous

A fool and his money are soon partying.
—Anonymous

He's a self-made man, but he's the most unskilled workman I've ever seen.
—Anonymous

You Are What You Ingest

and Medicine & Other Miseries

St. Ambrose

The precepts of medicine are contrary to celestial science, watching, and prayer.
— quoted by A.D. White in *The History of the Warfare Between Science and Theology*

St. Augustine

All diseases of Christians are to be ascribed to these demons; chiefly do they torment fresh-baptized Christians, yea, even the guiltless newborn infants.
— quoted by A.D. White

Ambrose Bierce

ABSTAINER, A weak person who yields to the temptation of denying himself a pleasure.

CABBAGE, A familiar kitchen-garden vegetable about as large and wise as a man's head.

FORK, An instrument used chiefly for the purpose of putting dead animals into the mouth.
— above definitions from *The Devil's Dictionary*

Rufus Choate

Well, it is better to have lunched and lost than never to have lunched at all.
— on seasickness (attributed)

Barry Goldwater

I have heard that the [National Press Club] serves only Texas chili. Tell me this is not true. A Texan does not know chili from leavings in a corral.
— attributed

King James I

A custom loathsome to the eye, hateful to the nose, harmful to the brain, dangerous to the lungs, and in the black, stinking fume thereof, nearest resembling the horrible Stygian smoke of the pit that is bottomless.
— *A Counterblaste to Tobacco*

Timothy Leary

Turn on. Tune in. Drop out.

Pope Leo X

This cross measured forty times makes the height of Christ in his humanity. He who kisses it is preserved for seven days from falling, sickness, apoplexy, and sudden death.
— Inscription on holy cards sold by the pontiff

Abraham Lincoln

If we take habitual drunkards as a class, their heads and their hearts will bear an advantageous comparison with those of any other class. There seems ever to have been a proneness in the brilliant and warm-blooded to fall into this vice. The demon of intemperance ever seems to have delighted in sucking the blood of genius and generosity.
— Address to the Washington Temperance Society, Springfield, Illinois, February 22, 1842

Martin Luther

Our bodies are always exposed to the attacks of Satan. The maladies I suffer are not natural, but Devil's spells.
— *Table Talk*

Satan produces all the maladies which afflict mankind for he is the prince of death.

Graphic by J. R. Swanson. Definition by Chaz Bufe.

DRUG ADDICTION, *n.* A popular method of dealing with day-to-day living in the United States.

Errico Malatesta

There are in France stringent laws against the traffic in drugs and against those who take them. And, as always happens, the scourge grows and spreads in spite, and perhaps because, of the laws...

It is the old mistake of legislators, in spite of experience invariably showing that laws, however barbarous they may be, have never served to suppress vice or to discourage delinquency. The more severe the penalties imposed on the consumers and traffickers of cocaine, the greater will be the attraction of forbidden fruits and the fascination of the risks incurred by the consumer, and the greater will be the profits made by the speculators, avid for money.

It is useless, therefore, to hope for anything from the law. We must suggest another solution. Make the use and sale of cocaine free, and open kiosks where it would be sold at cost or even under cost. And then launch a great propaganda campaign to explain to the public, and let them see for themselves, the evils of coaine; no one would engage in counter-propaganda because nobody could exploit the misfortunes of cocaine addicts.

Certainly the harmful use of cocaine would not disappear completely, because the social causes which create and drive those poor devils to the use of drugs would still exist. But in any case the evil would decrease, because nobody could make profits out of its sale... and for this reason our suggestion either will not be taken into account, or it will be considered impractical and mad.

— *Umanita Nova*, August 10, 1922

Rabbit Maranville

There is much less drinking now than there was before 1927, because I quit drinking on May 24, 1927.

— attributed

Wendell Phillips

In a recent speech before an audience of three thousand people in New York, I alluded to the governor's argument that alcohol was "food," and had nutritive properties as well as beef. Without consulting authorities, if alcohol is food, and any one will prove to me that beef causes two thirds of the pauperism and crime in the community, then I demand the prohibition of beef.

— *Christianity a Battle, Not a Dream*

Mary Pettibone Poole

Culture is what your butcher would have if he were a surgeon.

— attributed

George Bernard Shaw

My dear Barbara: Alcohol is a very necessary article...It makes life bearable to millions of people who could not endure their existence if they were quite sober. It enables Parliament to do things at eleven at night that no sane person would do at eleven in the morning.

— *Major Barbara* (Undershaft speaking)

I have never smoked in my life and look forward to a time when the world will look back with amazement and disgust to a practice so unnatural and offensive.

— quoted in the *New York Herald Tribune*, April 14, 1946

Percy Bysshe Shelley

It is only by softening and disguising dead flesh by culinary preparation that it is rendered susceptible of mastication or digestion, and that the sight of its bloody juices and raw horror does not excite intolerable loathing and disgust.

Lysander Spooner

A government that shall punish vices impartially is so obviously an impossibility that nobody was ever found, or ever will be found, foolish enough to propose it. The most that any one proposes is that government shall punish some one, or at most a few, of what he esteems the grossest of them. But this discrimination is an utterly absurd, illogical and tyrannical one. What right has any body of men to say, "The vices of other men *we* will punish; but our vices nobody shall punish? *We* will restrain other men from seeking their own happiness, according to their own notions of it; but nobody shall restrain *us*, from seeking our own happiness according to our own notions of it? *We* will restrain other men from acquiring any experimental knowledge of what is conducive or necessary to their own happiness; but nobody shall restrain *us* from acquiring an experimental knowledge of what is conducive or necessary to our own happiness?"

Nobody but knaves or blockheads ever thinks of making such absurd assumptions as these. And yet, evidently it is only upon such assumptions that anybody can claim the right to punish the vices of others, and at the same time claim exemption from punishment for his own.

— *Vices Are Not Crimes*

It is of no use to say that drunkenness, or any other vice, only adds to their miseries; for such is human nature — the weakness of human nature, if you please — that men can endure but a certain amount of misery, before their hope and courage fail, and they yield to almost anything that promises present relief or mitigation;...

— Ibid.

The really unanswerable objection to Prohibition was always the Prohibitionists...it was quickly manifest that improving the world was the last consideration in their minds. What moved them was simply a violent desire to satisfy their egos by harassing their fellow-men. It quickly became apparent that Prohibition actually made the world worse, and yet they continued to be hot for it and, in fact, with increasing fervor. Toward the end they refused to hear any evidence against their delusion. They became mere brutal bullies, who, having discovered a way to work their will upon their betters, pursued it recklessly and relentlessly. The same thing is true of all other moral reformers. Their altruism is always only an afterthought. What really motivates them is an insensate desire to wreak vengeance...

— Ibid.

Charles T. Sprading

The case of the total abstainer is worse than that of the overindulger. The second is curable, the first is hopeless.

— *Freedom and its Fundamentals*

Robert Tefton

DRUNKENNESS, n. A temporary but popular cure for Catholicism.

SMOKER, n. A person who believes he has the right to annoy and poison those around him. Unlike the user of non-addictive drugs, the smoker is to be pitied and tolerated rather than persecuted and imprisoned. See also "Asshole."

TOBACCO, n. A toxic, addictive substance, the chief drawback of which is that it does not kill its users more quickly.

Andrew Dickson White

The enormous development of miracle and fetish cures in the Church continued during century after century...the Church supposed herself in possession of something far better than scientific methods in medicine...

Thus the water in which a single hair of a saint had been dipped was used as a purgative; water in which St. Remy's ring had been dipped cured fevers; wine in which the bones of a saint had been dipped cured lunacy; oil from a lamp burning before the tomb of St. Gall cured tumours; St. Valentine cured epilepsy; St. Christopher, throat diseases; St. Eutropius dropsy; St. Ovid, deafness; St. Gervase, rheumatism; St. Apollonia, toothache; St. Vitus, St. Anthony, and a multitude of other saints, the maladies which bear their names. Even as late as

1784 we find certain authorities in Bavaria ordering that any one bitten by a mad dog shall at once put up prayers at the shrine of St. Hubert, and not waste his time in any attempts at medical or surgical cure. In the twelfth century we find a noted cure attempted by causing the invalid to drink water in which St. Bernard had washed his hands...The pulpit everywhere dwelt with unction on the reality of fetish cures...

Still another method evolved by this theological pseudo-science was that of disgusting the demon with the body which he tormented: hence the patient was made to swallow or apply to himself various unspeakable ordures, with such medicines as the livers of toads, the blood of frogs and rats, fibres of the hangman's rope, and ointment made from the body of gibbeted criminals. Many of these were survivals of heathen superstitions, but theologic reasoning wrought into them an orthodox significance. As an example of this mixture of heathen with Christian magic, we may cite the following from a medieval medical book as a salve against "nocturnal goblin visitors": "Take hop plant, wormwood, bishopwort, lupine, ash-throat, henbane, harewort, viper's bugloss, heathberry plant, cropleek, garlic, grains of hedgerlife, githrife, and fennel. Put these worts into a vessel, set them under the altar, sing over them nine masses, boil them in butter and sheep's grease, add much holy salt, strain through a cloth, throw the worts into running water. If any ill tempting occur to a man, or an elf or goblin night visitors come, smear his body with this salve, and put it on his eyes, and cense him with incense, and sign him frequently with the sign of the cross. His condition will soon be better.

...theological reasoning developed an idea... that Satan, in causing pestilences, used as his emissaries especially Jews and witches. The proof of this belief in the case of the Jews was seen in the fact that they escaped with a less percentage of disease than did the Christians in the great plague periods ...Certainly they observed more careful sanitary rules and more constant abstinence from dangerous foods than was usual among Christians; but the public at large could not understand so simple a cause, and jumped to the conclusion that their immunity resulted from protection by Satan, and that this protection was repaid and the pestilence caused by their wholesale poisoning of Christians. As a result of this mode of thought, attempts were made in all parts of Europe to propitiate the Almighty, to thwart Satan, and to stop the plague by torturing and murdering the Jews. Throughout Europe during great pestilences we hear of extensive burnings of this devoted people. In Bavaria, at the time of the Black Death, it is computed that twelve thousand Jews thus perished; in the small town of Erfurt the number is said to have been three thousand; in Strasburg, the Rue Brulee remains a monument to the two thousand Jews burned there for poisoning the wells and causing the plague

of 1348; at the royal castle of Chinon, near Tours, an immense trench was dug, filled with blazing wood, and in a single day one hundred and sixty Jews were burned.

Accounts of the filthiness of Scotch cities and villages, down to a period well within this [19th] century, seem monstrous. All that in these days is swept into the sewers was in those allowed to remain around the houses or thrown into the streets. The old theological theory, that "vain is the help of man,"

checked scientific thought and paralyzed sanitary endeavour. The result was natural: between the thirteenth and seventeenth centuries thirty notable epidemics swept the country, and some of them carried off multitudes; but as a rule these never suggested sanitary improvement; they were called "visitations," attributed to Divine wrath against human sin, and the work of the authorities was to announce the particular sin concerned and to declaim against it.

— above quotations from *The History of the Warfare Between Science and Theology*

PARENTS! IS YOUR BABY

ALIVE WITH PLEASURE?!?

Well then it's time to begin channeling that pleasure into useful consumption habits that will become the backbone of American Commerce. Forget about a SuperBaby— **Sign up your newborn to be a**

BUTT BABY!

Graphic from *Processed World*. Illustration by J.R. Swanson.

A consortium of U.S. tobacco companies is offering new parents a special deal: Sign your child up before they're two years old and s/he will qualify for a special drawing to win **HUGE SCHOLARSHIPS!!** And they will get free cigarettes while in college, the military, or incarcerated (forever!). A **free signing bonus is yours:** a rubber-lined, specially designed oversized ashtray/crib

Oscar Wilde

One knows so well the popular idea of health. The English country-gentleman galloping after a fox — the unspeakable in full pursuit of the uneatable.
— *A Woman of No Importance*

Frank Zappa

Speed will turn you into your parents.
— attributed

Anonymous & Multiple Author

Better belly burst than good drink lost.
— English proverb

Over 1 Billion Sold
— Hamburger stand sign

Over 1 Billion Dead
— Graffiti

Reality is for those too weak to handle drugs.
— Graffiti

LSD consumes 47 times its own weight in excess reality.
— Graffiti

Smoking is pulmonary rape.
— Bumpersticker

Kissing a smoker is like licking an ashtray.
— Anonymous

You are what you eat.
— "New Age" bromide

A note on brains: "You are what you eat" shouldn't be taken too literally; unlike some primitive tribesmen, you needn't fear that eating the brains of the wealthy will endow you with their personality traits and transform you overnight into an avaricious, exploitative parasite. This is no more possible than the eating of cow brains causing you to give milk and begin mooing!
— *To Serve The Rich*

Clean, Sober, and Bored Shitless
— Bumpersticker

I drink, therefore I am.
— Anonymous

The best cure for drunkenness is, when sober, to look at a drunken man.
— Chinese proverb

Dyslexics of the world untie!
— Graffiti

New! Improved! *INSTANT ASSHOLE*...Just Add Alcohol!
— Bumpersticker

Sex

St. Alphonsus

Young woman, if you are going to be married to that young man, I will tell you what to do. First, try as much as you can not to be *alone* with him, especially at *night*, or in the *dark*, or in *secret*, or in *lonesome places*. Try not to have *long conversations* with him, or have *long walks* with him.

—quoted by Reverend J. Furniss in *Tracts for Spiritual Reading*

Melvin Anchell

Pornography embellishes the physical sex life of free lovers and perverts.

The regressive effect of pornography on sexual behavior brings on premature death.

The debased sexual behavior that frequently becomes the life style for persons devoid of religion produces the first crack in the mental dam holding back regression to savagery.

Normally, public displays of nudity and sex cause embarrassment; they rouse feelings of disgust and shame. These feelings are natural barriers to perversion.

Our modern culture is spawning indifferent youths devoid of idealized love. Its members have adopted cave-man sex practices consisting of promiscuity and deviances replete with exhibitionism, voyeurism and other unmentionable practices. Many of them, then, commit suicide...

Better to go through life crippled than sexually perverted.

—*Pornography, a Psychiatrist's Verdict* (officially approved Catholic pamphlet)

St. Thomas Aquinas

When children are born of the intercourse of devils with human beings, they do not come from the seed of the devil or of the human body he has assumed, but of the seed which he has extracted from another human being [as a succubus]. The same devil who, as a woman, has intercourse with a man, can also, in the form of a man, have intercourse with a woman...

—quoted by McCabe in *A History of Satanism*

T.S. Atarov

Under Soviet conditions masturbation is no longer the mass phenomenon it was in the past.

—quoted by Brinton in *The Irrational in Politics*

St. Augustine

Give me chastity and continence, but do not give it yet.

—*Confessions*

How much better could two men live and converse together than a man and a woman.

—*On Genesis*

Sinful lust is not nature but a disease of nature.

—*On Continence*

The children of the flesh can never be compared to the glory of holy virginity.

—*On Holy Virginity*

Intercourse with even a lawful wife is unlawful and wicked if the conception of offspring be prevented.

—*Conjugal Adultery*

Nothing so much casts down the mind of man from its citadel as do the blandishments of women, and that physical contact without which a wife cannot be possessed.

—*Soliloquies*

Nothing is so much to be shunned as sex relations.

—Ibid.

Second marriages are lawful, but holy widowhood is better.

—*On the Good of Widowhood*

If a man leaves his wife and she marries another, she commits adultery.

—*On the Good of Marriage*

Marriage is not good, but it is good in comparison with fornication.

—Ibid.

Suppress prostitution and capricious lust will overthrow society.

Honore de Balzac

The majority of husbands remind me of an orang-utang trying to play the violin.

— *The Physiology of Marriage*

Ambrose Bierce

LOVE, A temporary insanity curable by marriage.

— *The Devil's Dictionary*

MARRIAGE, The state or condition of a community consisting of a master, a mistress and two slaves, making in all, two.

— Ibid.

Edward Carpenter

The commercial prostitution of love is the last outcome of our whole social system, and its most clear condemnation. It flaunts in our streets, it hides itself in the garment of respectability under the name of matrimony...it is fed by the oppression and the ignorance of women, by their poverty and denied means of livelihood, and by the hypocritical puritanism which forbids them by millions not only to gratify but even to speak of their natural desires; and it is encouraged by the callousness of an age which has accustomed men to buy and sell for money every most precious thing — even the life-long labor of their brothers, therefore why not also the very bodies of their sisters.

— *Love's Coming of Age*

St. John Chrysostom

Virginity stands as far above marriage as the heavens above the earth.

— *On Virginity*

Clement of Alexandria

Fornication is just a lapse from one marriage into many.

Anatole France

Of all the sexual aberrations, chastity is the strangest.

— attributed

Benjamin Franklin

It is the Man and Woman united that makes the complete Human Being...A single man has not nearly the Value he would have in that State of Union. He is an incomplete Animal. He resembles the odd Half of a Pair of Scissors.

— Letter to a Young Friend, June 25, 1745

...in your Amours you should *prefer old Women to Young ones*. This you call a Paradox and demand my reasons. They are these:

...covering all above with a Basket, and regarding only what is below the Girdle, it is impossible of two Women to know an old from a young one. And as in the Dark all Cats are grey, the Pleasure of Corporeal Enjoyment with an old Woman is at least equal and frequently superior; every Knack being by Practice capable by improvement.

...lastly. They are so grateful!!!

— Ibid.

Rev. J. Furniss, C.S.S.R.

Did you ever see two deadly vipers fly at each other? Their eyes burn with rage. They shoot out their poisoned stings. They struggle to give each other the death-blow. They struggle till they have torn the flesh and blood from each other. You may see the like of this in hell. See that young man and young woman — how changed they are! They loved each other so much on earth, that for this they broke the laws of God and man. But now they fight each other like two vipers, and so they will fight for all eternity.

— *Tracts for Spiritual Reading* (a Catholic *children's* book)

Emma Goldman

Love, the strongest and deepest element in all life, the harbinger of hope, of joy, of ecstasy; love, the defier of laws, of all conventions; love, the freest, the most powerful molder of human destiny; how can such an all-compelling force be synonymous with that poor little State- and church-begotten weed, marriage?

— *Marriage and Love*

Free love? as if love is anything but free. Man has bought brains, but all the millions in the world have failed to buy love.

— Ibid.

On rare occasions one does hear of a miraculous case of a married couple falling in love after marriage, but on close examination it will be found that it is a mere adjustment to the inevitable.

— Ibid.

Marriage is primarily an economic arrangement, an insurance pact. It differs from the ordinary life insurance agreement only in that it is more binding, more exacting. Its returns are insignificantly small compared with the investments. In taking out an insurance policy one pays for it in dollars and cents, always at liberty to discontinue payments. If, however, woman's premium is a husband, she pays for it with her name, her privacy, her self-respect, her very life, "until death doth part." Moreover, the marriage insurance condemns her to life-long dependency, to parasitism, to complete uselessness, individual as well as social...

Thus Dante's motto over Inferno applies with equal force to marriage: "Ye who enter here leave all hope behind."
—Ibid.

As a matter of fact, prostitution is no more a safeguard for the purity of the home than rigid laws are a safeguard against prostitution. Fully fifty per cent of married men are patrons of brothels. It is through this virtuous element that the married women—nay, even the children—are infected with venereal diseases. Yet society has not a word of condemnation for the man, while no law is too monstrous to be set in motion against the helpless victim. She is not only preyed upon by those who use her, but she is also absolutely at the mercy of every policeman and miserable detective on the beat, the officials at the station house, the authorities in every prison.
— *The Traffic in Women*

If love does not know how to give and take without restrictions, it is not love, but a transaction that never fails to lay stress on a plus and a minus.
— *The Tragedy of Women's Emancipation*

St. Gregory of Nazianzum

Blessed is the one who leads a celibate life and soils not the divine image within him with the filth of concupiscence.

Cardinal P.J. Hayes

Heinous is the sin [of birth control] against the creative act of God...To take life after its inception is a *horrible crime*, but to *prevent* human life that the Creator is about to bring into being is *Satanic*. In the first instance the body is killed while the soul lives on...In the latter not only a body but an immortal soul is denied existence, in time and eternity. It has been reserved to our day to see advocated shamelessly the legalizing of such a diabolic thing.
—quoted in *The New York Times*, December 18, 1921

Adolf Hitler

And marriage cannot be an end in itself, but must serve the one higher goal, the increase and preservation of the species and the race. This alone is its meaning and its task.
— *Mein Kampf*

Our whole public life today is like a hothouse for sexual ideas and stimulations. Just look at the bill of fare served up in our movies...this must cause great damage in our youth.
—Ibid.

Public life must be freed from the stifling perfume of our modern eroticism...
—Ibid.

J. Edgar Hoover

I regret to say that we of the FBI are powerless to act in case of oral-genital intimacy, unless it has in some way obstructed interstate commerce.
—attributed

Henry Hudson

If we relied exclusively on scientific data for every one of our findings, I'm afraid all our work would be inconclusive.
—on Reagan's anti-pornography commission (of which Hudson was chair), quoted in the *San Francisco Chronicle*, July 14, 1987

Aldous Huxley

Chastity: the most unnatural of the sexual perversions.
—attributed

St. Jerome

If it is good not to touch a woman, then it is bad to touch a woman.
— *Epistle 48* (refers to 1 Corinthians 7:1)

Matrimony is always a vice, all that can be done is to excuse it; therefore it was made a religious sacrament.

Virginity can be lost by a thought.

...marriage is good for those who are afraid to sleep alone at night.
— *Attack on Jovinian*

Of all the Roman ladies, only one had the power to tempt me, and that one was Paula. She mourned and she fasted. She was squalid with dirt; her eyes were dim from weeping...The Psalms were her only songs; the gospel her only speech; continence her one indulgence; fasting her staple of life.
— *Epistle 45*

I praise marriage only because it gives me virgins.
— *Epistle 22*

It is time to cut down the forest of marriage with the ax of virginity.
— *Epistle 123*

Florynce Kennedy

If men could get pregnant, abortion would be a sacrament.
—attributed

Ellen Key

Love has been in perpetual strife with monogamy.
— quoted by Sprading in *Liberty and the Great Libertarians*

A great poet has seldom sung of lawfully wedded happiness, but of free and secret love; and in this respect, too, the time is coming when there will no longer be one standard of morality for poetry and another for life. To anyone tender of conscience, the ties formed by a free connection are stronger than the legal ones...
— Ibid.

V.I. Lenin

Thirst must be satisfied—but will the normal man in normal circumstances lie down in the gutter and drink out of a glass with a rim greasy from many lips?
— on sexual freedom, quoted by Brinton in *The Irrational in Politics*

Pople Leo XIII

Divorce is born of perverted morals, and leads, as experience shows, to vicious habits in public and private life.
— *Arcanum divinae sapientiae*

When Christianity is rejected, marriage inevitably sinks into the slavery of man's vile passions.
— Ibid.

Joseph McCabe

This indissoluble monogamous marriage is supposed to be the grandest of institutions, radiating sunshine from happy homes. Yet the same apologist who assures us of this now offers us a picture of the race boiling with rebellious lust, so eager to throw off all restraint that it is ready to bring about its own destruction, held within the bonds of marriage only by the sure and certain knowledge that if a man does not submit to them [the church's prohibitions] he will spend all eternity in an underground tank of burning sulphur.
— *The Catholic Church and the Sex Question*

Harvey Milk

If we are not truly free to be ourselves in that which is most important of all human activities, the expression of love, then life itself loses its meaning.
— attributed

Michel de Montaigne

A good marriage would be between a blind wife and a deaf husband.
— *Essays*

Friedrich Nietzsche

...marriage, as we have said, *cannot* be founded on "love"—it is founded on sexual impulse, on the impulse to possess property (woman and child as property), on the *impulse to rule*, which constantly organizes for itself the smallest type of sovereignty (family), which *needs* children and heirs to maintain physiologically an acquired measure of power, influence and riches...
— *The Twilight of the Idols*

A pair of powerful spectacles has sometimes sufficed to cure a person in love...
— *Human, All Too Human*

Christianity gave Eros poison to drink; he did not die of it, certainly, but degenerated to Vice.
— *Beyond Good and Evil*

Max Nordau

A woman who sells herself to buy bread for her aged mother or her child, stands upon a higher moral plane than the blushing maiden who marries a money bag, in order to gratify her frivolous appetite for parties and travel. Of two men, he is the less deceived, the more logical and rational, who pays his companion of an hour in cash, each time, than he who gets a companion for life by the marriage contract, whose society was purchased as much as in the former case. Every alliance between man and woman in which either one is influenced by the substantial or selfish advantage to be gained by it, is prostitution...
But this is the character of almost all marriages ...Poor girls are carefully warned by their parents to stifle the dangerous natural impulses of their hearts, and to gauge the sweetness of their smile by the figure of the bachelor's income.
— *Conventional Lies of Our Civilization*

Unconditional fidelity is not an attribute of human nature...That we exact it is an outcome of our egotism. The individual wishes to reign entirely alone in the heart of the beloved, to fill it completely, to see only his reflection in the mirror, because... selfishness or vanity can conceive of no more perfect gratification than the observation of such a phenomenon.
— Ibid.

Origen

Marriage is something unholy and unclean, a means of sensuality.

Pope Pius XI

Any use whatsoever of matrimony exercised in such a way that the act is deliberately frustrated in its natural power to generate life is an offense against the law of God and of nature, and those who indulge in such are branded with the guilt of a grave sin.

— *Casti Connubii*

Since the conjugal act is designed primarily by nature for the begetting of children, those who in exercising it deliberately frustrate its natural power and purpose sin against nature and commit an act which is shameful and inherently vicious.

— Ibid.

Cardinal Joseph Ratzinger

Christians who are homosexual are called, as all of us are, to a chaste life. When they engage in homosexual activity, they confirm within themselves a disordered sexual inclination which is essentially self-indulgent.

— *Pastoral Letter on the Care of Homosexual Persons* (1986)

You cannot belong to Christ unless you crucify all self-indulgent passions and desires.

— Ibid.

Wilhelm Reich

. . . the goal of sexual repression is that of producing an individual who is adjusted to the authoritarian order and will submit to it in spite of all misery and degradation.

— *The Mass Psychology of Fascism*

The sexual morality that inhibits the will to freedom, as well as those forces that comply with authoritarian interests, derive their energy from repressed sexuality. . . *sexual inhibition changes the structure of economically suppressed man in such a way that he acts, feels and thinks contrary to his own material interests.*

— Ibid.

For what sociological reasons is sexuality suppressed by the society and repressed by the individual? The church says it is for the sake of salvation beyond the grave; mystic moral philosophy says that it is a direct result of man's eternal ethical and moral nature; the Freudian philosophy of civilization contends that this takes place in the interest of "culture." One becomes a bit skeptical and asks how is it possible for the masturbation of small children and the sexual intercourse of adolescents to disturb the building of gas stations and the manufacturing of airplanes. It becomes apparent that it is not cultural activity itself which demands suppression and repression of sexuality, but only the present *forms* of this activity. . .

— Ibid.

The moral inhibition of the child's natural sexuality, the last stage of which is the severe impairment of the child's *genital* sexuality, makes the child afraid, shy, fearful of authority, obedient, "good," and "docile" in the authoritarian sense of the words. It has a crippling effect on man's rebellious forces because every vital life impulse is now burdened with severe fear; and since sex is a forbidden subject, thought in general and man's critical faculty also become inhibited. In short, morality's aim is to produce acquiescent subjects who, despite distress and humiliation, are adjusted to the autoritarian order. Thus, the family is the authoritarian state in miniature, to which the child must learn to adapt himself as a preparation for the general social adjustment required of him later. *Man's authoritarian structure* — this must be clearly established — is basically produced by this embedding of sexual inhibitions and fear in the living substance of sexual impulses.

— Ibid.

John Rush

Expectant parents who want a boy will get a girl, and vice versa; those couples who practice birth control will get twins.

Marriage turns lovers into relatives.

Margo St. James

In this prostituting society, we all have to hustle, and I'd rather suck cock than kiss ass!

— attributed

Theodore Schroeder

Obscenity is not a quality inherent in a book or picture, but is solely and exclusively a contribution of the reading mind, and hence cannot be defined in terms of the qualities of a book or picture.

Has it ever occurred to you that the witchcraft superstition was almost identical, in its essence, with the present superstitious belief in the reality of the "obscene," as a thing outside the mind?

Fanatical men and pious judges, otherwise intelligent, have affirmed the reality of both, and, on the assumption of their inerrancy in this, have assumed to punish their fellow men. It is computed from historical records that 9,000,000 persons were put to death for witchcraft after 1484. The opponents of witch-belief were denounced just as disbelievers in the "obscene" are now denounced. Yet witches ceased to be, when men no longer believed in them. Think it over and see if the "obscene" will not also disappear when mean cease to believe in it.

. . . Obscenity and witches exist only in the minds and emotions of those who believe in them, and neither dogmatic judicial dictum nor righteous vituperation can ever give them any objective existence.

— quoted by Charles Sprading in *Liberty and the Great Libertarians*

George Bernard Shaw

Although romantic idealists generally insist on self-surrender as an indispensable element in true womanly love, its repulsive effect is well known and feared in practice by both sexes.

— quoted by Charles Sprading in *Liberty and the Great Libertarians*

Percy Bysshe Shelley

Love withers under constraints: its very essence is liberty: it is compatible neither with obedience, jealousy, nor fear: it is there most pure, perfect, and unlimited where its votaries live in confidence, equality and unreserve.

— *Queen Mab* notes

Robert Tefton

MASTURBATION, n. An extremely disgusting act performed on a regular basis by everyone *else*.

MONOGAMY, n. A common misspelling. See "Monotony."

Tertullian

We Christians regard a stain upon our chastity as more dreadful than any punishment, or even death itself.

— *Apologeticus*

Nicolas Walter

We [anarchists] are in favor of free love, but this does not mean that we advocate universal promiscuity; it means that all love is free, except prostitution and rape, and that people should be able to choose (or reject) forms of sexual behaviour and sexual partners for themselves. Extreme indulgence may suit one person, extreme chastity another — though most anarchists feel that the world would be a better place if there had been a lot less fussing and a lot more fucking.

— *About Anarchism*

Colin Ward

Those who have prophesied dreadful consequences as a result of the greater sexual freedom which the young assert — unwanted babies, venereal disease and so on — are usually the very same people who seek the fulfilment of their prophecies by opposing the free availability to the young of contraception and the removal of the stigma and mystification that surround venereal disease.

— *Anarchy in Action*

Anarchists, from Emma Goldman to Alex Comfort, have observed the connection between political and sexual repression and although those who think sexual liberation is necessarily going to lead to political and economic liberation are probably optimistic, it certainly makes people happier.

— Ibid.

Oscar Wilde

One should always be in love. That is why one should never marry.

Young men want to be faithful and are not; old men want to be faithless and cannot.

— *The Picture of Dorian Grey*

Anonymous & Multiple Author

Joey is a switch hitter and he's still batting zero.
— Graffiti, San Francisco, 1986

Virginity is like a bubble — one prick and it's gone.
— Graffiti

Abortion, which destroys life, is inadmissible in any country. Soviet woman has the same rights as Soviet man, but that does not absolve here from the great and honorable duty imposed on her by nature: she is to be a mother. She is to bear life. And this is certainly not a private matter but a public matter of great social significance.
— *Trud* (official Soviet trade union paper), April 27, 1936

You can catch VD in this john — but the floor is awfully cold.
— Graffiti

Sexism is a social disease.
— Graffiti

Oklahoma: Where men are men and sheep are *nervous*.
— Bumpersticker

Texas: The state where men are still men and sheep walk bow-legged.
— Graffiti

INCHES: The Magazine for Men Who Think BIG
— Title of gay porn magazine

Look at this. . . a new ideology! It's great, it makes you feel *really* guilty!
— *Processed World* No. 7, on *The Dialectic of Sex*

This is the worst chewing gum I've ever tasted.
— Graffiti on the side of a truckstop condom machine

Frank grinds his chuck daily.
— Sign on a hamburger stand.

If you think sex is a pain in the ass, try a new position.
— Graffiti

I'm a Christian auto-eroticist — I pound it!
— *The National Armbiter*, 1977

Support women's lib. Make *him* sleep on the wet spot.
— Bumpersticker

The heart of the question that the comrades are asking is this: is it anti-communist to have sexual relations with other than husband or wife, is it anti-communist to have sexual relations before marriage?
— *Proletariat* (organ of the Communist Labor Party), Spring 1974

In posing an individual solution to the contradictions of monopoly capitalism, homosexuality is an ideology of the petty bourgeoisie, and must be clearly distinguished from proletarian ideology.
— *On Homosexuality*, Revolutionary Union (U.S. maoist group)

The only real liberation, the only real road to real happiness for homosexuals — like all people caught in the mire and muck of bourgeois decadance — is to eliminate the reactionary, rotting system that drives them to homosexuality; . . .
— Ibid.

It's been so long since I got laid that I've forgotten who gets tied up.
— Anonymous

The Ultimate in Safe Sex: *Vinyl Sheep*
— Marquee sign on Kit Kat Theater, San Francisco, 1989

Nine out of ten men who prefer camels end up with women.
— Anonymous

Marriage is an institution.
Marriage is love.
Love is blind.
Therefore, marriage is an institution for the blind.
— Anonymous

What Causes Heterosexuality?
— Bumpersticker sighted in (where else?) San Francisco, 1991

Most men are like chicken wings — all promise and no meat.
— Graffiti

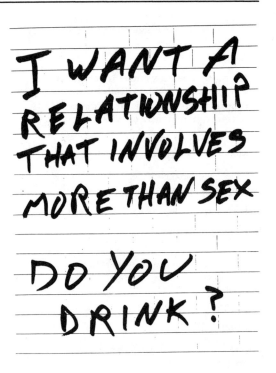

I WANT A RELATIONSHIP THAT INVOLVES MORE THAN SEX

DO YOU DRINK?

The reason so many women fake orgasms is that so many men fake foreplay.
— Graffiti

Astronomers Do It Nightly
— Bumpersticker

Men are like snow storms. You never know how many inches you're going to get or how long they're going to last.
— Graffiti, Boise, Idaho, 1978

Whosoever undertakes to artificially restrict the natural fertility of the German people to the injury of the nation, or by spoken word, writing, printing, picture, or any other means furthers such attempts . . . shall be punished for racial treason.
— Nazi addition to Criminal Code, introduced on March 12, 1930

The preservation of the form of the large family is a matter of national, cultural and political necessity . . . This view is also strictly opposed to the repeal of paragraph 218 [penal code provision prohibiting abortion], and it holds pregnancy to be inviolable. The termination of pregnancy is at variance with the meaning of the family, whose task is precisely the education of the coming generation — apart from the fact that the termination of pregnancy would mean the final destruction of the large family.
— *Volkischer Beobachter* (official Nazi organ), October 14, 1931

The whore and the whoremonger shall be scourged with a hundred stripes.
— *Koran*, 24:2

The quick brown fox jumped over the lazy dog, and then he rimmed him to death.
— Paper in used typewriter, Gay Community Thrift Store, San Francisco, 1987

Out of the closet and into the store!
— Motto of Gay Community Thrift Store

Loose tongues get into tight places.
— Sign on Baptist Church

A good man is hard to find, and a hard man is good to find.
— Graffiti

Sex is a misdemeanor. The more I miss the meaner I get.
— Graffiti

You can get laid — ask me how!
— Bumpersticker

Now I Lay Me Down to Cheat
— C&W song title

When the *putz* becomes erect, common sense is buried in the ground.
— Yiddish proverb

Are you going to come quietly, or will I have to use earplugs?
— Anonymous

Whosoever saith that marriage is to be put above virginity or celibacy, and that it is not more blessed to remain chaste than to marry, let him be anathema.
— Resolution of the Council of Trent

Jesus is coming [in different handwriting] *and we won't even make him clean it up!*
— Graffiti

I'm horny enough to fuck a snake if someone would pry its jaws open.
— Idaho folk saying

TOADY LITTLE CREEP NEEDS YOU: You must be willing to go out in public with me.
— Personals ad, *Bay Guardian*

JERK SEEKS CHICK: Stupid, lazy, insensitive, insecure SWM seeks SWF. I hate the arts, travel, reading and anything new. I love sitting, sleeping, drinking beer and TV. You are a former cheerleader with a lobotomy, earn 110K, and would like nothing more than spending a nice romantic evening at my home cleaning and doing laundry.
— Personals ad, *Bay Guardian*

BAD PROSPECT SEEMS MATE: Lazy, spoiled, irresponsible, desperate, flaccid wimp. Into Andre Kostelanetz, Nancy Sinatra, Rod McKuen, Keane and Dali paintings, tuna noodle casserole, and miniature golf.
— Personals ad, *Bay Guardian*

BISEXUAL SEEKS LOVER: Gender unimportant, but pleas be one or the other.
— Personals ad, *Bay Guardian*

Ex-Wife for Sale: *Take Over Payments*
— Bumpersticker

The Arts

St. Augustine

Poetry is the Devil's wine.
— *Contra Academicos*

Ludwig von Beethoven

Music is a higher revelation than philosophy.
— Letter to Bettina von Arnim, 1810

Ambrose Bierce

NOVEL, A short story padded...
— *The Devil's Dictionary*

PIANO, A parlor utensil for subduing the impenitent visitor. It is operated by depressing the keys of the machine and the spirits of the audience.
— Ibid.

PLAGIARIZE, To take the thought or style of another writer whom one has never, never read.
— Ibid.

If there had been no Washington, American independence would nevertheless have been won and the American republic established. But suppose that he alone had taken up arms. He was neither indispensable nor sufficient. Without Lincoln the great rebellion would have been subdued and negro slavery abolished. What kind of greatness is that— to do what another could have done anyhow? I call it pretty cheap work. Great statesmen and great soldiers are as common as flies; the world is lousy with them. We recognize their abundance in the saying that the hour brings the man. We do not say that of a literary emergency. There the demand is always calling for the cupply, and usually calling in vain. Once or twice in a century, it may be, the great man of thought comes, unforeseen and unrecognized, and makes the age and the glory thereof all his own by saying what none but he could bear. All round him swarm the little great men of action, laying sturdily about them with mace and sword, changing boundaries which are afterward changed back again, serving fascinating principles from which posterity turns away, building states that vanish like castles of cloud, founding thrones and dynasties with which Time plays at pitch-and-toss. But through it all, and after it all, the mighty thought of the man of words flows on and on with the restless sweep of "the great river where De Soto lies" [the Mississippi]—an unchanging and unchangeable current of eternal good.
— *Who Are Great?*

Nicolas Boileau

Whatever we conceive well we express clearly.

St. John Chrysostom

And as swine flock together where there is a mire, by where there is aroma and incense there bees abide, so demons congregate where there are licentious chants;...
— *Homily on the First Psalm*

Spending time in theaters produces fornication, intemperance, and every kind of impurity.
— *Homilies*

Noel Coward

Get all the lines right and don't trip over the furniture.
— advice to aspiring actors (attributed and probably spurious)

Ricardo Flores Magon

This "Art for Art's sake" is an absurdity and its defenders have always grated on my nerves. I feel such love and reverence for Art that it saddens me to see it prostituted by persons who have neither the power to make others feel as they feel, nor the ability to make others see things as they see things; they hide their impotency under the cloak of "Art for Art's sake."
— *Epistolario revolucionario e íntimo*

John Galsworthy

A true story, if told sincerely, is the strongest moral argument that can be put on stage.

— quoted by Emma Goldman in *The Social Significance of Modern Drama*

J.W. von Goethe

At bottom, however, we are all collective beings, pose however we please. For how little we have and how little we are that we can, in the strictest sense call our own! We must all receive and learn as well from those who were before us as from those who are with us. Even the greatest genius would not get far if he wished to owe everything to what he had within him. But very many worthy men do not understand this and, with their dreams of originality, grope half their lives in the dark. I have known artists who boasted of having no master, rather of owing everything to their own genius. The fools! As if that happened anywhere! And as if the world were not pressing on them at every step and, in spite of their stupidity, making something out of them.

— quoted in Eckermann's *Conversations with Goethe in the Last Years of His Life*

It is true that during my long life I have undertaken and accomplished a great variety of things of which, perhaps, I might boast. But what did I have if we want to be honest, that was really my own except the ability and the inclination, too, to see and to hear, to decide and to choose, and to animate what I had seen and heard with my own spirit and reproduce it with some skill. I owe my works in no way to my own wisdom alone, but thousands of things and persons outside me offered me the material for them.

— Ibid.

. . . the chief thing is that one have a great will and possess skill and persistence to carry it out; all the rest does not matter.

— Ibid.

Emma Goldman

The reason that many radicals as well as conservatives fail to grasp the powerful message of art is perhaps not far to seek. The average radical is as hidebound by mere terms as the man devoid of all ideas. "Bloated plutocrats," "economic determinism," "class consciousness," and similar expressions sum up for him the symbols of revolt.

— Foreword to *The Social Significance of Modern Drama*

Both radical and conservative have to learn that any mode of creative work, which with true perception portrays social wrongs earnestly and boldly, may be a greater menace to our social fabric and a more powerful inspiration than the wildest harangue of the soapbox orator.

— Ibid.

Publishers, theatrical managers, and critics ask not for the quality inherent in creative art, but will it meet with a good sale, will it suit the palate of the the people? Alas, this palate is like a dumping ground; it relishes anything that needs no mental mastication.

— *Minorities versus Majorities*

Robert Ingersoll

It was thought at one time by many that science would do away with poetry — that it was the enemy of the imagination. We know that it is in the highest degree poetic and that the old ideas once considered so beautiful are flat and stale. Compare Kepler's laws with the old Greek idea that the planets were boosted or pushed by angels. The more we know, the more beauty, the more poetry we find. Ignorance is not the mother of the poetic or artistic.

— *Science and Sentiment*

The greatest poet is the one who selects the best, the most appropriate symbols to convey the best, the highest, the sublimest thoughts.

— *Testimonial to Walt Whitman*

Is rhyme a necessary part of poetry? In my judgment, rhyme is a hindrance to expression. The rhymer is compelled to wander from his subject, to say more or less than he means, to introduce irrelevant matter that interferes continually with the dramatic action and is a perpetual obstruction to sincere utterance.

— *Testimonial to Walt Whitman*

Hans Johst

When I hear the word culture, I release the safety catch on my revolver.

W.L. Judson

There is no surer sign of the decadence of art than the search after formulae, striving to lay down rules in imitation of the methods of the past, as if discovery were dead.

— quoted by Sprading in *Liberty and the Great Libertarians*

Every young artist will base his method on the work of some master, perhaps many masters in succession. Gradually his own individuality begins to emerge and he adopts a manner of his own. Every man has his own ideal or personal convention in composition by which he selects his subject or into which he makes his subject fit.

— Ibid.

Jack London

It is the hardest thing in the world to put feeling, and deep feeling, into words. From the standpoint of expression, it is easier to write a *Das Kapital* in four volumes than a simply lyric of as many stanzas.

Mao Tse Tung

Literature and art are subordinate to politics...

Yenan Forum on Literature and Art

What we demand is the unity of politics and art...

—Ibid.

Then does not Marxism destroy the creative mood? Yes, it does. It definitely destroys creative moods that are feudal, bourgeois, petty-bourgeois, liberalistic, individualist, nihilist, art-for-art's sake, aristocratic, decadent or pessimistic, and every other creative mood that is alien to the masses of the people and to the proletariat. So far as proletarian writers and artists are concerned, should not these kinds of creative moods be destroyed? I think they should; they should be utterly destroyed.

—Ibid.

Karl Marx

The writer must earn money in order to be able to live and to write, but he must by no means live and write for the purpose of making money.

—*Herr Vogt*

Michelangelo

Trifles make perfection—and perfection is no trifle.

—attributed

Modest Mussorgsky

Art is not an end in itself, but a means of addressing humanity.

Friedrich Nietzsche

Without music life would be a mistake.

—attributed

...Art for Art's sake—a serpent which bites its own tail.

—*Twilight of the Idols*

No one, ultimately, can spend more than he has. This holds good for individuals as it does for nations. If you expend yourself for power, for politics, for commerce, for agriculture, electoralism, military interests—if you spend that amount of reason, sincerity, will, self-mastery, which constitutes your true self, for the one thing, you will not have it for the other. Culture and the State—let no one be deceived about this—are antagonistic. The "Cultural State" is only a modern concept. One lives off the other; one flourishes at the expense of the other. All great cultural periods are periods of political decline. Whatever is culturally great is non-political, even anti-political.

—Ibid.

The happiest fate is that of the author who, as an old man, is able to say that all there was in him of life-inspiring, strengthening, exalting, enlightening thoughts and feelings still lives on in his writings, and the he himself now only represents the gray ashes, whilst the fire has been kept alive...

—*Human, All Too Human*

The thinker, as likewise the artist, who has put his best self into his works, feels an almost malicious joy when he sees how mind and body are being slowly damaged and destroyed by time, as if from a dark corner he were spying a thief at his money-chest, knowing all the time that it was empty and his treasures in safety.

—Ibid.

Let us consider...the kind of melodies and songs in which the most vigorous, unspoiled and true-hearted classes of the population find genuine delight...is it not the worst music at present produced that is loved and, one might say, cherished? He who speaks of deeper needs and unsatisfied yearnings for art among the people, as it is, is a crank or an impostor. Be honest!

—Ibid.

Pope Pius XI

Everyone knows that damage is done to the soul by bad motion pictures.

—*Vigilanti Cura*

The more marvelous is the progress of the motion picture art and industry, the more pernicious and deadly has it shown itself to morality, to religion, and even to the very decencies of human society.

—Ibid.

Alexander Pope

The secret of writing well is to know thoroughly what one writes about, and not to be affected.

—attributed

Elvis Presley

I don't know anything about music. In my line of work I don't have to.

—attributed

Rudolf Rocker

Where the influence of political power on the creative forces in society is reduced to a minimum, there culture thrives the best, for political rulership always strives for uniformity and tends to subject every aspect of social life to its guardianship. And in this, it finds itself in inescapable contradiction to the creative aspirations of cultural development, which is always on the quest for new forms and fields of social activity, and for which freedom of expression, the many-sidedness and the continual changing of things, are just as vitally necessary as rigid forms, dead rules, and the forcible suppression of ideas are for the conservation of political power. Every successful piece of work stirs the desire for greater perfection and deeper inspiration; each new form becomes the herald of new possibilities of development. But power always tries to keep things as they are, safely anchored to stereotypes.

—*Anarchism and Anarcho-Syndicalism*

Charles T. Sprading

To coerce the artist is to destroy the work.

The public generally has poor taste, and is far behind the thinking part of the race, so it exercises its power to compel conformity, and the artist must be strong indeed to withstand the inducement of success on the one hand and the pressure of boycott and ostracism on the other.

Conformity may make one rich, but it can never make one great. A true artist ignores the public.

When the artist paints what the public demands, it is not art, but business.

Who ever heard of a real poet singing of slavery?

—above quotations from *Freedom and its Fundamentals*

August Strindberg

People clamour for the joy of life, and the theatrical managers order farces, as though the joy of life consisted in being foolish, and in describing people as if they were each and all afflicted with St. Vitus' dance or idiocy.

—quoted by Emma Goldman in *The Social Significance of Modern Drama*

Robert Tefton

ARTIST, n. One to whom it is unwise to lend money.

MUSIC, n. An area of universal expertise. The less formal musical training persons have, the more certain they are to know what is "good," and the more certain they are that their opinions are just as valid as those of persons who have spent their lives playing and composing music.

POET, n. A person who cannot write prose. See also "Narcissist."

POETRY, n. The French Poodle of the arts. An expression of egomania.

Tertullian

A certain woman went to the theater and brought the Devil home with her. And when the unclean spirit was pressed in the exorcism, and asked how he durst attack a Christian, "I have done nothing," says he, "but what I can justify, for I seized her upon my own ground."

—*De spectaculis*

Voltaire

The only reward to be expected from literature is contempt if one fails and hatred if one succeeds.

—Letter to Mlle. Quinault, August 16, 1738

Colin Ward

The system makes its morons, then despises them for their ineptitude, and rewards its "gifted few" for their rarity.

—*Anarchy in Action*

Oscar Wilde

Art is Individualism, and Individualism is a disturbing and disintegrating force. Therein lies its immense value. For what it seeks to disburb is monotony of type, slavery of custom, tyranny of habit, and the reduction of man to the level of a machine.

The fact is, the public make use of the classics of a country as a means of checking the progress of Art. They degrade the classics into authorities. They use them as bludgeons...They are always asking a writer why he does not write like somebody else, or a painter why he does not paint like somebody else, quite oblivious of the fact that if either of them did anything of the kind he would cease to be an artist. A fresh mode of Beauty is absolutely distasteful to them, and whenever it appears they get so angry and bewildered that they always use two stupid expressions—one that the work of art is grossly unintelligible; the other, that the work of art is grossly immoral. What they mean by these words seems to me to be this. When they say a work is grossly unintelligible, they mean that the artist has said or made a beautiful thing that is new; when they describe a work as grossly immoral, they mean that the artist has said or made a beautiful thing that is true.

The true artist is a man who believes absolutely in himself, because he is absolutely himself.

An unhealthy work of art...is a work whose style is obvious, old-fashioned and common, and whose subject is deliberately chosen, not because the artist has any pleasure in it, but because he thinks that the public will pay him for it.

Art is this intense form of Individualism that makes the public try to exercise over it an authority that is as immoral as it is ridiculous, and as corrupting as it is contemptible. It is not quite their fault. The public has always, and in every age, been badly brought up. They are continually asking Art to be popular, to please their want of taste, to flatter their absurd vanity, to tell them what they have been told before, to show them what they ought to be tired of seeing, to amuse them when they feel heavy after eating too much, and to distract their thoughts when they are wearied of their own stupidity. Now Art should never try to be popular. The public should try to make itself artistic.

The one thing that the public dislikes is novelty. Any attempt to extend the subject-matter of art is extremely distasteful to the public; and yet the vitality and progress of art depends in a large measure on the continual extension of subject-matter. The public dislikes novelty because it is afraid of it.

. . . whenever a community or a powerful section of a community, or a government of any kind, attempts to dictate to the artist what he is to do, Art either entirely vanishes, or becomes stereotyped, or degenerates into a low and ignoble form of craft.

A work of art is the unique result of a unique temperament. Its beauty comes from the fact that the author is what he is. It has nothing to do with the fact that other people want what they want. Indeed, the moment that an artist takes notice of what other people want, and tries to supply the demand, he ceases to be an artist, and becomes a dull or an amusing craftsman, an honest or dishonest tradesman. He has no further claim to be considered as an artist.

Art is the most intense mode of Individualism that the world has known.

In Art, the public accepts what has been because they cannot alter it, not because they appreciate it. They swallow their classics whole, and never taste them. They endure them as inevitable, and, as they cannot mar them, they mouth them.

A true artist takes no notice whatever of the public.

People sometimes inquire what form of government is most suitable for an artist to live under. To this question there is only one answer. The form of government that is most suitable to the artist is no government at all.

— above quotations from *The Soul of Man Under Socialism*

Anybody can write a three-volumed novel. It merely requires a complete ignorance of both life and literature.

— *The Critic as Artist*

I am certain that, as civilization progresses and we become more highly organized, the elect spirits of each age, the critical and cultured spirits, will grow less and less interested in actual life, and will seek to gain their impressions almost entirely from what Art has touched. For life is terribly deficient in form. Its catastrophes happen in the wrong way and to the wrong people. There is a grotesque horror about its comedies, and its tragedies seem to culminate in farce.

— Ibid.

There are moments when art attains almost to the dignity of manual labor.

— attributed

Frank Zappa

Most people wouldn't know music if it be 'em on the ass.

— attributed

Anonymous & Multiple Author

There are three sexes: men, women, and tenors.

— old musical joke

Science &
Scientific Thinking

St. Ambrose

We must remember that the light of day is one thing and the light of the sun, moon, and stars another—the sun by his rays appearing to add lustre to the daylight. For before sunrise the day dawns, but is not in full refulgence, for the sun adds still further to its splendour.

— quoted by White in *The History of the Warfare Between Science and Theology*

St. Thomas Aquinas

It is a dogma of faith that the demons can produce wind, storms, and rain of fire from heaven.

— *Summa Theologica*

Matthew Arnold

Faith in machinery is our besetting danger; often in machinery absurdly disproportioned to the end which this machinery, if it is to do any good at all, is to serve; but always in machinery, as if it had a value in and for itself.

— *Culture and Anarchy*

Marcus Aurelius

He is a true fugitive who flies from reason.

Michael Bakunin

The immense advantage of positive science over theology, metaphysics, politics and judicial right consists in this—that, in place of the false and fatal abstractions set up by these doctrines, it posits true abstractions which express the general nature and logic of things...

— *God and the State*

Ambrose Bierce

ACCIDENT, An inevitable occurrence due to the action of immutable natural laws.

— *The Devil's Dictionary*

Henry Thomas Buckle

If on any point we have attained to certainty, we make no further inquiry...doubt must intervene before the investigation can begin...the necessary antecedent, of all progress. Here we have that skepticism, the very name of which is an abomination to the ignorant; because it troubles their cherished superstitions; because it imposes on them the fatigue of inquiry; and because it arouses even sluggish understandings to ask if things are as they are commonly supposed...

— *The Wisdom of Thomas Buckle*

In science, originality is the parent of discovery, and is, therefore, a merit; in theology, it is the parent of heresy, and is, therefore, a crime.

— Ibid.

Luther Burbank

The scientist is a lover of truth for the very love of truth itself, wherever it may lead.

— *Why I Am an Infidel*

John Calvin

Who will venture to place the authority of Copernicus above that of the Holy Spirit?

— quoted by White in *The History of the Warfare Between Science and Theology*

Chapman Cohen

If there are certain scientists today who are ready to compromise with religion, it is also true that never before were there so many men of science who are openly disdainful of all religious theories.

Auguste Comte

All good intellects have repeated, since Bacon's time, that there can be no real knowledge but that which is based on observed facts.

— *The Positive Philosophy*

Clarence Darrow

I know the weakness of human reason... but it is all we have, and the only safety of man is to cultivate it and extend his knowledge so that he will be sure to understand life and as many of the mysteries of the universe as he can possibly solve.

— *Absurdities of the Bible*

William Drummond

He who will not reason is a bigot; he who cannot is a fool; and he who dares not is a slave.

— *Academical Questions*

Albert Ellis

...if people were thoroughly unbelieving of any dogmas, if they were highly skeptical of all hypotheses and theories that they formulated, if they believed in no kinds of gods, devils, or other supernatural beings, and if they subscribed to no forms of absolutistic thinking, they would be minimally emotionally disturbed and maximally healthy. Stated a little differently: if you, I, and everyone else in the world were thoroughly scientific, and if we consistently used the scientific method in our own lives and in our relationships with others, we would rarely upset ourselves about anything—and I mean *anything!*

— *The Case Against Religiosity*

Galileo Galilei

I, Galileo, being in my seventieth year, being a prisoner and on my knees, and before your Eminences, having before my eyes the Holy Gospel, which I touch with my hands, abjure, curse, and detest the error and heresy of the movement of the earth [around the sun].

— Recantation before the Inquisition, 1633

William Godwin

He that resigns his understanding upon one particular topic, will not exercise it vigorously upon others. If he be right in any instance, it will be inadvertently and by chance. A consciousness of the degradation to which he is subjected will perpetually haunt him; or at least he will want that intrepid perseverance, that calm self-approbation that grows out of independence. Such beings are the mere dwarfs and mockery of men, their efforts compara-

tively pusillanimous, and the vigor with which they should execute their purposes, superficial and hollow.

Strangers to conviction, they will never be able to distinguish between prejudice and reason.

— *An Inquiry Concerning Political Justice*

J.I. Guillotin

My machine will take off a head in a twinkling and the victim will feel nothing but a refreshing coolness. We cannot make too much haste, gentlemen, to allow the nation to enjoy this advantage.

— Speech to the French National Assembly, 1789

Thomas Huxley

Logical consequences are the scarecrows of fools and the beacons of wise men.

— *On the Hypothesis That Animals Are Automata*

Science is simply common sense at its best—that is, rigidly accurate in observation, and merciless to fallacy in logic.

Robert Ingersoll

Science denies the truth of myth and miracle, denies that human testimony can substantiate the miraculous, denies the existence of the supernatural. Science asserts the absolute, the unvarying uniformity of nature. Science insists that the present is the child of the past—that no power can change the past, and that nature is forever the same...

The uniformity of Nature renders a belief in "special providence" impossible. Prayer becomes a useless agitation of the air, and religious ceremonies are but motions, pantomimes, mindless and meaningless.

The naked savage, worshiping a wooden god, is the religious equal of the robed pope kneeling before an image of the Virgin. The poor African who carries roots and bark to protect himself from evil spirits is on the same intellectual plane of one who sprinkles his body with "holy water."

All the creeds of Christendom, all the religions of the heathen world are equally absurd. The cathedral, the mosque and the joss house have the same foundation. Their builders do not believe in the uniformity of Nature, and the business of the priests is to induce a so-called infinite being to change the order of events, to make causes barren of effects and to produce effects without, and in spite of, natural causes. They all believe in the unthinkable and pray for the impossible.

— *Myth and Miracle*

Science always has been, is, and always will be modest, thoughtful, truthful. It has but one object: The ascertainment of truth...It is for this world, for the use of man...It does not try to conceal, but to reveal...It does not pretend to be "holy" or "inspired." It courts investigation, criticism and even denial. It asks for the application of every test, for trial by every standard...The good that springs from a knowledge of the truth is the only reward it offers, and the evil resulting from ignorance is the only punishment it threatens.

— Ibid.

Reason, Observation and Experience — the Holy Trinity of science — have taught that happiness is the only good; that the time to be happy is now, and the way to be happy is to make others so. This is enough for us. In this belief we are content to live and die. If by any possibility the existence of a power superior to, and independent of Nature, shall be demonstrated, there will then be time enough to kneel. Until then, let us stand erect.

— quoted in *Ingersoll the Magnificent*

For ages, a deadly conflict has been waged between a few brave men and women of thought and genius upon the one side, and the great ignorant religious mass on the other. This is the war between Science and Faith. The few have appealed to reason, to honor, to law, to freedom, to the known, and to happiness here in this world. The many have appealed to prejudice, to fear, to miracle, to slavery, to the unknown, and to misery hereafter. The few have said, "Think!" The many have said, "Believe!"

Man must learn to rely upon himself. Reading Bibles will not protect him from the blasts of Winter, but houses, fires and clothing will. To prevent famine, one plow is worth a million sermons.

— Ibid.

Thomas Jefferson

Error of opinion may be tolerated where reason is left free to combat it.

— Inaugural address, 1801

Peter Kropotkin

More than a century has passed since science laid down sound propositions as to the origin of the universe, but how many have mastered them or possess the really scientific spirit of criticism? A few thousand at the outside, who are lost in the midst of hundreds of millions still steeped in prejudices and superstitions worthy of savages, who are consequently ever ready to serve as puppets for religious impostors.

— *An Appeal to the Young*

The most important thing is to spread the [scientific] truths already acquired, to practice them in daily life, to make of them a common inheritance. We have to order things in such wise that all humanity may be capable of assimilating and applying them, so that science ceasing to be a luxury becomes the basis of everyday life. Justice requires this.

— Ibid.

Martin Luther

Reason is the greatest enemy that faith has: it never comes to the aid of spiritual things, but — more frequently than not — struggles against the Divine Word, treating with contempt all that emanates from God.

— *Table Talk*

People gave ear to an upstart astrologer [Copernicus] who strove to show that the earth revolves, not the heavens or the firmament, the sun and the moon. Whoever wishes to appear clever must devise some new system, which of all systems is of course the very best. This fool wishes to reverse the entire science of astronomy; but sacred Scripture tells us that Joshua commanded the sun to stand still, and not the earth.

— quoted by White in *The History of the Warfare Between Science and Theology*

We know, on the authority of Moses, that longer ago than six thousand years the world did not exist.

— Ibid.

Joseph McCabe

There is much light mockery of Humanism for its faith in the saving power of Science. It must be understood that this phrase chiefly means that we are going to substitute a most careful study of the conditions of happiness for the haphazard appeals and transcendental preaching of the past. Science is not a new goddess, nor a patent medicine for life's disorders. It is knowledge, but knowledge gleaned with particular care. On the practical side it is opposed to quackery: it is effective or practical knowledge gained, not by chance experiment, but by a most rigorous series of tests. We mean, then, that we are going to study this life, and extract from it the secret of happiness or unhappiness with a care and rigor that have not been applied to the task before. He who scorns this hardly commends his own philosophy of life.

— *Religion of Woman*

H.L. Mencken

The idea that science is arid is due to a lack of imagination in those who propagate it. What was arid in the work of Koch? Or in that of Pasteur? Or even in that of Darwin? The same people who make this argument are usually prepared to believe that theology is a rich and charming science, or that Marx and his disciples were profound thinkers. They are the kind of men who dislike instinctively whatever is intellectually decent and probably true. Such men exist in large numbers. They are as easily recognizable as the men who dislike physical cleanliness.

— *Minority Report*

The essence of science is that it is always willing to abandon a given idea for a better one; the essence of theology is that it holds its truths to be eternal and immutable. To be sure, theology is always yielding a little to the progress of knowledge, and only a Holy Roller in the mountains of Tennessee would dare to preach today what the popes preached in the Thirteenth Century...

— Ibid.

Science has another and even more dubious rival [than quackery] in metaphysics, which operates on a higher level. Its recurrent resurrections are all based on the fact that many presumably educated men are quite incapable of grasping scientific concepts. The business is too laborious for them, too troublesome. They thus seek answers to their questions in much smoother waters. In other words, they seek them in speculation, not in experiment and study...The essential part is always quite simple. It is nothing more or less than a silly denial that facts are important. As commonly encountered, it takes the form of the doctrine that materialism is somehow sordid, and even more or less immoral. Yet it is materialism operating on the plane of common sense, that has brought the human race all the progress it has seen in five hundred years.

— Ibid.

Friedrich Nietzsche

...it is at an end with priests and gods, if man becomes scientific! — Moral: science is the thing forbidden in itself — it alone is forbidden. Science is the *first* sin, the germ of all sin, *original* sin. *This alone is morality* — "Thou shalt *not* know." All the rest follows from it.

— *The Anti-Christ*

On the whole, scientific methods are at least as an important result of investigation as any other result, for the scientific spirit is based upon a knowledge of method, and if the methods were lost, all the results of science could not prevent the renewed prevalence of superstition and absurdity. Clever people may *learn* as much as they like of the results of science, but one still notices in their conversation, and especially in the hypotheses they make, that they lack the scientific spirit; they have not the instinctive distrust of the devious courses of thinking which, in consequence of long training, has taken root in the soul of every scientific man...In the case of an unexplained matter they become heated for the first idea that comes into their heads which has any resemblance to an explanation — a course from which the worst results constantly follow, especially in the field of politics. On that account everybody should nowadays have become thoroughly

Graphic by Adam Cornford & Dennis Hayes

acquainted with at least *one* science, for then surely he knows what is meant by method, and how necessary is the extremest carefulness.

— *Human, All Too Human*

Origen

It is demons which produce famine, unfruitfulness, corruptions of the air, pestilences; they hover concealed in clouds in the lower atmosphere, and are attracted by the blood and incense which the heathen offer to them as gods.

— quoted by A.D. White in *The History of the Warfare Between Science and Theology*

Thomas Paine

The most formidable weapon against errors of every kind is reason. I have never used any other, and I trust I never shall.

— *The Age of Reason*

It is a fraud of the Christian system to call the sciences human invention; it is only the application of them that is human. Every science has for its basis a system of principles as fixed and unalterable as those by which the universe is regulated and governed. Man cannot make these principles; he can only discover them.

— Ibid.

Pope Paul V

The doctrine of the double motion of the earth about its axis and about the sun is false, and entirely contrary to Holy Scripture.

Karl Pearson

There is no short cut to truth, no way to gain knowledge except through the gateway of the scientific method. The hard, stony path of classifying facts and reasoning upon them is the only way to ascertain truth.

— quoted by Charles Sprading in *Science Versus Dogma*

John Ray

A man without reason is a beast in season.

— *English Proverbs*

Ronald Reagan

Approximately 80 percent of our air pollution stems from hydrocarbons released by vegetation, so let's not go overboard in setting and enforcing tough emission standards from man-made sources.

— quoted in *Sierra*, September 10, 1980

Herbert Spencer

By science, constant appeal is made to individual reason. Its truths are not accepted upon authority alone, but all are at liberty to test them — nay, in many cases, the pupil is required to think out his own conclusions. Every step in a scientific investigation is submitted to his judgment. He is not asked to admit it without seeing it to be true. And the trust in his own powers thus produced is further increased by the constancy with which nature justifies his conclusions when they are correctly drawn. From all which there flows that independence which is a most valuable element in character.

— *Education*

Science is simply a higher development of common knowledge; and if Science is repudiated, all knowledge must be repudiated along with it.

It is hard to bear the display of the pride of ignorance which so far exceeds the pride of science.

Benedict Spinoza

He alone is free who lives with free consent under the entire guidance of reason.

— *Theologico-Political Treatise*

Charles T. Sprading

Knowledge consists in understanding the evidence that establishes the fact, not in the belief that it is a fact.

— *Science Versus Dogma*

Criticism of science because It is limited is a criticism of knowledge as well, for knowledge is comparative and therefore limited.

— Ibid.

Charles Steinmetz

In the realm of science, all attempts to find any evidence of supernatural beings, of metaphysical conceptions, as God, immortality, infinity, etc., thus far have failed, and if we are honest, we must confess that in science there exists no God, no immortality, no soul or mind as distinct from the body.

— quoted in *The American Freeman*, July 1941

Leo Tolstoy

If there is no higher reason — and there is none — then my own reason must be the supreme judge of my life.

— *My Confession*

Pope Urban VIII

It would be an evil example for the world if such honours were rendered to a man who had been brought before the Roman Inquisition for an opinion so false and erroneous; who had communicated it to many others, and who had given so great a scandal to Christendom.

— on erection of a monument to Galileo, quoted by White in *The History of the Warfare Between Science and Theology*

John Wesley

Sin is the moral cause of earthquakes, whatever their natural cause may be.

— *The Cause and Cure of Earthquakes*

Andrew Dickson White

The establishment of Christianity, beginning a new evolution of theology, arrested the normal development of the physical sciences for over fifteen hundred years. The cause of this arrest was twofold: First, there was created an atmosphere in which the germs of physical science could hardly grow — an atmosphere in which all seeking in Nature for truth as truth was regarded as futile. The general belief derived from the New Testament Scriptures was, that the end of the world was at hand; that the last judgment was approaching; that all existing physical nature was soon to be destroyed: hence, the greatest thinkers in the Church generally poured contempt upon all investigators into a science of Nature, and insisted that everything except the saving of souls was folly . . .

Then, too, there was established a standard to which all science which did struggle up through this atmosphere must be made to conform — a standard which favoured magic rather than science, for it was a standard of rigid dogmatism obtained from literal readings in the Jewish and Christian Scriptures. The most careful inductions from ascertained facts were regarded as wretchedly fallible when compared with any view of nature whatever given or even hinted at in any poem, chronicle, code, apologue, myth, legend, allegory, letter, or discourse of any sort which had happened to be preserved in the literature which had come to be held as sacred.

Like all else in the Middle Ages, this sacred science [biology] was developed purely by theological methods. Neglecting the wonders which the dissection of the commonest animals would have afforded them, these naturalists attempted to throw light into Nature by ingenious use of scriptural texts, by research among the lives of the saints, and by the plentiful application of metaphysics. Hence even such strong men as St. Isidore of Seville treasured up accounts of the unicorn and dragons mentioned in the Scriptures and of the phoenix and basilisk in profane writings. Hence such contribu-

tions to knowledge as that the basilisk kills serpents by his breath and men by his glance, that the lion when pursued effaces his tracks with the end of his tail, that the pelican nourishes her young with her own blood, that serpents lay aside their venom before drinking, that the salamander quenches fire, that the hyena can talk with shepherds, that certain birds are born of the fruit of a certain tree when it happens to fall into the water, with other masses of science equally valuable.

"What caused the creation of the stars on the fourth day?" . . . "Why were only beasts and birds brought before Adam to be named?" "Why did the Creator not say, "Be fruitful and multiply," to plants as well as to animals?"

Sundry answers to these and similar questions formed the main contributions of the greatest of the Latin fathers to the scientific knowledge of the world, after a most thorough study of the biblical text and a most profound application of theological reasoning. The results of these contributions were most important. In this, as in so many other fields, Augustine gave direction to the main current of thought in western Europe, Catholic and Protestant, for nearly thirteen centuries.

When the Copernical doctrine was upheld by Galileo as a *truth*, and proved to be a truth by his telescope [Copernicus'] book was taken in hand by the Roman curia. The statements of Copernicus were condemned, "until they should be corrected"; and the corrections required were simply such as would substitute for his conclusions the old Ptolemaic theory [that the Earth is the center of the universe].

That this was their purpose was seen in that year when Galileo was forbidden to teach or discuss the Copernical theory, and when were forbidden "all books which affirm the motion of the earth."

The Pope himself, Paul V . . . ordered that Galileo be brought before the Inquisition. Then the greatest man of science in that age was brought face to face with the greatest theologian — Galileo was confronted by [Cardinal] Bellarmin. Bellarmin shows Galileo the error of his opinion and orders him to renounce it. De Lauda, fortified by a letter from the Pope, gives orders that the astronomer be placed in the dungeons of the Inquisition should he refuse to yield. Bellarmin now commands Galileo, "in the name of His Holiness the Pope and the whole Congregation of the Holy Office [the Inquisition], to relinquish altogether the opinion that the sun is the center of the world and immovable, and that the earth moves, nor henceforth to hold, teach, or defend it in any way whatsoever, verbally or in writing." This injunction Galiloe acquiesces in and promises to obey.

So important was it thought to have "sound learning" guarded and "safe science" taught, that in many of the universities, as late as the end of the seventeenth century, professors were forced to take an oath not to hold the "Pythagorean" — that is, the

New from ChéGene
(Sperm and Ovum Bank)

Revolutionary World Leaders and Martyrs!

Thanks to socialist biotechnology and generous contributions of genetic material by our greatest leaders, ChéGene can produce clones ready for election to *your* Central Committee within 18 months!

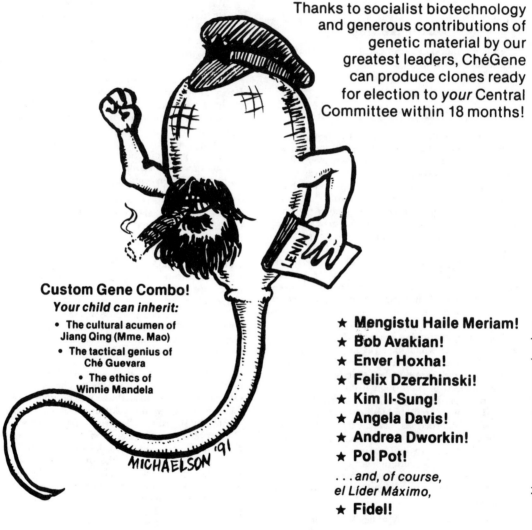

Custom Gene Combo!
Your child can inherit:

- The cultural acumen of Jiang Qing (Mme. Mao)
- The tactical genius of Ché Guevara
- The ethics of Winnie Mandela

★ **Mengistu Haile Meriam!**
★ **Bob Avakian!**
★ **Enver Hoxha!**
★ **Felix Dzerzhinski!**
★ **Kim Il-Sung!**
★ **Angela Davis!**
★ **Andrea Dworkin!**
★ **Pol Pot!**
. . . and, of course, el Líder Máximo,
★ **Fidel!**

All sales final—No Returns.

Graphic by M.C.B. & Louis Michaelson. Used by permission.

Copernican—idea as to the movement of the heavenly bodies. As the contest went on, professors were forbidden to make known to students the facts revealed by the telescope. Special orders to this effect were issued by the ecclesiastical authorities to the universities and colleges of Pisa, Innsbruck, Louvain, Douay, Salamanca, and others. . .nowhere were the facts confirming the Copernican theory more carefully kept out of sight than at Wittenberg—the university of Luther. . .

— above quotations from *The History of the Warfare Between Science and Theology*

Walt Whitman

Science, testing absolutely all thoughts, all works, has already burst well upon the world—a sun, mounting, most illuminating, most glorious, surely never again to set. But against it, deeply entrench'd, holding possession, yet remains...the fossil theology of the mythic-materialistic, superstitious, untaught and credulous, fable-loving, primitive ages of humanity.

Oscar Wilde

Up to the present, man has been, to a certain degree, the slave of machinery, and there is something tragic in the fact that as soon as man had invented a machine to do his work he began to starve. This, however, is of course the result of our property system and our system of competition. One man owns a machine which does the work of five hundred men. Five hundred men are, in consequence, thrown out of employment...Were the machine the property of all, everybody would benefit by it.

— *The Soul of Man Under Socialism*

Anonymous & Multiple Author

Rationalism may be defined as the mental attitude which unreservedly accepts the supremacy of reason and aims at establishing a system of philosophy and ethics verifiable by experience and independent of all arbitrary assumptions of authority.

— Rationalist Press Association (London), *Aims and Objects*, 1905

The first proposition, that the sun is the center and does not revolve about the earth, is foolish, absurd, false in theology, and heretical, because it is expressly contrary to Holy Scripture. The second proposition, that the earth is not the center but revolves about the sun, is absurd, false in philosophy, and, from a theological point of view at least opposed to the true faith.

— Roman Inquisition, judgment on the writings of Galileo, 1615

The doctrine of the double motion of the earth about its axis and about the sun is false, and entirely contrary to Holy Scripture.

— Congress of the Index of Prohibited Books Decree, 1616

HYDROGEN: a light, colorless, odorless gas which, given enough time, turns into people.

— Anonymous

Real programmers don't write documentation. It was hard to write, it *should* be hard to understand.

— Anonymous

Real men don't have floppy disks.

— Bumpersticker

Religion

Abu'l Ala Al Ma'arri

The world holds two classes of men—intelligent men without religion, and religious men without intelligence.

— attributed

John Adams

This would be the best of all possible worlds if there were no religion in it.

— quoted by American Atheists

Michael Bakunin

People go to church for the same reasons they go to a tavern: to stupefy themselves, to forget their misery, to imagine themselves, for a few minutes anyway, free and happy...

— *A Circular Letter to My Friends in Italy*

Divine morality is based upon two immoral principles: respect for authority and contempt for humanity. Human morality, on the contrary, is based only upon contempt for authority and respect for liberty and humanity.

— *Integral Education*

Of all the despotisms, that of the doctrinaires or inspired religionists is the worst. They are so jealous of the glory of their God and of the triumph of their idea that they have no heart left for the liberty of real men. Divine zeal, preoccupation with the idea, finally dry up the tenderest souls, the most compassionate hearts, the sources of human love. Considering all that is, all that happens in the world from the point of view of eternity or of the abstract idea, they treat passing matters with disdain, but the whole life of real men, of men of flesh and bone, is composed only of passing matters...

— *God and the State*

Alexander Berkman

What you personally believe in is indeed your private affair; but when you get together with other people and organize them into a body to impose your belief on others, to force them to think as you do, and to punish them (to the extent of your power) if they entertain other beliefs, then it is no more your "private matter." You might as well say that the Inquisition, which tortured and burned people alive as heretics, was a "private matter."

— *What Is Communist Anarchism?*

It was one of the worst betrayals of the cause of liberty by the Socialists, this declaration that religion is a "private matter." Mankind has slowly grown out of the fearful ignorance, superstition, bigotry, and intolerance which made religious persecution and inquisitions possible. The advance of science and invention, the printed word and means of communication have brought enlightenment, and it is that *enlightenment* which has to some extent freed the human mind from the clutches of the church.

— Ibid.

Ambrose Bierce

ADORE, To venerate expectantly.

ALTAR, The place whereon the priest formerly raveled out the small intestine of the sacrificial victim for the purposes of divination...The word is now seldom used, except with reference to the sacrifice of their liberty and peace by a male and a female fool.

CLAIRVOYANT, A person...who has the power of seeing that which is invisible to her patron—namely that he is a blockhead.

FAITH, Belief without evidence in what is told by one who speaks without knowledge, of things without parallel.

FEAST, A festival. A religious celebration usually signalized by gluttony and drunkenness, frequently in honor of some holy person distinguished for abstemiousness.

HEATHEN, A benighted creature who has the folly to worship something that he can see and feel.

INDIGESTION, A disease which the patient and his friends frequently mistake for deep religious conviction and concern for the salvation of mankind. As the simple Red Man of the western wild put it, with, it must be confessed, a certain force: "Plenty well, no pray; big bellyache, heap God."

MAGIC, An art of converting superstition into coin.

PALMISTRY, The 947th method...of obtaining money by false pretenses. It consists in "reading character" in the wrinkles made by closing the hand. The pretense is not altogether false; character can really be read very accurately in this way, for the wrinkles in every hand submitted plainly spell the word "dupe." The imposture consists in not reading it aloud.

PRAY, To ask that the laws of the universe be annulled in behalf of a single petitioner confessedly unworthy.

RELIGION, A daughter of Hope and Fear, explaining to Ignorance the nature of the Unknowable.

REVERENCE, The spiritual attitude of a man to a god and a dog to a man.

WORSHIP, ...A popular form of abjection, having an element of pride.
— above definitions from *The Devil's Dictionary*

The religious mind, it should be understood, is not logical...That is merely to say that a mind congenitally gifted with the power of logic and accessible to its light and leading does not take to religion.
— *Collected Works*

Religions are conclusions for which the facts of nature supply no major premises.
— Ibid.

When the anointed minister of Heaven spreads his palms and uprolls his eyes to beseech a general blessing or some special advantage is he the celebrant of a hollow, meaningless rite, or the dupe of a false promise? One does not know, but if one is not a fool one does know that his every resultless petition proves him by the inexorable laws of logic to be one or the other.
— Ibid.

Josh Billings

It's better to know nothing than to know what ain't so.

William Blake

Remove away that black'ning church:
Remove away that marriage hearse:
Remove away that man of blood:
You'll quite remove the ancient curse.

— *An Ancient Proverb*

Napoleon Bonaparte

Society cannot exist without inequality of property and the inequality not without religion. A man who is dying of hunger, next to one who has too much, could not possibly reconcile himself to it if it were not for a power which says to him: "It is the will of God that here on Earth there must be rich and poor, but yonder, in eternity, it will be different."
— quoted by Rocker in *Nationalism and Culture*

How can you have order in a state without religion? For, when one man is dying of hunger near another who is ill of surfeit, he cannot resign himself to this difference unless there is an authority which declares "God wills it thus." Religion is excellent stuff for keeping people quiet.
— a different translation of the preceding quotation.

Baron Bowen

A metaphysician is a man who goes into a dark cellar at midnight without a light looking for a black cat that is not there.

Luther Burbank

Those who take refuge behind theological barbed wire fences, quite often wish they could have more freedom of thought, but fear the change to the great ocean of scientific truth as they would a cold bath plunge.
— *Why I Am an Infidel*

Most people's religion is what they want to believe, not what they do believe.
— Ibid.

Rupert Burley

Don't religious beliefs give those who hold them a type of commitment, "something to build their lives around"? Religious belief certainly fills that need— so does heroin addiction.
— *The Match!*, No. 76

Bruce Calvert

Believing is easier than thinking. Hence so many more believers than thinkers.

John Calvin

God preordained, for his own glory and the display of His attributes of mercy and justice, a part of the human race, without any merit of their own, to eternal salvation, and another part, in just punishment of their sin, to eternal damnation.
— *Institutes of the Christian Religion*

Thomas Carlyle

There is no more fruitless endeavour than this, which the Metaphysician proper toils in; to educe Conviction out of Negation...Metaphysical Speculation, as it begins in No or Nothingness, so it must needs end in Nothingness; circulates and must circulate in endless vortices; creating, swallowing—itself.
— *Characteristics*

Clarence Darrow

The origin of the absurd idea of immortal life is easy to discover; it is kept alive by hope and fear, by childish faith, and by cowardice.
— *The Wisdom of Clarence Darrow*

Benjamin Disraeli

Where knowledge ends, religion begins.
— attributed

Albert Ellis

Masochistic self-sacrifice is an integral part of most major organized religions: as shown, for example, in the ritualistic self-deprivation that Jews, Christians and Muslims must continually bear if they are to keep their faith. Orthodox religions deliberately instil guilt (self-damnation) in their adherents and then give these adherents guilt-soothing rituals to (temporarily) allay this kind of self-damning feeling...

Devout religionists (both secular and divine) are almost necessarily dependent and other-directed rather than self-sufficient. To be true to orthodoxies, they first must immolate themselves to their god or god-like hero; second, to the religious hierarchy that runs their church or organization; and third, to all the other members of their religious sect, who are eagle-eyedly watching them to see if they deflect an iota from the conduct that their god and their churchly leadership define as proper.

If devout religiosity, therefore, is often masochism, it is even more often dependency. For humans to be true believers and to also be strong and independent is well nigh impossible. Religiosity and self-sufficiency are contradictory terms.

According to orthodox religious *shalts* and *shalt nots,* you become not only a *wrong-doer,* but an arrant *sinner* when you commit ethical and religious misdeeds; and, as a sinner, you become worthless, undeserving of any human happiness, and deserving of being forever damned (excommunicated) on earth and perhaps roasted eternally in hell.

...Religiosity, then, by setting up absolute standards of godly or proper conduct, makes you intolerant of yourself and others when you or they slightly dishonor these standards. Born of this kind of piety-inspired intolerance of self and others, come some of the most serious of emotional disorders—such as extreme anxiety, depression, self-hatred, and rage.

If one of the requisites for emotional health is acceptance of ambiguity and uncertainty, then divinity-oriented religiosity is the unhealthiest state imaginable: since its prime reason for being is to enable the religionist to believe in god-commanded certainty. Just because life is so uncertain and ambiguous, and because millions of people think that they cannot bear its vicissitudes, they invent absolutistic gods, and thereby pretend that there is some final, invariant answer to human problems. Patently, these people are fooling themselves—and instead of healthfully admitting that they do not need certainty, but can live comfortably in this often disorderly world, they stubbornly protect their neurotic beliefs by insisting that there must be the kind of certainty that they wrongly believe they need.

Pious religious commitment, however, frequently has its serious disadvantages, since it tends to interfere with other kinds of healthy commitments —such as deep involvements in sex-love relationships, in scientific pursuits, and even in artistic endeavors (because these may interfere with or contradict the religious commitments). Moreover, religious commitment is an absorption that is often motivated by guilt or hostility and that may consequently serve as a frenzied covering-up mechanism that masks, but that does not really eliminate, these underlying disturbed feelings. Pious god-inspired commitment, moreover, is frequently the kind of commitment that is based on falsehoods and illusions and that therefore easily can be shattered, thus plunging the previously committed individual into the depths of disillusionment and despair.

Not all forms of commitment, in other words, are equally healthy or beneficial. The grand inquisitors of the medieval Catholic church were utterly dedicated to their "holy" work and Hitler and many of his associates were fanatically committed to their Nazi doctrines.

In regard to risk-taking, I think it is fairly obvious that pious theists are highly determined to avoid adventure and to refuse to take many of life's normal risks. They strongly believe in rigid and unvalidatable assumptions precisely because they are often afraid to follow their own preferences and aims. They demand a guarantee that they will be safe and secure, come what may; and since the real world does not provide them with any such guarantee, they invent some god or other higher power that will presumably give it to them. Their invention of this deity, and their piously subjugating themselves to it, thereby confirms their view that the world is too risky and gives them a further excuse for sticking to inhibiting straight and narrow (and often joyless) paths of existence.

In regard to self acceptance, it seems clear that devout religionists cannot accept themselves just because they are alive and because they have some power to enjoy life. Rather, orthodox theists make their self-acceptance quite contingent on their being accepted by the god, the church, the clergy, and the other members of the religious denomination in which they believe. If all these extrinsic persons and things accept them, then and then only are they able to accept themselves. Which means that these religionists define themselves only through the reflected appraisals of god and of other humans. Fanatical religion, for such individuals, almost necessarily winds up with lack of unconditional self-acceptance and, instead, with a considerable degree of self-abasement and self-abnegation—as, of course, virtually all the saints and mystics have found.

Devout theistic religionists refuse to accept reality...(1) They are frequently sure they see things —e.g., gods, angels, devils, and absolute laws of the universe—for which there is no confirmatory empirical data and that in all probability do not actually exist. And they refuse to see some obvious things—such as the ubiquity of human fallibility... (2) They often whine and scream...when they see something "bad." They especially indulge in childish whining and in temper tantrums when other religionists or non-believers refuse to see the virtues of the devout theists' favorite religious dogmas. (3) Instead of working hard to change grim reality, they often pray to their god(s) to bring about such changes while they impotently sit on their rumps waiting for their prayers to be answered. When certain obnoxious things are unchangeable—such as the propensity of humans to become ill and to die—they refuse to accept these realities and often invent utopian heavens where humans presumably live forever in perfect bliss...Obviously, therefore, devout theists often ignore, deny, and hallucinate about reality; and the more devout they are—as the long history of religion shows—the more delusionary and hallucinatory they seem to be.

— above quotations from *The Case Against Religiosity*

Ralph Waldo Emerson

As men's prayers are a disease of the will, so are their creeds a disease of the intellect.
— *Representative Men*

Sebastian Faure

For centuries kings, rulers, churches, leaders have been treating the people like a vile, miserable herd to be fleeced and butchered. And for centuries the disinherited—thanks to the deceitful marriage of Heaven and the terrible, frightful vision of Hell— have been docile and have stood misery and slavery. It is time that this odious sacrilege, this abominable fraud came to an end!

...The heaven of which they have incessantly spoken to you, the heaven with which they try to lessen your misery, deaden your pain and suffocate the protest which, in spite of everything, comes from your heart, is unreal and deserted. Only your hell is populated and exists...
— *Twelve Proofs of the Nonexistence of God*

G.W. Foote

The mental serf is a bodily serf too, and spiritual fetters are the agencies of political thraldom. The man who worships a tyrant in heaven naturally submits his neck to the yoke of tyrants on earth. He who bows his intellect to a priest will yield his manhood to a king.
— *Flowers of Freethought*

Benjamin Franklin

When a religion is good, I conceive it will support itself; and when it does not support itself, and God does not care to support it—so that its professors are obliged to call for help of a civil power— it is a sign, I apprehend, of its being a bad one.

In the Affairs of this World Men are saved, not by Faith, but by Want of it.
— *Poor Richard's Almanac*, 1754

Frederick the Great

Religion is a fraud, but it must be maintained for the masses.
— attributed

Jeff Gallagher

A church that is prohibited from saying mass and denied access to spread its theology will surely shrivel up like a snake denied rodents to feed on.
— *Black Star*, Spring 1986

Edward Gibbon

A state of scepticism and suspense may amuse a few inquisitive minds. But the practice of superstition is so congenial to the multitude that, if they are forcibly awakened, they still regret the loss of their pleasing vision...So urgent on the vulgar is the necessity of believing, that the fall of any system of mythology will most probably be succeeded by the introduction of some other mode of superstition.

— *The Decline and Fall of the Roman Empire*

The various modes of worship which prevailed in the Roman world were all considered by the people as equally true; by the philosopher as equally false; and by the magistrate as equally useful.

— Ibid.

Joseph Goebbels

Faith in the fuhrer is enveloped, it could almost be said, in a mysterious, unfathomable mysticism.

— *The Struggle Over Berlin*

Emma Goldman

...while charity and religion are supposed to minister to the poor, both institutions derive their main revenue from the poor by the perpetuation of the evils both pretend to fight.

— *The Social Significance of Modern Drama*

All progress has been essentially an unmasking of "divinity" and "mystery," of alleged sacred, eternal "truth"; it has been a gradual elimination of the abstract and the substitution in its place of the real, the concrete. In short, of facts against fancy, of knowledge against ignorance, or light against darkness.

— *The Individual, Society and the State*

Praxedis Guerrero

Religion, by whatever name, is the most terrible enemy of woman. Pretending consolation, it destroys her consciousness. In the name of a sterile love, it snatches away real love, the source of life and human happiness...

— Speech in Los Angeles, 1910

Religion is the tool of tyrants in both home and presidential palace; its mission is to break people's spirits.

Religion is the right arm of domestic and national despots, its mission is to domesticate; through the caress or whip, cage or noose, it's all employed toward one end: to tame. First the woman, because the woman is the mother and teacher of the child, and the child will be the man.

— *Regeneración*, November 12, 1910

E. Haldeman-Julius

After all, the principal objection which a thinking man has to religion is that religion is not true — and is not even sane.

— *The Meaning of Atheism*

Religion, throughout the greater part of its history, has been a form of "holy" terrorism... wherever there is devout belief — there is also the inseparable feeling of fear.

— Ibid.

Perhaps religion might be dismissed as unimportant if it were merely theoretical... but there is and has always been sternly and largely a disposition of religion to enforce its theory in the conduct of life; religion has meant not simply dogmatism in abstract thinking but intolerance in legal and social action. Religion interferes with life and, being false, it necessarily interferes very much to the detriment of the sound human interests of life.

— Ibid.

Herman von Helmholtz

Metaphysicians, like other men who cannot give convincing reasons for their statements, are usually not very polite in controversy. One's success against them may be measured approximately by the increasing want of politeness in their replies.

— *Das Denken in der Medizin*

Joe Hill

Long-haired preachers come out every night,
Try to tell you what's wrong and what's right;
But when asked 'bout something to eat,
They will tell you with voices so sweet:

You will eat, by and bye,
In the glorious land above the sky;
Work and pray, live on hay,
You'll get pie in the sky when you die.

— *The Preacher and the Slave*

Adolf Hitler

...I believe that I am acting in accordance with the will of the Almighty Creator: *by defending myself against the Jews, I am fighting for the Lord.*

— *Mein Kampf*

Baron d'Holbach

The doctrine of spirituality, such as it now exists, offers nothing but vague ideas, or rather, is the absence of all ideas.

If we go back to the beginning we shall find that ignorance and fear created the gods; that fancy, enthusiasm, or deceit adorned or disfigured them; that weakness worships them; that credulity preserves them; and that custom respects and tyranny supports them in order to make the blindness of men serve its own interests.

Thomas Hood

Faith is a kind of parasitic plant,
That grasps the nearest plant with tendril-rings;
And as the climate and the soil may grant,
So is the sort of tree to which it clings.

— *Ode to Rae Wilson*

E.E. Howe

Religion is like an oil well — a promise of great happiness and prosperity — *in the future.*

— attributed

Elbert Hubbard

A Miracle: An event described by those to whom it was told by men who did not see it.

— *Epigrams*

L. Ron Hubbard, Sr.

Money! Repeat money! Repeat money! Repeat money!

— quoted by Bent Corydon and L. Ron Hubbard, Jr. in *L. Ron Hubbard: Messiah or Madman?*

There are men dead because they attacked us...

— Ibid.

Robert Ingersoll

I have had some little experience with political editors, and am forced to say, that until I had read religious papers, I did not know what malicious and slimy falsehoods could be construed from ordinary words. The ingenuity with which the real and apparent meaning can be tortured out of language, is simply amazing.

— Introduction *Atheist Truth vs. Religion's Ghosts*

The dead are orthodox, and your cemetery is the most perfect type of a well regulated church. No thought, no progress, no heresy there. Slowly and silently, side by side, the satisfied members peacefully decay. There is only this difference — the dead do not persecute.

— *Heretics and Heresy*

Theology makes God a monster, a tyrant, a savage; makes man a servant, a serf, a slave; promises heaven to the obedient, the meek, the frightened, and threatens the self-reliant with the tortures of hell.

It denounces reason and appeals to the passions —to hope and fear. It does not answer the arguments of those who attack, but resorts to sophistry, falsehood and slander. It is incapable of advancement.

—*Myth and Miracle*

Theology bears the same relation to science that the black art does to chemistry, that magic does to mathematics...It is not only unknowable, but unthinkable.

—Ibid.

Through hundreds and thousands of generations men have been discussing, wrangling and fighting about theology. No advance has been made. The robed priest has only reached the point from which the savage tried to start.

—Ibid.

It would be hard to overstate the time and talent wasted in the study of this so-called science. The men who believed in astrology thought that they lived in a supernatural world—a world in which causes and effects had no necessary connection with each other—in which all events were the result of magic and necromancy.

Even now, at the close of the nineteenth century, there are hundreds of men who make their living by casting the horoscopes of idiots and imbeciles.

—*Which Way?*

If the people were a little more ignorant, astrology would flourish—if a little more enlightened, religion would perish!

—*Some Mistakes of Moses*

To hate man and worship God seems to be the sum of all creeds.

—Ibid.

Belief is not a voluntary thing. A man believes or disbelieves in spite of himself. They tell us that to believe is the safe way; but I say, the safe way is to be honest.

—*Some Reasons Why*

It certainly cannot be necessary to throw away your reason to save your soul, because after that your soul is not worth saving.

—Ibid.

When I see an exceedingly solemn man, I know he is an exceedingly stupid man. No man of any humor ever founded a religion—never. Humor sees both sides. While reason is the holy light, humor carries the lantern, and the man with a keen sense of humor is preserved form the solemn stupidities of superstition.

—*What Must Be Done To Be Saved*

It seems almost impossible for religious people to really grasp the ideas of intellectual freedom. They seem to think that man is responsible for his honest thoughts; that unbelief is a crime; that investigation is sinful; that credulity is a virtue, and that reason is a dangerous guide. They cannot divest themselves of the idea that in the realm of thought there must be government—authority and obedience—laws and penalties—rewards and punishments, and that somewhere in the universe there is a penitentiary for the soul.

—Preface to *Atheist Truth vs. Religion's Ghosts*

The destroyer of weeds, thistles and thorns is a benefactor, whether he soweth grain or not.

—Inscription to Volume I, *Collected Works*

I simply ask you to be honest. Divest your minds, for a moment at least, of all religious prejudice. Act, for a few moments, as though you were men and women.

—*The Liberty of Man, Woman, and Child*

What harm does superstition do? What harm in believing in fables, in legends?

To believe in signs and wonders, in amulets, charms, and miracles, in gods and devils, in heavens and hells, makes the brain an insane ward, the world a madhouse, takes all certainty from the mind, makes experience a snare, destroys the kinship of effect and cause...Nature becomes a puppet of the unseen powers. The fairy, called the supernatural, touches with her wand a fact, it disappears. Causes are barren of effects, and effects are independent of all natural causes. Caprice is King...Reason abdicates and superstition wears her crown.

The heart hardens and the brain softens.

The energies of man are wasted in a vain effort to secure the protection of the supernatural. Credulity, ceremony, worship, sacrifice and prayer take the place of honest work, of investigation, of intellectual effort, of observation, or experience. Progress becomes impossible.

—*Superstition*

The worshiper always regrets that he is not the worshiped.

—*Individuality*

Religion does not, and cannot, contemplate man as free. She accepts only the homage of the prostrate, and scorns the offerings of those who stand erect. She cannot tolerate the liberty of thought. The wide and sunny fields belong not to her domain. The star-lit heights of genius and individuality are above and beyond her appreciation and power. Her subjects cringe at her feet, covered with the dust of obedience. They are not athletes standing posed by rich life and brave endeavor like antique statues, but shriveled deformities, studying with furtive glance the cruel face of power.

—Ibid.

Strange, but true, that those who have loved God most have loved man least.
— Speech in New York, April 25, 1881

It has always seemed absurd to suppose that a god would choose for his companions, during all eternity, the dear souls whose highest and only ambition is to obey.
— Ibid.

Nearly all people stand in great horror of annihilation, and yet to give up your individuality is to annihilate yourself. Mental slavery is mental death, and every man who has given up his intellectual freedom is the living coffin of his dead soul. In this sense, every church is a cemetery and every creed an epitaph.
— Ibid.

No one can overestimate the evils that have been endured by the human race by reason of a departure from the standard of the natural. The world has been governed by jugglery, by sleight-of-hand. Miracles, wonders, tricks, have been regarded as of far greater importance than the steady, the sublime and unbroken march of cause and effect. The improbable has been established by the impossible.
— *Professor Huxley and Agnosticism*

Nothing is more sickening than the "spiritual" whine—the pretense that crawls at first and talks about humility and then suddenly becomes arrogant and says "I am spiritual."
— *Spirituality*

Hands that help are nobler than lips that pray.
— quoted in *Ingersoll the Magnificent*

Fear paralyzes the brain. Progress is born of courage. Fear believes—courage doubts. Fear falls upon the earth and prays—courage stands erect and thinks. Fear retreats—courage advances. Fear is barbarism—courage is civilization. Fear believes in witchcraft, in devils and in ghosts. Fear is religion—courage is science.
— Ibid.

An infinite God ought to be able to protect Himself, without going in partnership with State Legislatures. Certainly He ought not so to act that laws become necessary to keep Him from being laughed at. No one thinks of protecting Shakespeare from ridicule, by the threat of fine and imprisonment. It strikes me that God might write a book that would not necessarily excite the laughter of His children. in fact, I think it would be safe to say that a real God could produce a work that would excite the admiration of mankind.
— Ibid.

Whenever a man believes that he has the exact truth from God, there is in that man no spirit of compromise. He has not the modesty born of the imperfections of human nature; he has the arro-

gance of theological certainty and the tyranny born of ignorant assurance. Believing himself to be the slave of God, he imitates his master, and of all tyrants the worst is a slave in power.
— *Some Reasons Why*

Thomas Jefferson

In every country and in every age the priest has been hostile to liberty; he is always in allegiance with the despot, abetting his abuses in return for protection of his own.
— Letter to Horatio Spofford, 1814

You judge truly that I am not afraid of priests. They have tried upon me all their various batteries, of pious whining, hypocritical canting, lying & slandering, without being able to give me one moment of pain. I have contemplated their order from the Magi of the East to the Saints of the West and I have found no difference of character, but of more or less caution, in proportion to their information or ignorance on whom their interested duperies were to be plaid off. Their sway in New England is indeed formidable. No mind beyond mediocrity dares there to develop itself.
— Letter to Horatio Spofford, 1816

On the dogmas of religion, as distinguished from moral principles, all mankind, from the beginning of the world to this day, have been quarreling, fighting, burning and torturing one another, for abstractions unintelligible to themselves and to all others, and absolutely beyond the comprehension of the human mind.
— Letter to Carey, 1816

Difference of opinion is advantageous in religion. The several sects perform the office of a *censor morum* over each other. Is uniformity attainable? Millions of innocent men, women and children since the introduction of Christianity, have been burnt, tortured, fined, imprisoned; yet we have not advanced one inch towards uniformity. What has been the effect of coercion? To make one half the world fools, and the other half hypocrites. To support rogeury and error all over the earth.
— *Notes on Virginia*

Anton Szandor LaVey

It's a living.
— on his job as head of the First Church of Satan, quoted in the *San Francisco Chronicle*, Oct. 31, 1986

How can you call yourself an expert on the occult when occult means hidden or secret?
— quoted Ibid.

Ervil LeBaron

The Lord wants this guy [killed] more than anything...simply do whatever has to be done. Anybody gets in the way—men, women or children—it doesn't make any difference.

—quoted by Van Atta and Bradlee in *Prophet of Blood*

You can lie, cheat and steal in the name of God, and it is all right.

—Ibid.

Gypsy Rose Lee

Praying is like a rocking chair—it'll give you something to do, but it won't get you anywhere.

—quoted by E. Haldeman-Julius

John Doyle Lee

...the people in Utah who professed the Mormon religion were at and for some time before the Mountain Meadows massacre [the mass murder of 120 men, women, and children on September 11, 1857 in southern Utah] full of wildfire and zeal, anxious to do something to build up the kingdom of God on earth and waste the enemies of the Mormon religion...The killing of Gentiles [non-Mormons] was a means of grace and a virtuous deed...

The Mormons believe in blood atonement. It is taught by the leaders, and believed by the people, that the Priesthood are inspired and cannot give a wrong order. It is the belief of all...that the authority that orders is the only responsible party and the Danite [member of the Sons of Dan—the Mormon KGB—which some say is still in existence] who does the killing only an instrument, and commits no wrong...

Punishment by death is the penalty for refusing to obey the orders of the Priesthood.

—*Being the Confession of John Doyle Lee, Danite,* quoted in *I Was a Mormon*

John Locke

I find every sect, as far as reason will help them, make use of it gladly; and where it fails them, they cry out, It is a matter of faith, and above reason.

—*Concerning Human Understanding*

Martin Luther

In our sad condition, our only consolation is the expectancy of another life.

—*Table Talk*

When a judge sentences a man to death who has done him no harm, he is not the man's enemy; he sentences him at God's behest.

Karl Marx

Religion is the sigh of the oppressed creature, the feeling of a heartless world, just as it is the spirit of unspiritual conditions. It is the opium of the people.

—*Critique of the Hegelian Philosophy of Right*

The first requisite for the happiness of the people is the abolition of religion.

—Ibid.

Nothing is easier than to invent mystical causes, that is to say, phrases which lack common sense.

—*The Wisdom of Karl Marx*

To want to renounce the illusions concerning our proper situation implies that we renounce the situation that needs such illusions. The critique of religion demands the critique of the valley of tears of which religion is the aureola...The critique of religion must rid man of his illusions in order that he may think, act and build his reality as a being who has finally become reasonable, in order that his world rotate about himself, that is to say, about his only true sun. Religion is merely an illusory sun.

—Ibid.

The imaginary flowers of religion adorn man's chains. Man must throw off the flowers and also the chains.

—Ibid.

The abolition of religion, as the illusory happiness of the people, is the demand for their real happiness.

—Ibid.

St. Maximus the Confessor

That mind is perfect which, through true faith, in supreme ignorance supremely knows the supremely Unknowable.

Joseph McCabe

The few mystics who stand outside all organizations differ from the rest of us in only one respect: they pretend to have a higher code of behavior, and where its clauses differ from ours they have no foundation that will survive examination.

—*The Menace of Mysticism*

H.L. Mencken

The cosmos is a gigantic fly wheel making 1,000 revolutions a minute. Man is a sick fly taking a dizzy ride on it. Religion is the theory that the wheel was designed and set spinning to give him the ride.

—*A Mencken Chrestomathy*

One of the strangest delusions of the Western mind is to the effect that a philosophy of profound wisdom is on tap in the East. I have read a great many expositions of it, some by native sages and the rest by Western enthusiasts, but I have found nothing in it save nonsense. It is fundamentally a moony transcendentalism almost as absurd as that of Emerson, Alcott and company. It bears no sort of relation to the known facts, and is full of assumptions and hypotheses that every intelligent man must laugh at. In its practical effect it seems as lacking in sense and as inimical to human dignity as Methodism, or even Mormonism.

— *Minority Report*

Men always try to make virtues of their weaknesses. Fear of death and fear of life both become piety.

— Ibid.

The belief that man is outfitted with an immortal soul, differing altogether from the engines which operate the lower animals, is ridiculously unjust to them. The difference between the smartest dog and the stupidest man — say a Tennessee Holy Roller — is really very small, and the difference between the decentest dog and the worst man is all in favor of the dog.

— Ibid.

Rev. Sun Myung Moon

I am your brain. What I wish must be your wish.

— message to his followers, quoted in the *San Francisco Examiner,* November 16, 1986

John Morley

All religions die of one disease, that of being found out.

— attributed

Johann Most

Among all mental diseases that have been systematically inoculated into the human cranium, the religious pest is the most abominable.

— *The God Pestilence*

The rich and mighty foster and nourish divine idiocy and religious stupidity. It is, in fact, part of their business; it is really a question of life or death to the domineering and exploiting classes whether the people at large are dumfounded religiously or not. With religious lunacy stands and falls their power. The more man clings to religion, the more he believes. The more he believes, the less he knows. The less he knows, the more stupid he is; the more stupid, the easier he is governed. The easier to govern, the better he may be exploited; the more exploited, the poorer he gets.

— Ibid.

Benito Mussolini

Fascism is a religious concept.

— *Fascism, Institutions and Doctrines*

Cardinal John Newman

It would be a gain to the country [England] were it vastly more superstitious, more bigoted, more gloomy, more fierce in its religion than at present it shows itself to be.

— *Apologia pro Vita Sua*

Friedrich Nietzsche

Faith, indeed, has up to the present not been able to move real mountains...But it can put mountains where there are none.

There is not sufficient love and goodness in the world to permit us to give some of it away to imaginary beings.

People to whom their daily life appears too empty and monotonous easily grow religious; this is comprehensible and excusable, only they have no right to demand religious sentiments from those whose daily life is not empty and monotonous.

Certain individuals have such great need of exercising their power and love of ruling that, in default of other objects, or because they have never succeeded otherwise, they finally excogitate the idea of tyrannizing over certain parts of their own nature, portions or degrees of themselves...This crushing of one's self, this scorn of one's own nature, this *spernere se sperni*, of which religion has made so much, is really a very high degree of vanity.

The commonest means which the ascetic and saint employs to render life still endurable and amusing consists in occasional warfare with alternate victory and defeat. For this he requires an opponent, and finds it in the so-called "inward enemy." He principally makes use of his inclination to vanity, love of honor and rule, and of his sensual desires, that he may be permitted to regard his life as a perpetual battle and himself as a battlefield upon which good and evil spirits strive with alternating success. It is well known that sensual imagination is moderated, indeed almost dispelled, by regular sexual intercourse, whereas, on the contrary, it is rendered unfettered and wild by abstinence or irregularity. The imagination of many Christian saints was filthy to an extraordinary degree; by virtue of those theories that these desires were actual demons raging within them they did not feel themselves to be too responsible; to this feeling we owe the very instructive frankness of their self-confessions. It was to their interest that this strife should always be maintained in one degree or another, because, as we have already said, their empty life was thereby entertained.

— above quotations from *Human, All Too Human*

The adoption of guiding principles without reasons is called *faith*.

...belief removes no mountains but places mountains where there are none. A hasty walk through a madhouse enlightens sufficiently on these matters. Not to a priest to be sure: for he denies by instinct that sickness is sickness and a madhouse is a madhouse.

Belief means *not wanting* to know what is true.

What alone did Mohammed borrow from Christianity? The invention of Paul, his expedient for priestly tyranny, for forming herds: the belief in immortality—*i.e., the doctrine of "judgment"* . . .

What a theologian feels as true, *must* be false: one has therein almost a criterion of truth.

The great lie of personal immortality destroys all reason, all naturalness in instinct—all that is beneficent, that is life-furthering. . .So to live that it has no longer any *significance, that* now becomes the significance of life. . .

"Salvation of the soul"—in plain words, "the world revolves around *me*."

Man is *not* to look outwards, he is to look inwards into himself, he is *not* to look prudently and cautiously into things as a learner, he is not to look at all, he is to *suffer*. . .And he is to suffer as to need the priest always. . .*A savior is needed.*

The concepts of guilt and punishment, inclusive of the doctrines of "grace," or "salvation," and of "forgiveness"—*lies* through and through. . .have been contrived to destroy the *causal sense* in man, they are an attack on the concepts of cause and effect!—And *not* an attack with the fists, with the knife, with honesty. . .But springing from the most cowardly, most deceitful, and most ignoble instincts! A *priest's* attack! A *parasite's* attack! A vampirism of pale, subterranean blood-suckers! When the natural consequences of a deed are no longer "natural," but are supposed to be brought about by the spectres of superstition, by "God," by "spirits," by "souls," as mere "moral" consequences, as reward, punishment, suggestion, or means of education, the prerequisite of perception has been destroyed—*the greatest crime against mankind has been committed.*

Sin, repeated once more, this form of human violation par excellence, has been invented for the purpose of making impossible science, culture, every kind of elevation and nobility of man; the priest *rules* by the invention of sin.

The ascetic makes a necessity of virtue.

If today persons are still to be found who do not know how *indecent* it is to be a "believer"—or in how far it is a symbol of *decadence,* of a broken will to live—they will know it tomorrow.
—above quotations from *The Anti-Christ*

It is the profound, suspicious fear, of an incurable pessimism, which compels whole centuries to fasten their teeth into a religious interpretation of existence . . .—Piety, the "Life in God," regarded in this light, would appear as the most elaborate and ultimate product of the *fear* of truth. . .as the will to inversion of truth, to untruth at any price.
—*Beyond Good and Evil*

Max Nordau

"The faith of the people must be maintained," is merely another way of syaing, "The submission of the people to their rulers, and their willingness to pay. . .taxes, must be maintained."

The first harmful effect of religion was that it satisfied man's desire for knowledge by means of a perfectly arbitrary invention. . . "The world was created by the Gods, who can free you from suffering and death; your souls are immortal," etc; and the timid questioners believed it, as children believe the answer their mother gives them. . . "The stork brought ye." Man asks for the bread of knowledge; religion gives him the stone of a fairy-tale, which, though indigestible, fills the stomach, gives a false satiety, and arrests the wholesome hunger. . .It was easier to give man a fictitious than a true answer to the questions about eternity that troubled him, but the effect was fatal, in so far as it led him to imagine that he had the knowledge he sought, and so arrested his natural impulse to win, through effort and mistakes, a real insight. . .

Religion no doubt has brought comfort to many. That this is so is not, however, to its credit. The practical utility of untruth is a cynical defense that all liars bring forward. No doubt the assurance of immortality robs the idea of death of its terrors. The promise of future reunion helps the mother to bear the loss of her child; the thought that eternal justice will be dealt out to good and evil deeds pours balsam in the wounds of the weak, down-trodden, and ill-used who have succumbed before the pride of the mighty. But the means by which these tortured spirits are soothed are unhealthy and immoral in the extreme—invented tales and arbitrary assertions. which cannot stand a moment's critical examination. The merit that belongs to the consolation of religion must be granted to every superstition—the amulet that averts the evil eye, spells, the interpretation of cards and dreams, the raising of spirits. All this hocus-pocus has lightened dark hours for millions who believed in it, given them confidence and self-reliance, lifted heavy burdens from their souls, and reconciled them to the hardness of their lot. Moreover, physical sedatives, like opium, morphia, and alcohol, must be assigned an equal value with religion. They, too, console; they, too, bring temporary oblivion of care and suffering; they, too, given an artificial sense of pleasure.

Copyright Bill Griffith, used by permission

No single fact supporting any of these hypotheses—the existence of the soul, its immortality, its sojourn in a supra-natural realm—has ever been cited in a material or intellectual form capable of analysis by a thinker worthy of being called one. Nevertheless, the majority go on persuading each other without any thought of proof...

Were anyone to say, "I am quite certain that I shall one day be rich: I have an intense desire for it, and a secret voice whispers to me that my desires will be realized," he would be laughed at...Yet this secret voice, this intense desire, are considered sufficient security for personal immortality.

The idea of immortality may have made death easier to many who found comfort in it. But the thought of his own death fills the most convinced believer with a terror that is meaningless if the grave be really the door into a new, eternal life, no longer shadowed by the fear of death.

Finally, the use of a jargon, remote alike from thought and reality, gave currency to the phrase, so often repeated in the last decades, that faith has nothing to do with knowledge, that they occupy distinct provinces in the realm of thought. Certainly a knowledge that rests upon the verifiable basis of experience has nothing to do with a faith whose content, even when dignified by the name of "inward events," is really from beginning to end nothing but subjective invention. The formula is, however, inadmissible, because it suggests that faith and knowledge, though different from and independent of each other, possess equal value. To assume this is to put dream, chimera, and delirium on the same level as the results of strict observation and the evidence obtained from the senses after careful examination and experimentation.

— above quotations from *The Interpretation of History*

Rev. John Osbourne

Give until it hurts. And then give until it starts feeling good.

— TV Broadcast, August 24, 1986

Thomas Paine

All national institutions of churches, whether Jewish, Christian, or Turkish, appear to me no other than human inventions, set up to terrify and enslave mankind, and monopolize power and profit.

— *The Age of Reason*

The world is my country, to do good my religion.

Albert Parsons

Those pious frauds who profess their faith in the "power" of God, while they employ the police, the militia and other armed hirelings to enforce their man-made laws and maintain their "power" over their fellow men. Oh, consistency, indeed thou art a jewel! These hypocrites, who always did, and do today, employ brute force to compel their fellow men to obey and serve them, while they whine and snivel behind their sanctimonious masks about the "love for man and the power of God."

— *The Philosophy of Anarchism*

Blaise Pascal

Men never do evil so completely and cheerfully as when they do it from religious conviction.

— attributed

Wendell Phillips

You and I are called "infidels," which means, merely, that we do not submit our necks to yokes.

— *The Bible and the Church*

Bhagwan Shree Rajneesh

Nature does not care about us, so why should we care about nature?

— quoted by Hugh Milne in *Bhagwan: The God that Failed*

Wilhelm Reich

...what religion calls freedom from the outside world really means fantasized substitute gratification for actual gratification.

Every form of mysticism is reactionary, and the reactionary man is mystical.

The cult of the Virgin Mary is drawn upon very successfully as a means of inculcating chastity... The same vital energy and enormous love that a healthy young man puts forth in an orgastic experience with his loved on is used by the mystical man to support the mystical cult of the Virgin Mary, *after* genital sensuality has been suppressed. This is the source from which mysticism draws its forces. Being *unsatisfied* forces, they should not be underestimated. They make intelligible the age-old power of mysticism over man and the inhibitions that operate against the responsibility of the masses.

In this regard it is not a matter of the veneration of the Virgin Mary or any other idol. It is a matter of *producing a mystical structure in the masses* in every new generation. But mysticism is nothing other than unconscious longing for orgasm.

Clinical experience shows incontestably that religious sentiments result from inhibited sexuality, that the source of mystical excitation is to be sought in inhibited sexual excitation. The inescapable conclusion of all this is that a *clear sexual consciousness* and a *natural regulation of sexual life must foredoom every form of mysticism;* that, in other words, *natural sexuality is the arch enemy of mystical religion.* By carrying on an anti-sexual fight wherever it can, making it the core of its dogmas and putting it in the foreground of its mass propaganda, the church only attests to the correctness of this interpretation.

As time goes on, people who are incapable of release must begin to sense sexual excitation as torturous, burdensome, destructive. In fact, sexual excitation is destructive and torturous if it is not allowed to achieve release. Thus, we see that the religious conception of sex as an annihilating diabolical force, predisposing one for final doom, is rooted in actual physical processes. As a result the attitude toward sexuality is forced to become divided: The typical religious and moralistic valuations "good-bad," "heavenly-earthly," "divine-diabolical," etc., become the symbols of sexual gratification on the one hand and the punishment thereof on the other hand.

The emotional structure of the genuinely religious man can be briefly described as follows: biologically, he is subject to sexual tensions just as all other human beings and creatures. Owing, however, to his assimilation of sex-negating religious conceptions, and especially to the fear of punishment that he has acquired, he has completely lost his ability to experience natural sexual tension and release. Consequently, he suffers from a chronic state of physical excitation, which he is continuously compelled to master. He is not only shut off from earthly happiness — it does not even appear desirable. Since he expects to be rewarded in the Beyond, he succumbs to a feeling of being *incapable of happiness* in this world. In view of the fact that he is a biologic creature and *cannot* under any circumstances forego happiness, release, and gratification, he seeks *illusionary* happiness.

— above quotations from *The Mass Psychology of Fascism*

Ernest Renan

No miracle has ever taken place under conditions which science can accept. Experience shows, without exception, that miracles occur only in times and in countries in which miracles are believed in, and in the presence of persons who are disposed to believe them.

— *The Life of Jesus*

Rev. Pat Robertson

People have immortal spirits with incredible power over elemental things. The way to deal with inanimate matter is to talk to it.

— quoted in the *San Francisco Examiner*, Sept. 7, 1986

If you wanted to get America destroyed, if you were a malevolent, evil force and you said, "How can I turn God against America? What can I do to get God mad at the people of America to cause this great land to vomit out the people?" Well, I'd pick five things. I'd begin to have incest, I'd begin to commit adultery wherever possible, all over the country, and sexuality. I'd begin to have them offering up and killing their babies. I'd get them having homosexual relations, and then I'd have them having sex with animals.

— Ibid.

Arthur Schopenauer

...faith and knowledge are related as the two scales of a balance; when the one goes up, the other goes down.

The power of religious dogma, when inculcated early, is such as to stifle conscience, compassion and finally every feeling of humanity.

One may say generally that duties towards God and duties towards humanity are in inverse ratio. It is easy to let adulation of the Deity make amends for lack of proper behavior towards man. And so we see that in all times and in all countries the great majority of mankind find it much easier to beg their way to heaven by prayers than to deserve to go there by their actions. In every religion it soon comes to be the case that faith, ceremonies, rites and the like are proclaimed to be more agreeable to the Divine will than moral actions; the former, especially if they are bound up with emoluments of the clergy, gradually come to be looked upon as a substitute for the latter. Sacrifices in temples, the saying of masses, the founding of chapels, the planting of crosses by the road side, soon come to be the most meritorious works, so that even great crimes are expiated by them, as also by penance, subjection to priestly authority, confessions, pilgrimages, donations to the temples and the clergy, the building of monasteries and the like... Those devils in human form, the slave owners and slave traders in the Free States of North America (they should be called the Slave States) are, as a rule, orthodox, pious Anglicans who would consider it a grave sin to work on Sundays; and in confidence in this, and their regular attendance at church, they hope for eternal salvation.

For, as you know, religions are like glow worms; they shine only when it's dark. A certain amount of ignorance is the condition of all religions, the element in which alone they can exist.

If, in early childhood, certain fundamental views and doctrines are paraded with unusual solemnity, and an air of the greatest earnestness never before visible in anything else; if at the same time, the possibility of doubt about them be completely passed over, or touched upon only to indicate that doubt is the first step to eternal perdition, the resulting impression will be so deep that, as a rule, that is, in almost every case, doubt about them will be almost as impossible as doubt about one's own existence. Hardly one in ten thousand will have the strength of mind to ask himself seriously and earnestly — is that true? To call such as can do it strong minds, strong spirits, is a description apter than is generally supposed.

To free a man from error is to give, not take away.

— above quotations from *Religion, A Dialogue*

George Bernard Shaw

The fact that a believer is happier than a skeptic is no more to the point than the fact that a drunken man is happier than a sober one. The happiness of credulity is a cheap and dangerous quality of happiness, and by no means a necessity of life. Whether Socrates got as much out of life as Wesley [John Wesley, the founder of Methodism] is an unanswerable question, but a nation of Socrateses would be much safer and happier than a nation of Wesleys. . .

Percy Bysshe Shelley

How ludicrous the priest's dogmatic roar!
The weight of his exterminating curses,
How light! and his affected charity,
To suit the pressure of the changing times,
What palpable deceit! — but for thy aid,
Religion! but for thee, prolific fiend,
Who peopleth earth with demons, hell with men,
And heaven with slaves!

— *Queen Mab*

Benedict Spinoza

Philosophy has no end in view save truth; faith looks for nothing but obedience and piety.

— *Theological-Political Treatise*

Charles T. Sprading

A union of church and state means an alliance between tyranny and hypocrisy.

— *Freedom and its Fundamentals*

Bishop Jeremy Taylor

Ignorance is the mother of devotion.

— *To a Person Newly Converted to the Church of England*

A great fear, when it is ill-managed, is the parent of superstition; but a discreet and well-guided fear produces religion.

— *The Rule and Exercises of Holy Living*

Robert Tefton

CULT, n. 1) An unsuccessful religion; 2) A pejorative term employed by members of religious bodies to refer to other religious bodies.

FAITH, n. An attitude of desperation. An attempt to make the intolerable tolerable. When achieved, it gives a satisfying feeling of superiority over those so unfortunate as to see things as they are.

MORMON, n. A common misspelling. Only one "m" is necessary.

PRAYER, n. A form of begging, unusual in that it's often practiced as a solitary activity. When practiced in groups, it is normally referred to as "worship."

RELIGION, n. 1) The first refuge of the desperate; 2) A convenient means of avoiding such unpleasantries as independent thought and reality; 3) A means of feeling superior to others; 4) A cult which has achieved sufficient longevity, membership, and economic clout to merit social acceptance.

SPIRITUAL, adj. A term of self-congratulation employed to assert superiority over others.

Leo Tolstoy

The religious superstition is encouraged by means of the institution of churches, processions, monuments, festivities, from the money collected from the masses, and these, with the aid of painting, architecture, music, incense, but chiefly by the maintenance of the so-called clergy, stupefy the masses: their duty consists in this, that with their representations, the pathos of the services, their sermons, their interference in the private lives of the people — at births, marriages, deaths — they befog the people and keep them in an eternal condition of stupefaction.

— *The Kingdom of God Is Within You*

Mark Twain

There are those who scoff at the schoolboy, calling him frivolous and shallow. Yet it was the schoolboy who said "Faith is believing what you know ain't so."

— *Following the Equator*

[*The Book of Mormon* is] an insipid mess of inspiration. It is chloroform in print.

— *Roughing It*

Voltaire

Nothing can be more contrary to religion and the clergy than reason and common sense.
— *Philosophical Dictionary*

One does not speak of a Euclidian, an Archimedean. When truth is evident, it is impossible for parties and factions to arise. There has never been a dispute as to whether there is daylight at noon.
— Ibid.

When he to whom one speaks does not understand, and he who speaks himself does not understand, that is metaphysics.
— Ibid.

The man who says to men, "Believe as I do, or God will damn you," will presently say, "Believe as I do, or I shall kill you."
— *Selected Works*

Any worship that is not offered up to the true God is false and superstitious. The only true God is the God of our priests; the only true worship is that which seems the most fitting to them, and to which they have accustomed us from our earliest childhood; any other worship is clearly superstitious, false, and even ridiculous.

Vince Williams

Religion keeps the people happy, or, at least, willing to suffer.

Fred Woodworth

[Religion has] never done much but serve as food for nationalism and wars, a sort of dietary supplement of the State. Religion's "holy books" — the so-called Bible, the Koran, and the Book of Mormon, to name the most famous ones — are gibbering lunacy as ethics, and extreme authoritarianism as politics. As writing, they are staggering in their crudity...
— *Strike*, June 1984

Religion is a terrible and opportunistic thing. The fact is that something in it will always attempt to seize on anything in the world that will lever it into an even more secure position of dominance. If the spirit of the time is for slavery, then it is for slavery; if the tendency evolves toward Fascism, it is fascistic. And true to form when protest is the hallmark of an age, the churches turn into abodes of singing nuns with guitars, or earnest young ministers decrying nuclear weapons.
— Ibid.

Brigham Young

Shall I tell you the law of God in regard to the African race? If the white man who belongs to the chosen seed mixes his blood with the seed of Cain, the penalty, under the law of God, is death on the spot.
— *Journal of Discourses*, Vol. 10

Ham will continue to be the servant of servants, as the Lord has decreed, until the curse is removed. Will the present struggle free the slave? No...Can you destroy the decrees of the Almighty? You cannot.
— Ibid.

We [Mormons] consider it [slavery] to be of divine institution, and not to be abolished until the curse pronounced on Ham shall have been removed from his descendants.
— Interview with Horace Greeley, Salt Lake City, 1859

Emile Zola

Civilization will not attain to its perfection until the last stone from the last church falls on the last priest.
— attributed

Anonymous & Multiple Author

...morality and piety, rightly grounded on evangelical principles, will give the best and greatest security to government, and will lay, in the hearts of men, the strongest obligations to due subjection.
— Constitution of the State of New Hampshire

A man without religion is like a horse without a bridle.
— Latin proverb

They who believe not shall have garments of fire fitted unto them; boiling water shall be poured on their heads; their bowels shall be dissolved thereby, and also their skins, and they shall be beaten with maces of iron.
— *Koran*, 22:19-21

ENTRANCE: SPIRITUAL PATH (Delivery Vehicles Only)
— Sign at Harbin Hot Springs (new age health spa)

We believe that all men are bound to sustain and uphold the respective governments in which they reside...and that to the laws, all men owe respect and deference...
— *Doctrines and Covenants of the Church of Jesus Christ of Latter Day Saints* [Mormons], Section 134

...we do not believe it right to interfere with bond servants [slaves], neither preach the gospel to, nore baptize them, contrary to the will and wish of their masters, nor to meddle with or influence them in the least, to cause them to be dissatisfied with their situations in this life, thereby jeopardizing the lives of men; such interference we believe to be unlawful and unjust, and dangerous to the peace of every government allowing human beings to be held in servitude.

—Ibid.

Inasmuch as they will not hearken unto thy words they shall be cut off from the presence of the Lord...wherefore as they were white, and exceedingly fair and delightsome, that they might not be enticing unto my people the Lord God did cause a skin of blackness to come upon them.

— *The Book of Mormon,* 2 Nephi 5:20-21

The delegates of the annual conference are decidedly opposed to modern Abolitionism, and wholly disclaim any right, wish or intention to interfere in the civil and political relation between master and slave as it exists in the slave-holding states of the nation.

— Resolution of the General Conference of the Methodist Church, May 1836

God & Atheism

St. Thomas Aquinas

...punishment is meted according to the dignity of the person sinned against, so that a person who strikes one in authority receives a greater punishment than one who strikes anyone else. Now whoever sins mortally sins against God...But God's majesty is infinite. Therefore whoever sins mortally deserves infinite punishment; and consequently it seems just that for a mortal sin a man should be punished forever.

— *Summa Theologica*

Petronius Arbiter

It was fear that first brought gods into the world.

St. Augustine

This then is not God, if thou has comprehended it; but if this be God, thou hast not comprehended it.

— *Sermo LII*

Michael Bakunin

There is a class of people who, if they do not believe, must at least make a semblance of believing. This class, comprising all the tormentors, all the oppressors, and all the exploiters of humanity: priests, monarchs, statesmen, soldiers, public and private financiers, officials of all sorts, policemen, gendarmes, jailers and executioners, monopolists, capitalists, tax-leeches, contractors and landlords, lawyers, economists, politicians of all shades, down to the smallest vendor of sweetmeats, all will repeat in unison those words of Voltaire: "If God did not exist, it would be necessary to invent him."

— *God and the State*

For, if God is, he is necessarily the eternal, supreme, absolute master, and, if such a master exists, man is a slave...a master, whoever he may be and however liberal he may desire to show himself, remains nonetheless always a master. His existence necessarily implies the slavery of all that is beneath him. Therefore, if God existed, only in one way could he serve human liberty — by ceasing to exist.

A jealous lover of human liberty, and deeming it the absolute condition of all that we admire and respect in humanity, I reverse the phrase of Voltaire and say that *if God really existed, it would be necessary to abolish him.*

— Ibid.

The idea of God implies the abdication of human reason and justice; it is the most decisive negation of human liberty, and necessarily ends in the enslavement of mankind, both in theory and practice. Unless, then, we desire the enslavement and degradation of mankind...we may not, must not make the slightest concession either to the God of theology or to the God of metaphysics. He who, in this mystical alphabet, begins with A will inevitably end with Z; he who desires to worship God must harbor no childish illusions about the matter, but bravely renounce his liberty and humanity.

If God is, man is a slave; now, man can and must be free; then, God does not exist.

I defy anyone whomsoever to avoid this circle; now, therefore, let all choose.

— Ibid.

There exists, finally a somewhat numerous class of honest but timid souls who, too intelligent to take the Christian dogmas seriously, reject them in detail, but have neither the courage nor the strength nor the necessary resolution to summarily renounce them altogether. They abandon to your criticism all the special absurdities of religion, they turn up their noses at all the miracles, but they cling desperately to the principal absurdity; the source of all the others, to the miracle that explains and justifies all the other miracles, the existence of God. Their God is not the vigorous and powerful being, the brutally positive God of theology. It is a nebulous, diaphanous, illusory being that vanishes into nothing at the first attempt to grasp it...And yet they hold fast to it, and believe that, were it to disappear, all would disappear with it. They are uncertain, sickly souls...They have neither the power nor the wish nor the determination to follow out their thought, and they waste their time and pains in constantly endeavoring to reconcile the irreconcilable...

With them, or against them, discussion is out of the question. They are too puny.

—Ibid.

St. John Chrysostom

To be a man is to fear God.

Samuel Taylor Coleridge

Not one man in ten thousand has goodness of heart or strength of mind to be an atheist.

— Letter to Thomas Allsop, 1820

Clarence Darrow

If there is any God in the universe I don't know it. Some people say they know it instinctively. Well, the errors and foolish things that men have known instinctively are so many we can't talk about them.

As a rule, the less a person knows, the surer he is, and he gets it by instinct...

—*Absurdities of the Bible*

I don't believe in God, because I don't believe in Mother Goose.

Thomas Edison

What does God mean to me? Not a damned thing! Religion is all bunk.

— quoted by American Atheists

Jonathan Edwards

The God that holds you over the pit of hell, much as anyone holds a spider, or some loathsome insect, over the fire, abhors you and is dreadfully provoked; his wrath towards you burns like fire.

Albert Einstein

I cannot imagine a god who rewards and punishes the objects of his creation, whose purposes are modeled after our own—a god, in short, who is but a reflection of human frailty. Neither can I believe that the individual survives the death of his body, although feeble souls harbor such thoughts through fear or ridiculous egotism.

— attributed

Epicurus

Is god willing to prevent evil but not able? Then he is not omnipotent.

Is he able but not willing? Then he is malevolent.

Is he both able and willing? Then whence cometh evil?

Is he neither able nor willing? Then why call him god?

Sebastian Faure

Arise, ye men! On your feet! and with a rebellious cry of indignation declare an inexorable war against that God whose depressing veneration has been imposed upon you for so many years. Free yourselves of the imaginary tyrant, and shake the yoke of his self-appointed representatives on earth.

When you will have chased away both the earthly and the heavenly gods, when you will have liberated yourselves from the masters above and the masters below, when you will have completed this double act of liberation, then you will escape Hell and attain Paradise. Only then!

— *Twelve Proofs of the Nonexistence of God*

Anatole France

In order not to impair human liberty, I will be ignorant of what I know, I will thicken upon my eyes the veils I have pierced, and in my blind clear-sightedness I will let myself be surprised by what I have foreseen.

—*Penguin Island* (God explaining the doctrine of free will)

Remy de Gourmont

God is not all that exists; he is all that does not exist.

E. Haldeman-Julius

The fear of gods and devils is never anything but a pitiable degradation of the human mind.

Belief in gods and belief in ghosts is identical. God is taken as a more respectable word than ghost, but it means no more.

A God of love, a God of wrath, a God of jealousy, a God of bigotry, a God of vulgar tirading, a God of cheating and lying—yes, the Christian God is given all of these characteristics, and isn't it a wretched mess to be offered to men in this twentieth century?

A sober, devout man will interpret "God's will" soberly and devoutly. A fanatic, with bloodshot mind, will interpret "God's will" fanatically. Men of extreme illogical views will interpret "God's will" in eccentric fashion...

And of course this means that whatever happens

in life and in the world of nature...happenings of the most immensely variant and complex kind are ascribed to the will of God—a blanket phrase, and a bombastic one too, which explains absolutely nothing.

One of the most amusing arguments, frequently offered in defense of belief in the idea of a God, is that such a belief is a way of playing safe...

Doesn't the religious person who uses this argument realize that he is appealing to a particularly low form of intellectual cowardice? What men need is courage in their thinking...Instead religion harps on the emotion of fear and tells men that they should treat ideas merely as gambling chances and that it is *safer* (not intellectually the *better*, but the more *craven* part) to believe in a God...

Such weak arguments exemplify the decline of religion and show its utter intellectual bankruptcy.

— above quotations from *The Meaning of Atheism*

Robert Ingersoll

I know absolutely nothing about God. I have always lived, you see, in one of the rural districts of the universe.

— quoted in *Ingersoll the Magnificent*

Thomas Jefferson

To talk of immaterial existences is to talk of nothings. To say that the human soul, angels, God, are immaterial, is to say they are nothings, or that there is no God, no angels, no soul. I cannot reason otherwise.

— Letter to John Adams, 1820

Joseph McCabe

The Rationalist [Atheist] believes that, when our philosophy of life is wholly humanist, the humanity of men and women will be greater than ever. He would tear the veil from the heavens and reveal its emptiness, because he knows that then at last men will turn to the brightening and gladdening of earth.

— *Religion of Woman*

There is...a lack of intelligence in the idea that the individual or the society will tumble to ruin when belief in God or a future life decays...it seems an extraordinary notion to imagine that humanity should allow this life to take on the traditional features of hell because it discovers there is no heaven. It might occur to intelligent fok that we should be rather minded to build our Golden City here and now, when we find the long-cherished vision of one in the clouds to be a mirage.

— Ibid.

John Stuart Mill

God is a word to express, not our ideas, but the want of them.

— attributed

Johann Most

If god desires that we know, love and fear him, why does he not show himself?...If he is omniscient, why bother him with private affairs and prayers? If he is omnipresent, why build him churches? If he is omnipotent, how can he permit that we blaspheme? If he is just, why the supposition that man, whom he created full of faults, shall be punished? If we do good only by the grace of god, why should we be rewarded? If god is inconceivable, why should we occupy ourselves with him?

— *The God Pestilence*

Friedrich Nietzsche

...a God who cures us of the flu at the right time, or who bids us get into the carriage at the exact moment when a downpour commences, ought to be such an absurd God to us, that he would have to be done away with even if he existed. God as a domestic servant, as a postman, as an almanac-maker...[God] a word for the stupidest kind of accidents...

— *The Anti-Christ*

In God nothingness deified, the will to nothingness deified!

— Ibid.

...this pitiable God of Christian monotonotheism!...in which all cowardices and weaknesses of the soul have their sanction.

— Ibid.

One does not say *nothingness;* one says instead, "the other world," or "God"...

— Ibid.

...we recognize what is worshipped as God, not as "divine," but as pitiable, as absurd, as injurious—not only as an error, but as a crime against life...

— Ibid.

Which is it? Is man only a mistake of God? Or is God only a mistake of man?

— *Twilight of the Idols*

It is a curious thing that God learned Greek when he wished to become an author—and that he did not learn it better.

— *Beyond Good and Evil*

The only excuse for God is that he doesn't exist.

— attributed

Max Nordau

How could men who lived free and equal...ever have found in their experience the idea of a mighty God whose frequent anger had to be propitiated by currish fawning, supplication, flattery, and sacrifice...? — an idea quite natural to a pack of slaves, who imagined their God in the image of the despotic ruler who cracked the whip above their heads.

— *The Interpretation of History*

Rudolf Rocker

The sense of dependence on a higher power, that source of all religious and political bondage which ever chains man to the past and blocks the path to a brighter future, will yield place to an enlightenment which makes man himself the master of his fate.

— *Nationalism and Culture*

Only when man shall have overcome the belief in his dependence on a higher power will the chains fall away that up to now have bowed the people beneath the yoke of spiritual and social slavery.

— Ibid.

Arthur Schopenhauer

...princes use God as a kind of bogey with which to frighten grown-up children into bed, if nothing else avails; that's why they attach so much importance to the deity.

— *Religion, A Dialogue*

The chief objection I have to pantheism is that it says nothing. To call the world "God" is not to explain it; it is only to enrich our language with a superfluous synonym for the word "world"...Taking an unprejudiced view of the world as it is, no one would dream of regarding it as a god. It must be a very ill-advised god who knows no better way of diverting himself than by turning into such a world as ours, such a mean, shabby world, there to take the form of innumerable millions who live indeed, but are fretted and tormented...

— *A Few Words on Pantheism*

Percy Bysshe Shelley

The self-sufficing, the omnipotent,
The merciful, and the avenging God!
Who, prototype of human misrule, sits
High in heaven's realm, upon a golden throne,
Even like an earthly king; and whose dread work,
Hell gapes forever for the unhappy slaves
Of fate, whom he created for his sport
To triumph in their torments when they fell!
Earth heard the name; earth trembled as the smoke
Of his revenge ascended up to heaven,
Blotting the constellations; and the cries

Of millions butchered in sweet confidence
And unsuspecting peace, even when the bonds
Of safety were confirmed by wordy oaths
Sworn in his dreadful name, rung through the land;
Whilst innocent babes writhed on thy stubborn spear,
And thou didst laugh to hear the mother's shriek
Of maniac gladness, as the sacred steel
Felt cold in his torn entrails!

— *Queen Mab*

I was an infant when my mother went
To see an atheist burned. She took me there.
The dark-robed priests were met around the pile;
The multitude was gazing silently;
And as the culprit passed with dauntless mien,
Tempered disdain in his unaltering eye,
Mixed with a quiet smile, shone calmly forth;
The thirsty fire crept round his manly limbs;
His resolute eyes were scorched to blindness soon;
His death pang rent my heart! the insensate mob
Uttered a cry of triumph, and I wept.
"Weep not, child!" cried my mother, "for that man
Has said, There is no God!"

— Ibid.

The being called God bears every mark of a veil woven by philosophical conceit, to hide the ignorance of the philosophers even from themselves.

— *Queen Mab* notes

Every time we say that God is the author of some phenomenon, that signifies that we are ignorant of how such a phenomenon was caused by the forces of nature. It is thus that the generality of mankind, whose lot is ignorance, attributes to the divinity, not only unusual events, but also the simple events ...In a word, man has always been impressed by unknown causes, surprising effects that his ignorance kept him from unraveling. It was on this debris of nature that man raised the imaginary colossus of the divinity.

— Ibid.

A. Wakefield Slaten

Atheism is too strenuous an intellectual and spiritual test to become popular. Atheism is achieved, while current religion of whatever sort is received. It is more restful to take than to achieve.

— attributed

Robert Tefton

GOD, n. A three-letter justification for murder; 2) An unsavory character found in many popular works of fiction, both ancient and modern; 3) An explanation which means: "I have no explanation."

Voltaire

If God did not exist, it would be necessary to invent him.

— quoted by Bakunin in *God and the State*

Fred Woodworth

Atheism is not a blind or arbitrary dogma; it is a positive rebellion against a prevailing oppressiveness.

If "God" was necessary to create the real world, in its infinite complexity, then who was the necessary one who *created God*—as God is presumably still more complex, and in even greater need therefore of a creator himself?

— *There Is No God*

Some religionists seem to delight in ascribing to "God" the credit for having made apple trees in fields of green, under a blue sky; but where is their creator when we remember that there are tapeworms in the world? I think I would be embarrassed to have to admit that I believed in an "all-wise God" who made tapeworms.

— Ibid.

If he [god] is wise, why did he not compose a coherent account of what he wanted mankind to do? No, the Bible is not such an account; nobody can agree on what it says. The very god who, according to those who believe in him, made every last electron spin in its orbit everywhere throughout the universe, still cannot write a clear, unmistakable volume of instructions to human beings who are supposed to follow his wishes. Instead, he allegedly gives us the Bible or Koran, or some other jumble of ridiculous and ancient superstitions...

— Ibid.

Not the least evidence exists that there really is a god of any kind, and unless there is evidence, it is harmful to believe that any such god exists, because then the illogical way of thinking can be extended to other areas of society, as indeed it has. A civilization that holds that it is proper to believe positively in something for which there is no evidence at all, perverts the fundamental structure of logic upon which human civilization rests.

— Ibid.

There is no god; there is only the real world with its ugliness and beauty and violence and peace and happiness and pain. If the world is to be made beautiful and peaceful and happy, "God" won't do it. We will.

— Ibid.

Let's get a certain point straight here once and for all, shall we? Yes you *can* under many circumstances, prove a negative. You can do it when definitions are tight enough and when conditions are specific enough. For instance, anyone reading this magazine can prove instantly that the Declaration of Independence is not printed on page 13 of this issue. How? They turn to page 13 and look. It's when assertions become more and more general that they become more and more difficult to disprove. If somebody says that Jesus Christ is standing on the corner of Speedway and Alvernon dispensing tea in paper cups, all you have to do to prove it's not so is to go there and check...If somebody says that Jesus Christ is dispensing tea on an unnamed streetcorner in this city, you have a larger number of places you have to look before the idea percolates down through your little mind that, gosh, it may not be so after all.

If some whacko bellows that Jesus Christ is "somewhere" in the *universe* can you prove the he isn't? Strictly speaking, no. On the other hand, you don't have to; as specificity departs, a claim becomes more and more extraordinary, and as it does so another philosophical rule takes hold, which is that Extraordinary Claims Require Extraordinary Proof.

Lacking that extraordinary proof, we can maintain that there is no such god as the religionists claim.

— *Arizona Atheist*, February 1988

Anonymous & Multiple Author

God is not dead. He's alive, well, and living in Paraguay.

— Graffiti

"God" is a three-letter word meaning "I don't know."

— Anonymous

The religious papers are rather interesting reading just now. It appears that God wants peace in Britain. God wants peace in the United States. God wants peace in the Balkan States. God wants peace in France. God wants peace all over the world, but *Hitler won't let him have it.*

— *The Freethinker*, 1942

Christianity

St. Alphonsus

...when anyone is dying, the house is filled with devils. They come out and try and ruin the soul of him who is dying, by fearful temptations. Holy water, blessed by the Church, can send away the devils.

—quoted by Rev. J. Furniss in *Tracts for Spiritual Reading*

It would be a great advantage to suffer during all our lives all the torments of the martyrs in exchange for one moment of heaven. Sufferings in this world are a sign that God loves us and intends to save us.

—Ibid.

Let us not desire to live longer to do penance for our sins. The best penance we can do is to receive the sickness, because it is God's will.

—Ibid.

Arnold Amalric

Kill them all. God will easily recognize his own.

—advice to crusaders at the Beziers massacre during the extermination of the Albigensian heretics

Rev. Robert N. Anderson

Now, dear Christian brethren...if there be any stray goat of a minister among you, tainted with the blood-hound principles of abolitionism, let him be ferreted out, silenced, excommunicated, and left to the public to dispose of him in other respects. Your affectionate brother in the Lord.

—Letter to West Hanover Presbytery, quoted by Kirby Page in *Jesus or Christianity*

St. Angela of Foligno

Sufferings are most holy and precious. They pray for us before God.

—quoted by Rev. J. Furniss in *Tracts for Spiritual Reading*

St. Thomas Aquinas

Since the Jews are according to the law sentenced to perpetual slavery for their sins, the rulers of the countries in which they are found may seize their property, provided that they do not deprive them of the necessities of life.

—Letter to the Duchess of Brabant, quoted by Joseph McCabe

It is much graver to corrupt the soul than to corrupt the coinage, which serves only to meet the needs of the body. Hence if coining and other crimes are justly punished by death by secular princes, how much more ground there is not only to excommunicate heretics but to put them to death.

The spiritual life is better than the corporal. But we put to death murderers who take the life of the body so we are all the more bound to kill heretics who take away the spiritual life of man...It is just that the secular courts should put them to death and confiscate their property even though they do not corrupt others, because they blaspheme against God and observe a false faith.

—*Summa Theologica*

Pedro Arbues

Innocent or not, let the Jew be fried.

—quoted by Charles Lea in *History of the Inquisition*

St. Augustine

Being led...to prefer the Christian doctrine, I felt that her proceeding was more unassuming and honest in that she required to be believed things not demonstrated...

—*Confessions*

Nothing is to be accepted save on the authority of Scripture, since greater is that authority than all the powers of the human mind.

—*On Genesis*

The first cause of slavery, then is sin. That one man should be put in bonds by another—this happens only by the judgment of God, in whose eyes it is no crime.

—*The City of God*

The whole clay of humanity is condemned clay.
— Ibid.

Jim Bakker

You can either have revolution or you can have revival.
— PTL Club broadcast, 1986

Michael Bakunin

It was very fortunate for Christianity that it met a world of slaves.
— *God and the State*

The doctrine taught by the apostles of Christ, wholly consoling as it may have seemed to the unfortunate, was too revolting, too absurd from the standpoint of human reason, ever to have been accepted by enlightened men...
Indeed, there must have been a very deep-seated dissatisfaction with life, a very intense thirst of heart, and an almost absolute poverty of thought, to secure the acceptance of the Christian absurdity, the most audacious and monstrous of all religious absurdities.
— Ibid.

Christianity is precisely the religion *par excellence,* because it exhibits and manifests to the fullest extent, the very nature and essence of every religious system, which is *the impoverishment, enslavement, and annihilation of humanity for the benefit of divinity.*
God being everything, the real world and man are nothing. God being truth, justice, goodness, beauty, power and life, man is falsehood, iniquity, evil, ugliness, impotence, and death. God being master, man is the slave. Incapable of finding justice, truth, and eternal life by his own effort, he can attain them only through a divine revelation. But whoever says revelation, says revealers, messiahs, prophets, priests, and legislators inspired by God himself; and these, as the holy instructors of humanity, chosen by God himself to direct it in the path of salvation, necessarily exercise absolute power. All men owe them passive and unlimited obedience; for against the divine reason there is no human reason, and against the justice of God no terrestrial justice holds. Slaves of God, men must also be slaves of Church and State, in so far as the State is consecrated by the Church.
— Ibid.

St. Bernard

They [christian soldiers] are to wage the war of Christ their master without fearing that they sin in killing their enemies or of being lost if they are themselves killed, since when they give or receive the death blow, they are guilty of no crime, but all is to their glory. If they kill, it is to the profit of Christ; if they die, it is to their own.

Ambrose Bierce

CHRISTIAN, One who believes that the New Testament is a divinely inspired book admirably suited to the spiritual needs of his neighbor. One who follows the teachings of Christ in so far as they are not inconsistent with a life of sin.

RACK, An argumentative implement formerly much used in persuading devotees of a false faith to embrace the living truth.

SCRIPTURES, The sacred books of our holy religion, as distinguished from the false and profane writings on which all other faiths are based.
— above definitions from *The Devil's Dictionary*

Christians and camels receive their burdens kneeling.
— *Epigrams*

William Blake

As the caterpillar chooses the fairest leaves
To lay her eggs on, so the priest lays his curse
On the fairest joys.
— *Proverbs of Hell*

Henri Boguet

Germany is almost entirely occupied with building fires for them [witches]. Switzerland has been compelled to wipe out many villages on their account. Travellers in Lorraine may see thousands of the stakes to which witches are bound. We in Burgundy are no more exempt than other lands... there are witches by the thousands everywhere, multiplying on the earth even as worms in a garden.
— quoted by McCabe in *The History of Satanism*

Pope Boniface VIII

We declare, we say, we defend and pronounce that to every human creature it is absolutely necessary to salvation to be subject to the Roman Pontiff.
— *Unam sanctam*

Giordano Bruno

It is with greater fear that ye pass this sentence upon me than I receive it.
— upon being sentenced by the Holy Inquisition in 1600 to be burned alive

Comte de Buffon

I declare that I had no intention to contradict the text of Scripture; that I believe most firmly all therein related about the creation, both as to order of time and matter of fact. I abandon everything in

Graphic by J. R. Swanson. Definition by Chaz Bufe.

CATHOLICISM, *n.* A popular form of self-degradation involving ritual cannibalism.

my book respecting the formation of the earth, and generally all which may be contrary to the narrative of Moses.

—Recantation to Sorbonne faculty in the mid-18th century for writing that the earth rotates on its axis, quoted by Madalyn Murray-O'Hair in *Freedom Under Siege*

W.S. Byrne

...our Christian neighbors know better than we what is good for us, and their judgment being infallible, they legislate for us accordingly.

—quoted by Charles Sprading

St. John Chrysostom

Laughter does not seem to be a sin, but it leads to sin.

—*Homilies*

Slander is worse than cannibalism.

—Ibid.

Swearing is worse than theft.

—Ibid.

Clement of Alexandria

The sacrifice most acceptable to God is complete renunciation of the body and its passions. This is the only real piety.

—*Stromateis*

St. John Climacus

I saw there [an Egyptian monastery] such sights as the eye of slothful man never saw, the ear of the idle never heard of, and the heart of the coward never thought.

In that monastery they always fasted on bread and water for their sins. Some of them stood upright all night in the open air. When sleep tempted them they drove it away and reproached themselves for their cowardice. Some, with their eyes lifted up to heaven, and with a sorrowful voice, called upon God to have mercy on them. Others stood with their hands tied behind their backs, as if they were great criminals. They did not dare to lift up their eyes to Heaven, but remained silent. Others placed on sack-cloth and ashes, hid their heads betwixt their knees or beat their foreheads against the ground. You might see others striking their breasts, and thinking of the happy days before they had sinned. Others cried aloud that they were unworthy of pardon, but prayed that God would punish them in this world, and save them from eternal torments in the world to come. They were so humbled and so bent down under their sins, that the very stones might have pitied them. No laughter was ever heard amongst them. There was no vain-glory or pride seen. There was no care about their body,

what they should eat or drink, or what was pleasant to the taste. Even the desire of these things was no longer in their heart. They thought about nothing but their sins and death. Will God forgive us, they cried, has he heard our prayers? How will it be with us in the last moment of our lives? Will the gates of Heaven be opened to us?

...As for me, when I had seen and heard all these things, I was near falling into despair, for I remembered how little my own penance had been. I remained there a month. Then I left the monastery, feeling that I was unworthy of the company of these holy penitents.

—quoted by Rev. J. Furniss in *Tracts for Spiritual Reading*

Glen A. Dahlquist

The Catholic Church has a strong sanction against suicide because the view of life taught by the priests, in time, causes great despair.

Clarence Darrow

Preachers have wasted their time and their strength and such intelligence and learning as they can command, talking about God forgiving man, as if it was possible for man to hurt God...They pray that man be forgiven and urge that man should be forgiven. Nobody knows for what, but still it has been their constant theme.

—*The Wisdom of Clarence Darrow*

I never saw any Socialist who could be a Christian, or any Christian who could be a Socialist. Because either dope is enough to fill anybody. If a man is drunk on whisky he does not need morphine. If he has morphine he does not need whisky.

—Ibid.

The ostrich is the original Christian Scientist— he gets rid of fear by denying unpleasant thoughts.

—Ibid.

Pope Eugenius IV

We decree and order that from now on, and for all time, Christians shall not eat or drink with Jews, nor admit them to feasts, nor cohabit with them, nor bathe with them. Christians shall not allow Jews to hold civil honor over Christians, or to exercise public offices in the state.

—Decree, 1442, quoted by Joseph McCabe

Benjamin Franklin

If we look back into history for the character of the present sects in Christianity, we shall find few that have not in their turns been persecutors, and complainers of persecution. The primitive Christians thought persecution extremely wrong in the Pagans, but practiced it on one another. The first Protestants of the Church of England blamed persecution in the Romish Church, but practiced it upon the Puritans. These found it wrong in the Bishops, but fell into the same practice themselves both here and in New England.

Clay Fulks

Intellectually considered, the Fundamentalist fairly belongs to that funny old stage of culture wherein unkempt, unwashed men bartered half-wild cattle for their half-wild brides—or stole them by moonlight...Having Fundamentalists in a nation is like having congenital imbeciles in the family—it's a calamity. Allow their mountebank, swindling leaders enough control over society and though religious faith would flourish fantastically, society would revert to the sheep-and-goat stage of culture ...Wherefore it is perfectly irrelevant whether your Fundamentalist is honest or utterly hypocritical in his religious beliefs and "rattlesnake" rituals; it just doesn't matter. The question of his intellectual integrity will have to wait until he grows an intellect. In the meantime, however, what the forces of reaction are doing with him constitutes a continuing calamity.

— *Christianity, A Continuing Calamity*

Your professional Modernist [liberal clergyman], with his suave and slippery ambivalence, his simultaneous acceptance of the forms and usufructs of Christianity and sly rejection of its marrow, blood and spirit, is doing about all he can to sap and undermine the national integrity—what there is of it. His offense is not so much against enlightenment as against moral and intellectual health, resulting from his preposterous pretension that Christianity remains a religion even after its superstitions have all been taken out of it! But a firm faith in the supernatural is of the essence of Christianity, and belief in the supernatural constitutes superstition. Christianity is based squarely on the theory that Christ was the half-god son of a human mother. When that theory and all the other miracles of Christianity are admitted to be myths, then Christianity loses its religious character and becomes at best, some sort of ethical—or *un*ethical—society.

— Ibid.

Rev. J. Furniss, C.S.S.R

Never forget that you must die; that death will come sooner than you expect...God has written the letters of death upon your hands. In the inside of your hands you will see the letters M.M. It means "Memento Mori"—remember you must die.

— *Tracts for Spiritual Reading*

Edward Gibbon

A cruel unfeeling temper has distinguished the monks of every age and country: their stern indifference, which is seldom mollified by personal friendship, is inflamed by religious hatred; and their merciless zeal has strenuously administered the holy office of the Inquisition.

— *Decline and Fall of the Roman Empire*

It is incumbent on us diligently to remember that the kingdom of heaven was promised to the poor in spirit, and that minds afflicted by calamity and the contempt of mankind cheerfully listen to the divine promise of future happiness...

— Ibid.

But how shall we excuse the supine inattention of the Pagan and philosophic world to those evidences which were presented by the hand of Omnipotence, not to their reason, but to their senses? During the age of Christ, of his apostles, and of their first disciples, the doctrine which they preached was confirmed by innumerable prodigies. The lame walked, the blind saw, the sick were healed, the dead were raised, demons were expelled, and the laws of Nature were frequently suspended for the benefit of the church. But the sages of Greece and Rome turned aside from the awful spectacle, and, pursuing the ordinary occupations of life and study, appeared unconscious of any alterations in the moral or physical government of the world. Under the reign of Tiberius, the whole earth, or at least a celebrated province of the Roman empire, was involved in a preternatural darkness of three hours [supposedly at the crucifixion of J.C.]. Even this miraculous event, which ought to have excited the wonder, the curiosity, and the devotion of mankind, passed without notice in an age of science and history. It happened during the lifetime of Seneca and the elder Pliny, who must have experienced the immediate effects, or received the earliest intelligence, of the prodigy. Each of these philosophers, in a laborious work, has recorded all the great phenomena of Nature, earthquakes, meteors, comets, and eclipses, which his indefatigable curiosity could collect. Both the one and the other had omitted to mention the greatest phenomenon to which the mortal eye has been witness since the creation of the globe.

— Ibid.

E. Haldeman-Julius

Christian theology has taught men that they should submit with unintelligent resignation to the worst real evils of life and waste their time in consideration of imaginary evils in "the life to come."

— *The Meaning of Atheism*

Heinrich Heine

Christ rode an ass, but now asses ride on Christ.
— quoted by Ingersoll in *The Devil*

Adolf Hitler

. . . Loyalty and responsibility toward the people and the fatherland are *most deeply anchored in the Christian faith.*
— quoted by Reich in *The Mass Psychology of Fascism*

A.A. Hodge

The Savior found it around him, the Apostles met with it in Asia, Greece and Italy. How did they treat it? Not by denunciation of slaveholding as necessarily sinful.

George Jacob Holyoake

For myself, I flee the Bible as a viper, and revolt at the touch of a Christian.
— *The History of the Last Trial by Jury for Atheism*

Rupert Hughes

John Wesley said that if you give up witchcraft you must give up the Bible. He is right. The choice is easy . . .
— *Why I Quit Going to Church*

Robert Ingersoll

Most of the clergy are, or seem to be, utterly incapable of discussing anything in a fair and catholic spirit. They appeal, not to facts, but to passages of Scripture. They can conceive of no goodness, of no spiritual exaltation beyond the horizon of their creed. Whoever differs with them upon what they are pleased to call "fundamental truths," is, in their opinion, a base and infamous man. To re-enact the tragedies of the sixteenth century, they lack only the power. Bigotry in all ages has been the same. Christianity simply transferred the brutality of the Colosseum to the Inquisition. For the murderous combat of the gladiators, the saints substituted the *auto da fe* [burning of heretics]. What has been called religion is, after all, but the organization of the wild beast in man. The perfumed blossom of arrogance is heaven. Hell is the consummation of revenge.
— Preface to *Atheist Truth vs. Religion's Ghosts*

To succeed, the theologians invade the cradle, the nursery. In the brains of innocence they plant the seeds of superstition. They pollute the minds and imaginations of children. They frighten the happy with threats of pain — they soothe the wretched with gilded lies.
This perpetual insincerity stamps itself on the face — affects every feature. We all know the theological countenance — cold, unsympathetic, cruel, lights with a pious smirk — no line of laughter — no dimpled mirth — no touch of humor — nothing human.
— *Atheist Truth vs. Religion's Ghosts*

Every Sunday school is a kind of inquisition where they torture and deform the minds of children.
— Ibid.

. . . ministers say they teach charity. This is natural. They live on alms. All beggars teach that others should give.
— Ibid.

The popes and cardinals, the bishops, priests and parsons are all useless. They produce nothing. They live on the labor of others. They are parasites that feed on the frightened. They are vampires that suck the blood of honest toil. Every church is an organized beggar.
— Ibid.

. . . priests and clergymen insist that the Bible is superior to human reason — that it is the duty of man to accept it — to believe it, whether he really thinks it is true or not, and without the slightest regard to evidence or reason.
It is his duty to cast out from the temple of his soul the goddess Reason, and bow before the coiled serpent of Fear.
This is what the church calls virtue.
— Ibid.

To compel man to desert the standard of Reason, the church does not entirely rely on the threat of eternal pain to be endured in another world, but holds out the reward of eternal joy.
To those who believe, it promises the endless ecstasies of heaven. If it cannot frighten, it will bribe.
— Ibid.

Imagine a circle of iron, and on the inside a hundred points almost as sharp as needles. This argument was fastened about the throat of the sufferer [by inquisitors]. Then he could not walk, nor sit down, nor stir, without the neck being punctured by these points. In a little while the throat would begin to swell, and suffocation would end the agonies of that man. This man, it may be, had committed the crime of saying, with tears on his cheeks, "I do not believe that god, the father of us all, will damn to eternal perdition any of the children of men."
— *The Liberty of Man, Woman and Child*

If there is in heaven an infinite being, he never will be satisfied with the worship of cowards and hypocrites. Honest unbelief, honest infidelity, honest atheism, will be a perfume in heaven when pious hypocrisy, no matter how religious it may be outwardly, will be a stench.
— Ibid.

As an excuse for tyranny, as a justification of slavery, the church has taught that man is totally depraved. Of the truth of that doctrine, the church has furnished the only evidence there is.

—Ibid.

In his infinite goodness, God invented rheumatism and gout and dyspepsia, cancers and neuralgia, and is still inventing new diseases. Not only this, but he decreed the pangs of mothers, and that by the gates of love and life should crouch the dragons of death and pain. Fearing that some might by accident, live too long, he planted poisonous vines and herbs that looked like food. He caught the serpents he had made and gave them fangs and curious organs, ingeniously devised to distill and deposit the deadly drop. He changed the nature of the beasts, that they might feed on human flesh. He cursed a world, and tainted every spring and source of joy. He poisoned every breath of air; corrupted even light, that it might bear the double fruit of pain and joy; decreed all accidents and mistakes that maim and hurt and kill, and set the snares of life-long grief, baited with present pleasure—with a moment's joy. Then and there he foreknew and foreordained all human tears. And yet all this is but the prelude, the introduction, to the infinite revenge of the good God. Increase and multiply all human griefs until the mind has reached imagination's farthest verge, then add eternity to time, and you may faintly tell, but never can conceive, the infinite horrors of this doctrine called "The Fall of Man."

— Orthodoxy

Did it ever occur to you that if God wrote the Old Testament and told the Jews to crucify or kill anybody that disagreed with them on religion, and that this God afterward took upon himself flesh and came to Jerusalem, and taught a different religion, and the Jews killed him—did it ever occur to you that he reaped exactly what he had sown?

—Ibid.

Praying has become a business, a profession, a trade. A minister is never happier than when praying in public. Most of them are exceedingly familiar with their God. Knowing that he knows everything, they tell him the needs of the nation and the desires of the people, they advise him what to do and when to do it. They appeal to his pride, asking him to do certain things for his own glory. They often pray for the impossible. In the House of Representatives in Washington I once heard a chaplain pray for what he must have known was impossible. Without a change of countenance, without a smile, with a face solemn as a sepulchre, he said: "I pray thee, O God, to give Congress wisdom." It may be that ministers really think that their prayers do good and it may be that frogs imagine that their croaking brings spring.

— Which Way?

If Jehovah had been civilized he would have left out the commandment about keeping the Sabbath, and in its place would have said: "Thou shalt not enslave thy fellow-men."

—About the Holy Bible

If the devil had inspired a book, will some Christian tell us in what respect, on the subjects of slavery, polygamy, war and liberty, it would have differed from some parts of the Old Testament?

—Some Reasons Why

If Christ, in fact, said "I came not to bring peace but a sword," it is the only prophecy in the New Testament that has been literally fulfilled.

—Ibid.

The Episcopal creed is substantially like the Catholic, containing a few additional absurdities. The Episcopalians teach that it is easier to get forgiveness for sin after you have been baptized. They seem to think that the moment you are baptized you become a member of the firm, and as such are entitled to wickedness at cost.

— What Must We Do To Be Saved?

"The justification of a sinner by faith alone," without works—just faith. Believing something that you do not understand. Of course God can not afford to reward a man for believing anything that is reasonable. God rewards only for believing something that is unreasonable. If you believe something that is improbable and unreasonable, you are a Christian; but if you believe something that you know is not so, then—you are a saint.

—Ibid.

In every orthodox Sunday school children are taught to believe in devils. Every little brain becomes a menagerie, filled with wild beasts from hell. The imagination is polluted with the deformed, the monstrous and mailicious. To fill the minds of children with leering fiends—with mocking devils—is one of the meanest and basest of crimes.

So, I say to all fathers and mothers, keep your children away from priests...

They will teach them to believe in the Devil; in hell; in the prison of God...This dogma of hell is the infinite of savagery—the dream of insane revenge. It makes God a wild beast—an infinite hyena. It makes Christ as merciless as the fangs of a viper. Save poor children from the pollution of this horror.

— The Devil

It is far better to have no heaven than to have heaven and hell: better to have no God than God and devil: better to rest in eternal sleep than to be an angel and know that the ones you love are suffering eternal pain: better to live a free and loving life—a life that ends forever at the grave—than to be an eternal slave.

—Ibid.

I gave up the Old Testament on account of its mistakes, its absurdities, its ignorance and its cruelties. I gave up the New because it vouched for the truth of the Old. I gave it up on account of its miracles, its contradictions, because Christ and his disciples believed in the existence of devils—talked and made bargains with them, expelled them from people and animals.

This, of itself, is enough. We know, if we know anything, that devils do not exist—that Christ never cast them out, and that if he pretended to, he was either ignorant, dishonest or insane. These stories about devils demonstrate the human, the ignorant origin of the new Testament.

—Why I Am an Agnostic

Is it possible that the writer or writers of First and Second Kings were inspired, and that Gibbon wrote *The Decline and Fall of the Roman Empire* without supernatural assistance?...

I do not see how it is possible for an intelligent human being to conclude that the Song of Solomon is the work of God, and that the tragedy of Lear was the work of an uninspired man.

—Ibid.

To love God, to practice self-denial, to overcome desire, to despise wealth, to hate prosperity, to desert wife and children, to live on roots and berries, to repeat prayers, to wear rags, to live in filth, and drive love from the heart—these for centuries, were the highest and most perfect virtues, and those who practiced them were saints.

The saints did not assist their fellow-men. Their fellow-men assisted them. They were insane. They followed the teachings of Christ. They mutilated their bodies—scarred their flesh and destroyed their minds for the sake of happiness in another world. During the journey of life they kept their eyes on the grave.

—A Thanksgiving Sermon

Ministers ask: Is it possible for God to forgive man?

And when I think of what has been suffered—of the centuries of agony and tears, I ask: Is it possible for man to forgive God?

— The Foundations of Faith

According to that Holy Book, Jehova was a believer in witchcraft, and said to his chosen people: "Thou shalt not suffer a witch to live." [Ex. 22:18]

This one commandment — this simple line — demonstrates that Jehovah was not only not God, but that he was a poor, ignorant, superstitious savage. This one line proves beyond all possible doubt that the Old Testament was written by men, by barbarians.

—Superstition

JC's Holy City BBQ

Specially cooked

"Ribs seared by the Eyes of Christ"

Graphic from *Processed World*

Superstition, the mother of those hideous twins, Fear and Faith, from her throne of skulls, still rules the world, and will until the mind of woman ceases to be the property of priests.

— Individuality

According to orthodox logic, God having furnished us with imperfect minds, has a right to demand a perfect result.

—Ibid.

The Church hates a thinker precisely for the same reason a robber dislikes a sheriff, or a thief despises the prosecuting witness.

—Ibid.

The Church demands worship—the very thing that man should give to no being, human or divine. To worship another is to degrade yourself.

—Ibid.

Who at the present day can imagine the courage, the devotion to principle, the intellectual and moral grandeur it once required to be an infidel, to brave the Church, her racks, her fagots, her dungeons, her tongues of fire—to defy and scorn her heaven and her hell—her devil and her God?

—Ibid.

The Church has burned honesty and rewarded hypocrisy. And all this, because it was commanded by a book...

The Bible was the real persecutor. The Bible burned heretics, built dungeons, founded the inquisition, and trampled upon all the liberties of men.

How long, O how long will mankind worship a book? How long will they grovel in the dust before the ignorant legends of the barbaric past? How long, O how long will they pursue phantoms in a darkness deeper than death?

— *Heretics and Heresy*

Calvin was of a pallid, bloodless complexion, thin, sickly, irritable, gloomy, impatient, egoistic, tyrannical, heartless, and infamous. He was a strange compound of revengeful morality, malicious forgiveness, ferocious charity, egoistic humility, and a kind of hellish justice. In other words, he was as near like the God of the Old Testament as his health permitted.

— Ibid.

In 1208, the Inquisition was established. Seven years afterward, the fourth council of the Lateran enjoined all kings and rulers to swear an oath that they would exterminate heretics from their dominions. The sword of the church was unsheathed, and the world was at the mercy of ignorant and infuriated priests, whose eyes feasted upon the agonies they inflicted. Acting, as they believed or pretended to believe, under the command of God; stimulated by the hope of infinite reward in another world — hating heretics with every drop of their bestial blood; savage beyond description; merciless beyond conception — these infamous priests, in a kind of frenzied joy, leaped upon the helpless victims of their rage. They crushed their bones in iron boots; tore their quivering flesh with iron hooks and pincers; cut off their lips and eyelids; pulled out their nails, and into the bleeding quick thrust needles; tore out their tongues; extinguished their eyes; stretched them upon racks; flayed them alive; crucified them with their heads downward; exposed them to wild beasts; burned them at the stake; mocked their cries and groans; ravished their wives; robbed their children, and then prayed to God to finish the holy work in hell.

— Ibid.

Take from the Christian the history of his own church — leave that entirely out of the question — and he has no argument left with which to substantiate the total depravity of man.

— Ibid.

In the early days of Christianity, the "spiritual" renounced the world with all its duties and obligations. They deserted their wives and children. They became hermits and dwelt in caves. They spent their useless years in praying for their shriveled and worthless souls. They were too "spiritual" to love women, to build homes and to labor for children. They were too "spiritual" to earn their bread, so they became beggars and stood by the highways of life and held out their hands and asked alms of Industry and Courage. They were too "spiritual" to be merciful. They preached the dogma of eternal pain and gloried in "the wrath to come." They were too "spiritual" to be civilized, so they persecuted their fellow-men for expressing their honest thoughts. They were so "spiritual" that they invented instruments of torture, founded the Inquisition, appealed to the whip, the rack, the sword and the fagot. They tore the flesh of the fellow-men with hooks of iron, buried their neighbors alive, cut off their eyelids, dashed out the brains of babes and cut off the breasts of mothers. These "spiritual" wretches spent day and night on their knees, praying for their own salvation and asking God to curse the best and noblest of the world.

— *Spirituality*

Nothing is more amusing than to hear a clergyman denounce worldliness — ask his hearers what it will profit them to build railways and palaces and lose their own souls — inquire of the common folks before him why they waste their precious years in following trades and professions, in gathering treasures that moths corrupt and rust devours, giving their days to the vulgar business of making money — and then see him take up a collection...

— Ibid.

If commandments had been given against slavery and polygamy, against wars of invasion and extermination, against religious persecution in all its forms, so that the world could be free, so that the brain might be developed and the heart civilized, then we might, with propriety, call such commandments a moral guide.

Before we can truthfully say that the Ten Commandments constitute a moral guide, we must subtract. We must throw away some, and write others in their places.

— *What Would You Substitute for the Bible as a Moral Guide?*

I admit that there are many good things in the New Testament, and if we take from that book the dogmas of eternal pain, of infinite revenge, of the atonement of human sacrifice, of the necessity of shedding blood; if we throw away the doctrine of non-resistance, of loving enemies, the idea that prosperity is the result of wickedness, that poverty is a preparation for Paradise, if we throw all these away and take the good, sensible passages, applicable to conduct, then we can make a fairly good moral guide — narrow, but moral.

Of course, many important things would be left out. You would have nothing about human rights, nothing in favor of the family, nothing for education, nothing for investigation, for thought and reason, but still you would have a fairly good moral guide...

If you take the cruel passages, the verses that inculcate eternal hatred, verses that writhe and hiss

Illustration by J. R. Swanson. Definition by Chaz Bufe.

FUNDAMENTALIST, *n.* One in whom something is fundamentally wrong, most commonly lack of reasoning ability and vicious intolerance toward those not sharing the fundamentalist's delusions. Thus, fundamentalists are especially intolerant of those able to draw obvious conclusions from observed facts, those who refuse to seek shelter in comforting falsehoods, and those who wish to lead their own lives.

like serpents, you can make a creed that would shock the heart of a hyena.

It may be that no book contains better passages than the New Testament, but certainly no book contains worse.

Below the blossom of love you find the thorn of hatred; on the lips that kiss, you find the poison of the cobra.

The Bible is not a moral guide.

—Ibid.

Pope Innocent III

The Jews, like Cain, are doomed to wander the earth as fugitives and vagabonds, and their faces are covered with shame.

—Letter to Count de Nevers, early 13th century

Use against heretics the spiritual sword of excommunication, and if this does not prove effective, use the material sword.

Thomas Jefferson

The Christian god can be easily pictured as virtually the same as the many ancient gods of past civilizations. The Christian god is a three headed monster; cruel, vengeful and capricious.

If one wishes to know more of this raging, three headed beast-like god, one only needs to look at the caliber of the people who say they serve him. They are always of two classes: fools and hypocrites.

— Letter to his nephew, Peter Carr

The Christian God is a being of terrific character — cruel, vindictive, capricious, and unjust.

— *The Jefferson Bible*

I have recently been examining all the known superstitions of the world, and do not find in our particular superstition [christianity] one redeeming feature. They are all alike, founded upon fables and mythologies.

— Ibid.

We discover [in the gospels] a groundwork of vulgar ignorance, of things impossible, of superstition, fanaticism and fabrication.

— Ibid.

If we believe that he [J.C.] really countenanced the follies, the falsehoods, and the charlatanisms, which his biographers [writers of the New Testament] father upon him, and admit the misconstructions, interpolations, and theorizations of the fathers of the early and the fanatics of the latter ages, the conclusion would be irresistible by every sound mind that he was an impostor.

— Ibid.

It is between fifty and sixty years since I read the Apocalypse, and I then considered it merely the ravings of a maniac.

— Ibid.

The day will come when the mystical generation of Jesus by the Supreme Being will be classed with the fable of the generation of Minerva in the brain of Jupiter.

— Letter to Peter Carr, 1787

St. Jerome

Though thy father cling to thee, and thy mother rend her garments and show thee the breasts thou hast sucked, thrust them aside with dry eyes to embrace the cross.

— Letter to Heliodorus

The duty of a monk is not to teach, but to weep.

— quoted by Lecky in *History of European Morals*

Jesus

I do to you what my Heavenly Father did to me. I send you as many sufferings as you can bear.

— quoted by Rev. J. Furniss in *Tracts for Spiritual Reading*

Venerable John of Avila

When we find ourselves in good dispositions, although they are only moderately good, we ought to desire to die, to get away from the danger so frequent on the earth, of sinning and losing God's grace.

— quoted by Rev. J. Furniss in *Tracts for Spiritual Reading*

Henry Charles Lea

The brief reign of Philip [in 1506] led other sorely vexed communities to appeal to the sovereign for relief [from the Inquisition], and some of their memorials have been preserved. One from Jaen relates that the tribunal of that city procured from Lucero a useful witness whom for five years he had kept in the prison of Cordova to swear to what was wanted. His name was Diego de Algeciras and, if the petitioners are to be believed, he was, in addition to being a perjurer, a drunkard, a gambler, a forger and a clipper of coins. This worthy was brought to Jaen and performed his functions so satisfactorily that the wealthiest Conversos [Jews "converted" to Catholicism under threat of massacre] were soon imprisoned. Two hundred wretches crowded the filthy gaol and it was requisite to forbid the rest of the Conversos from leaving the city without a license. With Diego's assistance and the free use of torture, on both accused and witnesses, it was not difficult to obtain whatever evidence was desired. The notary of the tribunal, Antonio de Barcena, was especially successful in this. On one occasion he locked a young girl of fifteen in a room, stripped her naked and scourged her until she consented to bear testimony against her mother. A prisoner was carried in a chair to the auto da fe with his feet burnt to the bone; he and his wife were burnt alive and then two of their slaves were imprisoned and forced to give such evidence as was necessary to justify the execution. The cells in which the unfortunates were confined in heavy chains were narrow, dark, humid, filthy and overrun with vermin, while their sequestrated property was squandered by the officials, so that they nearly starved in prison while their helpless children starved outside.

— *A History of the Inquisition of Spain*

W.E.H. Lecky

If, indeed, we . . . consider the actual history of the Church since Constantine, we shall find no justification for the popular theory that beneath its influence the narrow spirit of patriotism faded into a wide and cosmopolitan philanthropy...The eighty or ninety sects (St. Augustine estimated 89), into which Christianity speedily divided, hated one another with an intensity that extorted the wonder of Julian and the ridicule of the Pagans of Alexandria...There is, indeed, something at once grotesque and ghastly in the spectacle. The Donatists, having separated from the orthodox simply on the question of the validity of the consecration of a certain bishop, declared that all who adopted the orthodox view must be damned...[they] beat multitudes to death with clubs, blinded others by anointing their eyes with lime...The Catholics tell how an Arian Emperor caused eighty orthodox priests to be drowned on a single occasion...the Arian Bishop of Alexandria caused the widows of the Athanasian party to be scourged on the soles of their feet, the holy virgins to be stripped naked, to be flogged with the prickly branches of palm trees or to be slowly scorched over fires till they abjured their creed...The followers of St. Cyril, who were chiefly monks, filled their city [Alexandria] with riot and bloodshed, wounded the prefect Orestes, dragged the pure and gifted Hypatia into one of their churches, murdered her, tore the flesh from her bones with sharp shells, and having stripped her body naked, flung her mangled remains into the flames...In the contested election that resulted in the election of St. Damasus as Pope of Rome, though no theological question appears to have been at issue, the riots were so fierce that one hundred and thirty-seven corpses were found in one of the churches.

It had been boldly predicted by some of the early Christians that the conversion of the world would lead to the establishment of perpetual peace. In looking back, with our present experience, we are driven to the melancholy conclusion that, instead of diminishing the number of wars, ecclesiastical influence has actually and very seriously increased it. We may look in vain for any period since Constantine, in which the clergy, as a body, exerted themselves to repress the military spirit, or to prevent or abridge a particular war, with an energy at all comparable to that which they displayed in stimulating the fanaticism of the crusaders, in producing the atrocious massacre of the Albigensians, in embittering the religious contests that followed the Reformation.

The military fanaticism evoked by the indulgences of the popes, by the exhortations of the pulpit, by the religious importance attached to the relics at Jerusalem, and by the prevailing hatred of misbelievers, has scarcely ever been equalled in its intensity, and it has caused the effusion of oceans of blood, and has been productive of incalculable misery to the world.

Slavery was distinctly and formally recognised by Christianity, and no religion ever laboured more to encourage a habit of docility and passive obedience.

Christianity for the first time gave the servile virtues the foremost place in the moral type. Humility, obedience, gentleness, patience, resignation, are all cardinal or rudimentary virtues in the Christian character; they were all neglected or underrated by the Pagans; they can all expand and flourish in a servile position.

But of all the evidences of the loathsome excesses to which this [ascetic] spirit was carried, the life of St. Simeon Stylites is probably the most remarkable. It would be difficult to conceive a more horrible or disgusting picture than is given of the penances by which that saint commenced his ascetic career. He had bound a rope around him so that it became embedded in his flesh, which putrefied around it. A horrible stench, intolerable to the bystanders, exhaled from his body, and worms dropped from him whenever he moved, and they filled his bed. Sometimes he left the monastery and slept in a dry well, inhabited, it is said, by demons. He built successively, three pillars, the last being sixty feet high and scarcely two cubits in circumference, and on this pillar, during thirty years, he remained exposed to every change of climate, ceaselessly and rapidly bending his body in prayer almost to the level of his feet. A spectator attempted to number these rapid motions, but desisted from weariness when he had counted 1,244. For a whole year, we are told, St. Simeon stood upon one leg, the other being covered with hideous ulcers, while his biographer [St. Anthony] was commissioned to stand by his side, to pick up the worms that fell from his body, and to replace them in the sores, the saint saying to the worms, "Eat what God has given you." From every quarter pilgrims of every degree thronged to do him homage. A crowd of prelates followed him to the grave. A brilliant star is said to have shone miraculously over his pillar; the general voice of mankind pronounced him to be the highest model of a Christian saint; and several other anchorites [christian hermits] imitated or emulated his penances.

There is, perhaps, no phase in the moral history of mankind of a deeper or more painful interest than this ascetic epidemic. A hideous, sordid, and emaciated maniac, without knowledge, without patriotism, without natural affection, passing his life in a long routine of useless and atrocious self-torture, and quailing before the ghastly phantoms of his delirious brain, had become the ideal of the nations which had known the writings of Plato and Cicero and the lives of Socrates and Cato. For about two centuries, the hideous maceration of the body was regarded as the highest proof of excellence. St. Jerome declares with a thrill of admiration, how he had seen a monk, who for thirty years had lived exclusively on a small portion of barley bread and of muddy water; another who lived in a hole and never ate more than five figs for his daily repast; a third, who cut his hair only on Easter Sunday, who never washed his clothes, who never changed his tunic till it fell to pieces, who starved himself till his eyes grew dim, and his skin "like a pumice stone"...

The cleanliness of the body was regarded as a pollution of the soul, and the saints who were most admired had become one hideous mass of clotted filth. St. Athanasius relates with enthusiasm how St. Antony, the patriarch of monachism, had never to extreme old age, been guilty of washing his feet.

St. Ammon had never seen himself naked. A famous virgin named Silvia, though she was sixty years old and though bodily sickness was a consequence of her habits, resolutely refused, on religious principles, to wash any part of her body except her fingers. St. Euphraxia joined a convent of one hundred and thirty nuns, who never washed their feet, and who shuddered at the mention of a bath.

The occasional decadence of the monks into habits of decency was a subject of much reproach. "Our fathers," said the abbot Alexander, looking mournfully back to the past, "never washed their faces, but we frequent the public baths."

— above quotations from *History of European Morals*

Pope Leo XIII

Catholicism cannot be reconciled with naturalism or rationalism.

— Immortale Dei

It is necessary not only that religious instruction be given to the young at certain fixed times, but also that every other subject taught be permeated with Christian piety.

— Militantes Ecclesiae

Abraham Lincoln

My earlier views at the unsoundness of the Christian scheme of slavation and the human origin of the scriptures, have become clearer and stronger with advancing years and I see no reason for thinking I shall ever change them.

— Letter to Judge J. Wakefield

St. Ignatius Loyola

We should always be disposed to believe that which appears white is really black, if the hierarchy of the Church so decides.

— Spiritual Exercises

Fr. Marianus de Luca

The Church has the right to inflict corporal punishment, even death.

— Institutionos Juris Ecclesiasticus Publici (Vatican Press, 1901)

...we affirm that the Church has a coercive power that includes even the right of the sword. We make it our first point to vindicate this right of the Church on account of critics who, because the Church once put heretics and especially leaders of heretics and apostates to death, loudly declare that Our Holy Mother the Church acted unjustly and wickedly, and because once the right to inflict capital punishment is proved the right to inflict lesser punishments follows... But it can assuredly happen that no other punishment than death will suffice to prevent the contagion of crime from spreading and so preserve the social order.

— Ibid.

The right of the sword is the necessary and effective means to attain its [the Catholic Church's] end when rebels in the Church and disturbers of the ecclesiastical peace and unity, especially obstinate heretics and the leaders, cannot be prevented in any other way from continuing to disturb the ecclesiastical order, and leading others to crime, particularly against the Church.

— Ibid.

...the preservation of the Church is far more important than the preservation of civil society... It therefore follows that if the Church has the power to impose a capital sentence it has the power to inflict other bodily punishments... we have the record of the Church condemning men to slavery, exile to a foreign land, or a distant province, imprisonment for life, incarceration in a monastery, and flogging.

— Ibid.

Martin Luther

When I was a child there were many witches, and they bewitched both cattle and men, especially children.

— Commentary on Galatians

Many demons are in woods, in waters, in wildernesses, and in dark poolly places ready to hurt and prejudice people; some are also in the thick black clouds, which cause hail, lightning and thunder, and poison the air, the pastures and grounds.

— Table Talk

The legends or stories of the saints which we have in the papacy are not written according to the norm of Holy Scripture. For it is nothing to wear a hood, fast, or undertake other hard works of that sort in comparison with those troubles which family life brings...

— Commentary on Genesis

I feel much freer now that I am certain the pope is the Antichrist.

— Letter to Spalatin, October 10, 1520

I would have no compassion for a witch; I would burn them all.

Snakes and monkeys are subjected to the demon more than other animals. Satan lives in them and possesses them. He uses them to deceive men and to injure them. Demons live in many lands, but particularly in Prussia.

As for the demented, I hold it certain that all beings deprived of reason are thus afflicted only by the Devil.

In Switzerland, not far from Lucerne, upon a very high mountain, there is a lake which is called Pilate's Pool. There the Devil gives himself up to all kinds of infamous practices. In my own country, upon a high mountain called Poltersberg, there is a pool. If one throws a stone into it, instantly a storm arises and the whole surrounding countryside is overwhelmed by it.

This lake is full of demons; Satan holds them captive there. A large number of deaf, crippled and blind people are afflicted solely through the malice of the demon. And one must in no wise doubt that plagues, fevers and every sort of evil come from him.

Thomas Macaulay

The Puritan hated bear-baiting, not because it gave pain to the bear, but because it gave pleasure to the spectators.

— *History of England*

George E. MacDonald

The church often claims to have been the repository of education and art during the Middle Ages. Whether or not that claim is true, she was apparently the patron of mechanics, since about all the inventions by which the era is marked were made under her auspices for the torturing of unbelievers.

I had in some way got the erroneous notion that thumbscrews were intended solely for compressing the thumbs and that they took their name from the members compressed. That, I now conclude, is not so, because they may be used on the wrists, legs, or to prize the offender's teeth apart so that the "blasphemous" tongue may be torn out with pincers furnished with still other thumbscrews. These instruments are of various sizes. But being always worked by a thumbscrew, like that which spreads and closes a pair of dividers for describing circles. . . The inner sides. . . are sometimes roughened like the sole of a rubber boot, so that the flesh is pierced by blunt protuberances; others have little spikes that penetrate the upper and lower sides of the thumbs. . . The large ones crush the shin bones, or the bones of the wrists. . . Here again appears the deadly thumbscrew, which runs through the whole system of religious torture as the cross runs through the system of worship. A comparison of the one and of the other upon the growth of christianity might be decided in favor of the screw.

Executioners' swords are numerous and ornamental. . . The condemned one sat in a chair, with bowed head; the executioner whirled his blade in the air and if sufficiently strong and expert severed the neck at a blow. The swords are piously inscribed with the names of the deity and Christ, or with rhymes that may be freely translated about like these:

"O God, this sinner to thy kingdom take
That he may taste of joy, for Jesus' sake."

"Christ is the judge, and I the instrument
To execute God's law from heaven sent."

"When I upraise the fatal knife
God give the sinner eternal life."

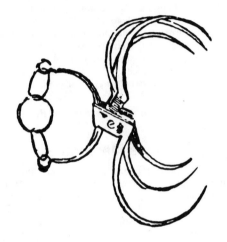

. . .let the women gaze on this horrible piece of ingenuity, the spider. It is a cluster of steel hooks pointed like needles. It is designed to be spread over the breast of the woman; the hand of the torturer grasps the central ring, drawing the points together, and then the flesh is torn away.

The "cradle of unrest," used to induce children to testify against their parents, is a cradle covered with wooden spikes. The headrest or cushion, also spiked, is movable. . .

As the church made a virgin the vehicle for bringing its alleged founder into the world, it naturally made another one the instrument for putting its enemies out of the world. Hence was invented the "Iron Virgin". . . She wears a cloak of wood and iron, which opens in front, revealing an interior lined with spikes shaped like harrow teeth, seven or eight inches in length and sharp as bayonets. Iron handles swing the virgin open and disclose the spikes. The figure stood above a trap-door opening into a moat or ditch, so that when the spikes let go of it the corpse dropped into the water and floated away. . . Two [spikes] are apparently aintended to enter the eyes, others the chest, and still others the abdomen. The virgin was the avenger of offenses against the Church such as doubt or unbelief.

Among the instruments of torture is a mouth opener used on blasphemers. It is made of two small iron plates. These are inserted between the upper and lower teeth and spread apart by turning the deadly screw. The jaws being thus forced open molten lead was poured down the throat or the tongue caught with pincers and either slitted, torn out, or cut off. The pincers used for this purpose have hooked teeth like the fangs of a serpent. The vicious little group which I have labeled "a trinity" includes the pincers for removing the tongue. The second member is a mask (put on red-hot); and the thing that looks like the skeleton of a snake is a metal scourge. This trinity was in its time of material service in stimulating the worship of that heavenly trinity in whose name the implements were manufactured and applied. There was a perforated iron spoon for dropping hot lead upon naked bodies.

The instruments for flaying do not indicate that a victim was skinned after the fashion adopted by butchers of cattle. The man or woman was strung up by the hands or feet, while the skin, with the flesh adhering to it, was dragged off with pronged hooks.

— above quotations from *Thumbscrew and Rack*

James Madison

During almost fifteen centuries has the legal establishment of Christianity been on trial. What has been its fruits? More or less, in all places, pride and indolence in the clergy; ignorance and servility in the laity; in both, superstition, bigotry and persecution.

— *A Memorial and Remonstrance* addressed to the General Assembly of the Commonwealth of Virginia, 1785

What influence, in fact, have ecclesiastical establishments had on society? In some instances they have been seen to erect a spiritual tyranny on the ruins of the civil authority; in many instances they have been seen upholding the thrones of political tyranny; in no instance have they been the guardians of the liberties of the people. Rulers who wish to subvert the public liberty may have found an established clergy convenient allies.

— Ibid.

Ferdinand Magellan

The Church says the earth is flat, but I know that it is round, for I have seen the shadow on the moon, and I have more faith in a shadow than in the church.

— attributed

Harriet Martineau

What an insult it is to our best moral faculties to hold over us the promises and threats of heaven and hell.

Joseph McCabe

I still have the two volumes (1,700 quarto pages) from which, 60 years ago, I learned "moral theology," or all that the Roman Church has to say about virtues and vices. It deals extensively and vehemently with vice while it devotes only 10 temperate lines to cruelty and does not even mention torture. This moral obliquity explains why the Church never condemned torture just as it never condemned slavery.

— *History of Torture*

All that is evil and brutal in life and history has been ascribed to "human nature"; all that is elevated and refined and heroic has been denied to human nature, and attributed to "grace" or miracle. This has begotten a dreary pessimism in the mind of Christian people. They find themselves incapable of thinking that man can be generous or just or temperate without the hope of a reward in heaven or the stimulus of pleasing God. The mind of the Rationalist [Atheist] is not warped by this illusion.

— *Religion of Woman*

But quite apart from the past errors of Christianity, we have the most indisputable grounds for opposing it today. We see this: if man can be persuaded that *he* is the maker of this world (on its moral side) and that there is no other world beside it, he will begin to work at its amelioration with an energy he never knew before.

— Ibid.

The world grows more humane as it discards Christianity. That is the subtle grievance of the modern priest.

— Ibid.

. . . Catholics and Fundamentalists would regard it as an outrage to be coupled together, and I have the tenderest regard for their feelings. Both believe in eternal torment, a blood-atonement, and so on. Both boast that they surrender not a tithe of ancient Christian doctrine at the bidding of modern culture. Yet there is a material difference. Catholic literature is generally written by men with a far more complete and lengthy education, and is therefore far more dishonest. . .

Not dishonesty, but ignorance, is the outstanding characteristic of Fundamentalist literature. . .

— *Lies of Religious Literature*

There is something miasmic about religion. Its defense is saturated with untruth; its defenders are less critical and scrupulous in their statements than the writers in almost any other department of literature. Claims which have been annihilated hundreds of times appear weekly in the religious press and are mellifluously broadcast from a thousand pulpits. And the crowning irony is to have these people assure us that, if the modern race discards their services and abandons their creeds, it is likely to lose the quick sense of honor and truthfulness which fifteen centuries of Christian education have implanted in it.

—Ibid.

"Eating the God"—that is to say, eating food in which the God is believed to be present so that some mysterious power or influence (grace) passes to the eater—is so natural a stage in the development of ritual religion that th Spanish missionaries who came out to convert the Aztecs found that they had that ceremony in a form that was weirdly like their own. It was common in Greece—in the cult of Ceres (the spirit of corn) and Bacchus (the spirit of the vine)—and was found in the Persian and Mithraic religions. Thus a sacred supper of bread and wine was very well known in all those cities of the Mediterranean coast in which Christianity arose.

...when, in the mass, the priest breathes over these the Latin for "This is my body" (*Hoc est corpus meum*, which the wicked Reformers shortened to Hocus-pocus) and "This is my blood," they are in the most literal sense converted into the living personality (body, mind, and divinity) of Jesus Christ.

— *The Holy Faith of Romanists*

Extreme Unction, or the Last Anointing, is a development of a pre-Christian medical practice of rubbing with oil, men who were very ill. It became a symbolical ceremony of touching with oil the parts of the body with which a man or woman had sinned. It was, however, apparently provided in the original blue-prints that when our wicked age supervened the anointing of "the loins" might be omitted. In the delicate and virtuous Middle Ages they just lifted up the dying person's smock and—Well, it is not clear in the ritual books what exactly the priest anointed.

—Ibid.

Holy water is not a sacrament but it is very valuable. It is water from which a priest has, with a pinch of salt...and various incantations driven out the devil, and he so dreads it ever after that the Catholic makes lavish use of it in church; where Catholic practice suggests—women still wear hats to keep the devil from entering by their ears—evil spirits are strangely numerous.

—Ibid.

At seven the normal child is introduced to the sacrament of Penance. The basis of this practice is ...revolting. It is that a child usually reaches "the age of reason" at that age and may incur eternal damnation. They are all treated as junior Dead-End Kids...

So begins the life-long comedy of the confessional.

—Ibid.

The crowd you will see on any Saturday night in a Catholic Church awaiting their turn to confess is enough to make you despair of modern intelligence in the mass. There are social moralists who shed tears over the crowds at baseball games or in cinemas. They would do better to be concerned about the intellectual level betrayed in these scenes in Catholic churches. Remember that I was once a father-confessor. They just reel off mechanically a list of lies, quarrels, thefts, drinking, etc. and in almost every case a few points about sex...And for every woman or girl who sincerely wants guidance there are fifty who just love the intimate talk about sex that is permitted with the priest in the confessional...That it promotes morals and reduces crime is bunk. The one object of it is to consolidate the power of the priest over the laity.

—Ibid.

A practice of voluntarily confessing sins was... inherited from the pre-Christian world, but it was not until after the year 200 that the Roman Church under a Pope of disreputable character (Callistus) discovered that the power to bind and loose, which Christ was supposed to have given to the apostles (Matt. 16:19), meant that the bishop could absolve from grave sins that were confessed to him, and other Churches pronounced this a scandalous misinterpretation of the Scriptures in the interest of the Roman clergy. In the Dark Age, naturally, the clergy made headway with their ambition to enslave the laity...The laity remained refractory until the most powerful and most arrogant of the popes, Innocent III, imposed the obligation of annual confession upon the entire Church (1215)... the law was followed by quite the most immoral and vicious period in the history of Europe (1200-1550). After this long and picturesque history the Council of Trent declared it a "sacrament."

—Ibid.

[Catholic] doctrine and practice "developed" in exactly the same way as a great store like Marshall Fields developed. New attractions were required to sustain or to increase profits. Age by age, the gothic structure of the faith, with its gargoyles and its buttresses, its dark corners and its theatrical mummery, was built up, and on every stone of the structure is stamped the word "Priestcraft."

—Ibid.

Al Medwin

I was negotiating a contract to accept Jesus as my personal savior, but he refused to recognize my free sex clause.

— Letter to the editor of this volume, 1986

John Stuart Mill

Christian morality (so called) has all the characters of a reaction; it is, in great part, a protest against Paganism. Its ideal is negative rather than positive; passive rather than active. Innocence rather than

Nobleness; Abstinence from Evil, rather than energetic Pursuit of Good; in its precepts..."thou shalt not" predominated unduly over "thou shalt." In its horror of sensuality, it made an idol of asceticism, which has been gradually compromised away into one of legality. It holds out the hope of heaven and the threat of hell, as the appointed and appropriate motives to a virtuous life—in this falling far below the best of the ancients, and doing what lies in it to give to human morality an essentially selfish character, by disconnecting each man's feelings of duty from the interests of his fellow-creatures, except so far as a self-interested inducement is offered to him for consulting them. It is essentially a doctrine of passive obedience; it inculcates submission to all authorities found established; who indeed are not to be actively obeyed when they command what religion forbids, but who are not to be resisted, far less rebelled against, for any amount of wrong to ourselves. And while, in the morality of the best Pagan nations, duty to the State holds even a disproportionate place, infringing on the just liberty of the individual, in purely Christian ethics, that grand department of duty is scarcely noticed or acknowledged.

— *On Liberty*

Thomas Muntzer

Bible, Babel, bubble!

Patriarch Nestorius

Give me, O Caesar!, give me the earth purged of heretics, and I will give you in exchange the kingdom of heaven.

— quoted by Gibbon in *The Decline and Fall of the Roman Empire*

Cardinal John Newman

The [Catholic] church holds that it were better for sun and moon to drop from heaven, for the earth to fail, and for all the many millions who are upon it to die of starvation in extremest agony, so far as temporal affliction goes, than that one soul, I will not say should be lost, but should commit one single venial sin, should tell one untruth, though it harmed no one, or steal one poor farthing without excuse.

— *On Anglican Differences*

Friedrich Nietzsche

...the domestic animal, the herd animal, the sick animal man—the Christian...

In Christianity neither morality nor religion is in contact with any point of reality. Nothing but imaginary *causes* ("God," "soul," "ego," "spirit," "free will"—or even "unfree will"); nothing but imaginary

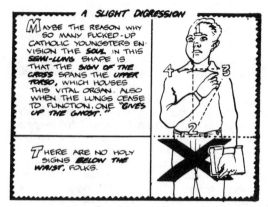

Copyright Justin Green, used by permission

effects ("sin," "salvation," "grace," "punishment," "forgiveness of sin"). An intercourse between imaginary *beings* ("Gods," "spirits," "souls"); an imaginary science of *nature* (anthropocentric; absolute lack of the concept of natural causes); an imaginary *psychology* (nothing but self-misunderstandings..."repentance," "remorse of conscience," "temptation by the devil," "presence of God"); an imaginary *teleology* ("the kingdom of God," "the last judgment," "everlasting life"). This purely *fictitious world* is, greatly to its disadvantage, distinguished from the dream-world in that while the latter *reflects* reality, the former falsifies, depreciates, and negates it. When once the concept of "nature" was devised as a concept antithetical to "God," "natural" had to be the word for "reprehensible"; that whole fictitious world has its root in *hatred* of the natural...

...the hiding place, the dark chamber are Christian. Here the body is despised, hygiene is repudiated as sensuousness; the church resists even cleanliness (the first Christian regulation, after the expulsion of the Moors, was the closing of the public baths...).

A certain sense of cruelty towards self and others is Christian; the hatred against those thinking differently; the will to persecute. Gloomy and exciting concepts are in the foreground; the most greatly coveted states, designated with the highest names, are epileptoid states...

The hatred of intellect, of pride, courage, freedom, libertinage of intellect, is Christian; the hatred of the senses, of the delights of the senses, of all delights, is Christian...

Christianity desires to become master of *beasts of prey*; its expedient is to make them sick—weakening is the Christian recipe for *taming*, for "civilization."

What is Jewish, what is Christian morality? Chance despoiled of innocence; misfortune befouled with the concept of "sin"; well-being as danger, as "temptation"...

...all the affairs of life are so regulated that the priest is *everywhere indispensable*; at all natural events of life, at birth, at marriage, in sickness, at death, not to speak of the sacrifice (the meal), the holy parasite appears in order to *denaturalize* them; in his language, to "sanctify" them.

...the concepts, "the other world," "last judgment," "immortality of soul," "soul" itself: they are torture instruments, they are systems of cruelty in virtue of which the priest became master...

...an absurd problem came to the surface: "How *could* God permit that [crucifixion of J.C.]!...the deranged reason of the little community found quite a frightfully absurd answer: God gave his Son for forgiveness, as a *sacrifice*...The *sacrifice for guilt*, and just in its most repugnant and barbarous form—the sacrifice of the innocent for the sins of the guilty! What horrifying heathenism!

...that little hypocrites and half-crazed people dare to imagine that on their account the laws of nature are constantly *broken*—such an enhancement of every kind of selfishness to infinity, to *impudence*, cannot be branded with sufficient contempt. And yet Christianity owes its *triumph* to this pitiable flattery of personal vanity.

One must not be misled: "judge not," they say, but send everything to hell which stands in their way. In making God judge, they themselves judge; in glorifying God, they glorify themselves.

Principle of Christian love: it wants to be well *paid*. [refers to Mat. 5:46]

...one does well to put on gloves when reading the New Testament. The proximity of so much filth almost compels one to do so.

Moral: every expression in the mouth of a "first Christian" is a lie, every action he does is an instinctive falsehood—all his values, all his aims are injurious, but *he* whom he hates, *that* which he hates, *has value*...

A religion like Christianity, which is not in touch with reality on any point, which immediately falls down as soon as reality gets its right even in a single point, must, of course, be mortally hostile to the "wisdom of the world," i.e., to *science*—it will approve of all expedients by which discipline of intellect, the noble coolness and freedom of intellect, can be poisoned, calumniated, and defamed. "Belief," as an imperative, is the veto against science—in practice, the lie at any price...

...one is not "converted to Christianity—one must be morbid enough for it...

We must never forgive Christianity for having taken advantage of the weakness of the dying to outrage their consciences...

— above quotations from *The Anti-Christ*

If we survey the separate moral demands of the earliest times of Christianity it will everywhere be found the requirements are exaggerated in order that man *cannot* satisfy them; the intention is not that he should become more moral, but that he should feel himself as *sinful as possible.*

— *Human, All Too Human*

If Christianity were right, with its theories of an avenging God, of general sinfulness, of redemption, and the danger of eternal damnation, it would be a sign of weak intellect and lack of character *not* to become a priest, apostle or hermit, and to work only with fear and trembling for one's own salvation; it would be senseless thus to neglect eternal benefits for temporary comfort. Taking it for granted that there *is* belief, the commonplace Christian is a miserable figure, a man that really cannot add two and two together, and who, moreover, just because of his mental incapacity for responsibility, does not deserve to be so severely punished as Christianity has decreed.

— Ibid.

Christianity...oppressed man and crushed him utterly, sinking him as if in deep mire; then into the feeling of absolute depravity it suddenly threw the light of divine mercy, so that the surprised man, dazzled by forgiveness, gave a cry of joy and for a moment believed that he bore all heaven within himself. All psychological feelings of Christianity work upon this unhealthy excess of sentiment, and upon the deep corruption of head and heart it necessitates; it desires to destroy, break, stupefy, confuse—only one thing it does not desire, namely *moderation*...

— Ibid.

...Christians call it "faith"...I call it "the herd"...

— *Beyond Good and Evil*

The Christian faith from the beginning, is self-sacrifice: the sacrifice of all freedom, all pride, all self-confidence of spirit; it is at the same time subjection, self-derision, and self-mutilation.

— Ibid.

If anyone seemed to have an equivocal attitude toward Christianity, I wouldn't have an ounce of confidence in him. There is only one possible attitude in this matter: absolute negation.

Max Nordau

Historical investigations have revealed to us the origin and growth of the Bible. We know that by this name we designate a collection of writings as radically unlike in origin, character and contents, as if the Nibelungen Lied, Mirabeau's speeches, Heine's love poems and a manual of zoology had been printed and mixed up promiscuously, and then bound into one volume.

We find collected in this book the superstitious beliefs of the ancient inhabitants of Palestine, with indistinct echoes of Indian and Persian fables, mistaken imitations of Egyptian theories, and customs, historical chronicles as dry as they are unreliable, and miscellaneous poems, amatory, human and Jewish-national, which are rarely distinguished by beauties of the highest order, but frequently by superfluity of expression, coarseness, bad taste, and genuine Oriental sensuality.

— *Conventional Lies of Our Civilization*

As a literary monument the Bible is of much later origin than the Vedas; as a work of literary value it is surpassed by everything written in the last two thousand years by authors even of the second rank, and to compare it seriously with the productions of Homer, Sophocles, Dante, Shakespeare or Goethe would require a fanaticized mind that had entirely lost its power of judgment. Its conception of the universe is childish, and its morality revolting.

— Ibid.

Thomas Paine

Whenever we read the obscene stories, the voluptuous debaucheries, the cruel and torturous executions, the unrelenting vindictiveness, with which more than half the Bible is filled, it would be more consistent that we called it the word of a demon, than the word of God. It is a history of wickedness, that has served to corrupt and brutalize mankind; and, for my part, I sincerely detest it, as I detest everything that is cruel.

— *The Age of Reason*

Theodore Parker

The Bible sanctions slavery. So much the worse for the Bible.

Vishnu with a necklace of skulls is a figure of love and mercy compared with the God of the Old Testament.

Wendell Phillips

...what was the New England Church, in its ideal, has come to be a mere yoke on which the awakened religious life was fastened, and it became a spiritual slavery, so that all the machineries of outside life were brought to bear as if for the manufacture of hypocrites. It has become the outer shed of the factory, the appendage of the shop, the rich man's kitchen. It contents itself with the policeman's duty of blinding the eyes of the working-men, and striving to make them contented. The undertone of its preaching is the clink of the dollar.
...The Pope himself...could not have devised machinerey more exactly suited to crush free thought, and to make each man a sham.

— *The Bible and the Church*

I affirm that the pulpit of this country...has a momentous influence, but it is only through dread and awe. It has made the masses afraid to think.

It has told them that thought is infidelity, that intellectual activity is ruin; and they look up to it thinking that stupidity is heaven, that chaining thought is agreeable to God, that suicide of the mind is doing honor to the Maker who gave us the mind; and having drilled the people into that superstition, the pulpit broods over it like a nightmare.

— *The Pulpit*

"I'm not going to inflict a sermon on you," says your generously considerate friend. What a testimony!

— *Christianity a Battle, Not a Dream*

Luther said, "A wicked tyrant is better than a wicked war." It was the essence of aristocracy. "Better submit to any evil than trust the masses."

— *The Puritan Principle and John Brown*

Pope Pius IV

We order that each and every Jew of both sexes in our temporal dominion, and in all the cities, lands, places and baronies subject to them, shall depart completely out of the confines thereof within the space of three months after these letters shall have been made public.

— Decree, 1569, quoted by Joseph McCabe

Pope Pius XI

A good Catholic, precisely because of his Catholic principles, makes the better citizen, attached to his country, and loyally submissive to constituted civil authority in every legitimate form of government.

— *Divini illius magistri*

Rev. J.C. Postell

So far from being a moral evil, slavery is a merciful visitation...It is the Lord's doing and it is marvelous in our eyes;...It is by divine appointment.

— quoted by Kirby Page in *Jesus or Christianity*

Wilhelm Reich

My medical experience has taught me that adolescents who are sexually sick have an unhealthy appreciation of the legend of Jesus.

— *The Mass Psychology of Fascism*

William Harris Rule

At Lisbon, the place of execution [by the Inquisition] was at the waterside. For each person to be burnt, whether dead or alive, a thick stake, or spar, was erected, not less than twelve feet above the ground; and within about eighteen inches of the top there was a thick cross-piece, to serve for a seat...for the condemned person, whom they compelled to mount, sit on the transverse piece, and there be chained fast. The priests then went up, delivered a hasty exhortation to repentance, and, that failing, declared that they left him to the devil, who was waiting to receive his soul. On perceiving this, the mob shouted, "Let the dog's beard be trimmed"; that is to say, let his face be scorched. This was done by tying pieces of furze [a dried plant] to the end of a long pole, and holding the flaming bush to his face until it was burnt black. The disfiguration of countenance and his cries for "mercy for the love of God," furnished great part of the amusement for the crowd...When "the beard" was trimmed, they lit the heap of furze at the foot of the stake, and if there was no wind, the flame would envelop the seat, and begin to burn the legs; but as there generally is a breeze on the banks of the Tagus, it seldom reached so high. If there was no wind he would be dead in half an hour; but the victim usually retained entire consciousness for an hour and a half, or two hours, in dire torment, which the spectators witnessed with such delight as could never be produced by any other spectacle.

— *History of the Inquisition*, Vol. 2

Marquis de Sade

Have no doubt on one point: at its very birth, this unworthy religion [christianity] would have been destroyed without shift, if only there had been employed against it no other weapon than the contempt it deserves—but it was persecuted, and so it grew. If today, the effort were made to cover it with ridicule, it would soon fall.

← *Philosophie dans le Boudoir*

Percy Bysshe Shelley

...humbly he came,
Veiling his horrible Godhead in the shape
Of man, scorned by the world, his name unheard
Save by the rabble of his native town,
Even as a parish demagogue. He led
The Crowd; he taught them justice, truth and peace,
In semblance; but he lit within their souls
The quenchless flames of zeal, and blessed the sword
He brought on earth to satiate with the blood
Of truth and freedom his malignant soul.
At length his mortal frame was led to death.
I stood beside him; on the torturing cross
No pain assiled his unterrestrial sense;
And yet he groaned. Indignantly I summed
The massacres and miseries which his name
Had sanction in my country, and I cried
"Go! Go!" in mockery.

— *Queen Mab*

Yes! I have seen God's worshippers unsheathe
The sword of his revenge, when grace descended,
Confirming all unnatural impulses,
To sanctify their desolating deeds;

And frantic priests waved the ill-omened cross
O'er the unhappy earth; then shone the sun
On showers of gore from the upflashing steel
Of safe assassination, and all crime
Made stingless by the spirits of the Lord,
And blood-red rainbows canopied the land.

— Ibid.

Barbara Simpson

As women's minds are freed by education the church will disappear; and high time too. It is entirely a man-made institution, even if it is woman supported, and I think that in the future every thinking woman will congratulate herself that her sex had no finger in that pie.

Charles Smith

The Bible is one of 27 books for which divine origin is claimed. Christians deny the divinity of all bibles but their own. We deny the divinity of only one more than they do.

Herbert Spencer

We hear with surprise of the savage who, falling down a precipice, ascribes the failure of his foothold to a malicious demon; and we smile at the kindred notion of the ancient Greek, that his death was prevented by a goddess who unfastened for him the thong of the helmet by which his enemy was dragging him. But daily, without surprise, we hear men who describe themselves as saved from shipwreck by "divine interposition," who speak of having "providentially" missed a train which met with a fatal disaster, and who call it a "mercy" to have escaped injury from a falling chimeny pot—men who, in such cases, recognize physical causation no more than do the uncivilized or semi-civilized. The Veddah who thinks that failure to hit an animal with his arrow resulted from inadequate invocation of an ancestral spirit, and the Christian priest who says prayers over a sick man in the expectation that the course of his disease will be so stayed, differ only in respect of the agent from whom they expect supernatural aid and the phenomenon to be altered by him: the necessary relations among causes and effects are tacitly ignored by the last as much as by the first.

Charles T. Sprading

Those who are now attempting to force people to read the Bible should do a little reading themselves of history; they tried this sort of thing during the middle ages, and that period is known as the "Dark Ages."

— *Freedom and Its Fundamentals*

The old Puritan came to America in order to worship God according to the dictates of his conscience—and to force everybody else to do the same.
—Ibid.

The Puritan...has the same aversion to strong characters that he has to strong minds; he believes in force, not reason. When he creates fear he thinks it is a virtue. When he compels obedience he calls it morality.

His attitude is renunciation for himself and denunciation for you...He believes that God implanted the instincts and desires in man, but that to gratify them is wrong and to crush them is right; to be happy is wicked, to be miserable is righteous.

...He measures the morality of an act, not by the pleasure it gives, but by the pain it causes. He is so constituted that the misery of others is his delight.
—Ibid.

Elizabeth Cady Stanton

The memory of my own suffering has prevented me from ever shadowing one young soul with the superstitions of the Christian religion.
— *Eighty Years and More*

I found nothing grand in the history of the Jews nor in the morals inculcated in the Pentateuch. I know of no other books that so fully teach the subjection and degradation of women.
—Ibid.

The Bible and Church have been the greatest stumbling blocks in the way of women's emancipation.
— *Free Thought Magazine*, September 1896

The whole tone of Church teaching in regard to woman is, to the last degree, contemptuous and degrading.
—Ibid.

Out of the doctrine of original sin grew the crimes and miseries of asceticism, celibacy and witchcraft; woman becoming the helpless victim of all these delusions.

Pope Stephanus V

The popes, like Jesus, are conceived by their mothers through the overshadowing of the Holy Ghost. All popes are a certain species of man-god, for the purpose of being the better able to conduct the functions of mediator between God and mankind. All powers in Heaven, as well as on earth, are given to them.
—attributed

Rev. Jimmy Swaggart

Go ahead! Give the Lord a hand!
—TV Broadcast, September 1986

Tacitus

The [christians] derived their name and origin from Christ, who, in the reign of Tiberius, had suffered death by the sentence of the procurator Pontius Pilate. For a while this dire superstition was checked, but it again burst forth; and not only spread itself over Judea, the first seat of this mischievous sect, but was even introduced into Rome, the common asylum which receives and protects whatever is impure, whatever is atrocious.
— quoted by Gibbon in *The Decline and Fall of the Roman Empire*

Robert Tefton

JESUS CHRIST, int. 1) A common exclamation indicating suprise or bewilderment; 2) n., A popular fictional character. Over the years controversy has arisen over his middle name, and even over his middle initial. Some have held that his proper name is Jesus H. Christ, with the "H" presumably standing for "Hubert." This is incorrect. The true name is Jesus F. Christ, but the vulgar presumption that the "F" stands for "Fucking" is wrong. The actual appellation of this unique character is the much more elegant Jesus Festering Christ.

St. Teresa

I have often found that there is nothing the devils fear so much as holy water. They fly away if you make the sign of the cross. But they come back again. When I have taken holy water, I always feel great delight and comfort. In taking holy water I feel like a person, who being very hot and thirsty, drinks a glass of cold water. I rejoice that the words used by the church in blessing holy water, have such great power over the devils.
— quoted by Rev. J. Furniss in *Tracts for Spriitual Reading*

Tertullian

The kindgom of heaven is open to all eunuchs.
— *On Monogamy*

Truth, from her first appearance, is an enemy.
— *The Christian's Defense*

And the Son of God dies; it is by all means to be believed, because it is absurd. And he was buried and rose again; the fact is certain because it is impossible.
— *The Testimony of a Christian Soul*

Demons are everywhere and the cursing of them universal.
—Ibid.

After Jesus Christ we have no need of speculation, after the Gospel no need of research. When we come to believe, we have no desire to believe anything else; for we begin by believing that there is nothing else which we have to believe...

My first principle is this. Christ laid down one definite system of truth which the world must believe without qualification.

Francisco (Pancho) Villa

The Spaniards inflicted upon us the worst superstition the world has ever known: the Catholic religion. For this alone they should all be shot.

— attributed

Voltaire

Crush the infamous thing!

— on superstition

I conclude that every sensible man, every honest man, ought to hold Christianity in abhorrence.

But what shall we substitute in its place? say you. What? A ferocious animal has sucked the blood of your relatives. I tell you to rid yourselves of this beast, and you ask me what shall you put in its place!

Evangelical sweetness consists in inculcating Faith by dint of abuse, threats, and tortures. It is by the aid of such "sweetmeats" as these that the Church causes her children to swallow the pill of Faith.

It is forbidden a Christian to end his days suddenly or to kill himself at one blow, but he may kill himself bit by bit, little by little, and then have nothing to fear. Indeed, such conduct on his part will be looked upon by other Christians as so edifying, so meritorious, that he may even hope to die in the odor of sanctity and even have his name in the almanac if he can manage to work a few miracles.

John Wesley

The giving up of witchcraft is in effect the giving up of the Bible.

— *Journal*, 1766–1768

E.A. Westermarck

Not one of the [Church] Fathers even hints that slavery is unlawful or improper. In the early age martyrs possessed slaves, and so did abbots, bishops, popes, monasteries and churches...So little was the abolition of slavery thought of that a Council at Orleans, in the middle of the Sixth Century, expressly decreed the perpetuity of servitude among the descendants of slaves...Throughout Christendom the purchase and sale of men, as property transferred from vendor to buyer, was recognized as a legal transaction of the same validity with the sale of other merchandise, land or cattle.

— *The Origin and Development of Moral Ideas*, Vol. 1

Andrew Dickson White

On the 7th of December, 1484, Pope Innocent VIII sent forth his bull *Summis Desiderantes*. Of all documents ever issued from Rome, imperial or papal, this has doubtless, first and last, cost the greatest shedding of innocent blood. Yet no document was ever more clearly dictated by conscience. Inspired by the scriptural command, "Thou shalt not suffer a witch to live," Pope Innocent exhorted the clergy of Germany to leave no means untried to detect sorcerers, and especially those who by evil weather destroy vineyards, gardens, meadows, and growing crops. These precepts were based upon various texts of Scripture, especially upon the famous statement in the book of Job; and, to carry them out, witch-finding inquisitors were authorized by the Pope to scour Europe, especially Germany, and a manual was prepared for their use—The Witch-Hammer, *Malleus Maleficarum*.

With the application of torture to thousands of women, in accordance with the precepts laid down in the *Malleus*, it was not difficult to extract masses of proof for this sacred theory of meteorology. The poor creatures writhing on the rack, held in horror by those who had been nearest and dearest to them, anxious only for death to relieve their sufferings, confessed to anything and everything that would satisfy the inquisitors and judges. All that was needed was that the inquisitors should ask leading questions and suggest satisfactory answers: the prisoners, to shorten their suffering, were sure sooner or later to give the answer required, even though they knew that this would send them to the stake or scaffold. Under the doctrine of "excepted cases," there was no limit to torture for persons accused of heresy or witchcraft; even the safeguards which the old pagan world had imposed upon torture were thus thrown down, and the prisoner *must* confess.

The theological literature of the Middle Ages was thus enriched with numberless statements regarding modes of Satanic influence on the weather. Pathetic, indeed, are the records; and none more so than the confessions of these poor creatures, chiefly women and children, during hundreds of years, as to their manner of raising hailstorms and tempests. Such confessions, by tens of thousands, are still to be found in the judicial records of Germany, and indeed of all Europe.

Typical as to the attitude both of Scotch and English Protestants were the theory and practice of King James I, himself the author of a book on *demonology*, and nothing if not a theologian...he applied his own knowledge to investigating the causes of the tempests which beset his bride on her voyage from Denmark. Skillful use of unlimited torture soon brought these causes to light. A Dr. Fian, while his legs were crushed in the "boots" and

©Justin Green. From *Binky Brown Meets the Holy Virgin Mary.* Used by permission.

wedges were driven under his finger nails, confessed that several hundred witches had gone to sea in a sieve from the port of Leith, and had raised storms and tempests to drive back the princess.

The *auto da fe* of Spain was celebrated in Scotland under a different name, and with Presbyterian ministers instead of Roman Catholic priests as the main attendants. At Leith, in 1664, nine women were burned together. Condemnations and punishments of women in batches were not uncommon. Torture was used far more freely than in England, both in detecting witches and in punishing them. The natural argument developed in hundreds of pulpits was this: If the All-wise God punishes his

creatures with tortures infinite in cruelty and duration, why should not his ministers, as far as they can, imitate him?

Down to the Christian era the fear of magic rarely led to any persecution very systematic or very cruel. While in Greece and Rome laws were at times enacted against magicians, they were only occasionally enforced with rigour, and finally, toward the end of the pagan empire, the feeling against them seemed dying out altogether...

Moreover, under the old empire a real science was coming in, and thought was progressing. Both the theory and practice of magic were more and more held up to ridicule...

But with the development of Christian theology came a change. The idea of the active interference of Satan in magic, which had come into the Hebrew mind with especial force from Persia during the captivity of Israel, had passed from the Hebrew Scriptures into Christianity, and had been made still stronger by various statements in the New Testament...

Hence it was that as soon as Christianity came into power it more than renewed the old severities against the forbidden art, and one of the first acts of the Emperor Constantine after his conversion was to enact a most severe law against magic and magicians, under which the main offender might be burned alive...

This severity went on increasing and threatened the simplest efforts in physics and chemistry; even the science of mathematics was looked upon with dread. By the twelfth and thirteenth centuries, the older theology having arrived at the climax of its development in Europe, terror of magic and witchcraft took complete possession of the popular mind.

Under paganism, the rule regarding torture had been that it should not be carried beyond human endurance...but when Christianity had become predominant throughout Europe, torture was developed with a cruelty never before known. There had evolved a doctrine of "excepted cases" — these "excepted cases" being especially heresy and witchcraft; for by a very simple and logical process of theological reasoning it was held that Satan would give supernatural strength to his special devotees — that is to heretics and witches — and therefore that, in dealing with them, there should be no limit to the torture.

In *[Spondent pariter]* and in sundry other bulls and briefs we find Pope John [XXII], by virtue of his infallibility as the world's instructor in all that pertains to faith and in morals, condemning real science and pseudo-science alike. In two of these documents supposed to be inspired by wisdom from on high, he complains that both he and his flock are in danger of their lives by the arts of sorcerers; he declares that such sorcerers can send devils into mirrors and finger rings, and can kill men and women by a magic word; that they tried to kill him by piercing a waxen image of him with needles in the name of the devil. He therefore called on all rulers, secular and ecclesiastical, to hunt down the miscreants who thus afflicted the faithful, and he especially increased the powers of inquisitors in various parts of Europe for this purpose.

From time to time men and women whose brains were disordered dreamed that they had been changed into various animals, and especially into wolves. On their confessing this, and often implicating others, many executions of lunatics resulted; moreover, countless sane victims, suspected of the same impossible crime, were forced by torture to confess it, and sent unpitied to the stake. The belief in such a transformation pervaded all Europe, and

lasted long even in the Protestant countries. Probably no article in the witch creed had more adherents in the fifteenth, sixteenth, and seventeenth centuries than this. Nearly every parish in Europe had its resultant horrors.

The result of...widespread terror was naturally therefore, a steady increase in mental disorders. A great modern authority tells us that, although modern civilization tends to increase insanity, the number of lunatics at present is far less than in the ages of faith and in the Reformation period. The treatment of the "possessed," as we find it laid down in standard treatises, sanctioned by orthodox churchmen and jurists, accounts for this abundantly. One sort of treatment used for all those accused of witchcraft will also serve to show this — the *tortura insomnia*. Of all things in brain-disease, calm and regular sleep is most certainly beneficial; yet, under this practice, these half-crazed creatures were prevented, night after night and day after day, from sleeping or even resting. In this way temporary delusion became chronic insanity, mild cases became violent, torture and death ensued, and the "ways of God to man" were justified.

By the investigations of George Smith among the Assyrian tablets of the British Museum, in 1872, and by his discoveries just afterward in Assyria, it was put beyond a reasonable doubt that a great mass of accounts in Genesis are simply adaptations of earlier and especially of Chaldean myths and legends. While this proved to be the fact as regards the accounts of Creation and the fall of man, it was seen to be most strikingly so as regards the Deluge. The eleventh of the twelve tablets, on which the most important of these inscriptions was found, was almost wholly preserved, and it revealed in this legend, dating from a time far earlier than that of Moses, such features peculiar to the childhood of the world as the building of the great ship or ark to escape the flood, the careful caulking of its seams, the saving of a man beloved of Heaven, his selecting and taking with him into the vessel animals of all sorts in couples, the impressive final closing of the door, the sending forth of different birds as the flood abated, the offering of sacrifices when the flood had subsided, the joy of the Divine Being who had caused the flood as the odour of the sacrifice reached his nostrils; while throughout all was shown that partiality for the Chaldean sacred number seven which appears so constantly in the Genesis legends and throughout the Hebrew sacred books.

— above quotations from *The History of the Warfare Between Science and Theology*

Oscar Wilde

Shallow speakers and shallow thinkers in pulpits and on platforms often talk about the world's worship of pleasure, and whine against it. But it is rarely in the world's history that its ideal has been one of joy and beauty. The worship of pain has far more often dominated the world. Medievalism, with its saints and martyrs, its love of self-torture, its wild passion for wounding itself, its gashing with knives, and its whipping with rods—Medievalism is real Christianity, and the medieval Christ is the real Christ.

— *The Soul of Man Under Socialism*

The pope may be cultivated. Many popes have been; the bad popes have been. The bad popes loved Beauty almost as passionately, nay, with as much passion as the good popes hated thought.

— Ibid.

Fred Woodworth

Christ's so-called purpose, to save man, is futile, since a god who could do all the rest could surely do this too without having to resort to an absurd ritual in Palestine.

Further, from the evidence of the holy wars and inquisitions carried out by those believing in Christianity, it must be concluded that Christ's advent was a major tragedy to the human species...

— *There Is No God*

[Fundamentalists] never wonder why, if herpes is sent by "god" to scourge "adulterers," whooping cough and measles weren't purposely created to lambaste children.

— *American Atheist,* January 1984

Victor Yarrow

The holy fraud, the inspired and sacred scriptures, a conglomeration of utterly unbelievable yarns, and the pious flapdoodle based upon them, would be vastly diverting were it not for the ugly fact that "it is a freedom-constricting, mind-dwarfing, meddlesome and irresponsible power"—a power that ought not to be tolerated outside of an insane asylum.

— Review of *Christianity, A Continuing Calamity*

Israel Zangwill

The Jews are a frightened people. Nineteen centuries of Christian love have broken down their nerves.

— attributed

Anonymous & Multiple Author

A foremost modern theologian, by no means of the radical school, has recorded his significant judgment that one of the main characteristics of [christian] apologetic literature is its lack of honesty; and no one who has studied theology can doubt that it has suffered more than any other science from equivocal phraseology [dishonest language].

— *Christian World,* August 20, 1903

If a cleric has fornicated with a quadruped let him do penance for, if he is a simple cleric, two years, if a deacon, three years, if a priest seven years, if a bishop ten years.

For fornication with his mother a man must do penance for 15 years. If with his daughter or sister 12 years. If with a natural brother he shall abstain from meat for 15 years.

— 8th-century Penitential (list of sins and punishments), quoted in A.A. Hadden's *Councils and Eccliastical Documents*

Blessed are the meek in heart and the poor of spirit, for they stand not the slightest chance of inheriting the Earth, but will slave on to the end like faithful sheep.

— Anonymous

...and as I laid my hands on the TV, my heart was filled with peace and mercy and joy and love.

— Audience member interviewed on the PTL Club

Christian teachers, following the example of St. Paul, implicitly accept slavery as not in itself incompatible with the Christian law. The Apostle counsels slaves to obey their masters and to bear with their conditions patiently. This estimate of slavery continued to prevail until it became fixed in the systematized ethical teaching of the schools; and so it remained without any conspicuous alteration until the end of the eighteenth century.

— *Catholic Encyclopedia* (1912)

A shipwrecked sailor, landing on a lonely beach, observed a gallows. "Thank God," he exclaimed, "I'm in a Christian country!"

— Anonymous

Jesus had his good points. So did Hitler.

— Graffiti

The reality of demoniacal possession stands upon the same evidence with the gospel system in general.

— *Encyclopedia Britannica* (1797)

By this Law, (1) Blasphemy against GOD, denying our Savior JESUS CHRIST to be the son of GOD, or denying the Holy TRINITY, or the Godhead of any of the Three Persons, &c. is to be Punished with Death, and Confiscation of Lands and Goods to the Lord Proprietary.

— *An Act Concerning Religion,* passed by the Maryland Colonial Assembly, April 21, 1649

(2) Persons using any reproachful Words or Speeches concerning the Blessed Virgin Mary, Mother of our Savior, or the Holy Apostles or Evangelists, or any of them for the 1st Offence to forfeit 5 pounds Sterling to the Lord Proprietary; or in default of Payment, to be publicly Whipped, and Imprisoned at the Pleasure of his Lordship, or his Lieut. General.

— Ibid.

Welcome to

Hell...

St. Thomas Aquinas

...Nothing should be denied to the blessed which belongs to the perfection of their beatitude. Now all things are the better known for being compared with their contrary. Consequently, in order that the happiness of the saints may be more delightful and that they may give to God more copious thanks for it, they are permitted perfectly to behold the sufferings of the damned...the saints will rejoice in the punishment of the damned.

St. Augustine

Hell was made for the inquisitive.
— *Confessions*

Let us go down to hell while we live, that we may not have to go down to hell when we die.
— quoted by Rev. J. Furniss in *Tracts for Spiritual Reading*

That hell, that lake of fire and brimstone shall be real, and the fire corporeal, burning both men and devils, the one in flesh, the other in air.
— quoted in *Hell, A Christian Doctrine*

Luther Burbank

The idea that a good God would send people to burning Hell is utterly damnable to me. The ravings of insanity! Superstition gone to seed! I don't want anything to do with such a God. No avenging Jewish God, no satanic devil, no fiery hell is of any interest to me.

John Calvin

Forever harrassed with a dreadful tempest, they shall feel themselves torn asunder by an angry God and transfixed and penetrated by mortal stings, terrified by the thunderbolts of God and broken by the weight of his hand, so that to sink into any gulf would be more tolerable than to stand for a moment in these terrors. Even infants bring their damnation with them.
— quoted in *Hell, A Christian Doctrine*

St. Cyprian

An ever-burning gehenna will burn up the condemned, and a punishment devouring with living flames...Souls with their bodies will be reserved in infinite tortures of suffering.

Jonathan Edwards

Reprobate infants are vipers of vengeance, which Jehovah will hold over hell in the tongs of his wrath until they turn and spit venom in his face.
— *The Eternity of Hell's Torments*

Can the believing husband in heaven be happy with his unbelieving wife in hell? Can the believing father in heaven be happy with his unbelieving children in hell? Can the loving wife in heaven be happy with her unbelieving husband in hell? I tell you, yea. Such will be their sense of justice, that it will increase rather than diminish their bliss.
— quoted by Ingersoll in *The Liberty of Man, Woman and Child*

St. Fulgentius

...little children who have begun to live in their mothers' womb and have there died, or who, having just been born, have passed away from the world without the sacrament of holy baptism... must be punished by the eternal torture of undying fire.
— quoted in *Hell, A Christian Doctrine*

Rev. J. Furniss, C.S.S.R.

Come into this room. You see it is very small. But see, in the midst of it there is a girl, perhaps about eighteen years old. What a terrible dress she has on — her dress is made of fire. On her head she wears a bonnet of fire. It is pressed down close all over her head; it burns her head; it burns into the skin; it scorches the bone of the skull and makes it smoke. The red hot fiery heat goes into the brain and melts it...there she will stand for ever burning and scorched! She counts with her fingers the moments as they pass away slowly, for each moment seems to her like a hundred years. As she counts the moments she remembers that she will have to count them for ever and ever.

Think of a coffin, not made of wood, but of fire, solid fire! And now come into this other room. You see a pit, a deep, almost bottomless, pit. Look down it and you will see something red hot and burning. It is a coffin, a red hot coffin of fire...It burns him from beneath. The sides of it scorch him. The heavy burning lid on the top presses down close upon him; he pants for breath; he cannot breathe; he cannot bear it; he gets furious...He tries with all his strength to burst open the coffin. He cannot

Thanks to American Atheists for this slogan

do it. He has no strength remaining. He gives up and sinks down again. Again the horrible choking. Again he tries; again he sinks down; so he will go on for ever and ever.

Look into this room. What a dreadful place it is! The roof is red hot; the walls are red hot; the floor is like a thick sheet of red hot iron. See, on the middle of that red hot floor stands a girl. She looks about sixteen years old. Her feet are bare, she has neither shoes nor stockings on her feet; her bare feet stand on the red hot burning floor.

Look into this little prison. In the middle of it there is a boy, a young man. He is silent; despair is on him...His eyes are burning like two burning coals. Two long flames come out of his ears. His breathing is difficult. Sometimes he opens his mouth and breath of blazing fire rolls out of it. But listen! There is a sound just like that of a kettle boiling. Is it really a kettle which is boiling? No; then what is it? Hear what it is. The blood is boiling in the scalding veins of that boy. The brain is boiling and bubbling in his head. The marrow is boiling in his bones. Ask him why he is thus tormented. His answer is that when he was alive, his blood boiled to do very wicked things.

You are going to see again the child about which you read in the Terrible Judgment, that it was condemned to hell. See! it is a pitiful sight. The little child is in this red hot oven. Hear the fire! It beats its head against the roof of the oven. It stamps its little feet on the floor. You can see on the face of this little child what you see on the faces of all in hell—despair, desperate and horrible...This child committed very bad mortal sins, knowing well the harm of what it was doing, and knowing that hell

would be the punishment. God was very good to this child. Very likely God saw that this child would get worse and worse, and would never repent, and so it would have to be punished much more in hell. So God, in His mercy, called it out of the world in its early childhood.

There are some diseases so bad, such as cancers and ulcers, that people cannot bear to breathe the air in the house where they are. There is something worse. It is the smell of death coming from a dead body lying in the grave. The dead body of Lazarus had been in the grave only four days. Yet Martha, his sister, could not bear that it should be taken out again. But what is the smell of death in hell? St. Bonaventure says that if one single body was taken out of hell and laid on the earth, in that same moment every living creature on the earth would sicken and die. Such is the smell of death from one body in hell.

— above quotations from *Tracts for Spiritual Reading* (an officially approved Catholic *Children's* book)
In his Approbation, William Meagher, Vicar-General of Dublin, states "I have carefully read over this Little Volume for Children and have found nothing whatever in it contrary to the doctrines of the Holy Faith; but on the contrary, a great deal to charm, instruct and edify the youthful classes for whose benefit it has been written."

Robert Ingersoll

The doctrine of eternal punishment was born in the glittering eyes of snakes—snakes that hung in fearful coils watching for their prey. It was born of the howl and bark and growl of wild beasts. It was born of the grin of hyenas and of the depraved chatter of unclean baboons. I despise it with every drop of my blood.
— *The Liberty of Man, Woman and Child*

Any man who believes it [hell] and has within his breast a decent, throbbing heart, will go insane. A man who believes that doctrine and does not go insane has the heart of a snake and the conscience of a hyena.
— Ibid.

Eternal punishment is eternal revenge, and can be inflicted only by an eternal monster.
— *Origin of God and the Devil*

Infinite punishment is infinite cruelty, endless injustice, immortal meanness. To worship an eternal jailer hardesn, debases, and pollutes even the vilest soul.
— Ibid.

The idea of hell was born of ignorance, brutality, fear, cowardice, and revenge. This idea testifies that our remote ancestors were the lowest beasts. Only from dens, lairs, and caves, only from mouths filled with cruel fangs, only from hearts of fear and hatred, only from the conscience of hunger and lust, only from the lowest and most debased could come this most cruel, heartless and bestial of all dogmas.

—Ibid.

The doctrine of eternal punishment is in perfect harmony with the savagery of the men who made the orthodox creeds. It is in harmony with torture, with flaying alive and with burnings. The men who burned their fellow-men for a moment, believed that God would burn his enemies forever.

— *Crumbling Creeds*

Who can estimate the misery that has been caused by this infamous doctrine of eternal punishment? Think of the lives it has blighted—of the tears it has caused—of the agony it has produced. Think of the millions who have been driven to insanity by this most terrible of dogmas. This doctrine renders God the basest and most cruel being in the universe. Compared with him, the most frightful deities of the most barbarous and degraded tribes are miracles of goodness and mercy. There is nothing more degrading than to worship such a god. Lower than this the soul can never sink.

— *Heretics and Heresies*

All the meanness, all the revenge, all the selfishness, all the cruelty, all the hatred, all the infamy of which the heart of man is capable, grew, blossomed and bore fruit in this one word—Hell.

— quoted in *Hell, A Christian Doctrine*

W.E.H. Lecky

A long series of monastic visions, of which that of St. Fursey, in the seventh century was one of the first, and which followed in rapid succession till that of Tundale, in the twelfth century, professed to describe with the most detailed accuracy the conditions of the lost.:.The devil was represented bound by red hot chains on a burning gridiron in the center of Hell. The screams of his never-ending agony made its rafters to resound; but his hands were free, and with these he seized the lost souls, crushed them like grapes against his teeth, and then threw them by his breath down the fiery cavern of his throat. Demons with hooks of red-hot iron plunged souls alternately into fire and ice. Some of the lost were hung up by their tongues, others were sawn asunder, other gnawed by serpents, others beaten together on an anvil and welded into a single mass, others boiled and then strained through a cloth, others twined in the embraces of demons whose limbs were of flame. The fire of earth, it was said, was but a picture of that of Hell. The latter was so immeasurably more intense that it alone could be called real. Sulphur was mixed with it, partly to increase its heat and partly, too, in order that an insufferable stench might be added to the misery of the lost; while, unlike other flames, it

emitted, according to some visions, no light, that the horror of darkness might be added to the horror of pain.

— *History of European Morals*

Illustration by J. R. Swanson

Joseph McCabe

Any body of men who believe in hell will persecute whenever they have the power.

— *What Gods Cost Men*

Bishop Jeremy Taylor

Husbands shall see their wives, parents their children, tormented before their eyes; the bodies of the damned shall be crowded together in hell, like grapes in a wine press, which press one another till they burst; every distinct sense and organ shall be assailed with its appropriate and most exquisite sufferings.

Tertullian

Ah! The broad magnificence of that scene! How shall I laugh and be glad and exult when I see these wise philosophers, who teach that the gods are indifferent and men soulless, roasting and browning before their own disciples in hell.

— *De Spectaculis*

You are fond of spectacles, except the greatest of all spectacles, the last and eternal judgment of the universe. How shall I admire, how laugh, how rejoice, how exult, when I behold so many proud monarchs, and fancied gods, groaning in the lowest abyss of darkness; so many magistrates, who persecuted the name of the Lord, liquefying in fiercer fires than they ever kindled against the Christians; so many sage philosophers blushing in red-hot flames with their deluded scholars; so many celebrated poets trembling before the tribunal, not of Minos, but of Christ, so many tragedians, more tuneful in the expression of their own sufferings; so many dancers.

—Ibid.

Voltaire

We are bound to believe, under pain of being damned, that the God of all mercy, to teach sinners how to live after their death, and to chastise those that are living who are blind, damns to all eternity the greater portion of mankind for venial faults, and that by special miracle of his divine love he causes them to endure everlastingly that he may everlastingly torture them.

—quoted in *Hell, A Christian Doctrine*

John Wesley

Fierce and poisonous animals were created for terrifying man, in order that he might be made aware of the final punishment.

—quoted in *Hell, A Christian Doctrine*

Is it not common to say to a child, "put your finger in that candle; can you bear it for even one minute?" How then will you bear hell-fire?

—Ibid.

Biblical Wisdom

Sex

It is good for a man not to touch a woman.
— *1 Corinthians 7:1*

For there are some eunuchs which were so born from their mother's womb; and there are some eunuchs which were made eunuchs of men; and there be eunuchs which have made themselves eunuchs for the kingdom of heaven's sake. He that is able to receive it, let him receive it.
— *Matthew 19:12* (J.C. speaking)

Dearly beloved, I beseech you as strangers and pilgrims, abstain from fleshly lusts, which war against the soul.
— *1 Peter 2:11*

For I would that all men were even as myself... I say therefore to the unmarried and widows. It is good for them if they abide even as I. But if they cannot contain, let them marry: for it is better to marry than to burn.
— *1 Corinthians 7:7-9*

Whosoever lieth with a beast shall surely be put to death.
— *Exodus 22:19*

And the man that committeth adultery with another man's wife, even he that committeth adultery with his neighbour's wife, the adulterer and the adulteress shall surely be put to death.
— *Leviticus 20:10*

If a man also lie with mankind, as he lieth with a woman, both of them have committed an abomination: they shall surely be put to death; their blood shall be upon them.
— *Leviticus 20:13*

And if a man lieth with a beast, he shall surely be put to death: and ye shall slay the beast.
— *Leviticus 20:15*

If a man be found lying with a woman married to an husband, then they shall both of them die...
— *Deuteronomy 22:22*

Now the works of the flesh are manifest, which are these; Adultery, fornication, uncleanliness, lasciviousness.
— *Galatians 5:19*

And whosoever lieth carnally with a woman, that is a bondmaid...she shall be scourged...And he shall bring his trespass offering unto the Lord...
— *Leviticus 19:20-21*

Behold, I was shapen in iniquity; and in sin did my mother conceive me.
— *Psalms 51:5*

If any man take a wife...and say, I took this woman, and when I came to her, I found her not a maid...if this thing be true...Then they shall bring out the damsel to the door of her father's house, and the men of the city shall stone her with stones that she die.
— *Deuteronomy 22:13-21*

And the daughter of any priest, if she profane herself by playing the whore, she profaneth her father: she shall be burnt with fire [to death].
— *Leviticus 21:9*

For to be carnally minded is death; but to be spiritually minded is life and peace.
— *Romans 8:6*

Women

Wives, submit yourselves unto your own husbands, as unto the Lord. For the husband is the head of the wife, even as Christ is the head of the church...
— *Ephesians 5:22-23*

Wives, submit yourselves unto your own husbands, as it is fit in the Lord.
— *Colossians 3:18*

Likewise ye husbands, dwell with them according to knowledge, giving honour unto the wife, as unto the weaker vessel...
— *1 Peter 3:7*

But I would have you know, that the head of every man is Christ; and the head of the woman is the man...

— *1 Corinthians 11:3*

Neither was the man created for the woman; but the woman for the man.

— *1 Corinthians 11:9*

Now that she is a widow indeed, and desolate, trusteth in God, and continueth supplications and prayers night and day. But she that liveth in pleasure is dead while she liveth.

— *1 Timothy 5:5-6*

Unto the woman He [god] said, "I will greatly multiply thy sorrow and thy conception; in sorrow thou shalt bring forth children; and thy desire shall be to thy husband, and he shall rule over thee.

— *Genesis 3:16*

How then can man be justified with God? or how can he be clean that is born of a woman?

— *Job 25:4*

These [redeemed] are they which were not defiled with women;...

— *Revelation 14:4*

But if thou has gone aside to another instead of thy husband, and if thou be defiled, and some man have lain with thee beside thine husband:
Then the priest shall charge the woman with an oath of cursing and the priest shall say unto the woman, The LORD make thee a curse and an oath among thy people, when the LORD doth make thy thigh [a euphemism for genitals] to rot and thy belly to swell;
And this water that causeth the curse shall go into thy bowels, to make thy belly to swell, and thy thigh to rot: and the woman shall say Amen, amen.

— *Numbers 5:20-22*

If a woman have conceived seed, and born a man child: then she shall be unclean seven days... but if she bear a maid child, then she shall be unclean two weeks...

— *Leviticus 12:2-5*

Let your women keep silence in the churches: for it is not permitted unto them to speak; but they are commanded to be under obedience, as also saith the law.

— *1 Corinthians 14:34*

Let the woman learn in silence with all subjection. But I suffer not a woman to teach, nor to usurp authority over the man, but to be in silence.

— *1 Timothy 2:11-12*

And every garment and every skin, whereon is the seed of copulation, shall be washed with water, and be unclean until the even. The woman also with whom man shall lie with seed of copulation, they shall both bathe themselves in water, and be unclean until the even. And if a woman have an issue, and her issue in her flesh be blood, she shall be unclean until the even. And whosoever toucheth any thing that she sat upon shall wash his clothes, and bathe himself in water, and be unclean until the even. And if any man lie with her at all, and her flowers be upon him, he shall be unclean seven days; and all the bed whereon he lieth shall be unclean... This is the law of him that hath an issue, and of him whose seed goeth from him, and is defiled therewith; And of her that is sick of her flowers, and of him that hath an issue, of the man, and of the woman, and of him that lieth with her that is unclean.

— *Leviticus 15:17-24, 32-33*

Slavery & Submission

Servants, be obedient to them that are your masters according to the flesh, with fear and trembling, in singleness of your heart, as unto Christ.

— *Ephesians 6:5*

Servants, obey in all things your masters according to the flesh; not with eyeservice, as menpleasers; but in singleness of heart, fearing God.

— *Colossians 3:22*

Exhort servants to be obedient unto their own masters, and to please them well in all things; not answering again; not purloining, but shewing good fidelity; that they may adorn the doctrine of God our Saviour in all things.

— *Titus 2:9-10*

And if a man smite his servant, or his maid with a rod, and he die under his hand; he shall be surely punished. Notwithstanding, if he continue a day or two, he shall not be punished: for he is his money.

— *Exodus 21:20-21*

If thou buy an Hebrew servant six years he shall serve: and in the seventh he shall go out free for nothing. If he came in by himself, he shall go out by himself: if he were married, then his wife shall go out with him. If his master have given him a wife, and she have born him sons or daughters; the wife and her children shall be her master's and he shall go out by himself. And if the servant shall plainly say, I love my master, my wife and my children; I will not go out free: Then his master shall bring him unto the judges; he shall also bring him to the door, or unto the door post; and his master shall bore his ear through with a ual; and he shall serve him for ever.

— *Exodus 21:2-6*

Both thy bondsmen, and thy bondsmaids, which thou shalt have, shall be of the heathen that are round about you: of them shall ye buy bondsmen and bondsmaids. Moreover of the children of the strangers that do sojourn among you, of them shall ye buy, and of their families that are with you, which they begat in your land: and they shall be your possession.

And ye shall take them as an inheritance for your children after you, to inherit them for a possession.

— Leviticus 25:44-46

Let every soul be subject unto the higher powers. For there is no power but of God: the powers that be are ordained of God. Whosoever therefore resisteth the power, resisteth the ordinance of God; and they that resist shall receive to themselves damnation.

— Romans 13:1-2

Submit yourselves to every ordinance of man for the Lord's sake: whether it be to the king, as supreme: or unto governors.

— 1 Peter 2:13-14

Servants, be subject to your masters with all fear; not only to the good and gentle, but also to the froward.

— 1 Peter 2:18

Let as many servants as are under the yoke count their own masters worthy of all honour, that the name of God and his doctrine be not blasphemed.

— 1 Timothy 6:1

The End of the World
(an unfulfilled prophecy)

And there shall be signs in the sun, and in the moon, and in the stars. . . Men's hearts failing them for fear. . . And then shall they see the Son of man coming in a cloud. . . This generation shall not pass till all be fulfilled.

— Luke 21:25-32

But the end of all things is at hand. . .

— 1 Peter 4:7

Little children, it is the last time: and as ye have heard that antichrist shall come, even now are there many antichrists; whereby we know that it is the last time.

— 1 John 2:18

Immediately after the tribulation of those days shall the sun be darkened, and the moon shall not give her light, and the stars shall fall from heaven. . . And then shall appear the sign of the Son of man in heaven, then shall all the tribes of the earth mourn, and they shall see the Son of man coming in the clouds of heaven. . . This generation shall not pass, till all these things be fulfilled.

— Matthew 24:29-34

And he [J.C.] said unto them, Verily I say unto you, That there be some of them that stand here, which shall not taste of death, till they have seen the Kingdom of God come with power.

— Mark 9:1

For the Son of man shall come in the glory of his Father with his angels; and then he shall reward every man according to his works. Verily I say unto you, there be some standing here, which shall not taste of death, till they see the Son of man coming in his kingdom.

— Matthew 16:27-28

But I tell you as a truth, there be some standing here, which shall not taste of death, till they see the kingdom of God.

— Luke 9:27

. . .the sun shall be darkened, and the moon shall not give her light And the stars of heaven shall fall . . .And then shall they see the Son of man coming in the clouds. . .And then shall he send his angels, and shall gather together his elect from the four winds, from the uttermost part of the earth. . . Verily I say unto you, that this generation shall not pass, till all these things be done.

— Mark 13:24-27, 30

Atrocities & Absurdities

And when the Lord thy God hath delivered it unto thine hands, thou shalt smite every male thereof with the edge of the sword: but the women, and the little ones, and the cattle, and all that is in the city, even the spoil thereof, shalt thou take unto thyself; and thou shalt eat the spoil of thine enemies, which the Lord thy God hath given thee.

— Deuteronomy 20:13-14

For my love they are my adversaries. . .When he shall be judged, let him be condemned. . .Let his days be few; and let another take his office. Let his children be continually vagabonds, and beg; let them seek their bread also out of their desolate places. Let the extortioner catch all that he hath; and let the strangers spoil his labour. Let there be none to extend mercy unto him: neither let there be any to favour his fatherless children. Let his posterity be cut off; and in the generation following let their name be blotted out.

— Psalm 109:4, 7-13

If any man will come after me [J.C.], let him deny himself, and take up his cross and follow me.

— Matthew 16:24

And if thy hand offend thee, cut it off: It is better for thee to enter into life maimed, than having two hands to go into hell, into the fire that never shall be quenched: where their worm dieth not, and the fire is not quenched.

— Mark 9:43-44

For rebellion is as the sin of witchcraft...
— *1 Samuel 15:23*

...I abhor myself, and repent in dust and ashes.
— *Job 42:6*

And these signs shall follow them that believe; in my name shall they cast out devils; they shall speak with new tongues; They shall take up serpents; and if they drink any deadly thing, it shall not hurt them; they shall lay hands on the sick, and they shall recover.
— *Mark 16:17-18*

Whosoever will come after me, let him deny himself, and take up his cross...
— *Mark 8:34* (J.C. speaking)

For ye, brethren, became followers of the churches of God which in Judea are in Christ Jesus: for ye also have suffered like things of your own countrymen, even as they have of the Jews: who both killed the Lord Jesus, and have persecuted us; and they please not God, and are contrary to all men.
— *1 Thessalonians 2:14-15*

But those mine enemies, which would not that I should reign over them, bring hither, and slay them before me.
— *Luke 19:27* (J.C. speaking)

He that believeth and is baptized shall be saved; but he that believeth not shall be damned. And these signs shall follow them that believe: In my name shall they cast out devils; they shall speak with new tongues; They shall take up serpents; and if they drink any deadly thing it shall not hurt them; they shall lay hands on the sick and they shall recover.
— *Mark 16:16-18*

Many of them also which used curious arts brought their books together and burned them...So mightily grew the word of God and prevailed.
— *Acts 19:19-20*

..if through my falsehood God's truthfulness abounds to his glory, why am I still being condemned as a sinner? And why not do evil that good may come? — as some people slanderously charge us with saying. Their condemnation is just.
— *Romans 3:7-8* (Revised Standard Edition)

For everyone that curseth his father or his mother shall be surely put to death.
— *Leviticus 20:9*

And he that blasphemeth the name of the LORD, he shall surely be put to death.
— *Leviticus 24:16*

Thou shalt not suffer a witch to live.
— *Exodus 22:18*

"We're all guilty!"

Graphic from *Freedom.*

Behold, I will corrupt your seed, and spread dung upon your faces.
— *Malachi 2:3*

And thou shalt eat it as barley cakes, and thou shalt bake it with dung that cometh out of man...
— *Ezekiel 4:12*

Lo, I have given thee cow's dung for man's dung and thou shalt prepare thy bread therewith.
— *Ezekiel 4:15*

Now therefore kill every male among the little ones, and kill every woman that hath known man by lying with him. But all the women children, that have not known a man by lying with him, keep alive for yourselves.
— *Numbers 31:17-18*

...Hath he not sent me to the men that sit upon the wall, that they may eat their own dung, and drink their own piss with you?
— *Isaiah 36:12*

Happy shall he be, that taketh and dasheth thy little ones against the stones.
— *Psalms 137:9*

Wherefore if thy hand or thy foot offend thee, cut them off, and cast them from thee: it is better for thee to enter into life halt or maimed, rather than having two hands or two feet to be cast into everlasting fire.
And if thine eye offend thee, pluck it out, and cast it from thee: it is better for thee to enter into life with one eye, rather than having two eyes to be cast into hell fire.
— *Matthew 18:8-9*

For if ye love them which love you, what reward have ye? Do not even the publicans do the same?
— *Matthew 5:46*

He that spareth the rod hateth his son.
— *Proverbs 13:24*

And Moses said, Thus saith the LORD, About midnight will I go out into the midst of Egypt: And all the firstborn in the land of Egypt shall die... even unto the firstborn of the maidservant...and all the firstborn of beasts.
— *Exodus 11:4-5*

Withhold not correction from the child: for *if* thou beatest him with the rod, he shall not die. Thou shalt beat him with the rod, and shalt deliver his soul from hell.
— *Proverbs 23:13-14*

If a man have a stubborn and rebellious son, which will not obey the voice of his father, or the voice of his mother, and *that*, when they have chastened him, will not hearken unto them: Then shall his father and his mother lay hold on him... And they shall say unto the elders of his city, This our son *is* stubborn and rebellious, he will not obey our voice; *he is* a glutton, and a drunkard. And all the men of his city shall stone him with stones, that he die.
— *Deuteronomy 21:18-21*

He that is wounded in the stones [testicles], or hath his privy member [penis] cut off, shall not enter into the congregation of the LORD.
— *Deuteronomy 23:1*

Contradictions

The son shall not bear the iniquity of the father.
— *Ezekiel 18:20*

...I the lord thy God am a jealous God, visiting the iniquity of the fathers upon the children unto the third and fourth generations.
— *Exodus 20:5*

...God cannot be tempted with evil, neither tempteth he any man.
— *James 1:13*

And it came to pass after these things, that God did tempt Abraham.
— *Genesis 22:1*

...for I am merciful, saith the Lord, and I will not keep anger forever.
— *Jeremiah 3:12*

Ye have kindled a fire in mine anger, which shall burn forever.
— *Jeremiah 17:4*

Lay not up for yourselves treasures upon the earth...
— *Matthew 6:19*

In the house of the righteous is much treasure...
— *Proverbs 15:6*

Honour thy father and thy mother.
— *Exodus 20:12*

If any man come to me, and hate not his father and mother, and wife, and children, and brethren, and sisters, yea, and his own life also, he cannot be my disciple.
— *Luke 14:26* (J.C. speaking)

...thou shalt give life for life, eye for eye, tooth for tooth, hand for hand, foot for foot, burning for burning, wound for wound, stripe for stripe.
— *Exodus 21:23-25*

...resist not evil; but whosoever shall smite thee on thy right cheek, turn to him the other also.
— *Matthew 5:39*

Happy is the man that findeth wisdom, and the man that getteth understanding.
— *Proverbs 3:13*

For in much wisdom is much grief; and he that increaseth knowledge increaseth sorrow.
— *Ecclesiastes 1:18*

...the earth abideth forever.
— *Ecclesiastes 1:4*

...the elements shall melt with fervent heat, the earth also and works that are therein shall be burned up.
— *2 Peter 3:10*

And God saw everything that he had made, and behold it was very good.
— *Genesis 1:31*

And it repented the Lord that he had made man on the earth, and it grieved at his heart.
— *Genesis 6:6*

Think not that I am come to send peace on earth: I came not to send peace, but a sword.
— *Matthew 10:34*

...all they that take the sword shall perish with the sword.
— *Matthew 26:52*

And no man hath ascended up to heaven, even the Son of man which is in heaven.

— *John 3:13*

. . . and Elijah went up by a whirlwind into heaven.

— *2 Kings 2:11*

If I bear witness of myself, my witness is not true.

— *John 5:31* (J.C. speaking)

I am one that bear witness of myself. . .

— *John 8:18* (J.C. speaking)

A good man leaveth an inheritance to his children's children. . .

— *Proverbs 13:22*

Sell that ye have and give alms. . .

— *Luke 12:33*

Blessed is the man that feareth the Lord. . . Wealth and riches shall be in his house. . .

— *Psalm 112:1-3*

It is easier for a camel to go through the eye of a needle, than for a rich man to enter the kingdom of God.

— *Matthew 19:24*

I and my father are one.

— *John 10:30* (J.C. speaking)

I go unto the Father: for my Father is greater than I.

— *John 14:28* (J.C. speaking)

. . . the hour is coming, in which all that are in the graves shall hear his voice, and come forth. . .

— *John 5:28-29*

As the cloud is consumed and vanisheth away: so he that goeth down to the grave shall come up no more.

— *Job 7:9*

I have seen God face to face, and my life is preserved.

— *Genesis 32:30*

No man hath seen God at any time.

— *John 1:18*

And I [god] will take away mine hand, and thou shalt see my back parts; but my face shall not be seen.

— *Exodus 33:23*

J.C. on the Bible

Think not that I am come to destroy the law or the prophets: I am not come to destroy, but to fulfil . . . Till heaven and earth shall pass, one jot or one tittle shall in no wise pass from the law. . .

— *Matthew 5:17-18*

Capsule Biographies

Abu'l-Ala-Al-Ma'arri—973-1057, Syrian poet
Lord Acton (John E.E. Dahlberg)—1834-1902, British historian
John Adams—1735-1826, second U.S. president
John Quincy Adams—1767-1848, sixth U.S. president
Gracie Allen—1906-1964, American comedienne
Grant Allen—1848-1899, British philosophical writer and novelist
St. Alphonsus—Catholic saint
Arnold Amalric—13th-century French theologian and papal official
St. Ambrose—340-397, Bishop of Milan
Melvin Anchell—contemporary American Catholic writer and M.D.
Rev. Robert N. Anderson—pre-Civil War American protestant clergyman
Stephen Pearl Andrews—1812-1886, American writer, linguist, lawyer, abolitionist, and anarchist.
Joaquin Andujar—contemporary major league baseball player
St. Angela of Foligno—1474-1550, founder of the Ursuline order
St. Anthony—251?-356?, Egyptian hermit, founder of monasticism
Susan B. Anthony—1820-1906, American feminist
St. Thomas Aquinas—1225-1274, Italian, the most important Catholic theologian
Petronius Arbiter—1st-century Roman writer
Pedro Arbues—15th-century Spanish Grand Inquisitor
Aristotle—384-322 b.c., Greek philosopher
Lord Armstrong (William George Armstrong)—1810-1900, British historian
Peter Arshinov—early 20th-century Russian anarchist, chronicler of the Makhnovist uprising in the Ukraine
T.S. Atarov—contemporary, physician emeritus of the Russian Soviet Socialist Republic
Athenagoras—20th-century Greek Orthodox patriarch
St. Augustine—340-430, church father, bishop of Hippo, theologian second in importance only to Aquinas
Marcus Aurelius—121-180, Roman emperor and stoic philosopher
Joan Baez—b. 1940, American folk musician
Jim Bakker—b. 1940, American televangelist and convicted swindler

Tammy Faye Bakker—b. 1942, ex-wife of televangelist Jim Bakker, a woman who stood by her man through thick and thin—until the going got a bit too thin (in 1992, during Jimbo's prison term)
Michael Bakunin—1814-1876, Russian revolutionary, anarchist and writer. His works include *God and the State, Letters to a Frenchman, Reaction in Germany, A Circular Letter to My Friends in Italy,* and *Federalism, Socialism, Anti-Theologism.* The best collection of his writings available in English is *Bakunin on Anarchy,* Sam Dolgoff, ed.
Adin Ballou—1803-1890, American abolitionist and christian advocate of nonresistance
Honore de Balzac—1799-1850, French novelist
Henry Ward Beecher—1813-1887, American clergyman and writer
Ludwig von Beethoven—1770-1827, German composer
Ernest Bennett—1868-1947, British journalist
Alexander Berkman—1870-1936, Russian-American anarchist and writer. He was imprisoned for 14 years for shooting robber baron Henry Clay Frick during the Homestead strike. He was later imprisoned for opposing conscription during World War I and was illegally deported in the Red Scare following the war. His best known works are *What Is Communist Anarchism, Prison Memoirs of an Anarchist,* and *The Bolshevik Myth.*
St. Bernard—1091-1153, French ecclesiastic
Yogi Berra—b. 1925, professional baseball player, manager, coach, and humorist
Albert Beveridge—1862-1927, U.S. senator
Ambrose Bierce—1842-1914, American journalist and iconoclast. He disappeared in Mexico during the Mexican Revolution. His best known work is *The Devil's Dictionary.*
Josh Billings (Henry Wheeler Shaw)—1818-1885, American humorist
William Blake—1757-1827, British poet
Henri Boguet—17th-century French judge
Nicolas Boileau—1631-1711, French poet
Napoleon Bonaparte—1769-1821, French politician, dictator, and militarist
Murray Bookchin—contemporary American anarchist and ecological writer. His works include *Post-Scarcity Anarchism* and *The Ecology of Freedom.*
Baron Bowen—1835-1894, British writer
John Bright—1811-1889, British liberal politician

Crane Brinton — 1898-1968, American writer

Maurice Brinton — contemporary British libertarian writer. His works include *The Irrational in Politics* and *The Bolsheviks and Workers Control*.

Giordano Bruno — 1548-1600, Italian scholar, burned at the stake by the Roman Inquisition for heresy.

Henry Thomas Buckle — 1821-1862, British historian

Comte de Buffon — 1707-1788, French naturalist

Nikolai Bukharin — 1888-1938, Russian writer and high-ranking Communist apparatchik. Executed during one of Stalin's purges.

Luther Burbank — 1849-1926, American horticulturist

Edmund Burke — 1729, 1797, Irish politician and writer

Rupert Burley — contemporary American anarchist writer

George Bush — b. 1924, American politician, 41st U.S. president

Samuel Butler — 1612-1680, English satirist

Smedley Butler — 1881-1940, U.S. Marine Corps major general and commandant

W.S. Byrne — early 20th-century American writer

Calgacus — 1st-century Roman orator

Bruce Calvert — 20th-century American publisher

John Calvin — 1509-1564, French protestant ascetic, dictator of Geneva

Simon Cameron — 1799-1889, U.S. Republican politician

Al Capone — 1899-1947, American businessman and firearms fancier

Thomas Carlyle — 1795-1881, Scottish historian

Edward Carpenter — 1844-1929, British libertarian, poet and essayist

Lewis Carroll (Charles Lutwidge Dodgson) — 1832-1898, British mathematician and author of children's books

Cornelius Castoriadis — b. 1922, leading libertarian theorist and writer

Anton Chekov — 1860-1904, Russian playwright

Lord Chesterfield (Philip Dormer Stanhope) — 1694-1733, British politician and writer

Rufus Choate — 1799-1859, American lawyer

Noam Chomsky — b. 1928, American scholar, the foremost authority on structural linguistics. His works include *American Power and the New Mandarins, For Reasons of State*, and *The Washington Connection and Third World Fascism*.

St. John Chrysostom — 347?-407, church father, patriarch of Constantinople

Winston Churchill, 1874-1965, British politician

Karl von Clausewitz — 1780-1831, German militarist and writer

Clement of Alexandria — 150?-215?, Greek theologian and church father

Voltairine de Cleyre — 1866-1912, American anarchist

William K. Clifford — 1845-1879, English mathematician and philosopher

St. John Climacus — Catholic saint

Chapman Cohen — early 20th-century British rationalist

Samuel Taylor Coleridge — 1772-1834, British poet

C.C. (Charles Caleb) Colton — 1780-1832, British writer

Alex Comfort — b. 1920, British writer, physician and libertarian, best known for *The Joy of Sex*

Auguste Comte — 1798-1857, French, founder of positivist philosophy

Confucius — 551?-478? b.c., Chinese philosopher

Calvin Coolidge — 1872-1933, 30th U.S. president

James Fenimore Cooper — 1780-1851, American novelist

Noel Coward — 1899-1973, British actor

Stephen Crane — 1871-1900, American novelist and poet

St. Cyprian — 200?-258, church father

Glen A. Dahlquist — contemporary American journalist

Richard Daley — 1902-1976, mayor of Chicago, Democratic Party political boss

Clarence Darrow — 1857-1938, American lawyer and author, defense attorney in the Scopes case and the Bill Haywood murder trial

Eugene V. Debs — 1855-1926, American socialist and orator, jailed for opposing World War I

Denis Diderot — 1713-1784, French philosopher, atheist, and encyclopedist

Everett Dirksen — 1896-1969, longtime Republican senator from Illinois

Benjamin Disraeli — 1804-1881, British politician

Sam Dolgoff — 1903-1991, American anarchist, translator, and writer. His works include *The Anarchist Collectives* and *Bakunin on Anarchy*.

Fyodor Dostoyevsky — 1821-1881, Russian novelist

William Drummond — 1585-1649, Scottish poet

Alexandre Dumas — 1824-1895, French Dramatist

Buenaventura Durruti — Spanish anarchist, killed in 1936 while fighting fascists on the Madrid front

Thomas Alva Edison — 1847-1931, American inventor

Jonathan Edwards — 1703-1758, American clergtyman, Yale University professor of theology

Albert Einstein — 1879-1955, German physicist and Nobel Prize winner, formulator of the theory of relativity

Dwight Eisenhower — 1890-1969, 34th U.S. president

Albert Ellis — b. 1913, American psychotherapist and writer, founder of the Rational Emotive Therapy (RET) school of psychotherapy, and a noted authority on sex. His works include *Sex Without Guilt, The Case for Sexual Liberty, Humanistic Psychotherapy: The Rational-Emotive Approach,* and *A New Guide to Rational Living* (w/ R. Harper)

Ralph Waldo Emerson — 1803-1882, American writer

George Engel — American anarchist and labor organizer, one of the Haymarket martyrs, murdered by the State of Illinois in 1887

Friedrich Engels — 1820-1895, British industrialist, friend and financial supporter of Karl Marx

Epicurus — 342?-270 b.c., Greek philosopher

Desiderius Erasmus — 1466-1536, Dutch humanist philosopher

Pope Eugenius IV — 1383-1447, pope 1431-1447

Luigi Fabbri — 1873-1935, Italian anarchist and writer

Warren Farrel — contemporary American writer, his best know work is *The Liberated Man*

Sebastian Faure — 1858-1942, French anarchist, atheist, writer and orator

Francisco Ferrer — 1859-1909, Spanish anarchist and educator, a founder of the modern school movement, murdered by the Spanish government

Adolph Fischer — American anarchist and labor organizer, one of the Haymarket martyrs, murdered by the State of Illinois in 1887

Camille Flammarion — 1842-1925, French astronomer and writer

Ricardo Flores Magon — 1873-1922, Mexican anarchist, writer, revolutionary, and founder of the Partido Liberal Mexicano. He was jailed many times in both Mexico and the United States for advocating unpopular causes. He died under mysterious circumstances in Leavenworth federal prison (probably murdered by guards), while serving a 21-year sentence for "seditious" writings.

John T. Flynn—1883-?, American libertarian writer
G.W. Foote—1850-1915, British rationalist and writer, responsible for production of *The Bible Handbook*
E.M. Forster—1879-1970, British writer, author of the popular "Hornblower" books
Jay Fox—early 20th-century American anarchist and writer
Vince Fox—contemporary American writer
Anatole France (Jacques Anatole Thibault)—1844-1924, French novelist, essayist, and Nobel Prize winner
Benjamin Franklin—1706-1790, American printer, diplomat, inventor, publisher, and writer
Frederick the Great—1744-1797, kind og Prussia and friend of Voltaire
Henry Clay Frick—1849-1919, American industrialist
St. Fulgentius—468-533, bishop and Catholic saint
Clay Fulks—mid-20th-century American atheist writer
Rev. J. Furniss, C.S.S.R.—19th-century Irish priest
Yekaterian Furtseva—contemporary, former USSR Minister of Cultural Affairs
Matilda Gage—1826-1898, American feminist
Galileo Galilei—1564-1642, Italian physicist and astronomer, first known user of a telescope for astronomical purposes, and discoverer of the moons of Jupiter. He died under house arrest imposed by the Holy Inquisition for pormoting the heretical doctrine (which he was forced to recant on his knees under threat of torture) that the earth revolves around the sun.
Jeff Gallagher—contemporary American anarchist, former editor of the periodical *Black Star*
John Galsworthy—1867-1933, English novelist and playwright
Victor Garcia—?-1991, exiled Spanish anarchist and writer who lived most of his life in Venezuela
James Garfield—1831-1881, 20th U.S. president
William Lloyd Garrison—1805-1879, American abolitionist, publisher of *The Liberator*
Henry George—1839-1897, American economist, reformer and writer, advocate of the "single tax" (on land)
Edward Gibbon—1737-1794, British historian
W.S. (William Schmenker) Gilbert—1836-1911, British librettist
William Godwin—1756-1836, British libertarian philosopher, and writer
Joseph Goebbels—1897-1945, Third Reich propaganda minister
J.W. (Johann Wolfgang) von Goethe—1749-1832, German poet, dramatist, novelist and philosopher
Emma Goldman—1869-1940, Russian-American anarchist, editor of *Mother Earth* She was jailed during World War I for opposing conscription, and was illegally deported during the post-war Red Scare. Her works include *Living My Life, Anarchistm and Other Essays* and *My Disillusionment in Russia.*
Oliver Goldsmith—1739-1774, Irish writer
Remy de Gourmont—1858-1915, French writer and poet
William B. Greene—1819-1873, American orator, radical, civil war colonel, and advocate of mutualism.
Pope Gregory XVI—1765-1846, pope 1831-1846
St. Gregory of Nazianzum—church father
Praxedis Guerrero—1882-1910, Mexican revolutionary and anarchist. A leading member of the Partido Liberal Mexicano, he was killed in a battle in the early days of the Mexican revolution.
J.J. Guillotin—1738-1814, French physician and inventor of the guillotine

E. (Emanuel) Haldeman-Julius—1889-1951, writer, atheist, and the most prolific publisher of radical materials in U.S. history. He died of a heart attack while being hounded to death by the IRS. His publishing firm, the Haldeman-Julius Company, published over 2,500 titles comprising over 500 million books and pamphlets between 1919 and 1951.
Robert Hall—1764-1831, British Baptist clergyman
H.W. (Henry Wager) Halleck—1815-1872, Union general in U.S. Civil War
Alexander Hamilton—1757-1804, First U.S. secretary of the treasury
Orrin Hatch—contemporary, Republican and Mormon U.S. senator from Utah
P.J. Hayes—20th-century U.S. Catholic cardinal
William Randolph Hearst—1863-1951, American newspaper publisher, sometimes "credited" as the originator of "yellow journalism"
Georg Hegel—1770-1831, German philosopher
Heinrich Heine—1797-1856, German poet
Herman von Helmholtz—1821-1894, German physicist
Claude Helvetius—1715-1771, French philosopher
Hans von Hentig—1887-?, criminologist
Auberon Herbert—1838-1906, British libertarian and writer
Jenny d'Hericourt—19th-century French feminist
George D. Herron—1862-1925, American socialist
Alexander Herzen—1812-1870, Russian revolutionary, exile, and publisher
Joe Hill—1879-1916, IWW songwriter, murdered by the state of Utah
Adolf Hitler—1889-1945, Austrian/German politician and dictator
A.A. Hodge—19th-century American professor of theology at Princeton University
Abbie Hoffman—1935-1989, American political activist and writer, founder of the Yippies
Baron d'Holbach (Paul Henry Thiry d'Holbach)—1723-1789, French rationalist philosopher
Oliver Wendell Holmes, Jr.—1841-1953, Associate Justice of U.S. Supreme Court
George Jacob Holyoake—1817-1906, last person imprisoned in England for being an atheist
Thomas Hood—1799-1845, British poet, principally remembered for his poem, "Song of the Shirt"
J. Edgar Hoover—1895-1972, head of the U.S. secret police (FBI) 1924-1972, and reputed closet case
Elbert Hubbard—1856-1915, American humorist, writer and publisher
L. Ron Hubbard, Sr.—1911-1986, pulp science fiction writer, millionaire, and founder of the Church of Scientology.
Henry Hudson—contemporary, American, chairman of the Meese Commission, Reagan's anti-pornography panel
Rupert Hughes—1872-1956, American writer
Aldous Huxley—1894-1963, British writer, best rememberd for *Brave New World*
Thomas Henry Huxley—1825-1895, British biologist and writer
Henrik Ibsen—1828-1906, Norwegian novelist and dramatist
Robert Ingersoll—1833-1899, "The Great Infidel," attorney and orator, the most influential American spokesman against christianity in the 19th century
Pope Innocent III—1161-1216, pope 1198-1216
Henry James—1843-1916, American novelist

King James I — 1566-1625, king of England

Thomas Jefferson — 1743-1826, third U.S. president

St. Jerome — 340?-420, church father, ascetic, main preparer of Vulgate version of the bible

Jesus of Nazareth — 4? b.c.-29? a.d., founder of influential religions cult

Venerable John of Avila — Catholic cleric

Judge Earl Johnson, Jr. — b. 1933, American jurist

Hiram Johnson — 1866-1945, U.S. senator from California

Samuel Johnson — 1709-1784, British lexicographer

Hans Johst — 1890-?, Nazi playwright

W.L. Judson — 19th-century American libertarian

Immanuel Kant — 1724-1804, German philosopher

Alphonse Karr — 1808-1890, French writer

Hellen Keller — 1880-1968, American educator and writer

Sally Kempton — contemporary American feminist

Florynce Kennedy — b. 1916, contemporary American feminist and attorney

John F. Kennedy — 1917-1963, 35th U.S. president and satyriasis victim

Frank Kent — 1877-?, American writer

Ellen Key — 1849-1926, Swedish feminist

Paul Krassner — contemporary American humorist, editor of *The Realist*

Peter Kropotkin — 1842-1921, Russian scientist, writer, revolutionary and anarchist. A Russian prince who forsook his privileges, he spent most of his life in exile or prison. His works include *Mutual Aid, The Conquest of Bread, The State: Its Historic Role, Fields, Factories and Workshops Tomorrow* and *Memoirs of a Revolutionist.*

Mike Krukow — contemporary, former starting pitcher for the San Francisco Giants, 20-game winner in 1986

Marquis de Lafayette — 1757-1834, French soldier and liberal poltiician

Lao Tse — 6th century b.c., founder of Taoism

Anton Szandor LaVey — contemporary, American, head of the First Church of Satan

Henry Charles Lea — 1825-1909, American writer, historian and publisher

Timothy Leary — b. 1920, contemporary, American, former Harvard psychology professor, LSD proponent in the 1960s

Ervil LeBaron — 1925-1981, 'the Mormon Manson,' head of polygamous religious cult and a multiple murderer

W.E.H. (William Edward Hartpole) Lecky — 1838-1903, Irish historian

Gypsy Rose Lee — 1914-1970, American burlesque and movie star

John Doyle Lee — 1812-1877, American Mormon, scapegoated and executed for his role in the 1857 Mountain Meadows Massacre

V.I. Lenin (Vladimir Ilyich Ulyanov) — 1870-1924, Russian, Communist politician and dictator

Pope Leo X — 1475-1521, pope 1513-1521

Pope Leo XIII — 1810-1903, pope 1878-1903

John L. Lewis — 1880-1969, American, president of the United Mine Workers

A.J. Liebling — 1904-1963, American writer

Laurel Limpus — contemporary British feminist

Abraham Lincoln — 1809-1865, 16th U.S. president

Louis Lingg — American anarchist and labor organizer, one of the Haymarket martyrs, murdered by the State of Illinois in 1887

John Locke — 1632-1704, British philosopher

Vince Lombardi — contemporary American retired NFL (football) coach

Jack London — 1876-1916, American socialist and novelist. His works include *The Sea Wolf* and *The Iron Heel*

Meyer London — 1871-1926, U.S. congressman

Huey Long — 1893-1935, governor of Louisiana

St. Ignatius Loyola — 1491-1556, Spanish priest, founder of the Society of Jesus (Jesuits)

Marianus de Luca — early 20th-century Italian priest

Martin Luther — 1483-1556, leader of the protestant reformation in Germany

George E. MacDonald — 1857-1943, British rationalist and writer

Thomas Macaulay — 1800-1859, Brisith historian

Niccolo Machiavelli — 1469-1527, Italian political writer

James Madison — 1751-1836, fourth U.S. president

Ferdinand Magellan — 1480?-1521, Portugese explorer

Errico Malatesta — 1853, 1932, Italian anarchist writer and revolutionary. His most important works are *Anarchy* and *Fra Contadini* ("Between peasants").

Malcolm X — 1925-1964, American black political activist and writer.

Mao Tse Tung — 1893-1975, Chinese Communist dictator and writer

Rabbit Maranville — early 20th-century American professional baseball player

Jean Paul Marat — 1743-1793, French revolutionary

Harriet Martineau — 1802-1876, British novelist, economist and feminist

Groucho Marx — 1891-1977, American comedian and movie/television star

Karl Marx — 1818-1883, German socialist, writer and economist

Guy de Maupassant — 1850-1893, French novelist and short story writer

G.P. (Gergori Petrovich) Maximoff — 1893-1950, Russian anarchist and revolutionary. He played an active part in the Russian Revolution and joined the Red Army, but was jailed and narrowly avoided being shot for opposing the dictatorial methods of the Bolsheviks.

St. Maximus the Confessor — Catholic saint

Joseph McCabe — 1867-1956, British, former Catholic priest and philosophy professor. He left the church while still a young man and became an atheist and a founder of the Rationalist Press Association. he authored hundreds of books and pamphlets, many published in the U.S. by the Haldeman-Julius Company.

Robert McFarlane — contemporary, Reagan National Security Adviser

Al Medwin — contemporary American anarchist and atheist

Philip Melancthon — 1497-1560, a leader of the protestant reformation in Germany and a close associate of Martin Luther

Richard B. Mellon — 1858-1933, American industrialist

H.L. (Henry Louis) Mencken — 1880-1956, American journalist, editor, and iconoclast. His works include *A New Dictionary of Quotations, The American Language, Prejudices* (six volumes) and *Minority Report.*

Karl Meninger — 1893-?, American psychiatrist

Jean Meslier — 1678-1733, French priest. His will, or "testament," in which he denounced christianity and proclaimed atheistic beliefs, was published by Voltaire.

William Messing — mid-20th century American attorney

Michelangelo (Michelangelo Buonarroti) — 1457-1564, Italian poet, artist, and architect

Harvey Milk — America's first openly gay elected public official, assassinated by Catholic Republican Dan White in 1977

Mohammed — 570-632, founder of influential religious cult

Michel de Montaigne — 1532-1592, French philosopher

Montesquieu (Charles Louis de Secondat) — 1689-1755, French philosopher

Maria Montessori — 1870-1952, Italian, originator of the Montessori method of early education

Sun Myung Moon — b. 1920, Korean, founder and head of the Unification Church religious cult and a farflung business empire which includes media outlet such as *The Washington Times*

Lewis Henry Morgan — 1818-1881, American anthropologist

John Morley — 1838-1923, British politician

Johann Most — 1846-1906, German anarchist, writer, and revolutionary. He became an anarchist after being elected to the Reichstag where he became disillusioned with government. He was later deported by both Germany and England, and finally emigrated to the U.S. where he was jailed many times for his writings.

Lewis Mumford — 1895-?, American writer

Thomas Muntzer — 16th-century, German, protestant mystic

Benito Mussolini — 1883-1945, Italian politician and dictator

Modest Mussorgsky — 1835-1881, Russian composer

Nestorius — 5th-century, patriarch of Constantinople

John Henry Newman — 1801-1890, British Catholic cardinal and theologian

Martin Niemoeller — 1892-?, protestant clergyman

Friedrich Nietzsche — 1844-1900, German philosopher. His works include *Human, All Too Human, Beyond Good and Evil,* and *The Anti-Christ.*

Swami Nirmalanda — contemporary Indian Tolstoyan anarchist

Richard Nixon — b. 1913, 37th U.S. president, forced from office because he made the mistake of using secret police 'dirty tricks' against mainstream political opponents rather than solely against 'radicals,' as is traditional in U.S. politics

Alfred Nobel — 1833-1896, Swedish, inventor of dynamite and originator of Nobel prizes

Max Nordau — 1849-1923, German physician and writer

Luke North — early 20th-century American writer and editor

Caliph Omar — 581?-644, the second caliph

Origen — 185?-254?, church father, theologian, and self-made eunuch (unlike today's lily-livered "fundamentalists," he interpreted Matthew 19:12 literally)

John Osbourne — contemporary American televangelist

Alvin M. Owsley — 1888-?, American lawyer and head of the American Legion

Leroy "Satchell" Paige — 1906-1982, American professional baseball player. One of the greatest pitchers to ever play the game, he was a victim of racism and made it into big leagues only when he was already well into his 40s, yet still enjoyed years of success

Thomas Paine — 1737-1809, British expatriate revolutionary and writer

Theodore Parker — 1810-1860, American preacher and abolitionist

Albert Parsons — 1848-1887, American anarchist, writer, labor organizer and editor of *The Alarm.* He was one of the Haymarket martyrs and was murdered by the State of Illinois in 1887.

Blaise Pascal — 1623-1662, French mathematician, philosopher and writer

Joseph Medill Patterson — 1879-1946, American newspaper publisher

Pope Paul V — 1552-1621, pope 1605-1621

Karl Pearson — 1857-1936, British statistician

William Penn — 1644-1718, American Quaker and founder of Pennsylvania

Wendell Phillips — 1811-1884, American abolitionist and social reformer

William Pitt, Jr. — 1759-1806, British politician

Pope Pius IV — 1499-1565, pope 1559-1565

Pope Pius XI — 1857-1939, pope 1922-1939

Plato — 427-347 b.c., Greek philosopher

Luis Polonia — contemporary professional baseball outfielder

Mary Pettibone Poole — no biographical information found

Alexander Pope — 1688-1744, British poet

Rev. J.C. Postell — pre-Civil War American clergyman

Eugene Pottier — 1816-1887, French socialist and writer

Elvis Presley — 1935-1977, American crooner, wildly popular for no discernible reason

Joseph Priestley — 1733-1804, British noncomformist cleric

Pierre Joseph Proudhon — 1809-1865, French anarchist, writer, and proponent of mutual aid and federalism. His works include *What Is Property?* and The General Idea of the Revolution in the 19th Century.

Isaac Puente — Spanish anarchist and physician, shot by fascists in the first days of the Spanish Civil War in 1936

Dan Quisenberry — b. 1952, American "submarine ball" baseball relief pitcher

Francois Rabelais — 1490?-1553, French satirist

Bhagwan Shree Rajneesh — b. 1931, Indian, head of religious cult

Joseph Ratzinger — contemporary, Catholic cardinal, head of the Congregation for the Doctrine of the Faith (formerly the Holy Inquisition)

John Ray — 1627-1705, British writer and philosopher

Ali Raza — contemporary, deposed Indian royalty

Ronald Reagan — b. 1911, 40th U.S. president

Elisee Reclus — late-19th/early 20th-century anarchist and historian

Wilhelm Reich — 1897-1957, a student of Freud and a leading psychoanalytic theorist. Reich's consistent investigations into the source and nature of energy in the neurosis led him to unexplored areas beyond psychoanalysis and to discovery of a measurable physical energy in all living substances and in the atmosphere. Reich called it "orgone energy." His works include *Character Analysis, The Mass Psychology of Fascism, The Function of the Orgasm,* and *The Cancer Biopathy.* (Biography as specified by Mr. Reich's estate)

Ernest Renan — 1823-1892, French hisorian

David Ricardo — 1772-1823, British economist

Allen Rice — contemporary American libertarian

Efrain Rios Montt — contemporary, former Guatemalan strongman and fundamentalist christian

Pat Robertson — b. 1930, American televangelist and Republican politician

Francois de La Rochefoucauld — 1613-1680, French moralist and epigramist

Rudolf Rocker — 1873-1958, German anarchist and historian. His works include *Nationalism and Culture* and *Anarchism and Anarcho-Syndicalism.*

Will Rogers — 1879-1935, American humorist

Franklin D. Roosevelt — 1882-1945, 32nd U.S. president

Jean Jacques Rousseau — 1712-1778, French philosopher

William Harris Rule — 19th-century historian

Richard Rumbold — 1622-1685, British rebel

John Rush — contemporary American anarchist and atheist

Marquis de Sade (Donatien Alphonse Francois de Sade) — 1740-1814, French writer

Margo St. James — contemporary, American, founder of C.O.Y.O.T.E. (Call Off Your Old Tired Ethics), the national prostitutes' rights organization

Margaret Sanger — 1883-1966, American feminist and advocate of reproductive rights

J.C.F. (Johann Christian Friedrich) **von Schiller** — 1759-1805, German poet

Arthur Schopenhauer — 1788-1860, German philosopher

Theodore Schroeder — early 20th-century American, attorney for the Free Speech League

Albert Schweitzer — 1875-1965, Alsatian writer, doctor, musician and missionary

Seneca — 4?-65 a.d., Roman philosopher

George Bernard Shaw — 1856-1950, Irish fabian socialist, writer, and Nobel Prize winner

Percy Bysshe Shelley — 1792-1822, British poet

William Tecumseh Sherman — 1820-1891, Union general in U.S. Civil War

Barbara Simpson — contemporary British writer

A. Wakefield Slaten — late 19th/early 20th-century American Unitarian clergyman

Charles Smith — 20th-century American journalist

J. Blair Smith — early 20th-century anarchist

Socrates — 469?-399? b.c., Greek Philosopher

Herbert Spencer — 1820-1903, British philosopher and writer

August Spies — American anarchist and labor organizer, one of the Haymarket martyrs, he was framed and murdered by the State of Illinois in 1887

Benedict (Baruch) Spinoza — 1632-1677, Dutch philosopher

Lysander Spooner — 1808-1887, American individualist anarchist, attorney, and writer. His works include *No Treason, Trial by Jury* and *Vices Are Not Crimes.*

Charles Sprading — early 20th-century American libertarian writer and editor

Hiram Stafford — 19th-century American abolitionist and socialist

Josef Stalin (Iosif Vissarionovich Dzhugashvili) — 1879-1953, Communist politician and dictator

Elizabeth Cady Stanton — 1815-1902, American feminist and suffragette

Gertrude Stein — 1874-1946, American expatriate writer

George Steinbrenner — contemporary, American, owner of the New York Yankees

Charles Steinmetz — 1865-1923, German-American electrical engineer and inventor

Pope Stephanus V — pope 885-891

Robert Louis Stevenson — 1850-1894, Scottish novelist and poet

Joseph Stilwell — 1883-1946, World War II U.S. Army general

Max Stirner — 1806-1856, German individualist

August Strindberg — 1849-1912, Swedish novelist and playwright

Don Sutton — contemporary American, former major league baseball pitcher

Jimmy Swaggart — contemporary American televangelist

Jonathan Swift — 1667-1745, British cleric and satirist

John Swinton — 1830-1901, American journalist

Tacitus (Publius Cornelius) — 55?-120?, Roman historian

Rober B. Taney — 1777-1864, chief justice of U.S. Supreme Court

Jeremy Taylor — 1613-1667, British clergyman

Tecumseh — 1768-1813, Shawnee chief

Robert Tefton — contemporary American anarchist and writer

St. Teresa — 1515-1582, Spanish Carmelite nun

Tertullian (Quintus Septimus Florens Tertulianus) — 160?-230?, Carthaginian theologian, church father

Theodorus — Greek philosopher

George Thomar — early 20th-century anarchist

Norman Thomas — 1884-1968, American socialist

Henry David Thoreau — 1817-1862, American naturalist, writer, and advocate of civil disobedience. He was jailed for refusing to pay taxes during the U.S. war against Mexico. His most important works are *Walden* and *On the Duty of Civil Disobedience.*

Thucydides — 460-400? b.c., Greek historian

Alexis de Tocqueville — 1805-1859, French writer and politician

Leo Tolstoy — 1828-1910, Russian pacifist anarchist (though he considered his approach "christian"), novelist and essayist

Heinrich von Treitschke — 1834-1896, German militarist

Benjamin Tucker — 1854-1939, American individualist anarchist, the editor of *Liberty*

Mark Twain (Samuel Clemens) — 1835-1910, American novelist, journalist, and humorist

Jesse Unruh — 1923-1987, California Democratic politician

Pope Urban VIII — 1568-1644, pope 1623-1644

William H. Vanderbilt — 1821-1885, American industrialist

Thorstein Veblen — 1857-1929, American economist

Francisco (Pancho) Villa — 1877-1923, Mexican revolutionary

Francois Voltaire — 1694-1778, French writer and philosopher

Nicolas Walter — contemporary British anarchist and rationalist writer, one of the editors of *Freedom*

Colin Ward — contemporary British anarchist and architect, and one of the editors of *Freedom*

Jack Warner — b. 1916, American film mogul

Josiah Warren — 1798-1874, American individualist anarchist, communitarian and inventor

Booker T. Washington — 1856-1915, American educator, founder of Tuskegee Institute

George Washington — 1732-1799, first U.S. president

Daniel Webster — 1782-1852, American politician

Simone Weil — 1909-1942, French writer and philosopher

John Wesley — 1703, 1791, British, founder of Methodism

A.E. Westermarck — 1862-1939, Finnish sociologist

Grover A. Whalen — 1886-?, American politician, New York City police commissioner

Andrew Dickson White — 1832-1918, American writer, educator and diplomat

Walt Whitman — 1819-1892, American poet

Oscar Wilde — 1854-1900, Irish poet, novelist, playwright, and essayist

Kaiser Wilhelm II — 1859-1941, German emperor
Vince Williams — contemporary American retired diplomat and anarchist
Charles E. Wilson — 1895-1961, American industrialist
Mary Wollstonecroft — 1759-1797, British feminist
Fred Woodworth — contemporary, American, editor and publisher of *The Match*, the longest-running U.S. anarchist periodical (since 1969)
Henry C. Wright — 19th-centry American, the most radical of the abolitionists
John Wycliffe — 1320?-1384, British reformer and bible translator
Philip Wylie — 1902-1971, American novelist and essayist
Jane Wyman — contemporary American actress, former wife of Ronald Reagan
Deng Xiaoping — b. 1906, Chinese Communist politician and dictator.
Victor Yarrow — early 20th-century American journalist, an associate of Clarence Darrow
Johnnie Yen — contemporary British anarchist writer
Brigham young — 1801-1877, head of Mormon church, successor of its founder, Joe Smith
Israel Zangwill — 1846-1926, British writer
Emiliano Zapata — 1877-1919, Mexican revolutionary
Frank Zappa — contemporary American rock musician, founder of the Mothers of Invention
John Peter Zenger — 1697-1746, American printer, journalist, and defender of free speech
Emile Zola — 1842-1902, French novelist

Index